DATE			

Time, Uncertainty,
and Information

Time, Uncertainty, and Information

JACK HIRSHLEIFER

Basil Blackwell

First published 1989

Basil Blackwell Ltd
108 Cowley Road, Oxford, OX4 1JF, UK

Basil Blackwell Inc.
432 Park Avenue South, Suite 1503
New York, NY 10016, USA

British Library Cataloguing in Publication Data

Hirshleifer, Jack
   Time, uncertainty and information.
   (Uncertainty and expectations in economics).
   1. Economics. Uncertainty
   I. Title II. Series
   330.15'4

   ISBN 0-631-16236-4

Library of Congress Cataloging in Publication Data

Hirshleifer, Jack.
   Time, uncertainty, and information/Jack Hirshleifer.
   p. cm. – (Uncertainty and expectations in economics)
   Includes index.
   ISBN 0-631-16236-4
   1. Uncertainty. 2. Investments – Decision making. 3.
   Risk. 4. Information theory in economics. I. Title. II.
   Series.
   HB615.H57 1989
   332.6 – dc 19   88-25129

Typeset in 10 on 11½ pt Times by Unicus Graphics Ltd,
Horsham
Printed in Great Britain by Bookcraft Ltd, Bath, Avon

Contents

List of Figures

List of Tables

Preface

Over the past decade, and increasingly so over the past five years, a large number of significant contributions have been made in the general area of uncertainty and expectations in economics. These cover the whole range of core economics, from the modeling of individual decision-making under uncertainty to the implications of rational expectations in temporary general equilibrium and macro models. These advances have contributed to a significant transformation in economic theory, and in economists' understanding of the economic world.

Until now, the majority of these advances have been published in prestigious academic journals, written by experts for fellow experts. In a few areas, books have appeared, but these have been scattered and isolated – lacking a central focus. The new series, *Uncertainty and Expectations in Economics*, aims to provide that focus. Moreover, it will provide an outlet so that the experts may synthesize and pass on their important new findings to interested non-experts.

We believe that developments in uncertainty and expectations will continue to set the pace for advances in economic theory generally over the coming years. We also believe that these developments should be quickly made accessible to the profession at large, and hence we believe that this new series will serve as an important forum for intellectual debate on issues of great importance.

We envisage books in a variety of areas within the general umbrella of *Uncertainty and Expectations in Economics*. Some examples are: criticisms and appraisals of subjective expected utility theory; alternative theories of individual and group behavior under risk and uncertainty; the formulation and adaptation of expectations; the implications of different expectational schemes within different areas of economics; psychological theories of behavior under uncertainty and expectations; asymmetric information; consumer and firm behavior under uncertainty; insurance; contract theory; labor markets under uncertainty; job search; consumer search; learning and adaptive behavior; auctions, contracts and bidding; value of life and safety; duopoly, oligopoly and monopolistic competition; strategic models; R&D; game theory; bounded rationality; rules of thumb; reasonable behavior; fix price 'disequilibrium' general equilibrium models; the principal/agent problem; macro disequilibrium models; conjectures and conjectural equilibrium; expectations in financial markets; models of monetary sequence economies; Keynesian models; econometric modeling and investigation of disequilibrium and search models; rational expectations.

The type of volume will vary from survey and synthesis, to collection of influential papers and research monographs. The level of books will range from undergraduate text to academic treatise.

J. L. Ford
John D. Hey
Mark Machina

University of Birmingham
University of York
University of California, San Diego

Introduction

I am grateful to the publishers and to the Series Editors, J. L. Ford, John D. Hey, and Mark Machina, for including this collection of my essays as a volume in the distinguished Basil Blackwell series *Uncertainty and Expectations in Economics*.

The topics of time, uncertainty, and information are intertwined in a number of ways. Most obviously, uncertainty normally increases as we peer further into the mists of the future. Conversely, uncertainty about the future is typically resolved, partially at least, as the passage of time provides information about the looming shape of things to come. This substantive association between uncertainty and futurity is a main theme in several of the chapters to follow, notably the papers on liquidity and the term structure (chapter 8) and on speculation (chapters 10–12).

But there is a subtler, methodological connection that runs as an even more central theme through these essays. Why have the economics of time and the economics of uncertainty and information proved to be such difficult topics in the history of economic thought? Because, or so I believe, in each case there was a preconception – more an implicit mindset than an explicit tenet of belief – that these topics were too "different" to be analyzed in terms of the standard economic theory of choice and equilibrium. In dealing with individual decisions and market relations involving time, for example, a whole corpus of thought called "capital theory" evolved with special terminological categories: interest, saving, investment, capital budgeting, period of production, rate of return over cost, etc. And the economics of uncertainty developed its own set of idiosyncratic rubrics, among them riskiness and risk-aversion, insurance, diversification, and debt *versus* equity finance.

As applied in each context, these novel categories were by no means useless or without meaning. But they deflected attention away from the step really needed for deeper understanding, *the unification of the economics of time and the economics of uncertainty with mainline price theory*. This unification rests upon appreciating that all the fundamental economic concepts – resources and commodities, preferences and production, income and wealth, exchange and prices – retain their relevance when we move from choices involving simple commodities into the domains of choices over time or choices subject to uncertainty.

One example: earlier writers were much exercised by *interest*, which they viewed as a peculiar phenomenon requiring a very special explanation. So they debated over its nature and essence: for example, whether it is subjective (due to human preferences) or objective (due to physical productivity of capital), or whether it is a real or a monetary phenomenon. But the generalized economic approach makes it immediately clear that, since the economics of time is simply price theory applied to choices involving dated commodities, "interest" is not a mystical category of its own. Rather, the rate of interest is simply an aspect of the ruling price ratio in markets where earlier-dated and later-dated claims are traded against one another. In other words, if you have a price ratio of dated claims, you have a rate of interest. And in the economics of uncertainty, a somewhat analogous development was the fruitless attempt by earlier economists (and regrettably, some later ones as well) to distinguish between "risk" and "uncertainty". As will be seen in several of the essays below, notably those in part II, the purported distinction (at least, as it is usually formulated) collapses when the problem is interpreted in terms of the economic theory of choice.

The essays collected here are grouped under three main headings. Part I (Time, Risk, and Uncertainty) covers the fundamentals of these two topics and some selected applications. The articles in part II (From Uncertainty Theory to Information Theory) review the advances of thought required to progress beyond merely *passive* adaptations to uncertainty – the balancing of risks – toward *active* adaptations taking the form of information-seeking behavior. Finally, in part III (Applications of the Economic Theory of Information) several papers utilize the economics of information to address three important categories of real-world phenomena: liquidity and the term-structure of interest rates, the return to inventive activity, and speculation.

All the essays in the volume appear here in their original form apart from correction of minor typographical and stylistic slips.

PART I

Time, Risk, and Uncertainty

1   On the Theory of Optimal Investment Decision*

Background and comments

The opening of this paper refers to Irving Fisher's justly famous works on interest. But at the time of writing such a description was more of a wish on my part than an actuality. The unification of the economics of time with the general theory of economic choice, referred to in the Introduction, had indeed been essentially achieved by Fisher in *The Rate of Interest* (1907). An improved and updated version was published as *The Theory of Interest* (1930). But Fisher's reputation went into a decline shortly thereafter, mainly owing to his supposed misreading of events in the course of the 1929–33 depression. It is true that his seminal contributions in many different areas – among them the theory of index numbers, monetary theory, and what we now call econometrics – were still valued in some circles. (I particularly remember the high regard for his work expressed by my teacher Joseph A. Schumpeter, not an easy person to please.) But Fisher's beautiful edifice of the general-equilibrium theory of intertemporal choice had been largely lost to view. It was totally ignored, for example, or referenced only in slighting and incidental ways, in standard treatises of the period that are now themselves largely forgotten.

The rehabilitation (if I may use an over-dramatic term reminiscent of the Gulag!) of Fisher's work on interest was the goal of the essay reprinted here. Since the paper has been reprinted in at least eight separate collections of essays before this one, I can perhaps dare hope that the aim has been achieved. Actually, the present paper covers only investment decision, a subdivision under the broader heading of the economics of time. My later book, *Investment, Interest, and Capital* (Prentice-Hall, 1970), went on to provide a unified Fisherian analysis of the inter-related problems of individual optimization and market equilibrium over time, together with the associated determination of intertemporal price ratios (i.e. of interest rates). The book dealt also with certain topics not thoroughly or successfully covered by Fisher, notably capital accumulation and models of uncertainty. These subjects are among those addressed in the essays below.

*This article originally appeared in *Journal of Political Economy*, vol. 66 (Aug. 1958), pp. 329–52. The permission of the University of Chicago Press to reprint in this volume is gratefully acknowledged.

I should like to express indebtedness to many of my colleagues, and especially to James H. Lorie and Martin J. Bailey, for valuable suggestions and criticisms.

This article is an attempt to solve (in the theoretical sense), through the use of isoquant analysis, the problem of optimal investment decisions (in business parlance, the problem of capital budgeting). The initial section reviews the principles laid down in Irving Fisher's justly famous works on interest[1] to see what light they shed on two competing rules of behavior currently proposed by economists to guide business investment decisions – the present-value rule and the internal-rate-of-return rule. The next concern of the paper is to show how Fisher's principles must be adapted when the perfect capital market assumed in his analysis does not exist – in particular, when borrowing and lending rates diverge, when capital can be secured only at an increasing marginal borrowing rate, and when capital is "rationed." In connection with this last situation, certain non-Fisherian views (in particular, those of Scitovsky and of the Lutzes) about the correct ultimate goal or criterion for investment decisions are examined. Section 1.3, which presents the solution for multiperiod investments, corrects an error by Fisher which has been the source of much difficulty. The main burden of the analysis justifies the contentions of those who reject the internal rate of return as an investment criterion, and the paper attempts to show where the error in that concept (as ordinarily defined) lies and how the internal rate must be redefined if it is to be used as a reliable guide. On the positive side, the analysis provides some support for the use of the present-value rule but shows that even that rule is at best only a partial indicator of optimal investments and, in fact, under some conditions, gives an incorrect result.

More recent works on investment decisions, I shall argue, suffer from the neglect of Fisher's great contributions – the attainment of an optimum through balancing consumption alternatives over time and the clear distinction between production opportunities and exchange opportunities. It is an implication of this analysis, though it cannot be pursued here in detail, that solutions to the problem of investment decision recently proposed by Boulding, Samuelson, Scitovsky, and the Lutzes are at least in part erroneous. Their common error lay in searching for a rule or formula which would indicate optimal investment decisions *independently of consumption decisions.* No such search can succeed, if Fisher's analysis is sound which regards investment as not an end in itself but rather a process for distributing consumption over time.

The present paper deals throughout with a highly simplified situation in which the costs and returns of alternative individual investments are known *with certainty*, the problem being to select the scale and the mix of investments to be undertaken. To begin with, the analysis will be limited to investment decisions relating to two time periods only. We shall see in later sections that the two-period analysis can be translated immediately to the analysis of investments in perpetuities. For more general fluctuating income streams, however, additional difficulties arise whose resolution involves important new questions of principle. The restriction of the solution to perfect-information situations is, of course, unfortunate, since ignorance and uncertainty are of the essence of certain important observable characteristics of investment decision behavior. The analysis of optimal decisions under conditions of certainty can be justified, however, as a first step toward a more complete theory. No further apology will be offered for considering this oversimplified problem beyond the statement that theoretical economists are in such substantial disagreement about it that a successful attempt to bring the solution within the standard body of economic doctrine would represent a real contribution.

1.1   TWO-PERIOD ANALYSIS

Borrowing rate equals lending rate (Fisher's solution)

In order to establish the background for the difficult problems to be considered later, let us first review Fisher's solution to the problem of investment decision.[2] Consider the case in which there is a given rate at which the individual (or firm)[3] may borrow that is unaffected by the amount of his borrowings; a given rate at which he can lend that is unaffected by the amount of his loans; and in which these two rates are equal. These are the conditions used by Fisher; they represent a perfect capital market.

In figure 1.1 the horizontal axis labeled K_0 represents the amount of actual or potential income (the amount consumed or available for consumption) in period 0; the vertical axis K_1 represents the amount of income in the same sense in period 1. The individual's decision problem is to choose, within the opportunities available to him, an optimum point on the graph – that is, an optimal time pattern of consumption. His starting point may conceivably be a point on either axis (initial income falling all in period 0 or all in period 1), such as points T or P, or else it may be a point in the positive quadrant (initial income falling partly in period 0 and partly in period 1), such as points W or S'. It may even lie in the second or fourth quadrants – where his initial situation involves negative income either in period 0 or in period 1.

The individual is assumed to have a preference function relating income in periods 0 and 1. This preference function would be mapped in quite the ordinary way, and the curves U_1 and U_2 are ordinary utility-indifference curves from this map.

Finally, there are the investment opportunities open to the individual. Fisher distinguishes between "investment opportunities" and "market opportunities." The former are real productive transfers between income in one time period and in another (what we usually think of as "physical" investment, like planting a seed); the latter are transfers through borrowing or lending (which naturally are on balance offsetting in the loan market). I shall depart from Fisher's language to distinguish somewhat more clearly

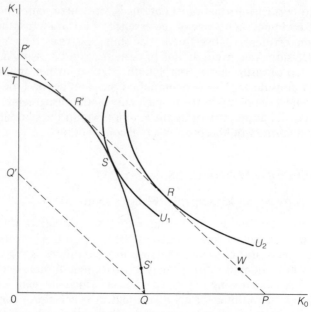

FIGURE 1.1 *Fisher's solution.*

between "production opportunities" and "market opportunities"; the word "investment" will be used in the more general and inclusive sense to refer to both types of opportunities taken together. Thus we may invest by building a house (a sacrifice of present for future income through a production opportunity) or by lending on the money market (a sacrifice of present for future income through a market or exchange opportunity). We could, equivalently, speak of purchase and sale of capital assets instead of lending or borrowing in describing the market opportunities.

In figure 1.1 an investor with a starting point at Q faces a market opportunity illustrated by the dashed line QQ'. That is, starting with all his income in time 0, he can lend at some given lending rate, sacrificing present for future income, any amount until his K_0 is exhausted – receiving in exchange K_1 or income in period 1. Equivalently, we could say that he can buy capital assets – titles to future income K_1 with current income K_0. Following Fisher, I shall call QQ' a "market line."[5] The line PP', parallel to QQ', is the market line available to an individual whose starting point is P on the K_0 axis. By our assumption that the borrowing rate is also constant and equal to the lending rate, the market line PP' is also the market opportunity to an individual whose starting point is W, within the positive quadrant.

Finally, the curve $QSTV$ shows the range of productive opportunities available to an individual with starting point Q. It is the locus of points attainable to such an individual as he sacrifices more and more of K_0 by productive investments yielding K_1 in return. This attainability locus Fisher somewhat ambiguously calls the "opportunity line"; it will be called here the "productive opportunity curve" or "productive transformation curve." Note that in its concavity to the origin the curve reveals a kind of diminishing returns to investment. More specifically, productive investment projects may be considered to be ranked by the expression $(\Delta K_1)/(-\Delta K_0) - 1$, which might be called the "productive rate of return."[5] Here ΔK_0 and ΔK_1 represent the changes in income of periods 0 and 1 associated with the project in question.

We may conceive of whole projects being so ranked, in which case we get the average productive rate of return for each such project. Or we may rank infinitesimal increments to projects, in which case we can deal with a marginal productive rate of return. The curve $QSTV$ will be continuous and have a continuous first derivative under certain conditions relating to absence of "lumpiness" of individual projects (or increments to projects), which we need not go into. In any case, $QSTV$ would represent a sequence of projects so arranged as to start with the one yielding the highest productive rate of return at the lower right and ending with the lowest rate of return encountered when the last dollar of period 0 is sacrificed at the upper left.[6] It is possible to attach meaning to the portion of $QSTV$ in the second quadrant, where K_0 becomes negative. Such points could not be optimal with indifference curves as portrayed in figure 1.1, of course, but they may enter into the determination of an optimum. (This analysis assumes that projects are independent. Where they are not, complications ensue which will be discussed below.)

As to the solution itself, the investor's objective is to climb onto as high an indifference curve as possible. Moving along the productive opportunity line $QSTV$, he sees that the highest indifference curve it touches is U_1 at the point S. But this is not the best point attainable, for he can move along $QSTV$ somewhat farther to the point R', which is on the market line PP'. He can now move in the reverse direction (borrowing) along PP', and the point R on the indifference curve U_2 is seen to be the best attainable.

The investor has, therefore, a solution in two steps. The "productive" solution – the point at which the individual should stop making additional productive investments – is at R'. He may then move along his market line to a point better satisfying his time preferences, at R. That is to say, he makes the best investment from the productive point of view and then "finances" it in the loan market. A very practical example is building a house and then borrowing on it through a mortgage so as to replenish current consumption income.

We may now consider, in the light of this solution, the current debate between two computing "rules" for optimal investment behavior.[7] The first of these, the present-value rule, would have the individual or firm adopt all projects whose present value is positive at the market rate of interest. This would have the effect of maximizing the present value of the firm's position in terms of income in periods 0 and 1. Present value, under the present conditions, may be defined as $K_0 + (K_1)/(1 + i)$, income in period 1 being discounted by the factor $1 + i$, where i is the lending-borrowing rate. Since the market lines are defined by the condition that a sacrifice of one dollar in K_0 yields $1 + i$ dollars in K_1, these market lines are nothing but lines of constant present value. The equation for these lines is $K_0 + (K_1)/(1 + i) = C$, C being a parameter. The present-value rule tells us to invest until the highest such line is attained, which clearly takes place at the point R'. So far so good, but note that the rule says nothing about the "financing" (borrowing or lending) also necessary to attain the final optimum at R.

The internal-rate-of-return rule, in the form here considered, would have the firm adopt any project whose internal rate is greater than the market rate of interest. The internal rate for a project in the general case is defined as that discounting rate ρ which reduces the stream of net returns associated with the project to a present value of zero (or, equivalently, which makes the discounted value of the associated cost stream equal to the discounted value of the receipts stream). We may write

$$0 = \Delta K_0 + \frac{\Delta K_1}{1 + \rho} + \frac{\Delta K_2}{(1 + \rho)^2} + \frac{\Delta K_n}{(1 + \rho)^n}. \tag{1.1}$$

In the two-period case ρ is identical with the productive rate of return, $(\Delta K_1)/(-\Delta K_0) - 1$. As in the discussion above, if infinitesimal changes are permitted, we may interpret this statement in the marginal sense. The marginal (two-period) internal rate of return is measured by the slope of the productive opportunity curve minus unity. In figure 1.1 at each step we would compare the steepness of $QSTV$ with that of the market lines. We would move along $QSTV$ as long as, and just so long as, it is the steeper. Evidently, this rule would have us move along $QSTV$ until it becomes tangent to a market line at R'. Again, so far so good, but nothing is said about the borrowing or lending then necessary to attain the optimum.

At least for the two-period case, then, the present-value rule and the internal-rate-of-return rule lead to identical answers[8] which are the same as that reached by our isoquant analysis, so far as *productive* investment decisions are concerned. The rules are both silent, however, about the market exchange between K_0 and K_1, which remains necessary if an optimum is to be achieved. This second step is obviously part of the solution. Had there been no actual opportunity to borrow or lend, the point S would have been the best attainable, and the process of productive investment should not have been carried as far as R'. We cannot say that the rules are definitely wrong, however, since with no such market opportunities there would have been no market rate of interest i for calculating present values or for comparison with the marginal internal rate of return. It remains to be seen whether these rules can be restated or generalized to apply to cases where a simple market rate of interest is not available for unlimited borrowing and lending. But it should be observed that, in comparison with isoquant analysis, each of the rules leads to only a partial answer.

When borrowing and lending rates differ

We may now depart from Fisher's analysis, or rather extend it, to a case he did not consider. The borrowing and lending rates are still assumed to be constant, independent of the amounts taken or supplied by the individual or firm under consideration. However, it is now assumed that these rates are not equal, the borrowing rate being higher than the lending rate.[9] In figure 1.2 there is the same preference map, of which only the isoquant U_1 is shown. There are now, however, two sets of market lines over the graph; the steeper (*dashed*) lines represent borrowing opportunities (note the direction of the arrows), and the flatter (*solid*) lines represent lending opportunities. The heavy solid lines show two possible sets of productive opportunities, both of which lead to solutions along U_1. Starting with amount OW of K_0, an investor with a production opportunity WVW' would move along WVW' to V, at which point he would *lend* to get to his time-preference optimum – the tangency with U_1 at V'. The curve STS' represents a much more productive possibility; starting with only OS of K_0, the investor would move along STS' to T and then *borrow* backward along the dashed line to get to T', the tangency point with U_1. Note that the total opportunity set (the points attainable through any combination of the market and productive opportunities) is WVV^* for the first opportunity, and $S'TT^*$ for the second.

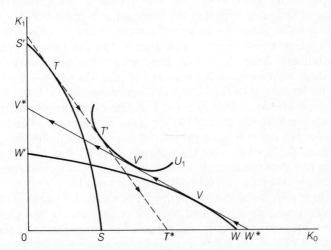

FIGURE 1.2 *Extension of Fisher's solution for differing borrowing and lending rates.*

More detailed analysis, however, shows that we do not yet have the full solution – there is a third possibility. An investor with a productive opportunity locus starting on the K_0 axis will never stop moving along this locus in the direction of greater K_1 as long as the marginal productive rate of return is still above the borrowing rate – nor will he ever push along the locus beyond the point where the marginal productive rate of return falls below the lending rate. Assuming that some initial investments are available which have a higher productive rate of return than the borrowing rate, the investor should push along the locus until the borrowing rate is reached. If, at this point, it is possible to move up the utility hill by borrowing, productive investment should cease, and the borrowing should take place; the investor is at some point like T in figure 1.2. If borrowing decreases utility, however, more productive investment is called for. Suppose investment is then carried on until diminishing returns bring the marginal productive rate of return down to the lending rate. If lending then increases utility, productive investment should halt there, and the lending take place; the investor is at some point like V in figure 1.2. But suppose that now it is found that lending also decreases utility! This can only mean that a tangency of the productive opportunity locus and an indifference curve took place when the marginal productive rate of return was somewhere *between* the lending and the borrowing rates. In this case neither lending nor borrowing is called for, the optimum being reached directly in the productive investment decision by equating the marginal productive rate of return with the marginal rate of substitution (in the sense of time preference) along the utility isoquant.

These solutions are illustrated by the division of figure 1.3 into three zones. In zone I the borrowing rate is relevant. Tangency solutions with the market line at the borrowing rate like that at T are carried back by borrowing to tangency with a utility isoquant at a point like T'. All such final solutions lie along the curve OB, which connects all points on the utility isoquants whose slope equals that of the *borrowing* market line. Correspondingly, zone III is that zone where the productive solution involves tangency with a lending market line (like V), which is then carried forward by lending to a final tangency optimum with a utility isoquant along the line OL at a point like V'. This line connects all points on the utility isoquants with slope equal to that of the *lending* market line. Finally, zone II solutions occur when a productive opportunity locus like QRQ' is steeper than the lending rate throughout zone III but flatter than the borrowing rate throughout zone I. Therefore, such a locus must be tangent to one of the indifference curves somewhere in zone II.

By analogy with the discussion in the previous section, we may conclude that the *borrowing* rate will lead to correct answers (to the productive investment decision, neglecting the related financing question) under the present-value rule or the internal-rate-of-return rule – when the situation involves a zone I solution. Correspondingly, the *lending* rate will be

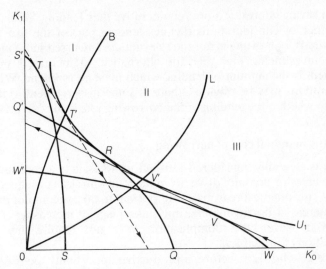

FIGURE 1.3   *Three solution zones for differing borrowing and lending rates.*

appropriate and lead to correct investment decisions for zone III solutions. For zone II solutions, however, neither will be correct. There will, in fact, be some rate between the lending and the borrowing rates which would lead to the correct results. Formally speaking, we could describe this correct discount rate as the marginal productive opportunity rate,[10] which will at equilibrium equal the marginal subjective time-preference rate. In such a case neither rule is satisfactory in the sense of providing the productive solution without reference to the utility isoquants; knowledge of the comparative slopes of the utility isoquant and the productive opportunity frontier is all that is necessary, however. Of course, even when the rules in question are considered "satisfactory," they are misleading in implying that productive investment decisions can be correctly made independently of the "financing" decision.

This solution, in retrospect, may perhaps seem obvious. Where the productive opportunity, time-preference, and market (or financing) opportunities stand in such relations to one another as to require borrowing to reach the optimum, the borrowing rate is the correct rate to use in the productive investment decision. The lending rate is irrelevant because the decision on the margin involves a balancing of the cost of borrowing and the return from further productive investment, both being higher than the lending rate. The lending opportunity is indeed still available, but, the rate of return on lending being lower than the lowest marginal productive rate of return we would wish to consider in the light of the borrowing rate we must pay, lending is not a relevant alternative. Rather the relevant alternative to productive investment is a reduction in borrowing, which in terms of saving interest is more remunerative than lending. Similarly, when the balance of considerations dictates lending part of the firm's current capital funds, borrowing is not the relevant cost incurred in financing productive investment. The relevant alternative to increased productive investment is the amount of lending which must be foregone. While these considerations may be obvious, there is some disagreement in the literature as to whether the lending or the borrowing rate is *the* correct one.[11]

Increasing marginal cost of borrowing

While it is generally considered satisfactory to assume a constant lending rate (the investor does not drive down the loan rate as a consequence of his lendings), for practical reasons it is important to take account of the case in which increased borrowing can only take place at increasing cost. As it happens, however, this complication does not require any essential modification of principle.

Figure 1.4 shows, as before, a productive opportunity locus $QR'T$ and an indifference curve U_1. For simplicity, assume that marginal borrowing costs rise at the same rate whether the investor begins to borrow at the

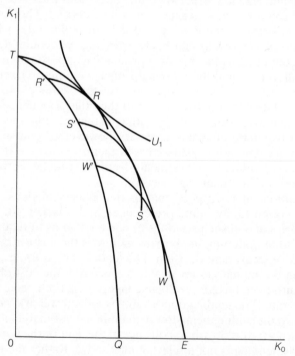

FIGURE 1.4 *Increasing marginal cost of borrowing.*

point R', S', or W' or at any other point along $QR'T$ (he cannot, of course, start borrowing at Q, having no K_1 to offer in exchange for more K_0). Under this assumption we can then draw market curves, now concave to the origin, like $R'R$, $S'S$, and $W'W$. The curve TE represents the total opportunity set as the *envelope* of these market curves, that is, TE connects all the points on the market curves representing the maximum K_0 attainable for any given K_1. By the nature of an envelope curve, TE will be tangent to a market curve at each such point. The optimum is then simply found where TE is tangent to the highest indifference curve attainable – here the curve U_1 at R. To reach R, the investor must exploit his productive opportunity to the point R' and then borrow back along his market curve to R.

The preceding discussion applies solely to what was called a zone I (borrowing) solution in the previous section. Depending upon the nature of the productive opportunity, a zone II or zone III solution would also be possible under the assumptions of this section. With regard to the present-value and the internal-rate-of-return rules, the conclusions are unchanged for zone II and III solutions, however. Only for zone I solutions is there any modification.

The crucial question, as always, for these rules is what rate of discount to use. Intuition tells us that the rate representing *marginal* borrowing cost should be used as the discount rate for zone I solutions, since productive investment will then be carried just to the point justified by the cost of the associated increment of borrowing.[12] That is, the slope of the envelope for any point on the envelope curve (for example, R), is the same as the slope of the productive opportunity curve at the correponding point (R') connected by the market curve.[13] If this is the case, the discount rate determined by the slope at a tangency with U_1 at a point like R will also lead to productive investment being carried to R' by the rules under consideration. Of course, this again is a purely formal statement. Operationally speaking, the rules may not be of much value, since the discount rate to be used is not known in advance independently of the utility (time-preference) function.

Rationing of "capital" – a current controversy

The previous discussion provides the key for resolving certain current disputes over what constitutes optimal investment decision under a condition of "capital rationing" or "fixed capital budget." This condition is said to exist when the firm, or individual, or perhaps department of government under consideration cannot borrow additional "capital" but is limited instead to making the best use of the "capital" already in its possession or allocated to it.[14] In theoretical literature a closely related idea is expressed by Scitovsky, who, regarding the availability of capital (in the sense of "current capital funds") as the fixed factor limiting the size of the firm, proposes as the investment criterion the maximization of "profit per unit capital invested."[15] Lutz and Lutz, in contrast, assert as their ultimate investment criterion the maximization of the rate of return on the entrepreneur's *owned* capital, which they regard as fixed.[16]

It is of some interest to analyze these concepts in greater detail in terms of our Fisherian model. Scitovsky defines "capital" as current capital funds (our K_0) required to bridge the time lapse between factor input and product output.[17] Under this definition, however, "capital" would be fixed to the firm only under rather peculiar conditions; specifically, if there is a discontinuity in the capital funds market such that the marginal borrowing rate suddenly becomes infinite at the firm's level of borrowings.[18] Without discontinuity, an infinitely high marginal borrowing rate could never represent an equilibrium position for the borrower, unless indeed his preference for present income over future income was absolute. And, of course, if the marginal borrowing rate is not infinite, current capital funds could not be said to be fixed. Nevertheless, while this case may be considered peculiar and unlikely to arise in any strict sense, it may be acceptable as a reasonable approximation of certain situations which occur in practice – especially in the short run, perhaps as a result of previous miscalculations. A division of a firm or a department of government may at times be said to face an infinite marginal borrowing rate once a budget constraint is reached – until the next meeting of the board of directors or the Congress provides more funds.

On the other hand, it is difficult to decipher the Lutzes' meaning when they speak of the firm's *owned* capital as fixed. In the Fisherian analysis, "ownership" of current or future assets is a legal form without analytical significance – to buy an asset yielding future income, with current funds, is simply to lend, while selling income is the same as borrowing. In a more fundamental sense, however, we could think of the firm as "owning" the opportunity set or at least the physical productive opportunities available to it, and this perhaps is what the Lutzes have in mind. Thus, Robinson Crusoe's house might be considered as his "owned capital" – a resource yielding consumption income in both present and future. The trouble is that the Lutzes seem to be thinking of "owned capital" as the *value* of the productive resources (in the form of capital goods) owned by the firm,[19] but owned physical capital goods cannot be converted to a capital *value* without bringing in a rate of discount for the receipts stream. But since, as we have seen, the relevant rate of discount for a firm's decisions is not (except where a perfect capital market exists) an independent entity but is itself determined by the analysis, the *capital value* cannot in general be considered to be fixed independently of the investment decision.[20]

While space does not permit a full critique of the Lutzes' important work, it is worth mentioning that – from a Fisherian point of view – it starts off on the wrong foot. They search first for an ultimate criterion or formula with which to gauge investment decision rules and settle upon "maximization of the rate of return on the investor's owned capital" on what seem to be purely intuitive grounds. The Fisherian approach, in contrast, integrates investment decision with the general theory of choice – the goal being to maximize utility subject to certain opportunities and constraints. In these terms, certain formulas can be validated as useful proximate rules for some classes of problems, as I am attempting to show here. However, the ultimate Fisherian criterion of choice – the optimal balancing of consumption alternatives over time – cannot be reduced to any of the usual formulas.

Instead of engaging in further discussion of the various senses in which "capital" may be said to be fixed to the firm, it will be more instructive to see how the Fisherian approach solves the problem of "capital rationing." I shall use as an illustration what may be called a "Scitovsky situation," in which the investor has run against a discontinuity making the marginal borrowing rate infinite. I regard this case (which I consider empirically significant only in the short run) as the model situation underlying the "capital rationing" discussion.

An infinite borrowing rate makes the dashed borrowing lines of figures 1.2 and 1.3 essentially vertical. In consequence, the curve OB in figure 1.3 shifts so far to the left as to make zone I disappear for all practical purposes. There are then only zone II and zone III solutions. An investment-opportunity locus like WVW' in figure 1.3 becomes less steep than the lending slope in zone III, in which case the investor will carry investment up to the point V where this occurs and then lend until a tangency solution is reached at V', which would be somewhere along the curve OL of figure 1.3. If an investment-opportunity locus like QRQ' in figure 1.3 is still steeper than the lending rate after it crosses OL, investment should be carried until tangency with an indifference curve like U_1 is attained somewhere to the left of OL, with no lending or borrowing taking place.

In terms of the present-value or internal-rate-of-return rules, under these conditions the decisions should be based on the *lending* rate (as the discounting rate or the standard of comparison) if the solution is a zone III one. Here lending actually takes place, since movement upward and to the left still remains desirable when the last investment with a rate of return greater than the lending rate is made. If the solution is a zone II one, the lending rate must not be used. Investments showing positive present value at the lending rate (or, equivalently, with an internal rate of return higher than the lending rate) will be nevertheless undesirable after a tangency point equating the investment-opportunity slope and the time-preference slope is reached. The correct rate, formally speaking, is the marginal opportunity rate.

The solution changes only slightly when we consider an isolated individual like Robinson Crusoe or a self-contained community like a nation under autarky (or like the world economy as a whole). In this situation neither borrowing nor lending is possible in our sense, only productive opportunities existing. Only zone II solutions are then possible. This case is the most extreme remove from the assumption of perfect capital markets.[21]

As in the case of the zone II solutions arising without capital rationing, the present-value or internal-rate-of-return rules can be formally modified to apply to the zone II solutions which are typical under capital rationing. The discount rate to be used for calculating present values or as a standard of comparison against the internal rate of project increments is the rate given by the slope of the zone II tangency (the marginal productive rate of return); with this rate, the rules give the correct answer. But this rate cannot be discovered until the solution is attained and so is of no assistance in reaching the solution. The exception is the zone III solution involving lending which can arise in a "Scitovsky situation." Here the lending rate should of course be used. The undetermined discount rate that gives correct results when the rules are used for zone II solutions can, in some problems, be regarded as a kind of shadow price reflecting the productive rate of return on the best alternative opportunity not being exploited.

The reader may be curious as to why, in the Scitovsky situation, the outcome of the analysis was not Scitovsky's result – that the optimal investment decision is such as to maximize the (average) internal rate of return on the firm's present capital funds (K_0). Thus, in figure 1.3, for a firm starting with OQ of K_0 and faced with the productive opportunity locus QRQ', the average rate of return (K_1 received per unit of K_0 sacrificed) is a maximum for an infinitesimal movement along QRQ', since, the farther it moves, the more the marginal and average productive rates of return fall. Such a rule implies staying at Q – which is obviously the wrong decision.

How does this square with Scitovsky's intuitively plausible argument that the firm always seeks to maximize its returns on the fixed factor, present capital funds being assumed here to be fixed?[22] The answer is that this argument is applicable only for a factor "fixed" in the sense of no alternative uses. Here present capital funds K_0 are assumed to be fixed, but not in the sense Scitovsky must have had in mind. The concept here is that no additional borrowing can take place, but the possibility of *consuming* the present funds as an alternative to investing them is recognized. For Scitovsky, however, the funds *must* be invested. If in fact current income K_0 had no uses other than conversion into future income K_1 (this amounts to absolute preference for future over current income), Scitovsky's rule would correctly tell us to pick that point on the K_1 axis which is the highest.[23] Actually, our time preferences are more balanced; there *is* an alternative use (consumption) for K_0. Therefore, even in Scitovsky situations, we will balance K_0 and K_1 on the margin – and not simply accept the maximum K_1 we can get in exchange for all our "fixed" K_0.[24] The analyses of Scitovsky, the Lutzes, and many other recent writers frequently lead to incorrect solutions because of their failure to take into account the alternative consumption opportunities which Fisher integrated into his theory of investment decision.

Non-independent investment opportunities

Up to this point, following Fisher, investment opportunities have been assumed to be independent so that it is possible to rank them in any desired way. In particular, they were ordered in figures 1.1–1.4 in terms of decreasing productive rate of return; the resultant concavity produced unique tangency solutions with the utility or market curves. But suppose, now, that there are two mutually exclusive sets of such investment opportunities. Thus we may consider building a factory in the East or the West, but not both – contemplating the alternatives, the eastern opportunities may look like the locus $QV'V$, and the western opportunities like $QT'T$ in figure 1.5.[25]

Which is better? Actually, the solutions continue to follow directly from Fisher's principles, though too much non-independence makes for troublesome calculations in practice, and in some classes of cases the heretofore inerrant present-value rule fails. In the simplest case, in which there is a constant borrowing-lending rate (a perfect capital market), the curve $QV'V$ is tangent to its highest attainable present-value line at V' – while the best point on $QT'T$ is T'. It is only necessary to consider these, and the one attaining the higher present-value line ($QT'T$ at T' in this case) will permit the investor to reach the highest possible indifference curve U_1 at R. In contrast, the internal-rate-of-return rule would locate the points T' and V' but could not discriminate between them. Where borrowing and

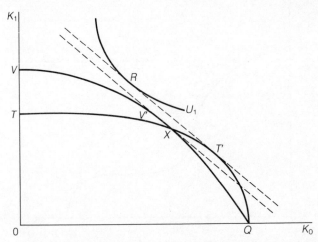

FIGURE 1.5 *Non-independent investment opportunities – two alternative productive investment loci.*

lending rates differ, as in figure 1.2 (now interpreting the productive opportunity loci of that figure as mutually exclusive alternatives), it may be necessary to compare, say, a lending solution at V with a borrowing solution at T. To find the *optimum optimorum*, the indifference curves must be known (in figure 1.2 the two solutions attain the same indifference curve). Note that present value is *not* a reliable guide here; in fact, the present value of the solution $V(= W^*)$ at the relevant discount rate for it (the lending rate) far exceeds that of the solution $T(= T^*)$ at its discount rate (the borrowing rate), when the two are actually indifferent. Assuming an increasing borrowing rate creates no new essential difficulty.

Another form of non-independence, illustrated in figure 1.6, is also troublesome without modifying principle. Here the projects along the productive investment locus QQ' are not entirely independent, for we are constrained to adopt some low-return ones before certain high-return ones. Again, there is a possibility of several local optima like V and T, which can be compared along the same lines as used in the previous illustration.

Conclusion for two-period analysis

The solutions for optimal investment decisions vary according to a two-way classification of cases. The first classification refers to the way market opportunities exist for the decision-making agency; the second classification refers to the absence or presence of the complication of non-independent productive opportunities. The simplest, extreme cases for the first classification are: (a) a perfect capital market (market opportunities

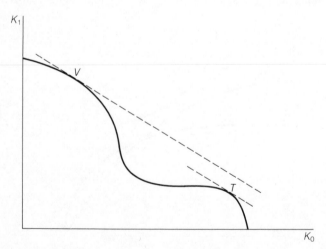

FIGURE 1.6 *Non-independent investment opportunities – poorer projects prerequisite to better ones.*

such that lending or borrowing in any amounts can take place at the same, fixed rate) and (b) no market opportunities whatsoever, as was true for Robinson Crusoe. Where there is a perfect capital market, the total attainable set is a triangle (considering only the first quadrant) like OPP' in figure 1.1, just tangent to the productive opportunity locus. Where there is no capital market at all, the total attainable set is simply the productive opportunity locus itself. It is not difficult to see how the varying forms of imperfection of the capital market fit in between these extremes.

When independence of physical (productive) opportunities holds, the opportunities may be ranked in order of descending productive rate of return. Geometrically, if the convenient (but inessential) assumption of continuity is adopted, independence means that the productive opportunity locus is everywhere concave to the origin, like $OS'TV$ in figure 1.1. Non-independence may take several forms (see figures 1.5 and 1.6), but in each case that is not trivial non-independence means that the effective productive opportunity locus is not simply concave. This is obvious in figure 1.6. In figure 1.5 each of the two alternative loci considered separately is concave, but the effective locus is the scalloped outer edge of the overlapping sets of points attainable by either – that is, the effective productive opportunity locus runs along $QT'T$ up to X and then crosses over to $QV'V$.

With this classification a detailed tabulation of the differing solutions could be presented; the following brief summary of the general principles involved should serve almost as well, however.

1 The internal-rate-of-return rule fails wherever there are multiple tangencies – the normal outcome for non-independent productive opportunities.

2 The present-value rule works whenever the other does and, in addition, correctly discriminates among multiple tangencies, whenever a perfect capital market exists (or, by extension, whenever a unique discount rate can be determined for the comparison – for example when all the alternative tangencies occur in zone I or else all in zone III).

3 Both rules work only in a formal sense when the solution involves direct tangency between a productive opportunity locus and a utility isoquant, since the discount rate necessary for use of both rules is the marginal opportunity rate – a product of the analysis.

4 The cases when even the present-value rule fails (may actually give wrong answers) all involve the comparison of multiple tangencies arising from non-independent investments when, in addition, a perfect capital market does not exist. One important example is the comparison of a tangency involving borrowing in zone I with another involving lending in zone III. Only reference to the utility map can give correct answers for such cases.

5 Even when one or both rules are correct in a not merely formal sense, the answer given is the "productive solution" – only part of the way toward

attainment of the utility optimum. Furthermore, this productive decision is optimal only when it can be assumed that the associated financing decision will in fact be made.

1.2   A BRIEF NOTE ON PERPETUITIES

A traditional way of handling the multiperiod case in capital theory has been to consider investment decisions as choices between current funds and perpetual future income flows. For many purposes this is a valuable simplifying idea. It cannot be adopted here, however, because the essence of the practical difficulties which have arisen in multiperiod investment decisions is the *reinvestment* problem – the necessity of making productive or market exchanges between incomes in future time periods. In fact, the consideration of the perpetuity case is, in a sense, only a variant of the two-period analysis, in which there is a single present and a single future. In the case of perpetuity analysis, the future is stretched out, but we cannot consider transfer between different periods of the future.

All the two-period results in section 1.1 can easily be modified to apply to the choice between current funds and perpetuities. In the figures, instead of income K_1 in period 1 one may speak of an annual rate of income k. Productive opportunity loci and time-preference curves will retain their familiar shapes. The lines of constant present value (borrow-lend lines) are expressed by the equation $C = K_0 + k/i$ instead of $C = K_0 + K_1/(1 + i)$. The "internal rate of return" will equal $k/(-\Delta K_0)$. The rest of the analysis follows directly, but, rather than trace it out, I shall turn to the consideration of the multiperiod case in a more general way.

1.3   MULTIPERIOD ANALYSIS

Considerable doubt prevails on how to generalize the principles of the two-period analysis to the multiperiod case. The problems which have troubled the analysis of the multiperiod case are actually the result of inappropriate generalizations of methods of solution that do lead to correct results in the simplified two-period analysis.

Internal-rate-of-return rule *versus* present-value rule

In the multiperiod analysis there is no formal difficulty in generalizing the indifference curves of Figure 1.1 to indifference shells in any number of dimensions. Also the lines of constant present value or market lines become hyperplanes with the equation (in the most general form)

$$K_0 + \frac{K_1}{1 + i_1} + \frac{K_2}{(1 + i_1)(1 + i_2)} + \ldots + \frac{K_n}{(1 + i_1)(1 + i_2)\ldots(1 + i_n)} = C, \qquad (1.2)$$

C being a parameter, i_1 the discount rate between income in period 0 and 1, i_2 the discount rate between periods 1 and 2, and so forth.[26] Where $i_1 = i_2 = \ldots i_n = i$, the expression takes on the simpler and more familiar form

$$K_0 + \frac{K_1}{1+i} + \frac{K_2}{(1+i)^2} + \ldots + \frac{K_n}{(1+i)^n} = C. \qquad (1.3)$$

The major difficulty with the multiperiod case turns upon the third element of the solution – the description of the productive opportunities, which may be denoted by the equation $f(K_0, K_1, \ldots, K_n) = 0$. The purely theoretical specification is not too difficult, however, if the assumption is made that all investment options are independent. The problem of non-independence is not essentially different in the multiperiod case and in the two-period case, and it would enormously complicate the presentation to consider it here. Under this condition, then, and with appropriate continuity assumptions, the productive opportunity locus may be envisaged as a shell[27] concave to the origin in all directions. With these assumptions, between income in any two periods K_r and K_s (holding K_t for all other periods constant) there will be a two-dimensional productive opportunity locus essentially like that in figure 1.1.[28]

Now suppose that lending or borrowing can take place between any two successive periods r and s at the rate i_s. The theoretical solution involves finding the multidimensional analogue of the point R' (in figure 1.1) – that is, the point on the highest present-value hyperplane reached by the productive opportunity locus. With simple curvature and continuity assumptions, R' will be a tangency point, thus having the additional property that, between the members of any such pair of time periods, the marginal productive rate of return between K_r and K_s (holding all other K_t's constant) will be equal to the discount rate between these periods. Furthermore, if the condition is met between all pairs of successive periods, it will also be satisfied between any pairs of time periods as well.[29] Again, as in the two-period case, the final solution will involve market lending or borrowing ("financing") to move along the highest present-value hyperplane attained from the intermediate productive solution R' to the true preference optimum at R. Note that, as compared with the present value or direct solution, the principle of equating the marginal productive rate of return with the discount rate requires certain continuity assumptions.

Now it is here that Fisher, who evidently understood the true nature of the solution himself, appears to have led others astray. In his *Rate of Interest* he provides a mathematical proof that the optimal investment decision involves setting what is here called the marginal productive rate of return equal to the market rate of interest *between any two periods*.[30] By obvious generalization of the result of the two-period problem, this condition is identical with that of finding the line of highest present value (the two-dimensional projection of the hyperplane of highest present value) between these time periods. Unfortunately, Fisher fails to state the qualification "between any two time-periods" consistently and at various places makes flat statements to the effect that investments will be made wherever the "rate of return on sacrifice" or "rate of return on cost" between any two options exceeds the rate of interest.[31]

Now the rate of return on sacrifice is, for two-period comparisons, equivalent to the productive rate of return. More generally, however, Fisher defines the rate of return on sacrifice in a *multiperiod* sense; that is, as that rate which reduces to a present value of zero the entire sequence of positive and negative periodic differences between the returns of any two investment options.[32] This definition is, for our purposes, equivalent to the so-called "internal rate of return."[33] This latter rate (which will be denoted ρ) will, however, be shown to lead to results which are, in general, not correct if the procedure is followed of adopting or rejecting investment options on the basis of a comparison of ρ and the market rate.[34]

Failure of the generalized "internal rate of return"

Recent thinking emphasizing the internal rate of return seems to be based upon the idea of finding a purely "internal" measure of the time productivity of an investment – that is, the rate of growth of capital funds invested in a project – for comparison with the market rate.[35] But the idea of rate of growth involves a ratio and cannot be uniquely defined unless one can uniquely value initial and terminal positions. Thus the investment option characterized by the annual cash-flow sequence $-1, 0, 0, 8$ clearly involves a growth rate of 100 percent (compounding annually), because it really reduces to a two-period option with intermediate compounding. Similarly, a savings deposit at 10 percent compounded annually for n years may seem to be a multiperiod option, but it is properly regarded as a series of two-period options (the "growth" will take place only if at the beginning of each period the decision is taken to reinvest the capital plus interest yielded by the investment of the previous period). A savings-account option without reinvestment would be: $-1, 0.10, 0.10, 0.10, \ldots,$ 1.10 (the last element being a terminating payment); with reinvestment, the option becomes $-1, 0, 0, 0, \ldots, (1.10)^n$, n being the number of compounding periods after the initial deposit.

Consider, however, a more general investment option characterized by the sequence $-1, 2, 1$. (In general, all investment options considered here will be normalized in terms of an assumed \$1.00 of initial outlay or initial receipt.) How can a rate of growth for the initial capital outlay be determined? Unlike the savings-account opportunity, no information is provided as to the rate at which the intermediate receipt or "cash throw-off" of \$2.00 can be reinvested. If, of course, we use some external discounting rate (for example, the cost of capital or the rate of an outside lending opportunity), we will be departing from the idea of a purely *internal* growth rate. In fact, the use of an external rate will simply reduce us to a present-value evaluation of the investment option.

In an attempt to resolve this difficulty, one mathematical feature of the two-period marginal productive rate of return was selected for generalization by both Fisher and his successors. This feature is the fact that, when ρ (in the two-period case equal to the marginal productive rate of return $[\Delta K_1]/[-\Delta K_0]-1$) is used for discounting the values in the receipt-outlay stream, the discounted value becomes zero. This concept lends itself to easy generalization: for any multiperiod stream there will be a similar discounting rate ρ which will make the discounted value equal to zero (or so it was thought). This rate seems to be purely internal, not infected by any market considerations. And, in certain simple cases, it does lead to correct answers in choosing investment projects according to the rule: Adopt the project if ρ is greater than the market rate r.

For the investment option $-1, 2, 1$ considered above, ρ is equal to $\sqrt{2}$, or 141.4 percent. And, in fact, if the borrowing rate or the rate on the best alternative opportunity (whichever is the appropriate comparison) is less than $\sqrt{2}$, the investment is desirable. Figure 1.7 plots the present value C of the option as a function of the discounting interest rate, i, assumed to be constant over the two discounting periods. Note that the present value of the option diminishes as i increases throughout the entire relevant range of i, from $i = -1$ to $i = \infty$.[36] The internal rate of return ρ is that i for which the present-value curve cuts the horizontal axis. Evidently, for any $i < \rho$, present value is positive; for $i > \rho$, it is negative.

However, the fact that the use of ρ leads to the correct decision in a particular case or a particular class of cases does not mean that it is correct

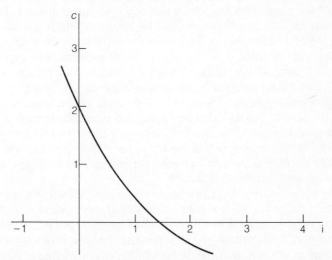

FIGURE 1.7 *Sketch of present value of the option $-1, 2, 1$.*

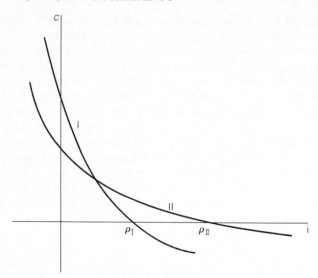

FIGURE 1.8 *Two alternative options.*

in principle. And, in fact, cases have been adduced where its use leads to incorrect answers. Alchian has shown that, in the comparison of two investment options which are alternatives, the choice of the one with a higher ρ is not in general correct – in fact, the decision cannot be made without knowledge of the appropriate external discounting rate.[37] Figure 1.8 illustrates two such options, I being preferable for low rates of interest and II for high rates. The *i* at which the crossover takes place is Fisher's rate of return on sacrifice between these two options. But II has the higher internal rate of return (that is, its present value falls to zero at a higher discounting rate) regardless of the actual rate of interest. How can we say that I is preferable at low rates of interest? Because its present value is higher, it permits the investor to move along a higher hyperplane to find the utility optimum attained somewhere on that hyperplane. If II were adopted, the investor would also be enabled to move along such a hyperplane, but a lower one. Put another way, with the specified low rate of interest, the investor adopting I could, if he chose, put himself in the position of adopting II by appropriate borrowings and lendings together with throwing away some of his wealth.[38]

Even more fundamentally, Lorie and Savage have shown that ρ may not be unique.[39] Consider, for example, the investment option $-1, 5, -6$. Calculation reveals that this option has a present value of zero at discounting rates of both 100 percent and 200 percent. For this investment option present value as a function of the discounting rate is sketched in figure 1.9. While Lorie and Savage speak only of "dual" internal rates of return, any

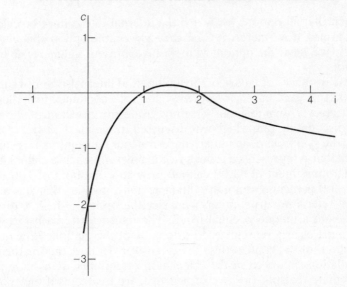

FIGURE 1.9 *Sketch of present value of the investment option* $-1, 5, -6.$

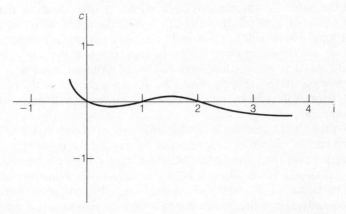

FIGURE 1.10 *Sketch of present value of the investment option* $-1, 6, -11, 6.$

number of zero values of the present-value function are possible in principle. The option $-1, 6, -11, 6$, illustrated in figure 1.10, has zero present value at the discounting rates 0 percent, 100 percent, and 200 percent, for example.[40]

In fact, perfectly respectable investment options may have *no* real internal rates (the present value equation has only imaginary roots). The option $-1, 3, -2\frac{1}{2}$ is an example; a plot would show that its present value is negative throughout the relevant range.[41] It is definitely not the case, however, that all options for which the internal rate cannot be calculated are bad ones. If we merely reverse the signs on the option above to get 1, -3, $2\frac{1}{2}$, we have an option with positive present value at all rates of discount.

These instances of failure of the multiperiod internal-rate-of-return rule (note that in each case the present-value rule continues to indicate the correct answer unambiguously, setting aside the question of the appropriate discounting rate which was discussed in section 1.1) are, of course, merely the symptom of an underlying erroneous conception. It is clear that the idea that ρ represents a growth rate in any simple sense cannot be true; a capital investment of $1.00 cannot grow at a rate both of 100 percent and of 200 percent. Even more fundamentally, the idea that ρ is a purely *internal* rate is not true either. Consider the option -1, 2, 1 discussed earlier, with a unique ρ equal to $\sqrt{2}$. The intermediate cash throwoff of $2.00 must clearly be reinvested externally of this option. How does the calculation of ρ handle this? This answer is that the mathematical manipulations involved in the calculation of ρ implicitly assume that all intermediate receipts, positive or negative, are treated as if they could be compounded at the rate ρ being solved for.[42] The rate ρ has been characterized rather appropriately as the "solving rate" of interest. But note that this mathematical manipulation, even where it does lead to a unique answer (and, in general, it will not), is unreasonable in its economic implications. There will not normally be other investment opportunities arising for investment of intermediate cash proceeds at the rate ρ, nor is it generally true that intermediate cash inflows (if required) must be obtained by borrowing at the rate ρ. The rate ρ, arising from a mathematical manipulation, will only by rare coincidence represent relevant economic alternatives.

The preceding arguments against the use of usual concept of the "internal rate of return" do not take any account of the possibility of non-constant interest rates over time. Martin J. Bailey has emphasized to me that it is precisely when this occurs (when there exists a known pattern of future variation of i) that the internal-rate-of-return rule fails most fundamentally. For in the use of that rule all time periods are treated on a par; the only discounting is via the solving rate defined only in terms of the sequence of cash flows. But with (a known pattern of) varying future i, shifts in the relative desirability of income in different periods are brought about. In the usual formulation the internal rate of return concept can take no account of this. In fact, in such a case one might have an investment for which ρ was well defined and unique and still not be able to determine the desirability of the investment opportunity (that is, depending upon the time pattern of future interest rates, present value might be either negative or positive).

The following remarks attempt to summarize the basic principles discussed in this section.

At least in the simplest case, where we do not worry about differences between borrowing and lending rates but assume these to be equal and also constant (constant with respect to the amount borrowed or lent – not constant over time), the multidimensional solution using the present-value rule is a straightforward generalization of the two-period solution. The principle is to push productive investment to the point where the highest attainable level of present value is reached and then to "finance" this investment by borrowing or lending between time periods to achieve a time-preference optimum.

The main burden of these remarks has been to the effect that the internal-rate-of-return rule, unlike the present-value rule, does not generalize to the multiperiod case if the usual definition of the internal rate ρ is adopted – that is, as that rate which sets the present value of the discounted income stream equal to zero. I have tried to show the multi-period generalization which *would* make the internal-rate-of-return rule still correct: between *every pair* of time periods, the marginal internal rate of return in the sense of the marginal productive rate of return between those two periods, holding income in other periods constant, should be set equal to the market discount rate between those periods. That the usual interpretation of the internal-rate-of-return rule is not in general correct has been illustrated by its failure in particular cases and has been explained by exposing the implicit assumption made in the mathematical manipulation which finds ρ – that all intermediate cash flows are reinvested (or borrowed, if cash flows are negative) at the rate ρ itself. In addition, ρ does not allow for varying interperiod preference rates (or interest rates) over time. This generalized multiperiod internal rate of return is, therefore, not really internal, nor is the assumption implied about the external opportunities generally correct or even generally reasonable.

1.4   CONCLUDING COMMENTS

The preceding analysis has slighted a great many questions. In addition, lack of time has precluded comparative discussion of the works of other authors, however helpful this might have been.[43]

I have not attempted to generalize the results to the multiperiod case with non-independent investments or with differing or non-constant borrowing and lending rates. On the latter points intuition suggests that whether the borrowing or lending rate in calculating present value is to be used for any time period does not depend upon any characteristics of the investment option under consideration in isolation; it depends rather upon the overall cash position after adoption of that option as an increment. If, after such adoption, time preference dictates shifting to less income in period r and more in period t, any income associated with the option in question falling in period r should be discounted back to the next earlier period at the lending rate (and that for period t at the borrowing rate). Income in any period s may then have been successively discounted at borrowing rates for a number of periods and lending rates for a number of others before being reduced to a present value.

The main positive conclusion of the paper is that the present-value rule for investment decisions is correct in a wide variety of cases (though not universally) and in a limited sense. The rule tells us to attain the highest possible level of present value, but the point at which this condition is satisfied (that is, the distribution of incomes in various time periods) is not the final solution. It is, rather, an intermediate "productive" solution which must then be modified by borrowing or lending ("financing") to find the overall optimum. This becomes particularly clear when we consider the case where lending and borrowing rates differ and thus enter the sub-controversy between those who favor the use of present-value discounting at the cost of capital and those who would discount at the alternative lending rate. Which is correct depends upon the financing necessary to approach the time-preference optimum. Furthermore, if a tangency takes place between the productive opportunity locus and the time-preference utility isoquant at a rate between the lending and the borrowing rates, the "productive" solution requires no financing and the present-value principle is only correct in a formal sense. The present-value rule fails to give correct answers only for certain cases which combine the difficulties of non-independent investments and absence of a perfect capital market. When a perfect capital market exists, the present-value rule is universally correct in the limited sense referred to above. With independent investments but an imperfect capital market, the present-value rule will give answers which are correct but possibly only in a formal sense (the discounting rate used is not an external opportunity but an internal shadow price which comes out of the analysis).

The main negative conclusion is that the internal-rate-of-return rule for the multiperiod case is not generally correct, if the usual definition of the internal rate is adopted as that discount rate which makes the present value of the income stream associated with an investment option equal to zero. The so-called internal rate will only give correct answers in general if restricted to two-period comparisons; I have called this two-period internal rate the productive rate of return. For multiperiod investments the usual internal-rate-of-return rule (compare ρ with the market rate r) is not generally correct; however, given certain continuity assumptions, the correct answer will be arrived at by setting the marginal productive rate of return between each *pair* of time periods equal to the discount or market rate between those periods.

More important than the specific detailed conclusions is the demonstration that the Fisherian approach – the analysis of investment decisions as a means of balancing consumption incomes over time, together with the distinction between productive and market investment opportunities – is capable of solving (in the theoretical sense) all the problems posed. This solution is, furthermore, not an excrescence upon the general economic theory of choice but entirely integrated with it, constituting another dimension, so to speak. Since Fisher, economists working in the theory of investment decision have tended to adopt a mechanical approach – some plumping for the use of this formula, some for that. From a Fisherian point of view, we can see that none of the formulas so far propounded is universally valid. Furthermore, even where the present-value rule, for example, is correct, few realize that its validity is conditional upon making certain associated financing decisions as the Fisherian analysis demonstrates. In short, the Fisherian approach permits us to define the range of applicability and the shortcomings of all the proposed formulas – thus standing over against them as the general theoretical solution to the problem of investment decision under conditions of certainty.

NOTES

[1] Irving Fisher, *The Theory of Interest* (New York: Macmillan Co., 1930), is most widely known. His earlier work, *The Rate of Interest* (New York: Macmillan Co., 1907), contains most of the essential ideas.

[2] Fisher's contributions to the theory of capital go beyond his solution of the problem discussed in this paper – optimal investment decision. He also considers the question of the equilibrium of the capital market, which balances the supplies and demands of all the decision-making agencies.

[3] This analysis does not distinguish between individuals and firms. Firms are regarded solely as agencies or instruments of individuals.

[4] The slope of the market line is, of course, $-(1 + i)$, where i is the lending-borrowing rate. That is, when one gives up a dollar in period 0, he receives in exchange $1 + i$ dollars in period 1.

[5] For the present it is best to avoid the term "internal rate of return." Fisher uses the expressions "rate of return on sacrifice" or "rate of return over cost."

[6] An individual starting at S' would also have a "disinvestment opportunity."

[7] The present-value rule is the more or less standard guide supported by a great many theorists. The internal-rate-of-return rule, in the sense used here, has also been frequently proposed (see, e.g., Joel Dean, *Capital Budgeting* [New York: Columbia University Press, 1951], pp. 17–19). Citations on the use of alternative investment criteria may be found in Friedrich and Vera Lutz, *The Theory of Investment of the Firm* (Princeton, NJ: Princeton University Press, 1951), p. 16. The internal-rate-of-return rule which we will consider in detail (i.e. adopt all projects and increments to projects for which the internal rate of return exceeds the market rate of interest) is *not* the same as that emphasized by the Lutzes (i.e. adopt that pattern of investments maximizing the internal rate of return). The rule considered here compares the incremental or marginal rate of return with a market rate; the other would maximize the average internal rate of return, without regard to the market rate. The latter rule will be shown to be fundamentally erroneous, even in the form the Lutzes accept as their ultimate criter-

ion (maximize the internal rate of return on the investor's owned capital). This point will be discussed in connection with capital rationing below.

[8] In fact, for the two-period case the rules are identical: it is possible to show that any project (or increment to a project) of positive present value must have an internal rate of return greater than the rate of interest.

[9] If the borrowing rate were lower than the lending rate, it would be possible to accumulate infinite wealth by borrowing and relending, so I shall not consider the possibility. Of course, financial institutions typically borrow at a lower average rate than that at which they lend, but they cannot expand their scale of operations indefinitely without changing this relationship.

[10] The marginal productive opportunity rate, or marginal internal rate of return, measures the rate of return on the best alternative project. Assuming continuity, it is defined by the slope of QRQ' at R in figure 1.3. Evidently, a present-value line tangent to U_1 and QRQ' at R would, in a formal sense, make the present-value rule correct. And comparing this rate with the marginal internal rate of return as it varies along QRQ' would make the internal-rate-of-return rule also correct in the same formal sense.

[11] The borrowing rate (the "cost of capital") has been recommended by Dean and by Lorie and Savage (see Joel Dean, *Capital Budgeting* [New York: Columbia University Press, 1951], esp. pp. 43–4; James H. Lorie and Leonard J. Savage, "Three Problems in Rationing Capital," *Journal of Business*, 28 [October, 1955], 229–39, esp. p. 229). Roberts and the Lutzes favor the use of the lending rate (see Friedrich and Vera Lutz, *op. cit.*, esp. p. 22; Harry V. Roberts, "Current Problems in the Economics of Capital Budgeting," *Journal of Business*, 30 [January, 1957], 12–16).

[12] I should like to thank Joel Segall for insisting on this point in discussions of the problem. Note that the rate representing marginal borrowing cost is not necessarily the borrowing rate on marginal funds – an increment of borrowing may increase the rate on infra-marginal units.

[13] While this point can be verified geometrically, it follows directly from the analytic properties of an envelope curve.

To simplify notation, in this note I shall denote K_1 of figure 1.4 as y and K_0 as x. The equation of the productive opportunity locus may be written

$$y_0 = f(x_0). \tag{a}$$

The family of market curves can be expressed by $y - y_0 = g(x - x_0)$, or

$$F(x, x_0) = f(x_0) + g(x - x_0). \tag{b}$$

An envelope, $y = h(x)$, is defined by the condition that any point on it must be a point of tangency with some member of the family (b). Thus we have

$$h(x) = F(x, x_0), \tag{c}$$

$$\frac{dh}{dx} = \frac{\partial F(x, x_0)}{\partial x}. \tag{d}$$

The second condition for an envelope is that the partial derivative of the function (b) with respect to the parameter must equal zero:

$$\frac{\partial F(x, x_0)}{\partial x_0} = 0. \tag{e}$$

But

$$\frac{\partial F(x, x_0)}{\partial x_0} = \frac{df(x_0)}{dx_0} + (-1) \frac{dg(x - x_0)}{d(x - x_0)}$$

Hence

$$\frac{df(x_0)}{dx_0} = \frac{dg(x - x_0)}{d(x - x_0)} .$$

Also

$$\frac{\partial F(x, x_0)}{\partial x} = \frac{dg(x - x_0)}{d(x - x_0)} .$$

So, finally,

$$\frac{df(x_0)}{dx_0} = \frac{dg(x - x_0)}{d(x - x_0)} = \frac{\partial F(x, x_0)}{\partial x} = \frac{dh}{dx} .$$

Thus the slope of the productive opportunity locus is the same as the slope of the envelope at points on the two curves connected by being on the same market curve.

[14] The expression "capital rationing" was used some time ago by Hart to refer to a non-price limitation on the acquisition of debt or equity financing (see A. G. Hart, "Anticipations, Business Planning, and the Cycle," *Quarterly Journal of Economics*, [1937], 273–97). His use of the term does not seem to imply a definitely fixed quantity available and can, in fact, be interpreted simply as indicating a rising marginal cost of capital funds. See also Joel Dean, *Managerial Economics* (Englewood Cliffs, NJ: Prentice-Hall, Inc., 1951), pp. 586–600. In the sense of a definitely fixed quantity of funds, the term has been used by various authors discussing business or government problems. See J. Margolis, "The Discount Rate and the Benefits-Cost Justification of Federal Irrigation Investment," (Department of Economics, Stanford University, Technical Report No. 23 [Stanford, Calif., 1955]); Lorie and Savage, *op. cit.*, and R. McKean, *Efficiency in Government through Systems Analysis* (New York: John Wiley & Sons, 1958).

[15] T. Scitovsky, *Welfare and Competition* (Chicago: Richard D. Irwin, Inc., 1951), pp. 208–9.

[16] *Op. cit.*, pp. 16–48, esp. pp. 17, 20, 42.

[17] *Op. cit.*, p. 194.

[18] Scitovsky appears to leap from the acceptable argument in the earlier part of his discussion that willingness to lend and to borrow are not *unlimited* to the unacceptable position in his later discussion that current capital funds are *fixed* (ibid., pp. 193–200, 208–9).

[19] Lutz and Lutz, *op. cit.*, pp. 3–13.

[20] It is possible, however, that the Lutzes had in mind only the case in which an investor starts off with current funds but no other assets. In this case no discounting problems would arise in defining owned capital, so their ultimate criterion could not be criticized on that score. The objection raised below to the

Scitovsky criterion, however – that it fails to consider the *consumption* alternative, which is really the heart of the question of investment decision – would then apply to the Lutzes' rule. In addition, a rule for an investor owning solely current funds is hardly of general enough applicability to be an ultimate criterion. The Lutzes themselves recognize the case of an investor owning no "capital" but using only borrowed funds, and for this case they themselves abandon their ultimate criterion (ibid., p. 42, n. 32). The most general case, of course, is that of an investor with a productive opportunity set capable of yielding him alternative combinations of present and future income.

[21] We could, following the principles already laid down, work out without great difficulty the solution for the case in which borrowing is permitted but only up to a certain fixed limit. The effect of such a provision is to provide a kind of "attainability envelope" as in figure 1.4, but of a somewhat different shape.

[22] *Op. cit.*, p. 209.

[23] That is, the point Q' in figure 1.3. This result is of course trivial. Scitovsky may possibly have in mind choice among non-independent sets of investments (discussed in the next section), where each set may have a different intersection with the K_1 axis. Here a non-trivial choice could be made with the criterion of maximizing the average rate of return.

[24] Scitovsky may have in mind a situation in which a certain fraction of current funds K_0 are set apart from consumption (on some unknown basis) to become the "fixed" current capital funds. In this case the Scitovsky rule would lead to the correct result if it happened that just so much "fixed" capital funds were allocated to get the investor to the point R on his productive transformation locus of figure 1.3.

[25] It would, of course, reduce matters to their former simplicity if one of the loci lay completely within the other, in which case it would be obviously inferior and could be dropped from consideration.

[26] I shall not, in this section, consider further the possible divergences between the lending and borrowing rates studied in detail in section 1.1 but shall speak simply of "the discount rate" or "the market rate." The principles involved are not essentially changed in the multiperiod case; I shall concentrate attention on certain other difficulties that appear only when more than two periods are considered. We may note that in the most general case the assumption of full information becomes rather unrealistic – e.g. that the pattern of interest rates i_1 through i_n is known today.

[27] As in the two-period case, the locus represents not all the production opportunities but only the *boundary* of the region represented by the production opportunities. The boundary consists of those opportunities not dominated by any other; any opportunity represented by an interior point is dominated by at least one boundary point.

[28] The assumption of n-dimensional continuity is harder to swallow than two-dimensional continuity as an approximation to the nature of the real world. Nevertheless, the restriction is not essential, though it is an enormous convenience in developing the argument. One possible misinterpretation of the continuity assumption should be mentioned: it does not necessarily mean that the only investment opportunities considered are two-period options between pairs of periods in the present or future. Genuine multiperiod options are allowable – for example, the option described by cash-flows of -1, $+4$, $+2$,

and $+6$ for periods 0, 1, 2, and 3, respectively. The continuity assumption means, rather, that if we choose to move from an option like this one in the direction of having more income in period 1 and less, say, in period 3, we can find other options available like -1, $+4+e_1$, $+2$, $+6-e_3$, where e_1 and e_3 represent infinitesimals. In other words, from any point on the locus it is possible to trade continuously between incomes in any pair of periods.

[29] Maximizing the Lagrangian expression $C - \lambda f(K_0, ..., K_n)$, we derive the first-order conditions

$$
\begin{cases}
\dfrac{\partial C}{\partial K_0} = 1 & -\lambda \dfrac{\partial f}{\partial K_0} = 0 \\[2ex]
\dfrac{\partial C}{\partial K_1} = \dfrac{1}{1+i_1} & -\lambda \dfrac{\partial f}{\partial K_1} = 0 \\[2ex]
\cdots\cdots\cdots\cdots\cdots\cdots\cdots\cdots \\[1ex]
\dfrac{\partial C}{\partial K_n} = \dfrac{1}{(1+i_1)(1+i_2)...(1+i_n)} - \lambda \dfrac{\partial f}{\partial K_n} = 0.
\end{cases}
$$

Eliminating λ between any pair of successive periods:

$$
\frac{\partial f / \partial K_r}{\partial f / \partial K_s} = \frac{(1+i_1)(1+i_2)...(1+i_r)(1+i_s)}{(1+i_1)(1+i_2)...(1+i_r)}
$$

$$
\frac{\partial K_s}{\partial K_r}\bigg|_{\substack{K_j \\ (j \neq r,s)}} = 1 + i_s.
$$

Between non-successive periods:

$$
\frac{\partial K_t}{\partial K_r}\bigg|_{\substack{K_j \\ (j \neq r,t)}} = (1+i_{r+1})(1+i_{r+2})...(1+i_{t-1})(1+i_t).
$$

[30] *Rate of Interest*, pp. 398–400. Actually, the proof refers only to successive periods, but this is an inessential restriction.

[31] Ibid., p. 155; *Theory of Interest*, pp. 168–9.

[32] *Rate of Interest*, p. 153; *Theory of Interest*, pp. 168–9.

[33] For some purposes it is important to distinguish between the rate which sets the present value of a series of receipts from an investment equal to zero and that rate which does the same for the series of *differences* between the receipts of two alternative investment options (see A. A. Alchian, "The Rate of Interest, Fisher's Rate of Return over Cost, and Keynes' Internal Rate of Return," *American Economic Review*, 45 [December, 1955], 938–43). For present purposes there is no need to make the distinction because individual investment options are regarded as independent increments – so that the receipts of the option in question are in fact a sequence of differences over the alternative of not adopting that option.

[34] As another complication, Fisher's mathematical analysis compares the two-period marginal rates of return on sacrifice with the interest rates between those two periods, the latter not being assumed constant throughout. In the multiperiod case Fisher nowhere states how to combine the differing period-to-period interest rates into an overall market rate for comparison with ρ. It is possible that just at this point Fisher was thinking only of a rate of interest which remained constant over time, in which case the question would not arise. The difficulty in the use of the "internal rate" when variations in the market rate over time exist will be discussed below.

[35] See K. E. Boulding, *Economic Analysis* (rev. ed.; New York: Harper & Bros, 1948), p. 819.

[36] Economic meaning may be attached to negative interest rates; these are rates of shrinkage of capital. I rule out the possibility of shrinkage rates greater than 100 percent, however.

[37] Alchian, *op. cit.*, p. 939.

[38] Some people find this so hard to believe that I shall provide a numerical example. For investment I, we may use the annual cash-flow stream $-1, 0, 4$ – then the internal rate of return is 1, or 100 percent. For investment option II, we may use the option illustrated in figure 1.7: $-1, 2, 1$. For this investment ρ is equal to $\sqrt{2}$, or 141.4 percent. So the internal rate of return is greater for II. However, the present value for option I is greater at an interest rate of 0 percent, and in fact it remains greater until the crossover rate, which happens to be at 50 percent for these two options. Now it is simple to show how, adopting I, we can get to the result II at any interest rate lower than 50 percent – 10 percent, for example. Borrowing from the final time period for the benefit of the intermediate one, we can convert $-1, 0, 4$ to $-1, 2.73, 1$ (I have subtracted 3 from the final period, crediting the intermediate period with $3/1.1 = 2.73$). We can now get to option II by throwing away the 0.73, leaving us with $-1, 2, 1$. The fact that we can get to option II by throwing away some wealth demonstrates the superiority of I even though $\rho_{II} > \rho_I$, provided that borrowing and lending can take place at an interest rate less than the crossover discounting rate of 50 percent.

[39] *Op. cit.*, pp. 236–9.

[40] The instances discussed above suggest that the alternation of signs in the receipt stream has something to do with the possibility of multiple ρ's. In fact, Descartes's rule of signs tells us that the number of solutions in the allowable range (the number of points where present value equals zero for $i > -1$) is at most equal to the number of reversals of sign in the terms of the receipts sequence. Therefore, a two-period investment option has at most a single ρ, a three-period option at most a dual ρ, and so forth. There is an interesting footnote in Fisher which suggests that he was not entirely unaware of this difficulty. Where more than a single-sign alternation takes place, he suggests the use of the present-value method rather than attempting to compute "the rate of return on sacrifice" (*Rate of Interest*, p. 155). That any number of zeros of the present value function can occur was pointed out by Paul A. Samuelson in "Some Aspects of the Pure Theory of Capital," *Quarterly Journal of Economics*, 51 (1936–7), 469–96 (at p. 475).

[41] Mathematically, the formula for the roots of a three-period option n_0, n_1, n_2 where $n_0 = -1$ is:

$$i = \frac{(n_1 - 2) \pm \sqrt{n_1^2 + 4n_2}}{2}.$$

If $-4n_2$ exceeds n_1^2, the roots will be imaginary, and an internal rate of return cannot be calculated. A necessary condition for this result is that the sum of the undiscounted cash flows be negative, but this condition should not rule out consideration of an option (note the option $-1, 5, -6$ in figure 1.9).

[42] The true significance of the reinvestment assumption was brought out in Ezra Solomon, "The Arithmetic of Capital-budgeting Decisions," *Journal of Business*, 29 (April, 1956), 124–9, esp. pp. 126–7.

[43] I should comment, though, on the important article by Samuelson, *op cit.* The results here are in part consistent with his, with the following main differences: (1) He limits himself to the analysis of a single investment, whereas I consider the entire investment-consumption pattern over time. (2) He concludes in favor of the present-value rule, discounting at *the* market rate of interest. I have attempted to consider explicitly the problem of what to do when the borrowing and lending rates diverge, or vary as a function of the amount borrowed, and I do not find the present-value rule to be universally valid. Of these differences, the first is really crucial. It is the heart of Fisher's message that investments *cannot* be considered in isolation but only in the context of the other investment and consumption alternatives available. Nevertheless, Samuelson's article suffices to refute a number of fallacies still current in this field of economic theory.

2   A Note on the Bohm-Bawerk/Wicksell Theory of Interest*

Background and comments

In his works on interest (briefly decribed in my note prefacing chapter 1), Irving Fisher did not attempt to incorporate a systematic theory of capital. By way of contrast, the contributions of Eugen v. Bohm-Bawerk to the theory of interest, as given classical interpretation by Knut Wicksell, were tied to a very specific model of capital: one in which accumulated investments at earlier dates contribute to output at later dates by allowing a more extended "period of production."

In my previously cited book *Investment, Interest, and Capital* I show that Bohm-Bawerk's concept is only one of several more or less equally valid images of capital. All of these constructs – in addition to Bohm-Bawerk's period-of-production concept these include the "Crusonia plant" of Frank Knight and the standard durable-instruments model – are simplifying metaphors for the complex process whereby the accumulated stock of produced means of production contributes to output. The essay here, working within the Bohm-Bawerk conceptualization, demonstrates that the Bohm-Bawerk/Wicksell model is logically incomplete; rather than determining the interest rate, it is consistent with any interest rate whatsoever. The flaw lies in the failure to provide properly for time-preference. Since the model is not a complete theory of interest, it cannot be validly used to demonstrate propositions such as that the rate of interest is determined by productive considerations alone. The paper also shows constructively how the Bohm-Bawerk/Wicksell model can be completed by incorporating a utility function in order to represent time-preferences.

*This article originally appeared in *Review of Economic Studies*, vol. 34 (April, 1967), pp. 191–9. The permission of The Society for Economic Analysis to reprint in this volume is gratefully acknowledged.

One of the most famous developments in the history of economic thought is the theory of Bohm-Bawerk (1891), as formalized by Wicksell (1954),[1] that relates the wage rate (w), the value of capital stock (K_0), the rate of interest (r), and the "period of production" (θ) in the stationary state. Dorfman has recently given a concise and instructive exposition of this system (Dorfman, 1959a, b).

Part I of this paper provides, on an elementary level, a critical interpretation of the Bohm-Bawerk/Wicksell system, leading (in increasing order of importance) to the following conclusions:

(1) That the approximation error in the Bohm-Bawerk/Wicksell capital-value formula is of far from negligible magnitude.
(2) That Wicksell's formalization constitutes an under-determined system, an incomplete theoretical structure.
(3) And, consequently, that the system is *not* a theory of interest; rather than determining the rate of interest, the equation system is consistent with any arbitrarily imposed exogenous interest rate.[2]

After some discussion of the nature of the analytical errors involved, in part II the Bohm-Bawerk/Wicksell system will be formally completed by bringing in time-preference considerations. A numerical example will be provided as an aid to intuition.

I

In the Bohm-Bawerk/Wicksell model of production, we can think of the individual productive unit under the metaphor of a *tree* to which labor services are applied, at a constant rate over time, from the moment of planting to the moment of cutting. The productive process is, therefore, of a continuous-input point-output nature so far as the individual unit (tree) is concerned. But it is assumed that stationary conditions apply – i.e. that the flow of output emerges at a constant rate over time. This is achieved by having in being a uniform age-distribution of trees at all levels of maturity, replanting taking place immediately upon harvesting a mature tree. Hence in aggregate there is a continuous level input of labor services, a continuous level output of timber (assumed to be a consumption-good for this example), and a constant stock of real-capital.

Even given the abstraction of a single class of capital-good (tree), the aggregate real-capital is not a simple scalar magnitude, however.[3] It is a complex of goods-in-process or potential "subsistences," distributed over all stages of maturation from 0 to θ. The function of the real-capital, of course, is to permit the utilization of relatively long-period ("roundabout") methods of production – the steady-state yields of which are (as an asserted technological fact) at least on the margin greater than the yields of more direct or shorter-period methods.

The first relationship of the Bohm-Bawerk/Wicksell system expresses the annual rate of output per laborer as a function of the period of production θ. Under the assumption of stationarity, the *current* rate of output per laborer, y_0/L, is equal to the *future* rate of output y_f/L. Subject to this understanding, we may write:

$$y_0/L = f(\theta). \tag{2.1}$$

Thus y_0 is the current rate of output capable of maintaining itself indefinitely – given continued labor input at the rate L and the real-capital aggregate implied by the level of θ. (In this presentation care is taken to distinguish the dating of economic magnitudes in order to facilitate the later incorporation of time-preference into the analytical system; in addition, the dating will help clarify the distinction between real-capital and capital-value – the latter being a discounted *present* worth of future returns.) As shown in figure 2.1, the rate of output per laborer y_0/L rises at a decreasing rate as the period θ increases: $f'(\theta) > 0, f''(\theta) < 0$.[4]

Equation (2.1) states that for a given period θ, the output y_0 is proportional to the labor L employed. This does not deny diminishing returns with respect to labor, because holding θ constant as L rises requires proportionately larger aggregates of real-capital in the form of "goods in process" or "subsistences." What is implied by (2.1) is constant returns to scale as labor and real-capital rise in the same proportion – so that other factors (e.g. land) are here assumed to be in unlimited supply.[5]

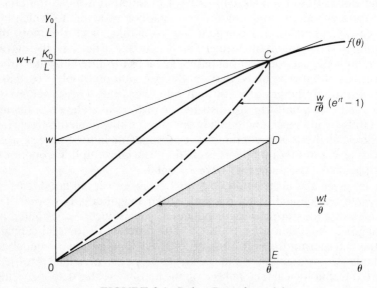

FIGURE 2.1 *Bohm-Bawerk model.*

Let us now consider further the meaning of "capital" in the Bohm-Bawerk model. The *real*-capital is an aggregate of not-yet-matured consumption goods continuously distributed over all stages of completion. Thus, if $\theta =$ ten years, one-tenth of the trees will be between nine and ten years old, one-tenth between eight and nine years old, etc. As already indicated, there is no natural way of measuring such a real-capital aggregate as a scalar quantity, since a unit of consumption-good ("subsistence") near maturity is intrinsically a different commodity from a unit far from maturity.[6] A young tree cannot be counted equally with a near-mature tree. Nor is the timber content a satisfactory measure; it is not the timber contained in a partially matured tree that is relevant, but only the timber it will contain *at maturity*, together with the remaining *time* required to reach maturity.

In their discussion of the productive role of capital, Bohm-Bawerk and Wicksell seem usually to be thinking of this real stock of partially matured subsistencies. But they go on to provide a scalar measure of something they call "capital," by simple addition of wage inputs. As they calculate "capital," a two-year-old tree counts for just twice as much as a one-year-old tree – the former incorporates twice the labor input of the other. Then, equation (2.2) is obtained:

$$K_0/L = \tfrac{1}{2}w\theta. \tag{2.2}$$

Here "capital" per laborer is measured by the amount necessary to subsist the laborer, at the wage rate w, for half the period of production θ. Putting it another way, for each laborer there will be in existence – under conditions of stationary equilibrium – $w\theta$ subsistence units evenly distributed over all stages of completion from 0 to θ, and so on the average half-completed. Geometrically, this wage-input measure of "capital" is represented by the shaded area under the line OD in figure 2.1.[7]

With current-output y_0 as the numeraire for values, K_0 has the dimensionality of present- or capital-*value* (which explains the K_0 symbolism used here); it is regularly expressed as a monetary value by Bohm-Bawerk and Wicksell. But under this interpretation, (2.2) is obviously erroneous as a capital-valuation equation. It fails to allow for simple, not to mention compound, interest over what may be a substantial period θ. The correct equation is:[8]

$$K_0/L = \frac{w}{r^2\theta}(e^{r\theta} - 1 - r\theta). \tag{2.2a}$$

Geometrically in figure 2.1, the correct capital-value measure of (2.2a) – if $\hat{\theta}$ is the equilibrium period – corresponds to the area under the dashed curve, OC. Obviously, as a condition of equilibrium, a practically matured subsistence must contribute to capital-value an amount almost equal to the value of an output unit $f(\theta)\,dt$, rather than only the uncompounded amount wdt. Specifically, in equilibrium the compounded capital-value of the just-matured "vintage" is:[9]

$$f(\theta) = \frac{w}{r\theta}(e^{r\theta} - 1).$$

This corresponds to the total vertical distance $\overline{EC}$. Algebraically, employing this equation and the capital-value measure of (2.2a), it may be verified that in equilibrium:[10]

$$f(\theta) = w + rK_0/L. \tag{2.3}$$

Then, if the distance $\overline{ED}$ corresponds to the wage w, the remaining vertical distance $\overline{DC}$ is the rate of continuous interest yield on the entire capital-value aggregate under the curve OC (as must be the case in equilibrium).

The scale of error involved in the use of (2.2) as a measure of K_0/L can be indicated by expressing $e^{r\theta}$ in (2.2a) as an infinite series.[11] Then:

$$K_0/L = \tfrac{1}{2}w\theta\left(1 + \frac{r\theta}{3} + \frac{(r\theta)^2}{12} + \ldots\right). \tag{2.2b}$$

If $r\theta$ were of small magnitude, (2.2) would be a tolerable approximation. But with, for example, $r = 10$ percent and $\theta = $ ten years, the first error term alone already represents a divergence factor of one-third. As will be seen below, the approximation error leads also to significant divergences in the derived results for w and θ.

What is rather more important than the erroneous form of (2.2) as a capital-value equation is the improper interpretation, by Wicksell at any rate, of "capital" K_0 as an autonomous constant rather than an endogenous variable of the system, Bohm-Bawerk and Wicksell speak of individual entrepreneurs, *and also of the community as a whole*, as possessing given "capitals" in money terms that can be utilized so as to freely select productive processes of greater or lesser θ. For example, if the wage rate w is 100 florins per annum, they say that a capitalist-entrepreneur with a "capital" of 1,200 florins can employ 24 laborers in a one-year process, 12 laborers if he chooses $\theta = 2$, six laborers with $\theta = 4$, etc. This is indeed true on the private level of analysis – aside from the approximation error of (2.2) as against 2.2a)[12] – since the individual entrepreneur under competitive conditions can take market values as given. But on the social level of analysis the wage w and the rate of interest r will both be functions of the θ adopted; there is no justification for taking the valuation of the *community*'s capital as invariant with respect to this decision. That K_0 need not be constant with respect to the choice of θ may be verified in the extreme case where the community shift to entirely non-capitalistic methods of production (selects $\theta = 0$).[13] Then whatever the original level of K_0, at the new stationary equilibrium K_0 would equal zero.

If on the other hand we interpret "capital" in the real sense, as Bohm-Bawerk and Wicksell sometimes appear to do, we cannot construct an equation in the form of (2.2) or (2.2a) at all. For the variables of these equations are scalars, whereas *real*-capital is a vector of quantities over all stages of completion. It is all the more true that we cannot then regard "capital" as constant with respect to choice of θ, since it is impossible to make two non-conformable vectors equal to one another. Thus, given 100 subsistences distributed uniformly over all stages of completion with $\theta = 4$, there is no uniform distribution with $\theta = 5$ that can be said to be "equal" to the original in *real* (vector) terms.

In what follows, the Bohm-Bawerk/Wicksell system will be corrected by treating capital-*value* K_0 as a variable. Assume that there is a "representative individual" whose productive (entrepreneurial) and consumptive decisions are a microcosm of those of the entire society. Hence, there is no need to distinguish in the symbolism between private and social magnitudes; the meaning will be clear from the context. First, we can set down again equations (2.1) and (2.2) – tolerating, for the moment, the approximation error in the incorrect form of (2.2):

$$y_0/L = f(\theta), \tag{2.1}$$

$$K_0/L = \tfrac{1}{2}w\theta. \tag{2.2}$$

Now, entrepreneurial[14] *profit per laborer* (as a continuous flow) can be written as $f(\theta) - w - rK_0/L$. Employing (2.2), and maximizing profit per laborer with respect to θ, the condition resulting is:

$$f'(\theta) = \tfrac{1}{2}rw. \tag{2.4}$$

Furthermore, in long-run competitive equilibrium the entrepreneurial profit must be zero. This leads to the equation (2.3) already obtained above:

$$f(\theta) = w + rK_0/L. \tag{2.3}$$

This equation could also, employing (2.2) and (2.4), be written in the form:

$$f(\theta) = w + \theta f'(\theta). \tag{2.3'}$$

Using (2.3'), the wage rate can then be shown geometrically as the intercept on the vertical axis of the line tangent to $f(\theta)$ in figure 2.1.

If indeed K_0 were a constant, equations (2.1), (2.2) and (2.4), plus either (2.3) or (2.3') would suffice in number[15] to determine the variables y_0, r, w and θ – treating $f(\theta)$ and $f'(\theta)$ as known functions. But since K_0 is also a variable, the system is under-determined.[16] To put the matter most forcefully, while Bohm-Bawerk's system (as formalized by Wicksell) purports to be a theory of interest it is actually consistent with any interest rate whatever! Given an arbitrary exogenously determined r, the rest of the system will adopt to conform to that r. Clearly, there is something missing from the model – and the missing element is the "subjective" or time-preference factor. In other words, this is a one-sided productivity model.

Some insight into this analytical system, as well as verification of the contentions above, can be obtained by employing a numerical illustration. Specifically, it will be assumed that $f(\theta)$ has the logarithmic form $a + b \ln \theta$ and that numerically $a = b = 10$. Furthermore, *the exogenous interest rate $r = 10$ percent will be arbitrarily imposed on the system.* It may be verified that the numerical solution for the equation system (2.1), (2.2), (2.3'), (2.4) – employing the inaccurate approximation (2.2) rather than the exact (2.2a) – is as follows (see table 2.1): the period of production $\theta = 9.07$ years, the wage $w = \$22.05$ (using dollars as unit of value), the capital-value per laborer $K_0/L = \$100.00$, and the output per laborer $y_0/L = \$32.05$. The capitalist earns at the rate $rK_0/L = \$10.00$, so that the total output is accounted for.

The error due to the incorrect formulation of K_0/L in (2.2) leads, as might be expected, to a violation of economic logic. The capitalist here is supposed to be satisfied with his earnings of $10.00 per laborer, believing that at 10 percent this is an appropriate return on his $100.00 of capital per laborer. But this belief is erroneous. Since he has laid out wage inputs over the entire period θ that could have been earning at 10 percent interest, his actual capital tied up in the process can be calculated as determined in equation (2.2a) to be approximately $138.57. Hence the return of $10.00 is only an earnings rate of some 7.22 percent per annum, quite inadequate given that the market interest rate $r = 10$ percent. Another way

TABLE 2.1 *Illustrative numerical solution for Bohm-Bawerk system*

		Incorrect capital-value equation	Correct capital-value equation
Period of production	θ	9.07 yrs	6.35 yrs
Output per laborer	y_0/L	$32.05	$28.52
Capital per laborer	K_0/L	100.00	81.04
Wage	w	22.05	20.42
Earnings of capital	rK_0/L	10.00	8.10
Prospective valuation of capital	$\dfrac{rK_0/L}{r}$	100.00	81.04
True retrospective valuation of capital from equation (2.2a)	...	138.57	81.04
Earnings rate on true retrospective valuation	...	7.22%	10%

Assumptions: $r = 10$ percent and $f(\theta) = 10(1 + \ln \theta)$

of looking at this is to notice that the *prospective* valuation of capital – the discounted present value of the infinite future flow of earnings at the rate $10.00 per annum – is

$$\frac{\$10.00}{r} = \$100.00,$$

while the restrospective valuation of the inputs invested equals $138.57 as shown above. The only possible conclusion is that capital accumulation has been carried beyond its economic limit; a period of 9.07 years is not warranted, given the rate of interest $r = 10$ percent.

The system employing the correct capital measure can be set down as follows:

$$y_0/L = f(\theta) \tag{2.1}$$

$$K_0/L = \frac{w}{r^2\theta}(e^{r\theta} - 1 - r\theta) \tag{2.2a}$$

$$f(\theta) = w + rK_0/L \tag{2.3}$$

$$f'(\theta) = \frac{w}{r\theta^2}[e^{r\theta}(r\theta - 1) + 1]. \tag{2.4'}$$

Equation $(2.4')$ here is obtained by maximizing profit per laborer with respect to θ, with capital per laborer given by $(2.2a)$.[17] Using the same illustration, letting $f(\theta) = a + b\ln\theta$ with $a = b = 10$ and $r = 10$ percent, the numerical results are compared in table 2.1 with those obtained earlier. Evidently, a considerably smaller degree of accumulation, as represented by the period $\theta = 6.35$ years, is economically warranted if the capitalists are actually to earn 10 percent on the value of their capital stocks. The wage rate and the earnings per laborer fall in a lesser proportion because of the working of diminishing returns as expressed in the form of $f(\theta)$.

Use of the approximate equation $(2.3')$, $f(\theta) = w + \theta f'(\theta)$, with the correct θ, $f(\theta)$, and $f'(\theta)$ would lead to a wage w of $18.42. The correct wage, $20.42, thus lies somewhat above the vertical intercept of the tangent line portrayed in figure 2.1.

II

That Bohm-Bawerk's system can be described as a one-sided productivity model may seem astonishing. Elsewhere in his work Bohm-Bawerk was at great pains to assert that among the reasons for an agio – a premium on present as against future goods – are differing circumstances of want and provision, as well as subjective underestimate of the future. Clearly, both of these reasons are connected with marginal time-preference valuations. The explanation seems to be that his conception was broader than the systematic treatment (in Bohm-Bawerk, 1891, Book VII, ch. 2) that was formalized in Wicksell's discussion. While Bohm-Bawerk does take the "Subsistence Fund" (K_0) as a constant in chapter 2, it is indicated in chapter 4 that time-preference elements enter into its determination. Any given Subsistence Fund implies a wage rate, a period of production, and a rate of interest, but it would appear that Bohm-Bawerk had in mind only *equilibrium* levels of the Subsistence Fund – i.e. levels implying rates of interest consistent with the capitalists' marginal time-preferences.[18] Wicksell, on the other hand, seems to have thought that Bohm-Bawerk's *was* a productivity theory and that the hypothesis of the stationary state sufficed to make the system of equations complete – since K_0 of equation (2.2) then becomes an "invariable magnitude."[19] There appears to be a confusion in Wicksell between constancy over time (which is what is assured by the stationary-state condition) and *functional* invariance within the equation system.

Leaving aside the question of what Bohm-Bawerk or Wicksell "really meant," to complete the Bohm-Wicksell formal system and actually determine the rate of interest, at least one other equation is needed – specifically, a time-preference relation or relations. The role of time-preference in the solution of the problem under discussion may be indicated by the following argument. Since $f'(\theta)$ is assumed to be always positive, indefinitely larger flows of *per-capita* income can be attained as θ is extended. What then keeps θ within bounds? Just the fact that extending θ requires tying up more and more potentiality of current or near-future consumption in the form of real-capital, the value of which is indicated in equations (2.2) or (2.2a). Of course, the consumption increment associated with augmenting real-capital arrives in the relatively distant future. In a sense the difficulty is always only one of transition, since once the larger θ is established a permanently increased flow of consumption can be obtained with no larger a flow of labor input – but this transition can only take place at the expense of current and near-future consumption.

Equations (2.5–2.8) below incorporate the time-preference conditions so as to complete Bohm-Bawerk's system.

$$c_0 = y_0/L \quad \text{Zero current-saving condition.} \tag{2.5}$$

This equation says that c_0, understood to refer to current individual consumption (*per-capita* consumption, given the "representative-individual" assumption) equals the current income per laborer. Hence, net saving and investment are zero, the capital being "maintained intact." Thus, (2.5) is a condition of stationary equilibrium.

$$c_f = rK_0/L + w \quad \text{Zero future-saving condition.} \tag{2.6}$$

This equation asserts that *future* consumption *per-capita*, regarded as a level perpetual flow, will always equal the wage plus interest on the constant capital-value per laborer ($=y_f$). It is also evident, from (2.1) and (2.3), that $c_f = c_0$ and $y_f = y_0$ (as required for stationarity).

$$\left. \frac{dc_f}{dc_0} \right|_U = \Phi(c_0, c_f) \quad \text{Time-Preference Function.} \qquad (2.7)$$

$$\left. \frac{dc_f}{dc_0} \right|_U = -r. \quad \text{Time-Preference Optimum.} \qquad (2.8)$$

Equation (2.7) defines the marginal rate of substitution (m.r.s.) in consumption, or marginal rate of time-preference between current rate of consumption and future perpetual flow of consumption, as a function of c_f and c_0. Equation (2.8) states that this subjective m.r.s. in consumption between c_0 and c_f must equal in absolute value the interest rate – the market rate at which current consumption c_0 can be converted into future perpetual flow c_f via exchange transactions. Note that in equations (2.7) and (2.8) we have shifted from a continuous-time to a discrete-period formulation, for ease of comprehension. The time-preference relations in a continuous-time model involve some technical complexities, which are relegated to a footnote.[20]

The entire system has eight equations to determine the eight variables y_0, K_0, w, θ, c_0, c_f, (dc_f/dc_0), and r. If the representative-individual assumption were dropped the system would, of course, become more complicated: with J individuals there would be (in the absence of firms) J each of the individual variables (all the above list except for the unique market variables w and r) and correspondingly many equations.

Returning to the question of the determinants of the rate of interest in the Bohm-Bawerk system, it could easily be the case that the time-preference equations alone fix the interest rate r at which stationarity could occur. If, for example, indifference curves drawn between current and future consumption as in figure 2.2 all have the same slope along the 45° line, then the absolute value of that constant slope would be the only rate of interest[21] consistent with stationarity (all stationary states must, of course, occur where $c_0 = c_f$ – along the 45° line). Then time-preference considerations alone would fix the rate of interest. Given the assumption of stationarity, the remainder of the equation system would have to adapt to the r thus determined.

A numerical utility function having this property[22] is $U = (c_0)^{1/11}(c_f)^{10/11}$. With this function the slope along the 45° line always equals -0.1. Hence the time-preference considerations dictate that stationarity can only be achieved with an interest rate $r = 10$ percent, the same rate as that imposed earlier as an arbitrary exogenous magnitude in the numerical example

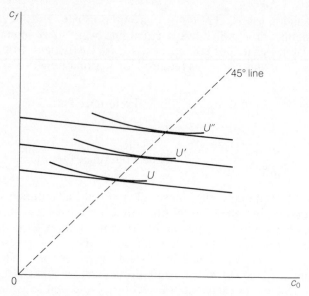

FIGURE 2.2   *Preference between present and future consumption.*

illustrating the Bohm-Bawerk/Wicksell system. More generally, of course, productive and time-preference considerations would interact to jointly determine the rate of interest.

REFERENCES

Bohm-Bawerk, E. von. *The Positive Theory of Capital*, transl. William Smart. New York: G. E. Stechert & Co., 1891, (especially Book VII, ch. 2).

Dorfman, R. "A Graphical Exposition of Bohm-Bawerk's Interest Theory", *Review of Economic Studies*, vol. 26 (1959a), pp. 153–8.

Dorfman, R. "Waiting and the Period of Production", *Quarterly Journal of Economics*, vol. 73 (1959b), pp. 351–72.

Neuburger, E. "Waiting and the Period of Production: Comment", *Quarterly Journal of Economics*, vol. 74 (1960), pp. 150–3.

Solow, R. M. "Notes Towards a Wicksellian Model of Distributive Shares", in F. A. Lutz and D. G. Hague, *The Theory of Capital*. London: Macmillan, 1961.

Stigler, J. G. *Production and Distribution Theories*. London: Macmillan, 1946.

Wicksell, K. *Lectures on Political Economy* (vol. 1), transl. E. Classen. London: George Routledge and Sons Ltd, 1934.

Wicksell, K. *Value, Capital and Rent*, transl. G. L. S. Shackle. London: George Allen and Unwin, 1954.

NOTES

[1] The exposition and analysis of Bohm-Bawerk's system here is based upon the formalization in Wicksell (1954, pp. 120–68). Here as in his *Lectures* (1934, vol. 1), Wicksell goes some way beyond the Bohm-Bawerk theory. We will not be concerned here with any conceptions original with Wicksell.

[2] The first of these points has already been suggested by Dorfman (1959b), and the second by Stigler (1946). The third point has possibly been made as well, but I have not seen it explicitly set down.

[3] Bohm-Bawerk and Wicksell were fully aware of the unrealism of assuming just one kind of capital-good. It is not so clear that they appreciated that, *even under this assumption*, real-capital could not be expressed as a scalar quantity.

[4] It should be appreciated that $f(\theta)$ is *not* a growth curve for the productive unit (tree). Given an established period θ^*, it will not in general be the case that the timber content of a tree aged $\theta^*/2$ is $f(\theta^*/2)$. For $f(\theta^*/2)$ refers to the *maximum* output per year achievable with a period of $\theta^*/2$. This might very well involve the choice of a species of tree with a better early-growth property than the species that would be selected for a period θ^*.

[5] The extension of the analysis to allow for other scarce factors creates no new essential difficulty. See Wicksell (1954, pp. 146–53).

[6] Disparate commodities such as shoes and apples cannot be aggregated in physical units, but only in terms of values – i.e. we must know the price ratio between the two. In exactly the same way, two subsistences of different times to maturity can only be aggregated in value terms, requiring a knowledge of their price ratio – which is a function of the rate of interest. So real-capital cannot here be quantified as a scalar independently of value considerations.

[7] Since labour contributes input to the productive process at the steady rate w spread over all "vintages" of trees, any particular age interval $d\tau$ receives input at the rate $wd\tau/\theta$. Then the accumulated wage input for a vintage begun t years ago is

$$\frac{w}{\theta}\int_0^t d\tau = \frac{wt}{\theta}.$$

Integrating over all vintages,

$$\frac{K_0}{L} = \frac{w}{\theta}\int_0^\theta t\,dt = \tfrac{1}{2}w\theta.$$

[8] The compounded wage input for a vintage begun t years ago is

$$\frac{w}{\theta}\int_0^t e^{r\tau}d\tau = \frac{w}{r\theta}(e^{rt}-1).$$

Integrating over all vintages, the equation in the text is obtained. This result is due to Dorfman, (1959a, pp. 157f).

[9] Derived from the equation for compounded wage input in the note above, substituting $t = \theta$.

[10] If $f(\theta)=(w/r\theta)(e^{r\theta}-1)$, then $f(\theta)-w=(w/r\theta)(e^{r\theta}-1-r\theta)=rK_0/L$.

[11] As an infinite series:

$$e^{r\theta}=1+\frac{r\theta}{1!}+\frac{(r\theta)^2}{2!}+\frac{(r\theta)^3}{3!}+\dots$$

Then, from (2.2a),

$$\frac{K_0}{L}=\frac{w}{r^2\theta}\left[\frac{(r\theta)^2}{2!}+\frac{(r\theta)^3}{3!}+\frac{(r\theta)^4}{4!}+\dots\right]=\frac{w\theta}{2}\left[1+\frac{r\theta}{3}+\frac{r^2\theta^2}{4\cdot3}+\dots\right].$$

See Dorfman (1959a, p. 158).

[12] With the correct formulation (2.2a), and assuming a rate of interest $r=10$ percent and a wage $w=100$, a "capital" of 1,200 florins employs just 23.2 laborers over a period θ of one year – and only 11.4 rather than 12 laborers if $\theta=2$, and 5.2 rather than six laborers if $\theta=4$.

[13] A zero production period is regarded as a possibility by Bohm-Bawerk (1891, pp. 376–8); see also Dorfman (1959a, p. 154). In figure 2.1, the positive intercept of the $f(\theta)$ function indicates that output per laborer y_0/L does not fall to zero at $\theta=0$. Of course, it is evident from the economics of the situation that such a choice will not make w or r infinite, so that K_0 is determinate and equal to zero. (It may be verified that K_0 in (2.2a) approaches zero as a limit as θ goes to zero.)

[14] This formulation will distinguish the entrepreneur from the capitalist. Bohm-Bawerk's own exposition, and all others known to me, combine the two roles and assume that the capitalist-entrepreneur maximizes a "profit" which is really interest. Here we will assume that the entrepreneur maximizes true profit (net of interest), but competition enforces a zero-profit condition. While our formulation is more modern, the result is unchanged.

[15] We pass over the additional restrictions necessary to guarantee a unique solution.

[16] It might be thought that an additional relation among the variables could be obtained by maximizing profit also with respect to the number of laborers employed. It can be verified that this does not provide an independent equation, but is instead another way of arriving at equation (2.3).

[17] Profit per laborer is $f(\theta)-w-rK_0/L$. Taking the derivative with respect to θ and setting equal to zero, the result (2.4') is obtained.

[18] I would like to thank referees of this paper for pointing out that an earlier version was unfair to Bohm-Bawerk on this score. See also Neuberger (1960). Of course, it must also be said that Bohm-Bawerk failed to provide any systematic description of how the equilibrating process for the magnitude of the Subsistence Fund – really, for the w, r and θ that determine this magnitude via (2.2) or (2.2a) – can incorporate time-preference. This is precisely what is provided in the text below.

[19] Wicksell (1954, p. 120). Stigler (1946) has also described the Bohm-Wicksell system as a productivity theory, and has noticed the incompleteness of the system. (See Stigler, 1946, pp. 218, 226, 283 n.) A similar point has been made by Solow (who credits the observation to Mrs Robinson) about Wicksell's later work on Akerman's problem. (See Solow, 1961.)

[20] Denote the time-length of the "current" period Δt. If $\Delta t = 1$ (i.e. the current period is one standard time-interval – let us say, a year) the market will permit exchanges of a perpetuity of $\$r$ per year, starting the year after the current one, against a current sacrifice of \$1 (i.e. against a c_0 of \$1 per time-unit extending over a period of one time-unit). If, on the other hand, the "current period" becomes vanishingly small, the market exchange rate and the marginal rate of substitution in consumption between c_f and c_0 both go to zero; no sacrifice of a rate of consumption c_0 over an instant of time can exchange in the market against, or can be preferred to, any non-zero future flow c_f over perpetual time. What does not go to zero as Δt diminishes (with c_0 held constant) is the market or preference ratio *per unit of time*

$$\frac{dc_f/dc_0}{\Delta t}.$$

The limit approached by this ratio has the dimensionality of the "instantaneous" (or "continuous") rate of interest. Given an instantaneous current period, then, the left-hand sides of (2.7) and (2.8) should be re-written as

$$\lim_{\Delta t \to 0} \frac{dc_f/dc_0}{\Delta t}.$$

[21] The absolute slope dc_f/dc_0 has the same dimensions as the annual rate of interest if $\Delta t =$ one year (see footnote above). For an instantaneous current period, the horizontal axis of figure 2.2 should be labeled

$$\lim_{\Delta t \to 0} (\Delta t)\, c_0.$$

Then the absolute slope will have the dimensionality of the instantaneous rate of interest $\Delta t \to 0$

$$\lim_{\Delta t \to 0} \frac{dc_f/dc_0}{\Delta t}.$$

[22] More generally, any homogeneous utility function will have this property.

3 "Sustained Yield" *versus* Capital Theory*

Background and comments

Capital theory – analysis of the use and accumulation of resources over time – is widely regarded as one of the more difficult branches of economics. At the same time, how to make correct investments is an issue of intense practical importance for decision-makers in business and government. There has been something of a mismatch here. Partly because the theory has tended toward the esoteric, it has been largely ignored by men and women of affairs.

This paper was originally presented at a symposium on The Economics of Sustained Yield Forestry held at the Collect of Forest Resources, University of Washington, in 1974. The intention of the organizers was to overcome the gap between capital theory and its evident practical application in forestry. Papers were presented by a number of distinguished economists – among them Paul Samuelson, Anthony Downs, John Ledyard and Leon Moses, and Marc J. Roberts.

The economists generally tended to argue that, owing to the sway of plausible yet irrational slogans like sustained yield, no drop-off, and never-declining yield, the vast resources of publicly owned timber were being inadequately harvested. But the implication that more logging should take place on public lands was unpalatable to many in the industry. As conservationists, officials charged with management of public forests are inclined to prefer timber in standing trees rather than in houses for people. And on the private side of the industry there was a very practical reason for distress: increased availability of public timber would reduce the value of privately owned forests, with possibly disastrous effects upon corporate balance sheets. Perhaps because of these reasons, the conference proceedings were not published as had originally been planned.

My own paper reproduced here attempts a straightforward presentation of the economic theory of use of resources over time. It goes on to deflate the supposed logic of current shibboleths like sustained yield, and to show some of the patho-

*This paper was presented at the symposium, The Economics of Sustained Yield Forestry, held at the College of Forest Resources, University of Washington, Seattle, Washington in November 1974.

logical consequences that stem therefrom. When a slogan like "no drop-off" is used, for example, redrawing the boundaries of the management unit can have drastic effects upon the allowable cut. Rationally speaking, of course, how boundaries are drawn should not affect the economics of whether or not to cut a stand of trees. And the paper goes to show how budgetary statistics demonstrate the extraordinarily low rate of return earned on the vast standing forest resources on public lands.

The religion of India dictates that cows are to be worshipped, but not eaten – a mistaken idea which converts a potential food resource into a drain sapping the economy of a nation. As a newcomer to forestry discussions. I had rather expected to find American foresters also to be very religious people – not cow worshippers, of course, but tree worshippers (modern Druids). Somewhat to my surprise, this did not prove to be the case. Foresters do seem willing to cut trees to serve the merely utilitarian purposes of mankind. But there is something that does seem to be irrationally worshipped in at least part of the forestry literature – a slogan called "sustained yield."

My thesis can be summarized briefly: sustained yield, which is a rational policy under very special conditions for an ultimate future, has been converted into a dangerously misleading rule for the actualities of the present – with seriously harmful consequences for the well-being of our nation. Instead of wandering cows we have standing trees. But in either case, a large part of a nation's capital is locked up in an untouchable and unremunerative form.

3.1   CAPITAL AND ITS YIELD

I have been asked to speak to you from the viewpoint of what economists call "capital theory." "Capital theory" may sound rather precious and abstruse, but it's actually a very practical subject. Men of affairs often claim to be free of concern about issues of theory. Usually this means they are acting on the basis of some theory whose validity they choose not to question. One allegedly "practical" contention sometimes encountered is the assertion that the *rate of interest* is an abstract or irrelevant nicety. Analytically, this usually amounts to a hidden assumption that the rate of interest should be treated as if it had a numerical value of zero. The impracticality of this assumption is readily discovered whenever one tries to borrow from a bank. Even the government of the United States cannot borrow from its citizens or from foreigners at zero interest rates.

Let me suggest how some fundamental features of capital theory bear upon the "sustained yield" issue. The upper panel of figure 3.1 illustrates the potential stream of *sustainable* annual yield, y, usually measured in terms of dollars per year, as a function of the magnitude of capital stock, K. Capital stock represents assets, and is usually measured in terms of dollars. Both the capital stock and its annual yield could as well be measured in other units.

Capital stock can take many forms. It might be a stand of trees yielding lumber, an inventory of houses yielding shelter, a population of chinchillas yielding fur coats, or a collection of factories or machines producing consumer goods. In each case we have a resource, whether originally God-

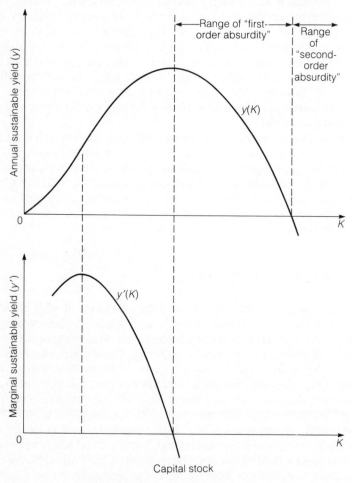

FIGURE 3.1 *Capital and its yield.*

given or man-made, which can be augmented or diminished by the actions of man. (A special case: some resources, like minerals, can be diminished but not augmented. They can, however, be recycled.) By currently using on net balance less than the sustainable annual yield, we may be able directly or indirectly to augment the capital stock; if we use more than is being replaced, the capital stock must of course decline.

The key feature to be emphasized is the curvature of the yield function $y(K)$. As capital stock increases, the annual sustainable yield rises at first (possibly at an increasing rate for small amounts of capital, but eventually at a decreasing rate), reaches a maximum, then finally begins to decline. This curvature reflects the famous law of diminishing returns.

Consider a capital stock of chinchillas. In the reasonable (or "non-absurd") range, the annual net yield of fur-coats rises as we acquire a larger population of the little beasts. At some point there will tend to be diminishing returns to further population increases – due to crowding, increased costs of labor, of fencing, etc. A similar effect is encountered with a population of trees. In the reasonable range of the annual yield function, larger inventories of standing timber will mean higher annual yields of lumber, but yields will rise at a decreasing rate due to pressure on limited amounts of cooperating resources such as land and labor.

Eventually, if we insisted on holding larger and larger capital stocks of either chinchillas or trees, we would find ourselves in the region labeled "first-order absurdity." In this range the capital yield $y(K)$ would be falling. The same yield y could be attained with a smaller capital stock K. We have, for example, so many chinchillas, so much crowding and the like, they are producing offspring and fur coats at a lower rate than a smaller population would. In the case of trees, the forest has become so dense that lumber yield is actually less than a smaller, less crowded, stand of trees would have produced.

These relations are further illustrated by the $y'(K)$ curve, in the lower panel of figure 3.1. The $y'(K)$ curve shows the *yield increment*, or "marginal" sustainable yield for each level of capital stock. In the reasonable region $y'(K)$ is positive (but falling). In the region of first-order absurdity, the *marginal* yield increment has fallen so far as to become negative. Whether yields and capital stocks are measured in the same physical units, or are reduced to a common dimension by converting them into dollars, marginal yields can be reinterpreted as the marginal percent *rate of return* (ROR) on the capital stock. A negative marginal yield implies a negative real rate of return being earned on the last unit of investment in capital stock. Society would be better off if some of this capital were reallocated elsewhere.

It is conceivable that capital stock might grow so large that the actual sustainable yield $y(K)$ in the upper panel of figure 3.1 becomes negative – the region labeled "second-order absurdity" in the diagram. This would be equivalent to trying to hold so many chinchillas that they are eating one another and not yielding, net, any fur coat values at all. In the case of forestry it might seem that this could not happen. Trees do not eat each other, and the capital stock (standing inventory) would surely always yield a positive harvest. But forest maintenance and logging are expensive. It is the net, or economic sustainable yield, that might actually be negative after these expenses are deducted. In the interests of suspense I will not disclose yet whether our current situation on private and public forest lands is either a first-order absurdity or a second-order absurdity.

3.2   A SECOND PROPOSITION ABOUT CAPITAL STOCK

The first important Proposition we learn from capital theory has already been seen: we should never maintain a capital stock so large that we operate in the region of a first-order absurdity or, *a fortiori*, in the region of a second-order absurdity. Another important Proposition I want to emphasize can be expressed as follows: *different types of capital stock should be adjusted in magnitude so as to equate their marginal rates of return.*

In figure 3.2 we see, for two different types of capital stock, K_1 and K_2, *marginal* yield curves $y'(K_1)$ and $y'(K_2)$. Interpreting these as curves of marginal rates of return, the vertical scales are measured in percent per unit time. The right-hand panel indicates a *relatively* plentiful type of capital, K_2. Capital type K_1 is *relatively* scarce in comparison with K_2 because the marginal ROR on the present stock K_1^0 is far higher than the marginal yield on the present relatively plentiful capital stock K_2^0. Note

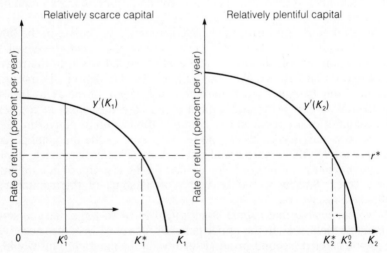

FIGURE 3.2 *Two types of capital stock – marginal yields.*

that K_2, while *relatively* plentiful, has a positive marginal yield, y'. It is not in either the region of a first-order or a second-order absurdity.

Nevertheless, rational policy still dictates that K_2 be decreased over time, as part of an economic process that brings about a corresponding increase of the relatively scarce capital K_1. This does not mean, of course, that we simply destroy the "excess" K_2. Rather, we *decumulate* it. We use it currently at a rate in excess of its present sustainable yield. This permits a faster rate of accumulation of the more productive capital resource K_1. A very practical example is the following. Suppose K_1 were *housing*, and K_2 *forests*. Then, if their relative yields are as shown, housing has a higher ROR on the margin than forests. We should expand the housing stock, even at the expense of a reduction in forest inventory.

How far should this process be carried? Far enough to make the marginal rates of return on both K_1 and K_2 equal to r^*, where r^* is the economy-wide real interest yield on capital in general. This process will not take place instantaneously. The adjustments of different types of capital stock to their proper sustainable-yield levels, where they are in balance with one another and with the real yield of capital in general in the economy, cannot take place except over a substantial time interval.

3.3   PATTERNS OF CAPITAL AND ITS YIELD OVER TIME

These propositions can now be used to explore the rational development over time of the capital stock and of its yield. In figure 3.3 the left-hand diagrams apply to the relatively scarce type of capital K_1 and the right-hand diagrams to the relatively plentiful capital K_2. The top pair of diagrams (figure 3.3a) suggests how the relatively scarce K_1 should be gradually augmented over time and the relatively plentiful K_2 gradually drawn down.

The middle pair of diagrams (figure 3.3b) shows more specifically how this is done. For the relatively scarce capital K_1, consumption in each period should be less than current sustainable yield. This would permit a positive net growth in the capital stock over time. For the relatively plentiful K_2, consumption should exceed current sustainable yield. There would be a negative net growth in capital. The crucial point is: *only in the limit should the "sustainable" yield approach a constant level so as to become a rationally justifiable "sustained" yield.* A premature policy of locking up an existing "sustainable" yield into a fixed "sustained" yield will preclude ever achieving a rational balance among different kinds of capital stocks.

The bottom pair of diagrams, finally, shows the implications of capital reallocation for the respective marginal rates of return over time. For K_1, the initially high level of ROR declines as the stock of K_1 rises. For K_2, a reverse pattern would occur, ROR rising as the stock of K_2 is drawn down.

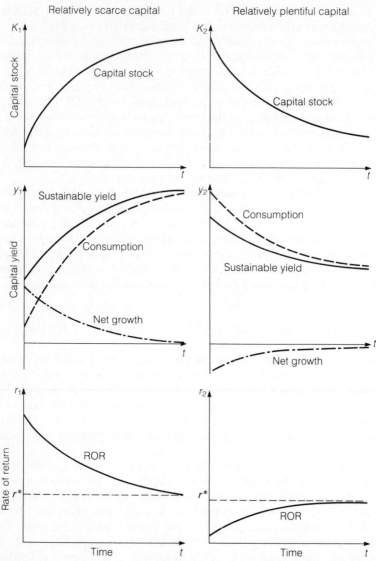

FIGURE 3.3 *Two types of capital stock – rational development over time.*

These rational patterns of capital adjustments, and their yields over time, are sensitive to a number of influences not shown in figure 3.3. One very important influence is *technological advance* over time. In general, prospective technological changes will allow us to get more yield from any given level of future capital stock. The prospect of technical advance justifies a greater degree of consumption today. Less current saving and investment are needed in the case of relatively scarce capital; a greater degree of draw-down can be justified for relatively plentiful capital. Another important influence that can work either way is the *relative price effect*. Suppose lumber and other forest products are expected to become relatively more valuable in the future than they are today. If so, we should consume less today than we otherwise would and save more for the future. But if forest products are expected to become relatively less valuable in the future, a greater cut would be justified today.

3.4 APPLICATIONS TO FORESTRY

Are forests in the United States today a *relatively* scarce type of resource, justifying a policy of accumulation, or a *relatively* plentiful form of capital justifying a degree of decumulation? The test is whether the real marginal rate of return (ROR) is greater than or less than the going real rate of interest in the economy. The latter rate reflects the ROR on real physical assets in general. (See figure 3.2.) If the ROR on forest investments is high, then a rational pattern of decision-making would lead to net growth. This appears to be what is actually happening today in the South. Without benefit of government ownership, any special regulations, or conservationist philosophy, both capital stock and sustainable yields of Southern woodlands are rapidly growing (Anderson, 1974). What about the West? I am too new in this field to hazard any comment about privately owned forests in the West. But we do have data that shed considerable light on the forest management practices of the US Forest Service. The national forests this agency manages are mostly located in the West.

The Forest Service administers a fantastically valuable resource, or at least a resource that has the potential of being highly valuable. What is being done with that resource? Budgetary estimates indicate USFS receipts of some $417,000,000 in 1974 (of which only $20,000,000 represented non-timber revenues). The expenses are over $695,000,000. That is a very large cash-flow deficit. To evaluate the current true yield we should deduct costs of non-forest activities, and separate capital investment from current expense categories. Deciphering the mish-mash of Federal budgetese, to isolate conclusively the current expenses chargeable against forestry operations, would unfortunately require a more elaborate investigation than I was able to undertake. Nevertheless, *expenses appear to exceed timber revenues*. (The single category "Forest protection and utilization" alone accounts for $372,000,000 of expenses. Substantially more costs are incurred for categories like "Forest roads and trails" and "Expenses, brush disposal.")

There are non-cash considerations that should also be counted on the credit side. These include growth of the capital stock in physical terms (increases in timber inventories) and increased accessibility (provision of roads by timber purchasers). A value of about $50,000,000 was estimated for the latter in 1971. Data for 1970 shown in table 3.1 reveal a net depletion of 0.42 percent of national forest inventory, compared with a cut of 1.29 percent. There may have been some accumulation (negative depletion) in 1974. Growth *before* cut in 1970 was only 0.88 percent. This would suggest current net growth cannot be large after corrections for cut.

Let me now relieve the earlier suspense I created. *There is a strong suggestion we are operating our national forests in the region not merely of first-order absurdity but of second-order absurdity!* That is, we appear to be reaping a negative income yield from this extremely valuable resource – not just a negative return at the margin but a negative return *in toto*. The plausibility of this conclusion is suggested by the tiny positive percent yield in physical terms (0.88 percent). This would very likely be negative if costs of operation were taken into account.

I cannot absolutely insist on this conclusion. There are a number of qualifications to be taken into account. First, perhaps more USFS expenses should be charged against non-timber forest operations. A smaller charge against timber revenues might result in a negative net economic yield becoming positive. Or, forests may be generating large "externality" benefits additional to timber production. (But note that this

TABLE 3.1 *Annual growth and removals of softwood sawtimber in relation to inventory, 1970*

Item	National forest	Other public	Forest industry	Other private	All owner-ships
Inventory in billions of board feet	982	223	318	382	1905
Percent of total inventory	51.6	11.7	16.7	20.0	100.0
Net annual growth in billions of board feet	8.6	4.0	10.0	17.7	40.3
Percent of inventory	0.88	1.79	3.14	4.63	2.11
Net annual removals in billions of board feet	12.7	4.2	16.3	14.5	47.7
Percent of inventory	1.29	1.88	5.13	3.80	2.50
Net annual depletion in billions of board feet (removals minus growth)	4.1	0.2	6.13	− 3.2[1]	7.4
Percent of inventory	0.42	0.09	1.98	− 0.84[1]	0.39

Source: Forest Service 1973.
[1] Negative depletion means an inventory increase.

does not justify a failure to maximize economic gain on timber production, unless somehow the externalities are more in evidence under low-yield than under high-yield timber management.) Perhaps most important of all, the 0.88 percent growth rate is a *physical* rather than an economic measure. It probably represents a mixture of two elements, zero or negative growth on some fully mature forests and a somewhat higher rate of growth on forest lands which have been cut over. Very likely some of the fully mature forests are relatively inaccessible or remote from markets, compared to newly established forests on cutover lands. Conceivably, physical growth that did take place on remote forests would have no market value. If zero rates of physical growth are taking place where their economic values are small, and positive growth is occurring where values are higher, then the average physical growth rate of 0.88 percent would underestimate the *economic* yield on timber capital. Another way of putting this: the average price per cubic foot of the wood being harvested is higher than the average price per cubic foot of wood remaining in inventory. To summarize, I cannot be certain about my drastic suggestion that we may be operating in the region of second-order absurdity. But there can be no doubt whatsoever that first-order absurdity has been "achieved!"

Is this an inference of concern only to dollar-grubbing accountants or economists, one that can be ignored by the forest practitioner? There is a serious question here suggested by the word stewardship. The citizens and taxpayers are the owners of the national forests. The question is, are the foresters, as stewards, making a proper use of this resource? If a potentially value asset is yielding zero total return, this is equivalent to saying we could simply deed our national forests to some Arab sheik and be no worse off. If we are reaping a negative return, we would actually be better off giving the forests away. The alternative, of course, would be to change the policies that have led us into this paradoxical situation. Even if we are not quite in the situation I have described, we are clearly earning an inadequate return on the valuable capital stock locked up in unproductive forests.

3.5   SUSTAINED YIELD AND THE NO-DROP-OFF CONSTRAINT

Why has this come about? There seem to have been two major analytical failings. The less serious is the technical issue of correct rotation age. The more serious is a truly pernicious notion of "no-drop-off" in the timber harvest rate. As I read the forestry literature of recent years, there has definitely been intellectual regress. Not too long ago "sustained yield" appeared to mean a level of yield to be attained at some point in the future. This yield was associated with a balanced age-class distribution of trees in the forest. In a homogeneous forest there would be equal acres in each age class from newly cutover lands to rotation age. It was recognized that allowable cut might rationally exceed current sustainable growth, especially if virgin forests are being harvested and second-growth stands are being established. Data for 1970 in table 3.1 do show net depletion – an excess of harvest over growth.

Even when this earlier and more justifiable concept of sustained yield was being used, the criterion for determining optimal rotation ages was incorrect. Cutting timber at an age which maximizes sustained yield (average annual growth) tells us nothing about how efficiently we are using our capital. This point is very clearly made in Professor Samuelson's paper. Nevertheless, the general approach was sound, sound in the sense that a rationally justifiable level of inventory is implicit. The realization that allowable cut must be permitted to exceed growth for a period of years until inventory is reduced to this level is also sound.

In recent years the interpretation of the phrase "sustained yield" has shifted to a notion of "no-drop-off" or "never declining yield." According to this notion, on no "working circle" (the administrative unit on national forests for planning timber harvests) should the allowable cut ever be so great that future harvests will have to be reduced. This guarantees that no progress can ever be made toward rationalizing the use of a relatively plentiful capital stock. As noted earlier, there is considerable evidence that the stock of timber capital on national forests in the West is indeed relatively plentiful.

The "no-drop-off" constraint has a number of specific pathological consequences. One is that working circle boundaries make a difference, sometimes rather large differences. Redrawing boundaries to combine a stand of fast-growing young timber with over-mature timber permits "earning" immediately the "right" to increase the rate of harvest of the latter. According to Mason and Henze (1959), by combining young-growth and old-growth lands in the Shelton Cooperative Sustained Yield Unit, a 50 percent increase in allowable cut (over the sum of separate cuts) was "earned." Rationally, of course, if a cut of over-mature timber is justified, it remains so whether or not a separate stand of young timber is included in the same working circle.

A second pathological consequence is revealed by a number of the cost-effectiveness calculations included in the "Douglas-fir Supply Study." (Forest Service, 1969). Generally, these calculations show astonishingly high rates of return, on the order of 40 percent to more than 100 percent, on investments in more intensive forestry practices. The increments to net worth are fantastic, on the order of $1.5 billion for the Douglas-fir region if capitalized at 5 percent. As I interpret the analysis, these incredibly high returns on investment are only incidentally due to their supposed cause, the intensified management practices. The crucial thing is that intensive management raises the *future* yield, and thereby permits "earning" a larger *current* harvest without violating the taboo against a later drop-off. This calculation is known as the "allowable cut effect" (Walker, 1971; Teeguarden, 1973). The increment to net worth is not due to the investment, rather *to the higher current harvest*. The investments for intensified management may or may not be independently justified, but the higher current harvest would vastly increase net even if no significant investment were undertaken.

The problem of the "allowable cut effect" is conclusively revealed in a Forest Service evaluation of management practices on the Gifford Pinchot National Forest (Forest Service, 1973). By combining intensified management and accelerated harvests, a net worth increment for this one national forest was estimated to be $238,000,000 if capitalized at a 5 percent interest rate, and $125,000,000 if capitalized at 10 percent. Then the interesting question was asked: "What if we pessimistically assumed intensified management practices are a total failure, they provide no future yield increment at all?" It turns out that these assumptions of utter disaster reduce the net-worth gain hardly at all! It falls off by only $12,400,000 at 5 percent interest and by an almost unbelievably low $180 (a misprint, perhaps?) at 10 percent interest! (See Forest Service, 1973, p. 36.) Evidently, practically all the gain is due to the accelerated harvest, and the intensified management makes little or no difference.

A similar phenomenon has been observed in Canada by Peter H. Pearse (1965). He reported that timber companies paid excessively high prices for cutover forest land in British Columbia. The reason was that under the sustained yield timber management plans in force, the inclusion of cutover land in a timber license area permitted a company to "earn" a larger harvest of mature timber. Cutover land that would otherwise be worthless has substantial value as a roundabout way of approaching economic efficiency.

The following metaphor may shed some light on the "allowable cut" issue. Suppose that instead of a "no-drop-off" constraint on harvest there was a "Druid-agreement" constraint. Before a tree could be cut, a Druid wizard would be hired to perform an incantation. Assume further that the tree is worth $200, and the wizard charges $100 per incantation. Simple arithmetic shows the rate of return on hiring the Druid to perform his incantation and then cutting the tree is 100 percent, a very profitable investment it would appear. We could do even better, of course, by dispensing with the wizard and just getting on with our timber harvesting.

3.6   SOME ADDITIONAL ISSUES

In closing, a number of additional issues are worth brief mention.

1 The Forest Service seems to place extraordinary emphasis on *economic stability* as an objective. This is reflected in slogans such as

"evenflow," "sustained yield," "no-drop-off," etc. On its face, it is ridiculous to rule out an attractive investment because it leads to a mild decline in timber harvest 120 years from now. In addition, as Professor Dowdle has repeatedly observed, imposing a rigidly even flow on timber harvests from national forests necessarily *increases instability elsewhere.* If public forest lands do not respond to changes in economic circumstances, then consumers must either suffer great price fluctuations or there will have to be greater swings in production on privately owned lands.

2 There seems to be very little discussion in recent forestry literature of what might be called the "cartelization" objective of low sustained-yield cuts. The Arab oil cartel has clearly shown us how producers can sometimes reap handsome returns at the expense of consumers by a cutback of output. This objective was apparently openly proclaimed by earlier exponents of sustained yield (Mason, 1927). There is an evident conflict of interest between private individuals and companies who benefit from low Forest Service harvests (to wit, the owners of private woodlands) and those who suffer from low Forest Service harvests. The latter group would include users of lumber, which is to say America's industry and consumers generally.

3 Finally, I have not seen any attempt to quantify the *environmental* damages that might ensue from more intensive use of forest lands. Increasing the rate of timber harvesting will presumably mean, at any moment of time, a greater fraction of land in a cut-over condition. This land may be subject to more erosion and may constitute a potential source of flooding. Another point: Would the net environmental effects of having a younger forest, on the average, be harmful or beneficial? Attempts should be made to measure these "external" considerations, to weigh them against the direct benefits of increasing the nation's available supply of forest products.

In conclusion, let me emphasize my main message. Suppose the 1970 estimate of 0.88 percent for annual sustainable yield (y/K) on our national forests is too low. We are not in the region of second-order absurdity, of negative total yields in economic terms, yet *marginal* yield y' is almost surely still negative. We still have what I have called a first-order absurdity. Rational policy dictates that this pitifully low-yielding stock of timber capital be drawn down, as illustrated on the right-hand side of figure 3.3. It should be reduced until marginal yields on our timber inventories approach a level which provides a reasonable return to the taxpayer-owners of this capital. We should be aiming at a real ROR, or *marginal sustainable yield* y', of perhaps 5 percent. This would be consistent with the rate of return on capital generally in our economy. If the marginal yield is 5 percent, the average annual yield overall as a percent of inventory (y/K) would be somewhat higher – perhaps 6 percent or 8 percent. This is what rational forest policy should be trying to achieve.

Such a policy would permit, in fact would require, that we cut and consume timber products now (and in the near future) at a rate greater than the current sustainable yield. This timber is urgently needed *now!* One hardly has to mention that a current increment of cut would benefit American consumers and American industry, most obviously through the impact on housing construction. But however rational, and however urgently needed, a present increment of cut is precisely what the "sustained yield" theory, or at least the "no-drop-off" interpretation of that theory, forbids. These slogans dictate, in short, that if it is a question of rational forest policy, "you just can't get there from here!"

3.7   DISCUSSION

Question: Do you have an estimate of the possible decline in the asset value of *private* forest land if *public* forest policy were to become rational? In other words, can the motivation for a public policy of sustained yield be attributed to lobbying to maximize the return on private assets?

Answer: That is a very good question, for which I have no accurate quantitative answer. Perhaps someone here, with more knowledge of the industry than I, does. To answer your question in qualitative terms, I am sure the effect would be large. If the harvest on the national forests were to be increased from around 1 percent to a still very modest 2 percent of inventory each year, there would be a big rise in wood supply. The impact on lumber prices would not be insignificant. Time would be required to construct access roads and otherwise prepare to market more timber. But subject to these kinds of lags, I think the impact on the value of privately held forest land would be substantial.

The next question is whether or not the policy of sustained yield, as I have described it, can be attributed to lobbying by private interests. I am just not familiar enough with the industry and its politics to answer this question. There is evidence that private industry lobbied to keep public timber off the market prior to World War II lest it depress price. On the other hand, since World War II there has been considerable lobbying on the part of plywood and lumber producers, who are substantially dependent upon public timber, to *increase* public timber harvests. Those who process their own timber are undoubtedly less enthusiastic about this prospect. The interests of companies with substantial timber holdings have not, to the best of my knowledge, manifested themselves recently in active and open lobbying to keep public timber off the market. Possibly this is because risks in other areas would be increased. Large timber-holding companies, for example, undoubtedly keep their eye on the local tax assessor and are reluctant to take any action that might lead him to conclude they are collecting cartel-like profits from a lumber scarcity.

When all these possibilities are balanced, I would still be doubtful that Forest Service timber harvesting policy is *mainly* a result of private lobbying efforts. The Forest Service's ideological rejection of the market has a long history and it seems to be deeply ingrained. I find it difficult to believe that the agency might now be a tool of large-scale capitalism.

Question: If the national forests were given an Arab sheik as you suggested, what would society do about the external benefits that would be lost? Perhaps the negative cash flow is a measure of these external values?

Answer: One of the points in my argument was that externalities should be considered. While conceding this in principle, I also noted that it would be useful if we could see some quantitative estimates in practice. If there are hidden defenses for policies that seem on their face indefensible, by all means they should be brought out where society as a whole can see and evaluate them.

Question: Haven't you oversimplified to the point that the force of your argument may be lost? Perhaps it would be better to isolate the timber cost-benefit data in the budget to support your position.

Answer: Simplification is a necessity if the essence of a complex issue is to be grasped. The question is whether or not the essence of the issue is lost in the process of simplification. I assume that this is what you mean by oversimplifying. The irrationality of the sustained-yield concept (in its "no-drop-off" interpretation, at least) is so painfully obvious it would be hard to lose by oversimplification.

Your second question is whether or not it would be better to isolate the timber cost-benefit data in the budget. I think it would. This would, of course, take time. In preparing my presentation, I juggled budget figures in an attempt to isolate the timber portion of the receipts and the timber portion of the benefits. When you do this, there are always questions. Without a lot more study, it would be impossible to give a definitive answer to your question. It was my impression that even if non-timber costs and benefits were included, the economic return on our national forest lands would be negative. If it is positive, it must be very small.

Question: Total National Forest expenses exceed total receipts, however, receipts for timber management alone are five or more times the expense for timber management. How do you explain this fact?

Answer: First, I disagree with the assertion that receipts from timber management are five or more times the expense of timber management. Such an assertion could be justified, if at all, only upon an exceedingly narrow concept of timber management. Consider 1974, for example. Total receipts were $417 million. One single category of expense, called "Forest Protection and Utilization," totaled $372 million. In other words, costs in just that one category of expense are nearly equal to overall receipts. A second item, "Forest Roads and Trails," came to an additional $98 million. It could hardly be claimed that these expenditures are not, in large part, for timber management.

Question: How would you feel about reducing the timber inventory in the San Bernardino National Forest, your own backyard?

Answer: I was afraid to bring my wife with me because I thought if she saw all these trees up here, she would never let me say we should cut more of them down. Personally, I feel very little loyalty and identification with the San Bernardino National Forest. I am just as loyal to and sympathetic with the national forests here in Washington. The relevant issue to me is whether or not they are managed efficiently. The only difference between San Bernardino and here that I can see, right off, might lie in the question of external benefits. If it could be demonstrated that the San Bernardino National Forest helps to reduce Los Angeles smog, or helps to avoid damaging flooding of a highly populated region, then these benefits should certainly be included as a big plus in determining how many trees to grow to what age in the San Bernardino Forest.

Question: Do the data for forest industry in your table 3.1 imply that private, as well as public, foresters should heed your lecture?

Answer: At first glance, a net annual growth rate for the private forest industry of 3.14 percent does appear to be low relative to competitive rates of return on capital. But recall this is a rate expressed in physical terms. It is the annual harvest of timber, expressed in board feet per year, divided by the inventory of timber capital expressed simply in terms of board feet. To express this ratio as a rate of return which could be compared with rates of return on other kinds of capital, we would have to multiply the numerator of our ratio, board feet per year, by the average price at which the annual harvest is sold. Similarly, we would have to multiply the denominator by the average price all the timber held in inventory would bring if the entire inventory were sold. Since much of the timber in the inventory is immature and will not be cut and sold to timber processors for several years, the average price implicit in the value of a timber inventory will be less than the average price of timber currently being sold as annual harvest.

Given the lengthy time period of production in forestry, it is not unreasonable to assume the average price of timber being harvested is two to three times as much as the average price of timber included in forest inventory. If so, the monetary rate of return would be between 6 and about 9 percent. This seems reasonable. In any case, the private yield is still over three times the growth rate on the national forests.

REFERENCES

Anderson, W. C., "The South – An Unregulated Forest Region", *Journal of Forestry*, vol. 72 (1974), pp. 221–3.

Mason, D. T., "Sustained Yield and American Forest Problems", *Journal of Forestry*, vol. 25 (1927), pp. 625–58.

Mason, D. T. and Henze, K. D., "The Shelton Cooperative Sustained Yield Unit", *Journal of Forestry*, vol. 57 (1959), p. 163–80.

Pearse, P. H., "Distortions in the Market for Forest Land", *The Forestry Chronicle*, vol. 41 (1965), pp. 406–18.

Teeguarden, D. E., "The Allowable Cut Effect: A Comment", *Journal of Forestry*, vol. 71 (1973), pp. 221–6.

Walker, J. L., "An economic model for optimizing the rate of timber harvesting", Ph.D. Thesis, University of Washington, 1971, 117 p.

US Department of Agriculture, Forest Service, "The Douglas-fir Supply Study", 1969, 53 p.

—— "Forest Regulation Study, Preliminary Draft", 1973a, 57 p.

—— "The Outlook for Timber in the United States", *Forestry Research Report* no. 20 (1973b), 367 p.

4 Investment Decision Under Uncertainty: Choice-theoretic Approaches*

Background and comments

Turning now from the economics of time to the economics of uncertainty, this and the following essay were initially composed as a single paper of rather unwieldy length. At the suggestion of the journal editors, the original version was separated into two articles. This first essay begins with a review of Irving Fisher's general-equilibrium model of *intertemporal* choice and equilibrium as a paradigm for the construction of a properly structured theory of decision and equilibrium *under uncertainty*. Curiously, Fisher himself failed to perceive this parallel. Instead, when in *The Theory of Interest* he had to deal with the inescapable problem of how uncertainty interacts with intertemporal choice, Fisher retreated to the uncharacteristically weak position that uncertainty was "unadapted to mathematical formulation!"

While several alternative approaches are reviewed here, the thrust of the article is to demonstrate that the "state-preference approach" is the proper formulation for unifying the economic theory of decision and equilibrium under uncertainty with general price theory.

Historically speaking, the key insight leading to this unification was provided in a paper by Kenneth Arrow. Once again, despite the author's many recognized previous achievements, it took time and effort before the path-breaking significance of this contribution was generally acknowledged. Arrow's pioneering article, published in a French journal in 1953, was in fact not even available in an English-language publication until 1964. Although in the intervening years the theory was notably extended by Gerard Debreu, and also applied in a number of contexts by a few other economists including the present author, the essay reprinted here did (I believe) play a role in winning more general acceptance for the state-preference model of uncertainty.

*This article orginally appeared in *Quarterly Journal of Economics*, vol. 74 (Nov. 1965), pp. 509–36. The permission of MIT Press and John Wiley and Sons to reprint in this volume is gratefully acknowledged.

Investment is, in essence, *present* sacrifice for *future* benefit. But the present is relatively well known, whereas the future is always an enigma. Investment is also, therefore, *certain* sacrifice for *uncertain* benefit. The theory of investment decision has been satisfactorily developed, in the great work of Irving Fisher,[1] only under the artificial assumption of certainty.[2] Despite the restrictiveness of this assumption, Fisher's theory does succeed in explaining substantial portions of observed investment behavior.[3] But other portions cannot apparently be explained without bringing in attitudes toward risk and differences of opinion, sources of behavior that only come into existence under uncertainty. Among the phenomena left unexplained under the certainty assumption are: the value attached to "liquidity," the willingness to buy insurance, the existence of debt and equity financing, and the bewildering variety of returns or yields on various forms of investment simultaneously ruling in the market.

The object of this paper is to develop, and show some of the implications of, a treatment of risky or uncertain choice that is a generalization of Fisher's theory of riskless choice over time (itself a generalization of the standard theory of timeless choice). In section 4.1 I provide an interpretation of Fisher's theory designed (a) to examine its character as a model of *choice-theoretic structure*, and (b) to introduce the *firm* as a decision-making unit, where Fisher treated only of atomic individuals. The next sections review alternative lines of approach to the theory of risky choice, showing how they diverge in specification of the *choice-objects* of individuals. The major analytical sections then follow, developing a theory of uncertain choice over time in terms of comparisons between consumption possibilities in different possible dated contingencies or "states of the world." A successor article[4] will apply this "time-state-preference" approach to several normative and positive issues: (1) risk aversion and the coexistence of gambling and insurance; (2) the Modigliani-Miller problem concerning the existence or non-existence of an optimum corporate financial structure (debt-equity mix); and (3) the discount rate to be employed in evaluating public investment projects not subject to the market test.

4.1   FISHER'S THEORY OF INVESTMENT DECISION: INTERPRETATION AND REFORMULATION

Only a brief exposition of Fisher's theory will be provided here, as a prelude to the introduction of the firm as an economic agent into Fisher's system. The concepts and terms of Fisher's presentation will be somewhat modified to suit my purposes. To avoid needless complications, the explicit presentation will be limited to two-period comparisons between the present (time 0) and the future (time 1).

In Fisher's system the primitive concept, in terms of which all others are defined, is *consumption*. The objects of choice are present consumption (c_0) and future consumption (c_1). The *time-preference* function for the j-th individual may be denoted $U^j = g^j(c_0^j, c_1^j), j = 1, 2, ..., J$. Each individual attempts to maximize utility within his *opportunity set*. It is useful to distinguish three different categories within the opportunity set: endowment, financial opportunities, and productive opportunities. The *endowment* $Y^j = (y_0^j, y_1^j)$ is the individual's initial position (see figure 4.1); it provides a base point for the analysis of investment as a redistribution of consumption opportunities over time. The endowment element y_0 may be interpreted as *current income* and y_1 correspondingly as *future income*. The justification for this interpretation (which departs from Fisher's terminology, but is consistent with the spirit of his analysis) is that y_0 is the amount that can be consumed without trenching on future consumptive possibilities.[5] We then define investment $i_0 = y_0 - c_0$, negative values of investment being possible.[6]

Financial opportunities for investment permit transformation of the endowment into alternative (c_0, c_1) combinations, but only by trading with other individuals. In such trading, motivated by disparities between

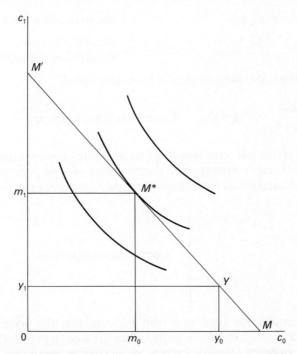

FIGURE 4.1 *Intertemporal choice – financial opportunities only.*

endowed or attained income-sequences and desired time-patterns of consumption, a rate of exchange between units of present consumption (present dollars) and of future consumption (future dollars) would be established in the market. This rate of exchange can be expressed as $(dc_1)/(dc_0) = -(1+r)$, where r is the *rate of interest*, or premium on current dollars. In figure 4.1 the financial opportunities facing the investor are shown by the "market line" MM' through Y. Along this market line *wealth* $W = c_0 + c_1/(1+r)$ equals $y_0 + y_1/(1+r)$, a constant, so that the market line is a budget or wealth constraint. The time-preference optimum for the individual under pure exchange (financial opportunities only) is M^*, and at the interest rate r he seeks to invest (lend) the amount $(y_0 - m_0)$. Under pure exchange the social totals of present and of future consumption,

$$\sum_j y_0^j \quad \text{and} \quad \sum_j y_1^j$$

are conserved, while the social total of investment is zero (for each borrower there is a lender). This condition determines the market interest rate r.

The basic equations under pure exchange may be represented as follows:

$$U^j = g^j(c_0^j, c_1^j) \qquad \text{Time-preference function} \quad (4.1)$$

$$c_0^j + c_1^j/(1+r) = y_0^j + y_1^j/(1+r) \qquad \begin{array}{l}\text{Wealth constraint, or} \\ \text{financial opportunities.}\end{array} \quad (4.2)$$

These equations also indicate that all loans are repaid.

$$\left.\frac{dc_1^j}{dc_0^j}\right|_{U^j} = -(1+r) \qquad \text{Time-preference optimum} \quad (4.3)$$

The symbol on the left represents the marginal rate of substitution of c_1 for c_0 that leaves utility constant – the marginal rate of time preference. Note that this is equated for all individuals (if we rule out corner solutions).

$$\left.\begin{array}{l}\displaystyle\sum_{j=1}^{J} c_0^j = \sum_{j=1}^{J} y_0^j \\[2em] \displaystyle\sum_{j=1}^{J} c_1^j = \sum_{j=1}^{J} y_1^j\end{array}\right\} \qquad \text{Conservation equations}[7] \quad (4.4)$$

These market-clearing equations also indicate that the social total of investment, $\Sigma(y_0 - c_0)$ is zero, as required for the case of pure exchange.

If the opportunity set also contains *productive opportunities*, then it is possible to engage in transactions with nature (e.g. planting a seed), as well as with other individuals. Under such circumstances, in Fisher's system the individual investor attains his utility optimum at X^* (in figure 4.2) by a two-step procedure. First, he moves from his endowment Y along his productive opportunity locus PP' (note that his opportunities are ordered according to diminishing marginal productivity of investment) to his productive optimum P^*. The productive optimum is characterized by attainment of the highest possible market line – that is, highest wealth level. The productive investor can then "finance" by borrowing, if need be, to attain his utility optimum X^*. In figure 4.2, his productive investment is $(y_0 - p_0)$, and he borrows $(x_0 - p_0)$ to replenish current consumption. It is the transaction with nature that creates wealth; the associated financial transfers leave wealth unchanged.

In the equations allowing productive opportunities, the elements (p_0, p_1) of the "productive solution" P^* appear as variables:

$$U^j = g^j(c_0^j, c_1^j) \qquad\qquad \text{Time-preference function} \quad (4.1')$$

$$c_0^j + c_1^j/(1+r) = p_0^j + p_1^j/(1+r) \quad \begin{array}{l}\text{Wealth constraint, or}\\\text{financial opportunities}\end{array} \quad (4.2')$$

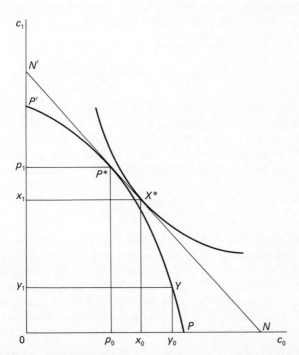

FIGURE 4.2 *Intertemporal choice – productive and exchange opportunities.*

The wealth level attained by productive transformations, rather than the endowment wealth level, becomes the financial constraint.

$$\frac{dc_1^j}{dc_0^j}\bigg|_{U^j} = -(1+r) \qquad \text{Time-preference optimum} \qquad (4.3')$$

$$p^j(p_0^j, y_1^j; y_0^j, y_1^j) = 0 \qquad \text{Productive opportunity set} \qquad (4.4')$$

$$\frac{dp_1^j}{dp_0^j} = -(1+r) \qquad \text{Productive optimum} \qquad (4.5')$$

This condition also represents attainment of maximum wealth or "present value."[8]

$$\left.\begin{array}{l} \displaystyle\sum_{j=1}^{J} c_0^j = \sum_{j=1}^{J} p_0^j \\[2em] \displaystyle\sum_{j=1}^{J} c_1^j = \sum_{j=1}^{J} p_1^j \end{array}\right\} \qquad \text{Conservation equations} \qquad (4.6')$$

These market-clearing equations make the interest rate depend upon the productive as well as the consumptive supply and demand for funds. The social total of current investment is

$$\sum_{j=1}^{J} i_0^j = \sum_{j=1}^{J} (y_0^j - p_0^j).$$

We may now introduce firms as the specialized agencies of individuals in their time-productive capacities. We specify: (a) firms do not consume; (b) firms have null endowments; and (c) all productive opportunities appertain to firms. Let there be F firms, and let o_f^j be the fraction of the f-th firm owned by the j-th individual. The o_f^j here are constants, such that

$$\sum_{j=1}^{J} o_f^j = 1, \text{ for } f = 1, 2, \dots, F.$$

The equilibrium of the firm (see figure 4.3) is the productive solution Q^* where the highest market line NN' is attained; this represents maximum wealth for the firm, and so for the owners. The firm, having null endowment, must borrow q_0, an amount equal to the productive investment. It repays lenders $-q_0(1+r) = q_1 - e_1$ (see figure 4.3). The firm income e_1^f is distributed to the owners as an increment to their endowments y_1^j.[9]

With the introduction of firms, the equation system may be represented:

$$U^j = g^j(c_0^j, c_1^j) \qquad \text{Time-preference function} \quad (4.1'')$$

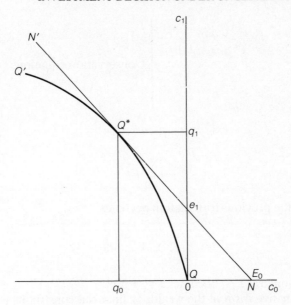

FIGURE 4.3 *The firm's investment decision.*

$$c_0^j + c_1^j/(1+r) = y_0^j + (y_1^j + \sum_{f=1}^{F} o_f^j e_1^f)/(1+r) \qquad \text{Wealth constraint}$$

$$(4.2'')$$

On this interpretation, the firms use no "equity" funds. In a world of certainty, full-debt financing is possible. However, the effect of profitable investment is an increment e_1^j to equity (wealth of owners) in time "1."

$$\left.\frac{dc_1^j}{dc_0^j}\right|_{U^j} = -(1+r) \qquad \text{Time-preference optimum} \qquad (4.3'')$$

$$q^j(q_0^f; q_1^f) = 0 \qquad \text{Productive opportunity set} \qquad (4.4'')$$

$$\frac{dq_1^f}{dq_0^f} = -(1+r) \qquad \text{Productive optimum} \qquad (4.5'')$$

The productive decisions are all made by the firms.

$$q_1^f = -q_0^f(1+r) + e_1^f \qquad \text{Firm's financial distributions} \qquad (4.6'')$$

Since the firm does not consume, it must distribute its productive gross earnings, q_1. This amount is divided between repayment of debt and equity income to owners.

$$\left.\begin{array}{l} \displaystyle\sum_{j=1}^{J} y_0^j + \sum_{f=1}^{F} q_0^f = \sum_{j=1}^{J} c_0^j \\[2em] \displaystyle\sum_{j=1}^{J} y_1^j + \sum_{f=1}^{F} q_1^f = \sum_{j=1}^{J} c_1^j \end{array}\right\} \text{Conservation equations} \qquad (4.7'')$$

Note that

$$\sum_{j=1}^{J} p_0^j$$

in $(4.6')$ of the previous formulation becomes

$$\sum_{j=1}^{J} y_0^j + \sum_{f=1}^{F} q_0^f$$

here, and similarly Σp_1^j becomes $\Sigma y_1^j + \Sigma y_1^f$.

An alternative form of the wealth or financial constraints is also useful. Let P_0 be the price of c_0, and P_1 the price of c_1. If c_0 is taken as numeraire we have $P_0 = 1$ and $P_1 = 1/(1 + r)$. Then:

Equation (4.2) becomes: $P_0 c_0 + P_1 c_1 = P_0 y_0 + P_1 y_1$.

Equation $(4.2')$ becomes: $P_0 c_0 + P_1 c_1 = P_0 p_0 + P_1 p_1$.

Equation $(4.2'')$ becomes: $P_0 c_0 + P_1 c_1 = P_0 y_0 + P_1 y_1 + \left(P_1 \left[\displaystyle\sum_{f=1}^{F} (o_f e_1^f) \right] \right)$.

And, after dividing through by $(1 + r)$, equation $(4.6'')$ becomes:

$$P_1 q_1 = -P_0 q_0 + P_1 e_1. \qquad (4.6''')$$

This can be given the interpretation: the "wealth of the firm" (i.e. the present worth of the firm's gross or productive income q_1) is the sum of the values of the debt and equity – the sum of the borrowings and the increment to wealth of the owners.[10]

4.2   CHOICE-THEORETIC APPROACHES TO INVESTMENT DECISION UNDER UNCERTAINTY

While Fisher's model is a special application to the problem of investment decision under certainty, it can also be regarded as an archetype of choice-theoretic system for any decision problem. By "choice-theoretic system" I will mean a model containing the following features: (1) objects of choice (commodities), and decision-making units (economic agents); (2) a preference function ordering such objects, for each economic agent; (3) an opportunity set, again for each agent, which is equivalent to specifying the constraints upon the agent's range of choice; and (4) balancing or conservation equations, which specify the social interactions among the individual decisions. The competing approaches to investment decision considered in this section diverge in their specification of the basic objects of choice.

Investment decision under uncertainty involves purchase of *assets* – more or less complex claims or titles to present and future incomes. The most direct theoretical formulation of this decision is the *Asset-preference Approach*; this postulates that assets themselves are the desired objects of choice. On the theoretical level, comparisons usually run in terms of exchanges between a riskless asset and one or more risky assets (or lotteries) with arbitrary but specified probability distributions.[11] The main appeal of this approach is the attractiveness of the direct analogy between assets in investment theory and the commodities of ordinary price theory. The central disadvantage of the approach is that assets are clearly not the elemental desired objects; what we would like to do analytically would be to show how the prices of assets are determined by the valuations placed by individuals upon the underlying income opportunities to which the assets represent claims. In other words, what we really are seeking is a means of resolving assets into more fundamental choice-objects. A second difficulty, which will reappear below in connection with each of the alternative formulations for the objects of choice, is that the total of the various types of assets cannot be assumed fixed, even under pure exchange. Thus, an individual owning a real asset can issue claims against the security of his original asset – i.e. he can "finance" his holdings of assets, and in doing so has a wide variety of options ("debt-equity mix"). But each such action generates a more or less complex pattern of new "financial" assets which can substitute for productive assets in the portfolios of investors. It is clear, therefore, that conservation relations do not hold in any simple way when the objects of choice are taken to be assets.

The approach currently most popular in the analysis of investment decision under uncertainty postulates that the fundamental objects of choice, standing behind the particularities of individual assets, are the *mean* and the *variability* of future return – where variability refers to probabilistic rather than chronological fluctuation. This *Mean, Variability Approach*, to be critically analyzed in the next section, reduces assets (or portfolios of assets) to underlying mean and variability measures which, it is postulated, enter into investors' preference functions. An alternative reduction will be developed next, under the heading of *State-preference Approach*. Here the underlying objects of choice are postulated to be contingent consumption opportunities or claims defined over a complete listing of all possible "states of the world." It will be shown that this latter approach can easily be developed into a choice-theoretic system that represents a natural extension of Fisher's into the domain of uncertainty.

4.3   THE MEAN, VARIABILITY APPROACH

The mean, variability approach to investment decision under uncertainty selects as the objects of choice *expected returns* and *variability of returns* from investment.[12] In accordance with the common beliefs of observers of financial markets, the assumption is made that investors desire high values of the former and low values of the latter – as usually measured by the mean (μ) and standard deviation (σ), respectively, of the probability distribution of returns – and show increasing aversion to σ as risk increases. Under these assumptions a preference function can be shown as in figure 4.4 ordering all possible (μ, σ) combinations.

Theorists following the mean, variability approach have concentrated upon the problem of portfolios, i.e. holdings of financial assets (securities). Little or no attention has been paid to productive assets or investments. Also, the usual portfolio analysis keeps constant the amount of current investment and concerns itself only with the distribution of that amount over the available securities. Neither restriction is, however, essential. The same approach could be extended, on the level of the individual investor, to include real productive investments in addition to a financial portfolio,[13] and a simultaneous solution could be provided for the amount of investment together with the choice of securities to be held.

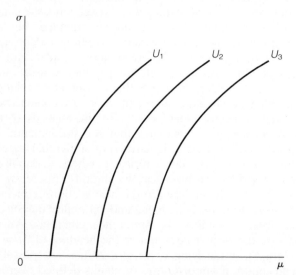

FIGURE 4.4   *Mean* versus *variability – preference function.*

For our purposes, it will suffice to present only the broad outlines of the mean, variability formulation. Turning first to the opportunity set, and letting X be the random variable of prospective gross portfolio value[14] consequent upon given current investment, the possible combinations of $\mu(X)$ and $\sigma(X)$ attainable by holding individual securities (i.e., combinations attainable in one-security portfolios) are suggested by the typical points B, C, D, etc., in figure 4.5. The point B is on the horizontal axis; it is intended to represent investment in riskless bonds. The solid curve shows the efficient frontier (minimum σ attainable for each possible value of μ) when the investor does *not* have the riskless opportunity B available. In general, one-security portfolios are not on the efficient frontier, because of the advantage of diversification: the overall μ for any mixed portfolio will be the weighted average of the component μ_i values for the individual securities, but the overall σ will in general be lower than the corresponding average of the σ_i.[15] However, the security G, whose expected future value is greater than any other security's, is an efficient one-security portfolio. This suggests why the efficient frontier is convex to the right: as we move to higher and higher portfolio μ, we are forced to concentrate increasingly on the small number of high-μ_i securities, thus progressively reducing the power of diversification. The introduction of the riskless security B, with mean future value μ_B, changes the opportunity set to incorporate the area bounded by the line through B and tangent at ϕ to the efficient frontier constructed from the risky securities.[16]

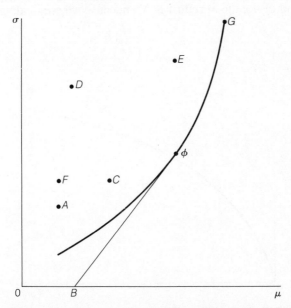

Figure 4.5 *Mean* versus *variability – opportunity set.*

The preference function has been the focus of attention in controversial discussion of the mean, variability approach. There have been attempts to derive indifference maps like that portrayed in figure 4.4 from the Neumann-Morgenstern axioms of rational choice – together with a specification of a concave-downward utility-of-income $v(X)$ function like that shown in figure 4.6. The latter shape is necessary in order to obtain risk aversion (positive-sloping U-curves in figure 4.4).[17] (Whether observed behavior can be regarded as reflecting risk aversion rather than risk preference, or some mixture of the two, is a subject of disagreement that will be considered in chapter 5.) Here v is the Neumann-Morgenstern utility indicator that permits use of the expected-utility theorem in rationalizing choice under uncertainty, and the argument X is really consumption income in the future period. It has been shown that a μ, σ indifference map can be derived (i.e., that each indifference curve represents a locus of constant expected utility-of-income) only if one of the following conditions obtains: (a) the utility-of-income function v is quadratic, or (b) in considering alternative portfolios, the investor's probability distributions for X under the various portfolios considered are all members of a two-parameter family.[18]

It is clear that a quadratic utility-of-income function is unacceptable. To make $v(X)$ concave downward with such a function, the coefficient of the squared term must be negative – but in this case a point must be reached where additional income decreases utility! Furthermore, we cannot accept the quadratic even as an approximation, however well it may fit in the neighborhood of the mean return $\mu(X)$, because we are dealing with risky

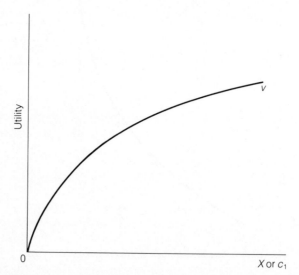

FIGURE 4.6 *Utility-of-income function with risk aversion.*

portfolios that require us to evaluate the utility of values for the random variable X diverging considerably from the mean.

One's first impression is that the second condition should be much more widely applicable. In particular, if (on the efficient frontier, at least) all portfolios consist of relatively large numbers of securities, the Central Limit Theorem indicates that the probability distributions for the returns X under any such "well-diversified" portfolio will approach normality – and, of course, the normal distribution is two-parameter. Nevertheless, this does not really help us, though to explain why will require an illustration anticipating the main ideas of the next section. Let us suppose that an investor contemplates the uncertain future as the set of three equally probable "states of the world" A, B, and C – one and only one of which will actually obtain. A "state" here is a complete world-environment for the individual. For two different portfolios, the distribution of future values over these states (X_A, X_B, X_C), might be $(3, 2, 1)$ and $(1, 2, 3)$ respectively. Since these two distributions or "prospects" have the same μ and σ, they would have to be identical in preference ordering in order for it to be possible to construct a preference map on μ, σ axes. But we have no right to assume that an investor would be indifferent between the two prospects. The nature of the world-environments A, B, and C might be such that he prefers the distribution biased toward wealth in state A over that biased toward wealth in state C. Here the *ordering* on A, B, and C of the elements of the distribution cannot be neglected; a distribution that is two-parameter disregarding ordering turns out to be insufficiently specified, for preference ranking purposes, by the mean and standard deviation.

One element of the choice-theoretic structure under the mean, variability approach has not received the attention it deserves: the role of conservation relations. Waiving the difficulties turning upon the existence and shape of μ, σ preference functions, and accepting the efficient frontier as defining the useful limits of the opportunity set, the individual will presumably attain a tangency solution. Note in figure 4.5 that there are two main classes of solutions: mixtures of riskless bonds and risky assets in the range $B\phi$, and portfolios excluding riskless bonds in the range ϕG.[19] But this is only an individual solution, not a market solution. The analytical system requires a specification of the social interactions that determine a set of asset prices P_i, which in turn modify the μ, σ_i, and σ_{ij} of the various securities until finally an equilibrium is reached.

In equations (4.4) describing Fisher's system, the social interaction takes the form of conservation equations fixing the social totals of the various objects of choice. Sharpe, apparently the first to realize the need for completion of the mean, variability theoretic structure, employed a formulation fixing the social totals of the various *securities* available. He has succeeded in deriving a number of theorems, based essentially upon the consideration that in equilibrium security prices P_i must be such as to permit the existing totals of securities to be exactly held in terms of the summation of the individuals' tangency solutions. These results are important, but they cannot be regarded as a final completion of the choice-theoretic system.[20] The reason is that securities are artificial commodities or objects of choice. Without changing the underlying real investment yields, alternative patterns of securities can be generated as claims to these real yields. On the individual or firm level, the question of the optimal pattern of securities to issue against one's assets – which latter may be real assets, or may themselves be securities one step or more removed from the ultimate real assets – is known in capital-budgeting literature as the "financing" problem, or in the simplest case as the problem of the "debt-equity mix." To complete the system fully under pure exchange, analysis must go beyond the principles on which individuals decide both to hold assets and to finance asset-holdings, to the social interactions that determine the equilibrium set of financial securities issued by all individuals together as the set of claims to the underlying real assets of the community. Presumably, these interactions will be governed by the μ and σ represented by the given real assets. And, when production is introduced, the real assets themselves can no longer be held constant, and analysis must go back to the forces determining the balance between μ and σ in the real investments undertaken. We are thus still a considerable distance from a market theory of the risk premium under the mean, variability approach.

4.4   THE STATE-PREFERENCE APPROACH

The approach to investment decision under uncertainty that begins by postulating the objects of choice to be contingent consumption opportunities, in alternative possible states of the world, is comparatively unfamiliar.[21] But it has great advantages. There is a close formal analogy with Fisher's model for riskless choice over time; in fact, the state-and-time-preference choice-theoretic model is a natural generalization of Fisher's system. The approach leads, we shall see, to important theorems concerning investment and financing decisions.

In the interest of minimizing complications, it will be assumed that there is only one present state; i.e. there is certainty as to the present (time 0). The future is represented by a point in time (time 1), in which there are two alternative "states of the world" (state a or state b must obtain). The two states might be thought of as war *versus* peace, or prosperity *versus* depression. Two-state uncertainty is, of course, a very radical over-simplification, adopted here for purposes of presentation only. In the two-period *certainty* case we needed to consider only the single type of exchange between present and future consumption, c_0 and c_1. But now there are three objects of choice: c_0, c_{1a}, and c_{1b}. We may think of two dimensions of choice: the contemporaneous balance of risky claims between c_{1a} and c_{1b} (figure 4.7), and the time-plus-risk exchange between

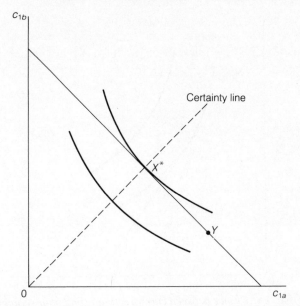

FIGURE 4.7   *Choice between contemporaneous state-claims.*

a present certain c_0 and a future uncertain c_{1b} or c_{1a} (figure 4.8 portrays the choice between c_0 and c_{1b}). We will consider here situations of pure exchange, deferring the problems introduced by the existence of productive opportunities.

Under the conditions of figure 4.7, the amount of c_0 is implicitly fixed so that we can deal with simple exchange between contemporaneous risky claims. The 45° line through the origin represents points along which $c_{1a} = c_{1b}$, so that the amount c_1 is sure to be received – this is the "certainty line." The figure portrays the preference function for an individual attaching subjective probabilities $\pi_a = \pi_b = 1/2$ to the two possible states.

The convex indifference curves shown in figure 4.7 can be justified on several levels. General observation of behavior probably suffices to convince us that almost no one is so reckless to prefer, if $\pi_a = \pi_b = 1/2$, the prospect $(c_{1a}, c_{1b}) = (1000, 0)$ to a prospect like $(500, 500)$. (It must be understood that the statement $c_{1b} = 0$ does not mean merely a possibly tolerable loss of a gamble, but an actual zero consumption level – starvation – if state b should occur.) Thus, even the very mild degree of conservatism, implicit in observed "non-specialization" among claims to consumption in alternative states of the world, requires convex utility isoquants.[22]

Interesting questions arise concerning the interpretation of the convex preference function in figure 4.7 in terms of subjective probabilities and Neumann-Morgenstern utilities. Let a Neumann-Morgenstern function

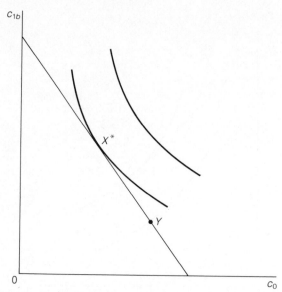

FIGURE 4.8   *Choice between current certainty and future contingency.*

$v(c_1)$ be postulated, concave downward as in figure 4.6, and assume that this function can be applied to the risky choice between c_{1a} and c_{1b}. This special assumption says that the function $v(c_1)$ is independent of the state – the world-environment – that obtains; it will be called the "uniqueness" assumption. Then concavity of $v(c_1)$, or "diminishing marginal utility of (consumption) income," implies convexity of the utility isoquants in figure 4.7. The converse also holds, so Neumann-Morgenstern risk aversion is implied by non-specialization of risky choice. (Convexity is more general than diminishing marginal utility, in that convexity at a particular (c_{1a}, c_{1b}) point does not necessarily imply diminishing marginal utility at c_{1a} and c_{1b} – but convexity *everywhere* requires diminishing marginal utility.)[23] In the special case where $\pi_a = \pi_b = 1/2$, and holding to the uniqueness assumption so that the single function $v(c_1)$ is applicable to consumption in state a or state b, concavity of $v(c_1)$ implies not merely convex indifference curves in figure 4.7 but indifference curves symmetrical about the 45° certainty line. For, with a single $v(c_1)$ function, utility of any prospect $(y, x; 1/2, 1/2)$ would then be the same as that of the prospect $(x, y; 1/2, 1/2)$.

Under the simplified model investigated here, any commodity basket consists of time-state consumption elements c_0, c_{1a}, and c_{1b}. In particular, the endowment Y may be denoted (y_0, y_{1a}, y_{1b}). Since we are considering a pure-exchange situation, there are no productive opportunities. But financial opportunities exist for individuals to trade elements of their endowed combinations. In such trading each is constrained by his endowed wealth: $W = P_0 c_0 + P_{1a} c_{1a} + P_{1b} c_{1b}$. Here P_0, P_{1a}, and P_{1b} are the prices of the correspondingly subscribed time-state claims – the commodities of this model. The constant W is determined by $P_0 y_0 + P_{1a} y_{1a} + P_{1b} y_{1b}$, the present value of the endowment. Let c_0 be the numeraire, so that $P_0 = 1$. At this point we may generalize the concept of discount rate by defining the *time-and-state discount rates* r_{1a} and r_{1b} in terms of the prices of the corresponding time-state claims: $P_{1a} = 1/(1 + r_{1a})$ and $P_{1b} = 1/(1 + r_{1b})$. Note that these rates discount for both futurity and probability (or, rather, improbability). In the degenerate case of only one future state, the riskless rate, discounting for time only, is defined in $P_1 = 1/(1 + r_1)$.

In the special case where $\pi_a = \pi_b = 1/2$, and if the price of claims to c_{1a} happens to equal that of claims to c_{1b}, under the uniqueness assumption the wealth constraint and preference function for contemporaneous exchanges (i.e. given the amount of c_0) are as portrayed in figure 4.7 – the former is a $135°$ line, and the latter is symmetrical about the $45°$ certainty line. Then, the state-preference tangency optimum must be along the certainty line. More generally, given uniqueness of $v(c_1)$, if the price ratio P_{1b}/P_{1a} is equal to the probability ratio π_b/π_a, the optimum is along the certainty line.[24] This result corresponds to the well-known theorem that, if $v(c_1)$ is concave, a fair gamble will not be accepted[25] (N.B. assuming the individual is already on the certainty line!).[26]

The final elements in the choice system are the conservation equations. These take on almost trivially simple forms: in each separate time-state, the total social endowment must be conserved (under pure exchange).

The entire time-and-state choice-theoretic system, for the special case of pure exchange with a single present state and two future states, and excluding generation of "financial" assets, may be summarized in the equations below:

$$U^j = g^j(c_0^j, c_{1a}^j, c_{1b}^j; \pi_a^j, \pi_b^j) \quad \text{Time-and-state Preference} \quad (4.8)$$
$$\text{Function}$$

This formulation emphasizes that utility depends upon the subjective probability estimates, π_a^j and π_b^j.[27]

$$c_0^j + \frac{c_{1a}^j}{1 + r_{1a}} + \frac{c_{1b}^j}{1 + r_{1b}} = y_0^j + \frac{y_{1a}^j}{1 + r_{1a}} + \frac{y_{1b}^j}{1 + r_{1b}} \quad \begin{matrix}\text{Wealth} \\ \text{constraint}\end{matrix} \quad (4.9)$$

$$\left.\frac{\partial c_{1a}^j}{\partial c_0^j}\right|_{U^j} = -(1 + r_{1a})$$

$$\left.\frac{\partial c_{1b}^j}{\partial c_0^j}\right|_{U^j} = -(1 + r_{1b}) \quad \left.\right\} \quad \text{Optimum conditions} \quad (4.10)$$

$$\left.\frac{\partial c_{1b}^j}{\partial c_{1a}^j}\right|_{U^j} = -\frac{1 + r_{1b}}{1 + r_{1a}}$$

$$\left. \begin{array}{l} \sum c_0^j = \sum y_0^j \\[2mm] \sum c_{1a}^j = \sum y_{1a}^j \\[2mm] \sum c_{1b}^j = \sum y_{1b}^j \end{array} \right\} \qquad \text{Conservation equations} \qquad (4.11)$$

A numerical illustration may help provide an intuitive grasp of the above relationships. Imagine a simple economy consisting of 100 identically situated individuals with one consumption commodity ("corn"). Each individual has an endowment distributed as follows: 100 bushels of present corn (y_0), and contingent claims to the future crop $y_{1a} = 150$ and $y_{1b} = 50$. Thus, the individual is entitled to 150 bushels if state a obtains, but only 50 bushels if state b obtains – only these two states, regarded as equally probable, being considered possible for the future crop. In a pure-exchange situation, it is impossible to change these endowments by planting seed, carry-over of crop, or "consumption of capital"; individuals can only modify their positions by trading. If, however, all individuals have identical preferences in addition to identical endowments and identical (null) productive opportunities, the markets must establish a set of prices such that each individual is satisifed to hold his original endowment. Let the numeraire $P_0 = 1$, and assume that with this time-state distribution there is on the margin for each individual zero time preference with respect to certainties. Thus, denoting the price of a certainty as P_1, where necessarily $P_1 = P_{1a} + P_{1b}$, we have $P_1 = 1$. To deal with the contemporaneous choices in time 1, it will be convenient to define a cardinal utility U_1 which assigns a numerical value to probabilistic combinations by the use of the expected-utility theorem and an underlying Neumann-Morgenstern utility-of-income function $v(c_1)$. Then $U_1 = 1/2 v(c_{1a}) + 1/2 v(c_{1b})$. For concreteness, we may use a logarithmic formulation: $v(c_1) = \ln c_1$. It may then be verified that the indifference curves are rectangular hyperbolas on axes as in figure 4.7 with slope $-c_{1b}/c_{1a}$, or at the endowment point $-1/3$. It follows that $P_{1a} = 1/4$, $P_{1b} = 3/4$, at which prices everyone prefers to hold his endowment rather than exchange it for any alternative combination. Our numerical assumptions have implied discount rates $r_{1a} = 300$ percent and $r_{1b} = 33\frac{1}{3}$ percent.

It is often illuminating to introduce the concept of the riskless ("pure") interest rate, which we have denoted r_1. This would represent the marginal *time* preference alone. The relation defining the riskless discount rate in terms of the more basic time-and-risk exchanges is:

$$\frac{1}{1+r_1} = \frac{1}{1+r_{1a}} + \frac{1}{1+r_{1b}}.$$

This follows immediately from $P_1 = P_{1a} + P_{1b}$ – that is, the price of a riskless holding is simply the sum of the prices of a corresponding holding for each possible contingency. It would then be possible to reformulate the choice situation in terms of future risky and future riskless assets. The set of objects of choice, instead of (c_0, c_{1a}, c_{1b}) would be (c_0, c_1, c_{1x}), where c_1 is the lesser of c_{1a} and c_{1b}, and c_{1x} is the excess of the greater over the lesser of these two. This route leads toward the asset-preference approach alluded to earlier; its disadvantage lies in obscuring the state in which the risky asset pays off (that is, it will in general make a difference to an individual if a unit of c_{1x} represents a claim to time-state $1a$ or $1b$).

Waiving explicit introduction of productive opportunities, and generalizations to T times and S states, it is possible in a few sentences to sum up the main nature of the results yielded by the time-and-state-preference approach. The discount rates are determined by the interaction of individual attempts to move to preferred time-and-state consumption combinations by productive and financial transformations. The equilibrium rates will depend upon the composition of endowments among individuals, states, and times; the natures of the productive and financial opportunities; and the time-and-state preferences of individuals, these in turn being connected with their subjective probability estimates for the states. In the case of certainty the interest rate was determined by the interaction of endowments, time preferences, and time productivity. The additional elements entering under uncertainty are state endowments, state productivity, and state preferences. Probability opinions will enter into state preferences.

Corresponding to the theorem under certainty that all investors (barring corner solutions) adapt their subjective marginal rates of time preference to the market rate of interest is the following: each investor will adapt his marginal rate of time-and-state preference to the market discount rate for claims of the corresponding state and time. This conclusion indicates that it is not necessary to allow an additional degree of freedom in the form of the interposition of a "personal discount rate" to reach an optimum under uncertainty.[28] The error here is analogous to that sometimes committed of imposing a personal *time-preference* discount rate on future certain returns – whereas attainment of an optimum requires adjusting the marginal personal rate of time preference to the objective market rate.

4.5   RISK AVERSION AND THE UNIQUENESS ASSUMPTION

In the section preceding, the observation of "non-specialization" among time-state contingencies was employed to justify convex indifference curves between state incomes. The further assumption of uniqueness of the underlying Neumann-Morgenstern utility-of-income $v(c_1)$ function, for uncertain future consumption, led to a kind of symmetry of state preferences such that if the price ratio for state incomes P_{1b}/P_{1a} is equal to the probability ratio π_b/π_a, the preferred combination will be along the certainty line. This last condition is the ordinary definition of risk aversion: given an initial combination along the certainty line, a fair gamble would not be accepted.[29]

But, it may be asked, if reasonable assumptions under the state-preference approach lead to risk aversion in the ordinary sense, what is the advantage of the approach over the mean, variability formulation that directly postulates aversion to variability risk? The crucial advantage, developed at length in the previous sections, is that time-state claims are commodities capable of being exchanged in markets – so that a complete choice-theoretic structure, including conservation equations, can be constructed as in equations (4.8) through (4.11) above. Mean return and variability of return are not commodities in this sense, or at least there are as yet unresolved difficulties in regarding them as such. Furthermore, even in terms of the preference function alone, there is a gain in depth of understanding in deriving risk aversion from more fundamental considerations as compared with merely postulating it.[30] But the consideration to be examined further in this section is whether some types of behavior that seem to violate risk aversion can be rationalized in terms of the state-preference approach.

If one asked a responsible family man why he carries life insurance, presumably he would give a reply consistent with our risk-avoiding picture in figure 4.7. Letting the state a represent the contingency "Breadwinner dies" and b the contingency "Breadwinner lives," our family man purchases life insurance to move his heirs in the direction of the certainty line. But a similarly thoughtful man, who happened to be a bachelor without family, would be unlikely to purchase insurance. Are we to say that he prefers risk? In a sense, perhaps, but it is more natural to explain his behavior by saying that a consumption opportunity contingent upon his death does not have the same appeal to the bachelor as it does to the family man.

This extreme case suggests the more general consideration that the utility-of-income function for any individual may not be invariant with respect to the state that obtains. It will be useful here to distinguish between true *gambles* (artificially generated risks, as at roulette) and natural *hazards*. There seems no reason to believe that anyone would rationally value consumption opportunities differently depending upon which end of a winning gamble he held. Money won on Black at roulette means exactly the same as an equivalent sum won on Red.[31] Therefore, within our model and ruling out pleasure-oriented gambling,[32] it continues to follow that fair *gambles* would never be accepted. A natural *hazard*, in contrast, will in general affect the external or internal context for choice by modifying the significance of the "same" consumption opportunity or sum of money.[33] We might say, somewhat loosely, that states may vary in respect to "non-pecuniary income." As a result, state preferences for income become asymmetrical. For the bachelor in the above example, occurrence of the state "Death" eliminates practically any significance he might otherwise place upon titles to consumption. Again, a particular individual might weight his present choices in such a way as to have *more* income in depression or famine than in prosperity, because he would then be able to assist his neighbors in their day of need. More typically, perhaps, we do not mind being poor so much if our neighbors (the Joneses) are also poor, since keeping up with them would then require less effort. The example cited in section 4.3, that an investor would not in general find the state-distributed portfolios $(3, 2, 1)$ and $(1, 2, 3)$ indifferent even if all three states were equally probable, would also be an instance of asymmetrical state-preferences.

In all these cases we would observe risk-taking at fair odds in the sense that the preferred state-distributions would not be along the certainty line (see figure 4.9). But the reason is not non-concavity of the $v(c_1)$ function – Neumann-Morgenstern risk-preference – but rather non-uniqueness. That is, we would have to admit that, in general, we would have differing *conditional* utility-of-income functions $v_{1a}(c_{1a})$ and $v_{1b}(c_{1b})$. These separate functions can, however, be given a common scaling[34] so that we can find the utility of any prospect $(c_{1a}, c_{1b}; \pi_a, \pi_b)$ via the expected-utility theorem:

$$U(c_{1a}, c_{1b}; \pi_a, \pi_b) = \pi_a v_{1a}(c_{1a}) + \pi_b v_{1b}(c_{1b}).$$

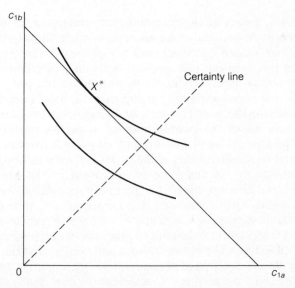

FIGURE 4.9 *Risk-taking due to asymmetrical state-preferences.*

Convexity of the state-distributed indifference curve follows, by the same reasoning employed in section 4.4, making use again of the "independence" postulate which asserts that the marginal utilities of income in state a are unaffected by the level of consumption available for state b, and vice versa. The equilibrium condition is

$$\frac{P_{1b}}{P_{1a}} = \frac{\pi_b v'_{1b}(c_{1b})}{\pi_a v'_{1a}(c_{1b})}.$$

However, since in general $v'_{1a}(c_{1a}) \neq v'_{1b}(c_{1b})$ when $c_{1a} = c_{1b}$, the tangencies will not occur on the certainty line, as was the case with a single utility-of-income function and consequent symmetrical state-preferences.

The situation portrayed in figure 4.9 can be interpreted as indicating that in hazard situations people will be inclined to take risks. This is true in an actuarial sense (the decision-maker prefers at fair odds to move away from the certainty line), and yet the behavior remains essentially conservative. The "risk" is undertaken because quantitative equality of incomes in the two states does not properly balance the marginal utilities. We have shown, therefore, that the state-preference approach leads to a generalized concept which might be called "conservative behavior" – of which ordinary risk aversion in the sense of minimizing variability of outcome is only a special case.

4.6   CONCLUDING REMARK

One surprising aspect of the time-and-state preference model is that it leads to a theory of decision under uncertainty while entirely excluding the "vagueness" we usually associate with uncertainty.[35] Uncertainty in this model takes the form not of vagueness but rather of completely precise beliefs as to endowments, productive opportunities, etc., just as in the case of certainty – the only difference being that the beliefs span alternative possible states of the world as well as successive time periods. Again, precise beliefs as to the probabilities of these alternative states are assumed. The assumption that uncertainty takes the form of precise beliefs about alternative possible states of the world certainly lacks psychological verisimilitude to the mental state of confusion and doubt commonly experienced in this connection. It is generally recognized, however, that descriptive reality of assumptions is no essential criterion for a useful theory. So far as vagueness is concerned, we have already in our simplest timeless and riskless models assumed a precision in preference (as when we draw maps of indifference between shoes and apples) that can scarcely be regarded as closely descriptive of mental states. A similarly "unrealistic" or "depsychologized" portraying of uncertainty may really be what is required for comparably fruitful results in our analysis of risky choice.

4.7   APPENDIX: SCALING OF UTILITY-OF-INCOME
FUNCTIONS CONDITIONAL UPON STATE

We seek to show informally here that conditional utility-of-income functions, each defined for a particular state of the world, can nevertheless be given a common utility scaling consistent with the Neumann-Morgenstern postulates. In the case of a single (independent of state) utility-of-income function $v(c)$,[36] unique up to a linear transformation, a convenient scaling *sets* $v(0) = 0$, and $v(\bar{M}) = 1$, where $\bar{M}$ is the maximum income (consumption) level contemplated. The scaling used here will preserve analogues of these properties, for a hazard situation consisting of two alternative states of the world a and b $(\pi_a + \pi_b = 1)$, and where $v_a(c_a)$ is not identical with $v_b(c_b)$. As before, the elemental object of choice is a *conditional* claim to consumption in a specified state of the world. The "independence axiom" continues to apply: that is, $v_a(c_a)$ is independent of c_b, and vice versa.

To fix our desired scaling, it will suffice to assign utility values to two incomes on each condition function: specifically to fix $v_a(0)$, $v_b(0)$, $v_a(\bar{M})$, and $v_b(\bar{M})$. We wish to continue assigning the utility value 1 to the certain receipt of $\bar{M}$, and the value 0 to the certain receipt of 0. Writing this in prospect notation, and using the expected-utility theorem:

$$U(\bar{M}, \bar{M}; \pi_a, \pi_b) = 1 = \pi_a v_a(\bar{M}) + \pi_b v_b(\bar{M})$$

$$U(0, 0; \pi_a, \pi_b) = 0 = \pi_a v_a(0) + \pi_b v_b(0).$$

We may now denote by the symbols X_a and X_b the prospects $(X, 0; \pi_a, \pi_b)$ and $(0, X; \pi_a, \pi_b)$, respectively. We can then adopt the scaling rule $v_a(X) = U(X_a)/\pi_a$, and similarly for $v_b(X)$. It follows immediately that $v_a(0) = v_b(0) = 0$, since 0_a and 0_b are identical and both have utility value zero; we may call this principle the Equivalence of Nulls. The interpretation is that, since we cannot do worse than zero in either state, a title or claim to zero in a particular state is worthless. Note that this does not deny that we might be happier with zero in state a (should state a obtain) than with zero in state b (should state b obtain) – but we cannot in fact ever be offered a choice among states, but only among claims to income conditional upon states occurring.

By the ordering postulate,[37] the individual can compare $\bar{M}_a$ with $\bar{M}_b$, and they need not be indifferent. Suppose he prefers the former. Then, by the continuity postulate[38] there is some probability π (in a pure gamble) such that $\bar{M}_b$ is indifferent to a lottery ticket offering $\bar{M}_a$ or zero.[39] Thus:

$$U(0, \bar{M}; \pi_a, \pi_b) = U[(\bar{M}, 0; \pi_a, \pi_b), 0; \pi, 1 - \pi]$$

$$\pi_b v_b(\bar{M}) = \pi \pi_a v_a(\bar{M}).$$

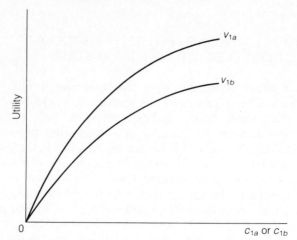

FIGURE 4.10   *Utility-of-income functions conditional upon state of the world.*

Using the property that the certain receipt of $\bar{M}$ has utility 1, we get the results $v_a(\bar{M}) = 1/(\pi_a + \pi_a\pi)$ and $v_b(\bar{M}) = \pi/(\pi_b + \pi_b\pi)$. The import of this is that we are now able, in principle, to use the two points thus provided for each state so as to construct in figure 4.10 two separate curves, $v_{1a}(c_{1a})$ and $v_{1b}(c_{1b})$, to serve as *conditional* utility-of-income scales. The expected-utility theorem can then be used with these scales to calculate the overall preference ordering of any income distribution over these states.

NOTES

[1] Irving Fisher, *The Theory of Interest*, New York: Macmillan, 1930; reprinted, Augustus M. Kelley, 1961. Fisher's earlier work, *The Rate of Interest*, New York: Macmillan, 1907, is also important.

[2] Fisher takes account of uncertainty in his "third approximation" to the theory of interest. Significantly, ch. 14 of *The Theory of Interest* is entitled: "The Third Approximation Unadapted to Mathematical Formulation."

[3] *Theory of Interest, op. cit.,* chs 18–19.

[4] "Investment Decision Under Uncertainty: Applications of the State-Preference Approach", *Quarterly Journal of Economics*, vol. 80 (1966), pp. 252–77 (reprinted as ch. 5 in this volume).

[5] "Income" is a troublesome concept. Fisher attempted to dispose of it by defining income as identical with consumption; this is unsatisfactory, since one cannot avoid distinguishing *actual* and *potential* consumption. Income is a potential-consumption concept: in principle, it is what can be consumed in the current period without impairing future income or consumption. But this statement of principle leaves open a number of possible interpretations. For accounting or tax purposes, a *net* concept of income is ordinarily adopted: the gross yield of any

income source in the current period is reduced by allowance for "depreciation of capital." Depreciation represents the amount which, if reinvested, would replenish the income source so as to permit maintenance of the net income to the time-horizon envisaged – under the ordinary assumption of an infinite horizon, this is equivalent to maintaining capital value intact. The analytical inconvenience of this concept, for our purposes, is that depreciation (and therefore net income) cannot in general be calculated independently of the rate of interest – which is what we seek to explain. For this reason the income concept used here is *gross* income: for any time-period, this is the corresponding element of the gross yield sequence (the endowment) itself, without any accounting adjustments. This interpretation qualifies as a potential-consumption concept; it is what can be consumed without borrowing, or (equivalently) without trenching on the future-consumption elements of the endowment itself.

6 This is a *gross* rather than a *net* investment concept (see note 5 above).

7 One of the conservation equations can be shown to follow from the remainder of the system.

8 In more general cases, where the productive opportunity locus need not have the simple concavity properties of figure 4.2 (because of lumpiness or interdependence among investments), the tangency condition of equation (4.5′) is insufficient to determine the optimum. The more general maximum-wealth condition permits selection among multiple local maxima, whether tangencies or corner solutions. See ch. 1.

9 Alternatively, in a world of certainty the firm's payout could be in current funds c_0. That is, the firm could immediately distribute to owners the amount E_0, the present value of the future net income e_1.

10 This looks very much like the famous "Proposition I" in F. Modigliani and M. H. Miller, "The Cost of Capital, Corporation Finance and the Theory of Investment", *American Economic Review*, vol. 48 (June 1958), p. 268. Of course, that the Modigliani-Miller theorem holds under conditions of certainty is not surprising; in ch. 5 it will be proved that the theorem continues to hold even under some forms of uncertainty.

11 An asset-preference approach is adopted in my paper, "Risk, the Discount Rate, and Investment Decisions," *American Economic Review*, vol. 51 (May 1961). A much more complete working out of this approach was independently developed by Gordon B. Pye in his 1963 M.I.T. Ph.D. thesis, "Investment Rules for Corporations."

12 The most complete development of this viewpoint is in H. M. Markowitz, *Portfolio Selection*, New York: Wiley, 1959. The earliest conception is apparently that of Fisher in *The Nature of Capital and Income*, New York: Macmillan, 1912. Other important contributions are J. R. Hicks, "A Suggestion for Simplifying the Theory of Money," *Economica*, N.S., vol. 2 (Feb. 1935); J. Marschak, "Money and the Theory of Assets," *Econometrica*, vol. 6 (Oct. 1938); and James Tobin, "Liquidity Preference as Behavior Towards Risk," *Review of Economic Studies*, vol. 25 (Feb. 1958). A convenient condensed formulation will be found in D. E. Farrar, *The Investment Decision Under Uncertainty*, Englewood Cliffs, NJ: Prentice-Hall, 1962. An important recent contribution, breaking into entirely new ground, is William F. Sharpe, "Capital Asset Prices: A Theory of Market Equilibrium under Conditions of Risk, *Journal of Finance*, vol. 29 (Sept. 1964).

[13] Although, as indicated above, such an extension would involve some difficulties in specifying conservation relations when both productive and financial assets are considered.

[14] Since a portfolio is a collection of assets, the gross value X cannot be negative.

[15] Let X be the future value of the overall portfolio, x_i the future value of the i-th security, a_i the fraction of the fixed original investment held in the i-th security, and n the number of securities. Then:

$$\text{(a)} \quad X = \sum_{i=1}^{n} a_i x_i$$

$$\text{(b)} \quad \mu = E(X) = \sum_{i=1}^{n} a_i \mu_i$$

$$\text{(c)} \quad \sigma = \left[\sum_{i=1}^{n} a_i^2 \sigma_i^2 + 2 \sum_{i=1}^{n} \sum_{j=1}^{i-1} a_i \sigma_{ij} a_j \right]^{1/2}$$

Here σ_{ij} is the covariance of the i-th and the j-th security.

There are two important exceptions to the statement that σ will be lower than the average of the σ_i: (1) if all the securities are perfectly correlated (each $\sigma_{ij} = \sigma_i \sigma_j$), or (2) if one security of a two-security portfolio has zero σ_i, from which it follows that covariance also equals zero. In either of these cases,

$$\sigma = \sum_{i=1}^{n} a_i \sigma_i.$$

[16] The portfolio μ and σ represented by combinations of B and the "security" ϕ (itself generally a combination of securities) plot along a straight line because σ_B and therefore $\sigma_{B\phi}$ equal zero (see note above).

[17] See M. Friedman and L. J. Savage, "The Utility Analysis of Choices Involving Risk," *Journal of Political Economy*, vol. 56 (Aug. 1948). Reprinted in American Economic Association, *Readings in Price Theory*, Homewood, Ill.: Irwin, 1952. Page references to the latter volume.

[18] Tobin, *loc. cit.*, pp. 74–7.

[19] Sharpe (*loc. cit.*) extends the line $B\phi$ beyond the point ϕ, arguing that the extension represents negative amounts of the asset B, or "selling B short" to hold more of the μ, σ combination represented by ϕ. But this amounts to the investor issuing a new bond to "finance" his asset-holdings – which is inconsistent with the spirit of Sharpe's analysis that postulates fixed social totals of each class of risky and riskless assets. (If the analysis were to permit the investor to issue new bonds, it should also permit him to issue new risky securities as well.)

[20] They are analogous to the results derived in ordinary price theory in the so-called "very short run" where, with fixed supplies, demand alone governs price.

[21] The pioneering work here is Kenneth J. Arrow, "Le Rôle des Valeurs Boursières pour la Répartition la Meilleure des Risques," *International Colloquium on Econometrics, 1952*, Centre National de la Recherche Scientifique (Paris, 1953). An English version appeared under the title "The Role of Securities in the Optimal Allocation of Risk-bearing," *Review of Economic Studies*, vol. 31 (April 1964). See also G. Debreu, *Theory of Value*, New York: Wiley, 1959, ch. 7, and

J. Hirshleifer, "Efficient Allocation of Capital in an Uncertain World," *American Economic Review*, vol. 54 (May 1964), 77–85.

[22] This statement is correct provided that the choice is between simple convex and simple concave curvature. Other, more complex, shapes would also be consistent with the observation.

[23] Convexity requires $(d^2 c_{1b})/(dc_{1a}^2) > 0$. Under the Neumann-Morgenstern postulates, it is possible to attribute a utility function $v(c_1)$ to "income" (here, to consumption) such that the utility of a risky prospect equals the expectation of the v's attached to the elements of the prospect. Then $U(c_{1a}, c_{1b}; \pi_a, \pi_b) = \pi_a v(c_{1a}) + \pi_b v(c_{1b})$, or, simplifying notation:

$$= \pi_a v_{1a} + \pi_b v_{1b}$$

$$\left. \frac{dc_{1b}}{dc_{1a}} \right|_U = -\frac{\partial U/\partial c_{1a}}{\partial U/\partial c_{1b}} = -\frac{\pi_a v'_{1a}}{\pi_b v'_{1b}}$$

$$\frac{d^2 c_{1b}}{dc_{1a}^2} = \frac{d}{dc_{1a}}\left(\frac{dc_{1b}}{dc_{1a}}\right) = \frac{\partial}{\partial c_{1a}}\left(\frac{dc_{1b}}{dc_{1a}}\right) + \frac{\partial}{\partial c_{1b}}\left(\frac{dc_{1b}}{dc_{1a}}\right) \cdot \frac{dc_{1b}}{dc_{1a}}$$

$$= -\frac{\pi_a v''_{1a}}{\pi_b v'_{1b}} + \frac{\pi_a v'_{1a} v''_{1b}}{\pi_b (v'_{1b})^2}\left(-\frac{\pi_a v'_{1a}}{\pi_b v'_{1b}}\right)$$

$$= -\frac{\pi_a v''_{1a}}{\pi_b v'_{1b}} - \frac{\pi_a^2 (v'_{1a})^2 v''_{1b}}{\pi_b^2 (v'_{1b})^3}.$$

It should be noted that

$$\frac{\partial v'_{1b}}{\partial c_{1a}} = \frac{\partial v'_{1a}}{\partial c_{1b}} = 0.$$

That is, the slope of the "utility-of-income" curve for state b is independent of the amount scheduled for consumption in state a, and vice versa. This follows from the Neumann-Morgenstern "independence" or "substitutability" postulate (R. D. Luce and H. Raiffa, *Games and Decisions* (New York: Wiley, 1957), p. 27). Since $\pi_a, \pi_b, v'_{1a}, v'_{1b} > 0$, diminishing marginal utility ($v''_{1a} < 0$ and $v''_{1b} < 0$) is sufficient for convexity but is not a necessary condition for convexity at (c_{1a}, c_{1b}); a sufficiently negative v''_{1a} may outweigh a positive v''_{1b}, or vice versa. But in this latter case it will be possible to find risky prospects for which v''_{1a} and v''_{1b} are both positive, so that convexity would not hold everywhere.

[24] The utility function is: $U = \pi_a v(c_{1a}) + \pi_b v(c_{1b})$. It is to be maximized subject to the constraint: $P_{1a} c_{1a} + P_{1b} c_{1b} = K$, a parameter equal to $W - c_0$. The condition resulting is:

$$\frac{P_{1b}}{P_{1a}} = \frac{\pi_a v'(c_{1b})}{\pi_a v'(c_{1a})}.$$

The equality of price and probability ratios must hold along the certainty line, since there $c_{1b} = c_{1a}$. Convexity of the indifference curves assures that the condition cannot be met elsewhere.

[25] Friedman and Savage, *loc. cit.*, pp. 73 ff.

[26] If the individual is not on the certainty line, there may exist "gambles" that can move him toward that line. We call such gambles "insurance." Under the present assumptions fair insurance will be purchased. It is important to note that, depending on the endowed or attained position, the same contractual arrangement could be a risk-increasing gamble for one person and a risk-decreasing insurance for another. A very clear case exists in the futures market, where the same contract can be either a hedge or a speculation, depending upon the risk status of the purchaser.

[27] But note that the subjective probability estimates nowhere appear in the equations directly, so that up to this point the formulation does not require the existence of subjective probabilities. Actually, it is not necessary to go behind the preference function in this way. After specifying the time-state consumption claims as the basic objects of choice, we could assert convexity of indifference curves as a generalization of ordinary consumption theory. This is indeed the line pursued by Arrow and Debreu, and has the advantage of parsimony of assumptions. On the other hand, explicit introduction of probabilities does enable us to derive results (e.g. about fair gambles) not otherwise attainable. For discussions of the conditions permitting the simultaneous identification of subjective probabilities and numerical utilities, see L. J. Savage, *The Foundations of Statistics*, New York: Wiley, 1954; and Jacques Drèze, "Fondements Logiques de la Probabilité Subjective et de L'Utilité," *La Décision*, Paris: Centre National de la Recherche Scientifique, 1961.

[28] Lacking a formal solution to investment decision under uncertainty, Fisher recommended discounting anticipated future receipts by a personal "caution coefficient" (*Rate of Interest, op. cit.*, p. 215). The analysis here indicates that the interaction of personal time-and-risk preferences will establish a *market* time-and-risk discount rate, to which individuals will adjust on the margin.

[29] As mentioned above, the proviso about the initial situation being one of certainty should not be omitted.

[30] In suppressing the information about the state-distributed composition of a particular combination being analyzed, essential information may be lost. One example would be the comparison of two-state prospects like $(3, 1)$ and $(6, 2)$ – where, for each combination, the first number gives the income for state a and the second for state b, the two states being equally probable. Evidently, the combination $(6, 2)$ is dominant. But in terms of mean and variability measures this would not be evident, since $(6, 2)$ has both a larger mean and a larger standard deviation. A somewhat related point is discussed in W. J. Baumol, "An Expected Gain-Confidence Limit Criterion for Portfolio Selection," *Management Science*, vol. 10 (Oct. 1963).

[31] Though one of the appeals of long-shot betting may be that it provides more thrill and conversation value than an equivalent sum won on favorites.

[32] The next chapter considers the question of how observed gambling can be rationalized.

[33] A rather similar conception has been put forward and analyzed by Jacques Drèze, *op. cit.*

[34] See appendix to this chapter.

[35] Compare Fisher's declaration: "The third approximation cannot avoid some degree of vagueness" (*Theory of Interest, op. cit.*, p. 227).

[36] The time subscript will be dropped in this appendix, which deals only with utility functions for synchronous decisions.

[37] Luce and Raiffa, *op. cit.*, p. 25.

[38] Ibid., p. 27.

[39] This π is a variable in an artificial gamble constructed to test preferences, whereas π_a and π_b are to be regarded as constants fixed by nature (or at least by belief) in a real hazard situation.

5 Investment Decision Under Uncertainty: Applications of the State-preference Approach*

Background and comments

As indicated above, this article originally formed part of a single long paper that began with the previous essay. When the papers were divided, the theoretical formulation of the state-preference approach in the previous essay was separated from the specific applications explored here. These explorations, intended to illustrate the power of the state-preference approach, address three important problems and controversies: the nature and extent of risk-aversion, the problem of the optimal debt-equity mix in corporate finance, and the appropriate discount rate for evaluating public investment proposals.

With regard to the second of these, the initially very controversial "Modigliani-Miller theorem" is shown here to follow in an extremely elementary way from the state-preference interpretation of uncertainty. This is now a generally accepted result. By way of contrast, in the area of public investment decision – where the thrust of the state-preference interpretation is that the discount rate should be the same as that employed for private investments of comparable risk – the lesson has not yet been generally accepted. The view that government (owing merely to its large size and consequent ability to internalize a large number of separate investments) can diversify productive risks in a way that private firms and investors cannot, although refuted here, remains prevalent in popular and even professional thinking. The mistake is the failure to appreciate that individuals and firms are able to *diversify their private risks through the markets for contingent claims*. (On a more sophisticated level, it is indeed possible to argue that the imperfections and incompleteness of state-claim markets limit the prospects for diversification through market transactions. But then a proper comparison would of course have to allow for the imperfections of government risk-spreading processes as well.)

*This article originally appeared in *Quarterly Journal of Economics*, vol. 80 (May 1966), pp. 252–77. The permission of MIT Press and John Wiley and Sons Inc. to reprint in this volume is gratefully acknowledged.

Chapter 4 examined alternative approaches to the problem of investment decision under uncertainty. It was shown there that the various formulations differ essentially in specifying the *objects of choice* (commodities). Two such specifications were reviewed in detail: (1) The *mean, variability* approach – this reduces the assets or securities traded in the market to underlying objects of choice in the form of mean-return and variability-of-return measures which, it is alleged, enter into investors' preference functions.[1] (2) The *state-preference* (or, more fully, *time-state-preference*) approach – which resolves the assets or securities into distributions of dated contingent claims to income defined over the set of all possible "states of the world."[2]

The preceding chapter showed that the more familiar mean, variability formulation has never been completed so as to constitute an acceptable choice-theoretic structure. If mean-return and variability-of-return are to be regarded as commodities, the analysis must go beyond the individual level of decision to show how the relative "prices" for mean-return and variability-of-return are determined in the market. There seem to be rather considerable difficulties facing theorists who attempt to fulfill this program.[3] In contrast, the state-preference approach was demonstrated to be the natural generalization of Fisher's theory of intertemporal choice,[4] into the domain of uncertainty. Where Fisher's objects of choice are titles to consumption as of differing dates, the generalization takes the fundamental commodities, underlying all market assets, to be contingent time-state claims – titles to consumption for specified dates and states of the world. While various assets may package these underlying claims into more or less complex bundles, the "market-clearing" or "conservation" equations determine prices for the elementary time-state claims to which asset prices must conform. The idealizing assumptions, necessary for this formal theoretical structure to hold, are in some respects akin to those of standard theory in requiring a kind of precision of knowledge or belief as to preferences and opportunities that is only very approximately true of the real world. Thus, the theory that results contains uncertainty, imperfect knowledge as to the state of the world that will actually obtain in the future, but does not contain the "vagueness" we usually find psychologically associated with uncertainty.

The present article is devoted to an examination of some implications and applications of the time-state-preference approach, that reveal its power by casting light upon a number of unresolved controversies. These include: (1) the nature and extent of risk aversion; (2) whether there is an optimal "debt-equity mix" in financing corporate undertakings (the Modigliani-Miller problem); and (3) the "appropriate" rate of discount to employ in cost-benefit calculations for government investments not subject to the market test.

In the very simplest illustration of time-state-preference, there is one commodity ("corn"), only one possible current state (i.e. the *present* is certain), and just two possible and mutually exclusive future states. The objects of choice then can be symbolized: c_0, c_{1a}, c_{1b} – present titles to consumption of, respectively, current or time-0 corn, corn at time-1 provided that state a obtains, and corn at time-1 provided that state b obtains. Each individual has an endowment of such claims, has preference relations ordering the combinations he could possibly hold,[5] and has certain opportunities for transforming his endowed bundle into alternative combinations. The possible transformations can take the form of market trading ("financial opportunities") or else of physical conversions ("productive opportunities") – transactions in the one case with other individuals, in the other case with Nature.

5.1   STATE PREFERENCE, RISK AVERSION, AND THE UTILITY-OF-INCOME FUNCTION

In this section we restrict ourselves to synchronous choice among claims to consumption in alternative future states; i.e. we are isolating the problem of risky choice from the problem of time choice. Under these circumstances the individual's situation may be portrayed as in figure 5.1, which shows an indifference map and financial or market opportunities for converting endowment Y into alternative combinations of c_{1a} and c_{1b}. The

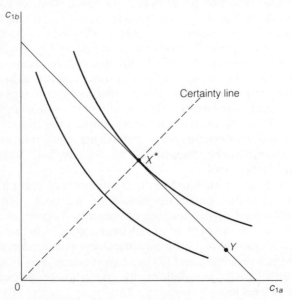

FIGURE 5.1 *Contemporaneous state-preferences and financial opportunities (state-preferences symmetrical, $\pi_a = \pi_b = 1/2$).*

assumption here is that the state probabilities $\pi_a = \pi_b = 1/2$. The wealth constraint upon the market opportunities can be written $W = P_0 c_0 + P_{1a} c_{1a} + P_{1b} c_{1b}$, where P_0, P_{1a}, and P_{1b} are the prices of the respective time-state claims, with c_0 here taken to be a constant holding of current corn. The wealth is in turn fixed by the value of the endowment: $W = P_0 y_0 + P_{1a} y_{1a} + P_{1b} y_{1b}$ – where the y's represent elements of the endowment vector. The 45° "certainty line" connects combinations for which $c_{1a} = c_{1b}$.

The convexity of the indifference curves between the commodities c_{1a} and c_{1b}, which corresponds to one concept of *risk aversion*, may be justified by appeal to the general principle of diminishing marginal rate of substitution that holds for ordinary commodities. A more convincing defense, perhaps, is the observation of "non-specialization" – that individuals almost universally prefer to hedge against many contingencies rather than place all their bets on one. It is of interest to relate this formulation to the Neumann-Morgenstern utility-of-income function $v(c_1)$ that permits use of the expected-utility theorem in rationalizing risky choice.[6] It was shown in chapter 4 that a concave $v(c_1)$ function, as plotted in figure 5.2 ("diminishing marginal utility of consumption income") is equivalent to a convex indifference map as in figure 5.1. In addition, the rather strong theorem was obtained that under these conditions, if the probability ratio for the two states π_b/π_a is equal to the price ratio P_{1b}/P_{1a}, the individual's optimum must be on the certainty line. This is completely consistent with the Friedman-Savage formulation in terms of the Neumann-Morgenstern function, which under the same conditions leads to the conclusions that a fair gamble would not be accepted and that the individual would be willing to insure at fair odds.[7]

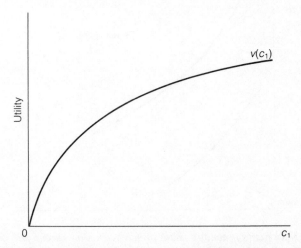

FIGURE 5.2 *Concave Neumann-Morgenstern utility-of-income function.*

However, one observes in the world instances of risk-preferring behavior. Some gambles are accepted at fair, or even adverse odds. We will be considering in this section alternative explanations for this phenomenon. First, however, it is necessary to clarify one point on which error is often committed. Whether a particular contract is a *gamble* – i.e. an arrangement moving the individual farther from the 45° certainty line – or a particular asset a risky one depends not upon the terms of the contract or the nature of the asset in isolation but upon the individual's total portfolio and endowed position. While common stocks are often regarded as riskier than bonds, their purchase may stabilize an overall portfolio with respect to the hazard of inflation; i.e. may move an investor *closer* to the 45° line. Similarly, for some individuals a futures contract may be very risky, but for a hedger the same contract is "insurance" rather than a gamble. The hedger, of course, is someone who starts with a risky endowment – i.e. he has an unbalanced endowed state-distribution of income – and a contract with an *offsettingly* uneven state-distribution of return serves to bring him nearer the certainty line.

The preceding chapter also showed that it was possible, by relaxing the assumption of *uniqueness* of the Neumann-Morgenstern $v(c_1)$ function, to combine convex indifference curves with solutions at fair odds that are off the 45° line (see figure 5.3). The assumption of a single $v(c_1)$ function implies a symmetry as to state preferences such that – adjusting for probabilities – marginal incomes, at any given level of income, are valued

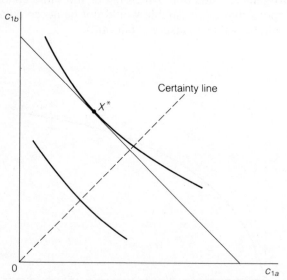

FIGURE 5.3 *Contemporaneous state-preferences and financial opportunities* ($\pi_a = \pi_b = 1/2$, *but state-preferences asymmetrical*).

equivalently in all states. But since the definition of a state of the world incorporates a description of an entire world-environment, there may well be "non-pecuniary" aspects of the respective situations that would warrant biasing the pecuniary-wealth position at fair odds. There would then be a different $v(c_1)$ function for each state, as portrayed for the two-state situation in figure 5.4, where the functions $v_a(c_{1a})$ and $v_b(c_{1b})$ are defined so as to continue permitting the use of the expected-utility theorem to rationalize uncertain choice. This relaxation leads to the conclusion that basically conservative behavior is still consistent with a certain amount of seeming risk preference – the risk preference being a kind of illusion due to looking only at the *pecuniary* income distribution. Still, this explanation hardly accounts for what we observe at Las Vegas, though it may tell us why bachelors commonly do not buy life insurance.[8]

A different explanation for the observed mixture of risk-avoiding and risk-preferring behavior has been offered by Friedman and Savage. They argue that in economic activities such as choices of occupation, business undertakings, and purchases of securities and real property, people generally prefer both low-risk and high-risk activities to moderate-risk activities. This is, assertedly, evidenced by relatively low realized average return (after allowance for unsuccessful as well as successful outcomes) on the former categories as compared with the latter.[9] To explain this, and certain other observed behavior patterns – of which the most significant is the simultaneous purchase of insurance and lottery tickets by low-income individuals – Friedman and Savage construct a Neumann-Morgenstern utility-of-income function of the special shape[10] illustrated in figure 5.5.

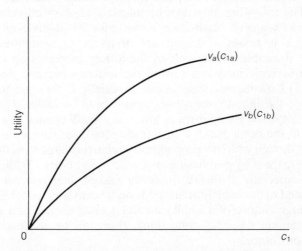

FIGURE 5.4 *Neumann-Morgenstern utility-of-income functions conditional upon state.*

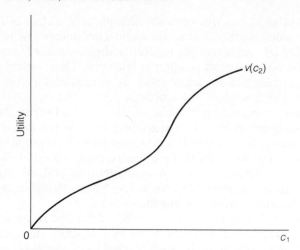

FIGURE 5.5   *Doubly inflected utility-of-income function.*

This doubly inflected curve has a concave segment at the low-income end, a convex segment for middle incomes, and finally another concave segment at the high-income end. For a lottery with only two outcomes, the relative desirability of taking or refusing the lottery is found by comparing the height along the straight line connecting the utilities of the outcomes (i.e. the expected utility of the lottery) with the height of the corresponding point along the doubly inflected curve – the utility of the certain income alternative. If the lottery is fair, the corresponding points are vertically aligned.[11] The following may then be inferred. (1) For individuals in the middle convex segment, small-scale fair lotteries at roughly even odds (e.g. bets on heads in tosses of a coin) are preferred to certainties, become increasingly desirable as the scale of the lottery increases up to a point, after which as scale increases further the lotteries become decreasingly desirable. (2) Low-income individuals, especially if they are toward the upper end of the initial concave segment, would be inclined to buy fair "long-shot" lotteries, giving them at low cost a small chance at a relatively big prize. On the other hand, if they find themselves subject to a hazard threatening (though with low probability) a relatively large loss, they will be inclined to escape it by purchasing insurance at fair odds. (3) High-income indivduals, especially if toward the lower end of their concave segment, will be inclined to bet heavily at fair odds on "short shots" (strong favorites, offering a large chance of a small gain and a small chance of a great loss) and, what amounts to the same thing, they will be inclined to avoid purchasing insurance.

Following the lead of Friedman and Savage, testable inferences can be derived if we interpret the three segments as corresponding at least roughly to three income classes. The behavior implied for the low-income class (most particularly, as we have noted, for the upper end of the low-income segment) is to some extent verified by common observation: many poor people place long-shot bets, and many purchase insurance to protect their modest sources of wealth. Actually, the data cited by Friedman-Savage[12] indicate that poorer people buy proportionately *less* insurance than other income groups; furthermore, the fraction of families purchasing insurance seems to rise smoothly with income. There is thus no indication of a risk-preferring middle segment. This evidence does not, therefore, support their position as against the alternative hypothesis of general risk aversion. The smaller purchases by poorer people may, perhaps, be explained away as due to relatively heavier transactions costs on smaller policies (leading to adverse "loading" of rates) or to possession of fewer insurable assets in proportion to income.

The behavior implied by the Friedman-Savage hypothesis for the upper-income group seems somewhat strange. Do we really see rich people failing to insure their *major* sources of wealth[13] – or, correspondingly, do we commonly observe them hazarding major sums on short-odds bets?[14] A possible defense here would be to bring in the asymmetrical income-tax treatment of gambling and casualty gains and losses, and the favorable treatment of insurance reserves – all of which combine to induce rich people to insure more and to gamble less than they otherwise would. On the other hand, it seems doubtful whether conservative behavior in these respects was really uncharacteristic of rich people even before the income tax.

But the crucial failure of the Friedman-Savage model lies in its implied behavior for the middle classes. This group, if they behaved as pictured, would be plungers of an extreme sort. They would stand ready, at any moment, to accept at fair odds a gamble of such a scale as to thrust them out of the convex segment and into (developing on the outcome) the poor-man or rich-man class. In addition, as we have remarked, it is the individual at the upper end of the low-income segment who is most inclined to take long-shot bets, and the individual at the lower end of the high-income segment who is most inclined to take short-odds bets. Thus, the model would have us believe, the solid risk-avoiders of our society are only the poorer poor, and the richer rich. Aside from the notorious lack of direct confirmation of these assertions, it is of interest to note how they conflict with observed stability patterns of the various income classes. With behavior as postulated, the middle ranks of incomes would be rapidly depopulated, the end result being a U-shaped distribution piled up at the extremes. Needless to say, this is not observed.

There is one important observation that should be considered part of the behavior that needs explaining in constructing a risk-preference model (utility-of-income function): gambling on a scale at all likely to *impoverish* is rarely observed in middle- and upper-income groups. One way to reconcile this observation with the Friedman-Savage model would be to shrink the middle convex segment to a narrow range.[15] To do this is, however, to lose the main point of the Friedman-Savage argument, since then risk aversion would be the predominant behavior pattern after all.[16] And the problem remains of combining the risk aversion necessary for observed diversification of assets and purchase of insurance with the existence of at least a modest amount of gambling at all income levels.[17]

An easy way out of the difficulty lies in recognizing that many people take pleasure in gambling *per se* (i.e. as a consumption good). A modest amount of *pleasure-oriented* gambling would then not be inconsistent with risk aversion (a concave utility-of-income function) for serious *wealth-oriented* activities.[18] To make this distinction workable, however, it must be possible to distinguish observationally between pleasure-oriented and wealth-oriented gambling, the latter being defined as a deliberate attempt to change wealth status. Fortunately, the two motives for gambling are observably distinct, because they imply radically different wagering procedures. If gambling is wealth-oriented, it will take the form of hazarding great sums (proportionate to one's endowment and hopes) on a single turn of a wheel or flip of a coin. Repetitive gambling at relatively small stakes would be absurd: the law of large numbers shrinks the variance of the overall outcome, whereas wealth-oriented gamblers are trying to achieve large changes. While repetitive small-stake gambling does not quite guarantee a final result near the mean, the likelihood of such outcomes is greatly increased; in any case, the average time required to win the desired sum (or lose the fortune hazarded) will be enormously extended. What we observe at Las Vegas is, of course, very much the repetitive, small-stake pattern. The combination of adverse odds and limited stakes assures a high probability that the final outcome for the gambler will be a modest loss – the price paid for the pleasure of gambling. All this is not to say that we never observe wealth-oriented gambling, but rather that it is not a sufficiently important phenomenon to dictate the main lines of our theory of risk.[19]

On our hypothesis, therefore, we expect to see risk aversion predominating in wealth-oriented activities at all income levels – thus explaining purchase of insurance all along the wealth scale. We also expect to see a moderate amount of pleasure-oriented gambling, again all along the wealth scale. Wealth-oriented gambling will not be a very important phenomenon, but such as exists would be concentrated among the poor.[20] This is in sharp contrast with the view of Friedman and Savage, whose theory indicates that wealth-oriented gambling will be very significant, and concentrated among the middle classes. We, on the contrary, would expect to find the middle classes to be the most insurance-minded. Insurance purchases by the poor would be deterred by the substantially higher transactions cost on the one hand, and the relief floor on the other. As for the rich, they are likely to possess a sufficient diversity of assets as to make self-insurance feasible (this consideration being counterbalanced somewhat by tax advantages where life insurance is concerned).

Leaving the sphere of gambling *versus* insurance, the most significant class of economic activity, in terms of implications for attitudes toward risk, is choice of occupation. Except in the very highest income brackets, this decision determines the nature of the major source of wealth. In addition, it is difficult to insure or diversify against certain hazards associated with occupational choice, such as cyclical unemployment and technological obsolescence. Insurance is available against physical hazards – but there will typically be penalty rates to pay for life or disability insurance in dangerous occupations. Consequently, on our hypothesis we would expect to observe relatively low returns in occupations that are highly secure in almost all respects, like teaching and civil service. In hazardous occupations such as mining, and insecure activities such as business entrepreneurship, we would expect higher average returns – even after allowing for injuries and failures. Unfortunately, the evidence available is difficult to interpret because of differences in personal qualities of individuals, non-pecuniary returns and differences of tastes with respect to them, tax and relief effects, and numerous difficulties with the data.[21]

The evidence on return to property in relation to risk is fortunately somewhat clearer. We must be careful to recollect here, however, that the "riskiness" (imbalance in the state-distribution of income) relevant for decisions is not that of particular assets in isolation. It is the variability of the state-distribution of consumption possibilities yielded by overall *portfolios* that is relevant. For some classes of assets (securities, in particular) it is relatively easy to obtain considerable diversification while holding individually risky assets. The main problem is posed by the overall swings of the business cycle, which limit the variance-minimizing effect of diversification by imposing high correlation among security returns – and, probably even more important, high correlation between overall property income and overall wage or other personal income. Consequently, and especially because of the intrinsically risky situation involved in occupational choice, the risk-aversion hypothesis would predict relatively high average return on procyclical securities and relatively low on stable or anticyclical securities. This is borne out by the historically realized yields on equities (highly procyclical in real terms).[22] Comparison of the cyclically unstable "industrial" equities with the more stable "utility" equities provides another confirmation.[23]

Thus, a combination of a risk-aversion hypothesis for wealth-oriented activities with recognition that, for many individuals, repetitive small-stake gambling (i.e. gambling guaranteed not to drastically transform the wealth level) is a pleasurable activity, serves to explain the available evidence. In contrast, the attempt to explain both insurance and gambling as reflecting a single utility-of-income function of peculiar shape leads to contradictions – in which the supposed risk-preferring group is first large and then small, first a stable and then a disappearing element, etc. – and is in conflict with more direct knowledge about the risk-seeking propensities of the various income groups.

5.2   OPTIMAL CAPITAL STRUCTURE

The analysis of risky investment decision in terms of state preferences may be applied in the area of corporate finance to the controversial "Proposition I" of Modigliani and Miller: "The market value of any firm is independent of its capital structure and is given by capitalizing its expected return at the rate ρ_κ appropriate to its class."[24] Our main concern here will be with the first part of the proposition, the assertion that market value is independent of capital structure. Symbolically, the contention is that $D_0 + E_0 = V_0 = \bar{X}/\rho_\kappa$, a constant – where D_0 is present (or market) value of the debt, E_0 the value of the equity, V_0 is the assertedly constant value of the firm, and $\bar{X}$ is the firm's given operating income. The language in the second part of the proposition, and elsewhere in their paper, indicate that Modigliani and Miller were employing a mean, variability approach to risk-bearing.[25]

In chapter 4, Fisher's analysis of individuals' investment decisions under certainty was generalized to include investment decisions of *firms*. The result was obtained, in equation (4.6′′′), that the market value (wealth) of the firm under certainty equals the present value of debt repayments plus (if the firm has productive opportunities that lead to an increase of wealth) the present value of any equity increment. This looks very much like the Modigliani-Miller theorem. In fact, it is easy to extend this result, via a state-preference analysis, to decisions under uncertainty so as to validate the Modigliani-Miller theorem. The extension is based on the premise that individuals and firms form a closed system, so that all assets or claims must be held by, and only by, individuals or firms. Furthermore, looking at the situation *ex post* of the production decisions (i.e. after commitment of funds to investment), the social totals of each time-state class of assets must then be constant. What this rules out are "external drains" of which the most crucial are personal and corporate taxes. Bankruptcy penalties, transactions and underwriting costs, etc., must also be excluded.

Continuing to employ our simplifying assumption of only two time-periods (dates 0 and 1), with only one present state but two future states (a and b), we first develop equations for the firm's capital input and the distribution of returns.

$$- q_0 = d_0 + e_0 \qquad \text{Capital input balance} \qquad (5.1)$$

Here q_0 is the total of corporate funds committed to investment at time-0; d_0 is the portion coming from borrowings, and e_0 the portion from equity funds.[26] (In chapter 4 we assumed $e_0 = 0$, all-debt financing being possible under certainty.)

$$\begin{cases} q_{1a} = d_{1a} + e_{1a} \\ q_{1b} = d_{1b} + e_{1b} \end{cases} \quad \text{Firm's financial distributions} \quad (5.2)$$

Equations (5.2) say that all gross asset earnings, in either state, are fully distributed and that the only recipients are the debt and equity owners. Here d_{1a} is the gross return to debtholders if state a obtains; the other claims are defined correspondingly. If the debt is riskless, $d_{1a} = d_{1b} = d_0(1 + r^*)$, where r^* is the promised interest rate on the bond. If the debt is risky so that in state b, let us say, $d_{1b} < d_0(1 + r^*)$ then $e_{1b} = 0$ – since the debt is a senior claim that must be paid first before equity receives any return.

We have here three types of future time-state claims: (physical) asset claims (q_{1a} and q_{1b}), debt claims (d_{1a} and d_{1b}) and equity claims (e_{1a} and e_{1b}). Under the single-price law of markets, unit claims to the same commodity must sell at the same price. Hence, unless there are differentiations due to such features as tax status (excluded by our assumption above), the single price P_{1a} must apply to q_{1a}, d_{1a}, and e_{1a} – and correspondingly P_{1b} is the price of q_{1b}, d_{1b}, and e_{1b}. Taking c_0 as numeraire so that $P_0 = 1$, the prices for the future claims can be written in the form $P_{1a} = 1/(1 + r_{1a})$ and $P_{1b} = 1/(1 + r_{1b})$, where r_{1a} and r_{1b} are the "time-and-risk" discount rates for contingent future incomes. There is a possible source of confusion here: it might be thought that the equity claim e_{1b} is "riskier" than the debt claim d_{1b}, for example, and so should sell at a lower price. But risk has already been taken account of in the *quantification* of d_{1b} and e_{1b} – in the example given just above, if state b obtains so that d_{1b} is less than $d_0(1 + r^*)$, then the junior claim $e_{1b} = 0$. Conditionally upon the occurrence of the specified state, the various claims all become certainties.[27]

If we define present values of the firm, of the debt, and of the equity return in the natural way for this problem (*ex post* of the investment decision),[28] we obtain:

$$\begin{cases} V_0 = P_{1a}q_{1a} + P_{1b}q_{1b} \\ D_0 = P_{1a}d_{1a} + P_{1b}d_{1b} \\ E_0 = P_{1a}e_{1a} + P_{1b}e_{1b} \end{cases} \quad (5.3)$$

Here again there is a possible source of confusion, in that it might seem plausible that the relative constancy of the d's as compared with the e's would be reflected by a kind of premium in the value D_0 as compared with E_0, given predominant risk aversion. But since each form of security is only a package of elementary claims to contingent incomes, market equilibrium requires that the value of the package equal the sum of the values of the components.[29]

The Modigliani-Miller Theorem follows immediately from (5.2) and (5.3):

$$V_0 = D_0 + E_0. \tag{5.4}$$

Our formulation makes it possible to observe that the proposition in question is a special case of a Fisherian theorem. Financing operations (i.e. market conversions among claims to income) take place *within* a wealth constraint – they do not change wealth. In the familiar Fisherian analysis of choices involving time, the market value of the productive solution determines wealth; borrowing and lending can then take place to achieve a different distribution of timed income claims, but all such transformations leave wealth unchanged. In the model considered here, the productive solution determines wealth by the condition $V_0 = \bar{X}/\rho_K$; financing via alternative debt-equity ratios then represent different possible ways of distributing this wealth over time-state claims. But all the attainable distributions have the same wealth-value.

We may now examine further the significance of the "closed system" or "no external drains" proviso stated earlier. Let us suppose that there is no corporate tax, but that equity claims are given preferential treatment with respect to the external drain of the *personal* income tax on the system composed of the individuals and firms.[30] This factor, other things equal, would raise the price (lower the discounting rate) of an equity claim relative to a debt claim – and also relative to asset claims assuming these latter have to be financed by mixes of debt and equity. Then the single-price law, for claims conditioned on a given state, could not be applied, and equations (5.3) and (5.4) would not hold. Alternatively, if we ignored the personal income tax but assumed the existence of an external drain on the corporation in the form of a *corporate* income tax, equations (5.2) would be modified so as to become (t_{1a} and t_{1b} indicating conditional tax liabilities):

$$\begin{cases} q_{1a} = d_{1a} + e_{1a} + t_{1a} \\ q_{1b} = d_{1b} + e_{1b} + t_{1b}. \end{cases} \tag{5.2'}$$

Equations (5.2′) indicate that there is an opportunity to increase wealth by tax-minimizing devices. Under the corporate income tax, debt and equity earnings are differentially treated; tax liability can be reduced by a high debt/equity fraction. The sum $d_{1a} + e_{1a}$ then, for example, would not be a constant independent of the ratio of the two – so that even though the prices (or discounting rates) for asset, debt, and (after-tax) equity earnings are identical, equation (5.4) would not follow.

We may conclude this section by noting that we have gone only a small step toward solving the problem of optimal capital structure in terms of a state-preference analysis. Doing so would require an integration of the personal-tax and corporate-tax effects, and consideration of other factors (such as the magnitude of bankruptcy penalties) to yield the optimal balance of debt and equity financing.[31] The limited purpose here was only to illustrate the use of a state-preference analysis in order to suggest the range of applicability and the crucial limitations of the much debated Modigliani-Miller "Proposition I."

5.3 UNCERTAINTY AND THE DISCOUNT RATE FOR PUBLIC INVESTMENT

The final application to be presented here of the model of time-state-preference concerns the much controverted question: What is the "appropriate" discount rate, for use under uncertainty, in present-worth calculations evaluating government investments not subject to the market test? Many conflicting recommendations have been expressed on this question, but only two of these will be examined here for consistency with Pareto efficiency in an uncertain world.[32] Of these, the first prescribes that the government employ as discount rate for a public project the same rate as would be applied, in principle, by a company evaluating a "comparable" project in the private sphere. The opposing position would have the government take advantage of its power to finance exceptionally cheaply by undertaking projects that are profitable when the returns are evaluated at the government's low borrowing rate. We may think of these two as prescriptions to employ, in the first case, a *risky*, and in the second case a *riskless*, rate – to discount the mathematical expectations of the uncertain returns.

The argument for use of the risky rate runs somewhat as follows.[33] The market rate of interest is generated by an equilibrium between marginal time preferences of consumers and the marginal time productivity of resources. If neither private nor public projects involved risk, it would obviously be inefficient to depart from this equilibrium rate in evaluating intertemporal transfers of income (i.e. investments) in the public sphere. It is true that in a risky world there are many "impure" time-plus-risk interest rates rather than one pure time-rate, but the way to take this into account is to use in the public sphere the rate employed for "comparable" invest-ments in the private sphere. Thus, if a power project would in the private sector be financed half from debt sources paying 4 percent (this being a riskless rate, let us say) and half from equity sources requiring an expected return of 6 percent, the government discount rate for a comparable project should be the same 5 percent the private company must employ. Then the marginally desirable project would, in either sector, yield 5 percent in terms of probabilistic expectation. (If corporate income tax is taken into account, the marginally desirable project in the private sphere must have an expected yield around 8.5 percent, and so the discount rate for government investment should be correspondingly higher.)[34] Failure to abide by this rule leads to obviously inefficient results. If the government, merely because it can finance entirely by riskless borrowing at, say 4 percent, employed the latter rate in its calculations, the marginally adopted project in the public sector would yield on the average but 4 percent while private projects with higher expected yields were failing of adoption.

The opposing recommendation is based upon the contention that the higher rates required to secure funds for private investments (e.g. the 6 percent equity yield in the illustration above) are a reflection of risk aversion – and that risk aversion is a private, not a social cost. The possibility of *pooling* independent risks is essential to this argument. AT&T can pool more risks than can a small local telephone company; it will therefore, be able to finance more cheaply and so to undertake projects with a lower expected yield than the small company can. The federal government can pool risks far more effectively than AT&T and so is as a practical matter quite justified in treating the expected project yield as if it were riskless. Consequently, the 4 percent riskless discount rate is the relevant one for its calculations.[35] (It should be noted, however, that the conclusion of this argument only follows in a "second-best" sense. For, granted the premises, it would clearly be most efficient for the government to borrow in order to subsidize the higher-expected-yield private investments – a larger subsidy to the small telephone company, a smaller one to AT&T – rather than for the purpose of undertaking lower-yield public investments. Only if this possibility is ruled out does it follow that lower-yielding government investments should be undertaken.)

A simple numerical illustration will indicate the incorrectness of the "pooling" argument *within the time-state model developed here*. Suppose the society consists of J identically placed individuals with identical tastes, and let the social endowment consist of $100J$ units of income (say, "corn") in time-0, $150J$ units in the time-state $1a$, and $50J$ units in time-state $1b$. Let the numeraire $P_0 = 1$. Suppose, for arithmetical convenience, that the state-probabilities $\pi_a = \pi_b = 1/2$, and that with this distribution of consumption opportunities there is on the margin zero time preference with respect to certainties: thus, the price of a unit of future certain income $P_1 = 1$ (and the riskless discount rate $r_1 = 0$ percent)[36] where, of course, $P_1 = P_{1a} + P_{1b}$. Since by hypothesis there is risk aversion, it must be the case that the overall value of the time-1 endowment for each person – 150 $(P_{1a}) + 50 (P_{1b})$ – must be less than the value of the average holding as a certainty, i.e. less than $100(P_{1a}) + 100(P_{1b}) = 100$. (If the prices P_{1a} and P_{1b} were such that the average holding certain *could* be purchased within the endowment wealth constraint, it *would* be, given risk aversion.) This requires that P_{1a} be less than $1/2$. For concreteness, let $P_{1a} = 0.4$, and hence $P_{1b} = 0.6$, thus determining the "impure" time-and-state discount rates $r_{1a} = 150$ percent, and $r_{1b} = 66.66$ percent.[37]

Now consider various investment opportunities, all of infinitesimal scale so that we can hold the price relationships unchanged (the opportunities are infinitesimal on the social scale, but not necessarily on the individual scale). It is immediately clear that, in terms of efficiency, either a private or public project whose returns fall *exclusively* in state $1a$ should have these returns discounted at the rate of 150 percent. To attempt to make a distinction between public and private here would be equivalent to charging different prices for the same commodity – c_{1a}. If the returns all fell in state $1b$, the discount rate should be 66.66 percent. For an investment yielding returns equally in either state (i.e. an investment whose returns are certain), the 0 percent rate would be appropriate. For a project yielding in the ratio of 3 in state $1a$ to 1 in state $1b$ (that is, in the same proportions as the private and social endowments) the appropriate discount (for application to the mathematical expectation of returns) is approximately 11.1 percent.[38] The appropriate discount rate would be much lower if, with the same mathematical expectation of returns, the state-distribution were reversed so as to pay off more heavily in the less well-endowed state $1b$ (the rate to use would be *minus* 9.1 percent, on our assumptions). In every case, of course, the "appropriate" discount rate is that which correctly distinguishes efficient from inefficient projects by showing positive or negative values in a present-worth calculation.

The foregoing indicates that there is a single definite discount rate to be used, *whether a project is private or public*, in making efficiency calculations for any given state-pattern of returns. This result supports, therefore, the "risky discount rate" position on the normative issue in question. The crucial proviso is that when the recommendation is made to employ for government investments the private market discount rate for "comparable" projects, it must be understood that *"comparable" projects are those having the same proportionate time-state distribution of returns*. In particular, note that the "risky" rate might be *lower* than the riskless rate.

It is correspondingly clear that within this model the position recommending the use of the riskless discount rate with the mathematical expectation of returns must be incorrect. We have just seen that it would fail to distinguish between, on the one hand, a project paying off more heavily in the better-endowed state and, on the other hand, a project with a quantitatively identical but reversed state-pattern paying off more heavily in the more urgently desired income of the poorer-endowed state. Or, to take another example, a project yielding only a dollar in state $1a$ would have that dollar reduced to $0.50 in taking the expectation, and then be discounted at the riskless rate (0 percent here). This is equivalent to letting $r_{1a} = 100$ percent, too lax a criterion since the correct $r_{1a} = 150$ percent. On the other hand, if the dollar were returned in state $1b$ the recommendation would indicate too stringent a criterion, employing 100 percent instead of the correct 66.66 percent. The basic reason, of course, is that the process of taking mathematical expectations considers dollars equivalent when they appertain to equally probable states – but as between two such states, the dollars in one may be much more highly valued on the margin than in the other. In other words, dollars in distinct time-states are different commodities within the model considered here, and it is as incorrect to average them as it would be to average shoes and apples.

We may now turn to the "pooling" argument. Suppose it were possible to pool two projects, one yielding a dollar in state 1 a and the other a dollar in state 1 b. Since the pooled return in thus riskless, it may seem plausible to employ the riskless rate 0 percent for the two, viewed in combination. But this is definitely incorrect. If the two projects were *necessarily* tied together, then the recommended procedure would be appropriate. But if they are really separable, they should be evaluated separately (for simplicity, we set aside complications such as possible interactions between the two). It could easily happen that the combination, if forced upon us as a combination, might be desirable – but that it might be more efficient to adopt one component and not the other, if we could separate the two. In short, the device of pooling provides no justification in efficiency terms for adopting what is incrementally a bad project, if in fact we can adopt the good one separately from the bad.[39]

Even if the "pooling" argument is rejected, it could still be maintained that the discount rate on public projects ought "usually" to be lower than those of private projects. All that is required to support this view is that government projects be "usually" (in contrast with private projects) such that they pay off in less well-endowed states. For example, a federal irrigation project pays off disproportionately when there would otherwise be a drought. Of course, some special argument is required to explain why private initiative does not exploit such opportunities. But if such opportunities are not privately exploited, then in fact the "usual" private investments would not be the *comparable* ones in the sense required by the "risky-discount-rate" position.

It may seem surprising, however, that so little can be made of "pooling" in view of the plausible arguments adduced in its favor. One can, in fact, construct a model in which the pooling argument makes more sense, and it will be instructive to compare that model with ours above. The key is to distinguish between private "states" and social "states." The idea here is related to a maxim often (rather too sweepingly) expressed in connection with life-insurance calculations: "We don't know who will die next year, but we do know how many!" Similarly, the social total of endowments might be constant (thus, there is really only one social state, ignoring distribution) and yet for each individual the endowment might be uncertain.[40] For concreteness, imagine the following situation. If state a obtains, every odd-numbered individual has an endowment of 50 and every even-numbered individual an endowment of 150; if state b obtains the positions are reversed. Let us suppose, in order to make the case as strong as possible, that the investments available to even and odd classes of individuals will have returns proportionate to their respective endowment distributions. Then the "even" individuals will, on the basis of risk aversion, have a bias against the investments available to them, and the "odd" individuals similarly against their investments – whereas, if pooled, the investments would tend to become certainties justifying no risk discount.

Consider investments of the form requiring a time-0 input of \$1, and yielding a time-1 return of \$1.50 in an individual's better-endowed and \$0.50 in his worse-endowed state, the states again assumed equally probable. If the subjective marginal value of a dollar in an individual's better-endowed state is 0.4 and in his poorer-endowed state is 0.6 (as before), then each individual would assign a present worth of − \$0.10 to the investment opportunity. But if an "odd" and an "even" investment opportunity were pooled, the return would be certain; at the riskless 0 percent rate the combination would have a zero present worth, and so be on the margin of desirability. Here pooling does not sneak in a bad project under the mantle of a good one. Rather, two projects separately bad (in terms of private calculations) may become a good project in terms of social calculations!

A model of this kind is what lies behind the usual "pooling" argument justifying the use of the riskless rate for evaluating government investments. The model diverges in two essential ways from that presented earlier justifying the employment of the risky rate. First is the assumption, already mentioned, that risk is private rather than social – i.e. that there is only one state with respect to social totals[41] but more than one state in terms of possible individual distributions within that total. Second, and this is the really critical point, is the assumption that markets are so imperfect that it is impossible for the individuals better-endowed in state a to trade claims to income in that state against the claims to income in state b that other individuals would like to sell. In short, *the single-price law of materials must be violated.*

Continuing our numerical example, the commodity c_{1a} had a subjective value equal to 0.4 for even-numbered individuals and 0.6 for odd-numbered individuals. If trade were permitted between the two classes, the two values would have to come into equality. Holding to the assumption that a riskless future claim has unit present value $(P_{1a} + P_{1b} = 1)$, P_{1a} and P_{1b} would then each have to equal 0.5. Then strictly private calculations, without any pooling, would show that the private investment opportunities of the example were on the margin of desirability. The discount rate for the "comparable" private investments would be 0 percent, so that proponents of the so-called "risky discount rate" for evaluation of public investment would be led by their analysis to the correct 0 percent rate in this case. In contrast, as we have seen, proponents of the so-called "riskless rate" – while also correct in favoring 0 percent as the discount rate *in this case* – would be led into definite error under conditions where private risks *are* reflective of social risks.

We may conclude, therefore, that the pooling argument rests ultimately for support upon market imperfections that prevent equivalent time-state claims from selling at a uniform price, thus hindering the possibility of private movements away from risky (unbalanced with respect to state) endowments by trading. Such imperfections may, of course, be very prevalent. One important example concerns assets whose productiveness has a personal element. Such an asset may be worth much in the hands of some Mr X, but little if traded to anyone else. It will, therefore, be difficult to reduce the riskiness associated with holding such assets.[42] Here is a case where, granted the other conditions in our illustration above, the pooling argument would have real force. But it is clear that the argument is incorrect on the level of generality at which it is usually propounded. If time-state claims can be regarded as commodities traded in perfect markets, the prescription for the use of the so-called "risky rate" – the discount rate implicit in the valuation of private projects with the *same proportionate time-state distribution of returns* – has been shown to be generally correct.

5.4   CONCLUDING REMARKS

To rationalize the process of investment decision under uncertainty, and to explain the price relationships among risky assets, two main conceptions of the choice process have been put forward by economic theorists. Both conceptions *reduce* the observed assets traded in the marketplace into more fundamental entities – choice-objects assertedly desired by investors. Under the first and more familiar approach, the more fundamental entities are represented by mean and variability measures, μ and σ, of overall return provided by any given portfolio of assets; under the second approach, the assets are regarded as packages of more fundamental contingent claims to income at specified dates and states of the world.

In chapter 4, it was shown that the state-preference formulation was the logical extension, to the world of uncertain choice, of Fisher's model of certain intertemporal choice. The various topics covered in this article were intended to serve as illustrations of the power and relevance of the state-preference approach, to show that some interesting and novel results in a number of areas can be obtained thereby. (1) As to risk aversion, under the mean *versus* variability approach the investor's attitude toward risk (whether σ is for him a good or a "bad") is a personal characteristic. It remains unclear how the risk-loving or risk-avoiding propensities of individuals are composed into an overall market premium or discount for risk. In contrast, under the state-preference approach the very elementary principle of nonspecialization of choice among time-state claims, leads to the inference that in their wealth-oriented decisions, and if asset prices represent fair odds, investors seek portfolios with balanced state-distributions of income. In general, however, they will not actually achieve perfect balance (zero σ), because the endowments and productive opportunities available to society are not symmetrically distributed over all the possible states. (2) As to the unresolved question about the existence of an optimal debt-equity ratio for financing corporate investment, the state-preference formulation leads directly to a set of idealizing assumptions ("no external drains") under which all possible ratios are equivalent in market value. Where the idealized conditions do not hold, there *will* in general be an optimal ratio. (3) With regard to the appropriate discount rate for evaluating government investments, rather vaguely stated ideas concerning risk aversion as a social or a private cost can be precisely formulated in terms of time-state preferences. It was shown that the efficient discount rate, assuming perfect markets, is the market rate implicit in the valuation of private assets whose returns are "comparable" to the public investment in question – where "comparable" means having the same proportionate time-state distribution of returns. The argument often encountered, to the effect that "risk aversion is a private cost and not a social cost," was shown to be mistaken unless two restrictive conditions both hold: (a) Private risks exist, but these do not represent social risks (as when the aggregate social endowment is constant, but its distribution over the individuals varies with state). (b) Markets are imperfect, so that the single-price law of markets does not hold for contingent time-state-claims as commodities.

Going beyond the ground covered by this article, there seem to be considerable difficulties of an operational nature in more direct empirical tests employing a state-preference formulation. The mean and the variability of return embodied in a given set of assets are already only implicitly observable; when the assets are interpreted instead as packages of claims to incomes in underlying hypothetical states of the world, the fundamental choice-objects have an even higher degree of invisibility. Assets ordinarily encountered in capital markets, such as corporate bonds or equities, represent complex aggregates of claims to income in an embarrassing multiplicity of possible states of the world. Nevertheless, in some cases the interpretation may be reasonably clear. Thus, the course of stock and bond prices since 1929 has certainly reflected investors' changing views of the probabilities of more and less prosperous states of the world occurring. Here, as elsewhere, progress will depend upon the discovery of strategic simplifications that reduce seemingly intractable problems into at least partially manageable ones.[43]

NOTES

[1] The most complete development is in H. M. Markowitz, *Portfolio Selection*, New York: Wiley, 1959; see also D. E. Farrar, *The Investment Decision Under Uncertainty*, Englewood Cliffs, NJ: Prentice-Hall, 1962.

[2] See K. J. Arrow, "The Role of Securities in the Optimal Allocation of Risk-Bearing," *Review of Economic Studies*, vol. 21 (April 1964); G. Debreu, *Theory of Value*, New York: Wiley, 1959, ch. 7; J. Hirshleifer, "Efficient Allocation of Capital in an Uncertain World," *American Economic Review*, vol. 54 (May 1964), 77–85.

[3] The furthest development to date seems to be that of W. F. Sharpe, "Capital Asset Prices: A Theory of Market Equilibrium Under Conditions of Risk," *Journal of Finance*, vol. 19 (Sept. 1964). This may be regarded as a theory of prices for mean and variability in the "very short run," with fixed supplies of productive and financial assets.

[4] Irving Fisher, *The Theory of Interest*, New York: Macmillan, 1930; reprinted, Augustus M. Kelley, 1955.

[5] Note that he can *hold* present claims or titles to both c_{1a}, and c_{1b}, although he cannot ultimately *consume* both since only one of the two states will actually obtain.

[6] As discussed, for example, in M. Friedman and L. J. Savage, "The Utility Analysis of Choices Involving Risk," *Journal of Political Economy*, vol. 56 (Aug. 1948). Reprinted in American Economic Association, *Readings in Price Theory*, Homewood, Ill.: Irwin, 1952. Page references are to the latter volume.

[7] Ibid., pp. 73–7.

[8] While a reasonable family man in his current decisions will attach considerable significance to income for his beneficiaries contingent upon his own death, a bachelor with only remote heirs has very asymmetrical state-preferences with respect to income accruing to him under the contingencies "Alive" or "Dead."

[9] Friedman and Savage, *op. cit.*, pp. 63–6.

[10] Ibid., p. 85.

[11] Justifications of these assertions are omitted because of their familiarity and availability in the cited source. The key to the proofs is the use of the expected-utility principle for risky outcomes.

[12] Ibid., pp. 66 f.

[13] Rich people would, on any risk-preference assumption, tend to self-insure (to save the transactions cost) against hazards threatening losses involving only minor fractions of their wealth. Thus we would expect to see them often foregoing the purchase of automobile collision insurance. But the Friedman-Savage assertion implies that they would omit insuring against potentially great losses such as those associated with accident liability claims, and physical disability or death of the main income-earner. Again their own evidence does not support Friedman and Savage here.

[14] Occasional racetrack betting on favorites, so long as the scale is minor, means little here. The main point of the Friedman-Savage assumption is that the rich man is willing, at fair odds, to accept a hazard that (if it eventuated) would thrust him entirely out of the concave segment – out of the rich-man class! This requires betting on a scale considered pathological in our culture (see Dostoyevsky, *The Gambler*).

[15] At one point (*op cit.*, p. 92) Friedman and Savage do suggest that relatively few individuals are in the middle segment.

[16] Substantial numbers of individuals in the middle segment are necessary to explain the alleged observation of preference for low-risk or high-risk as against moderate-risk economic activities.

[17] One possible way out would be to assert that the middle segment is small and, in addition, slides up and down as the individual's income level changes – see H. Markowitz, "The Utility of Wealth," *Journal of Political Economy*, vol. 60 (April 1952) – so that he is always willing to undertake a small amount of gambling from his present income level. As in the case of Ptolemy's geocentric system, when it becomes necessary to incorporate such *ad hoc* "epicycles" to save the phenomena, it is time for a new conception.

[18] The following may perhaps be an illuminating analogy. Men like to live in houses on solid foundations, with square corners, and level floors. And yet they may pay money to spend a few minutes at an amusement park in a "crazy-house" with quite the reverse characteristics.

[19] Some wealth-oriented gambling is based on "hunches" or "inside information" that, if true, would make the bet a lottery at *favorable* odds rather than the adverse gamble it appears – to others! Of course, given the belief in favorable odds, even a risk-avoider might gamble. There is also strictly rational wealth-oriented gambling, as in the classic case of the embezzler who plunges his remaining cash in the hope of being able to straighten out his accounts prior to an audit. Here the dollar in hand that the gambler risks is almost costless, as he cannot hope to salvage much of his illegal taking by conservative behavior. A somewhat similar argument may partially explain lower-class gambling: the floor on consumption provided by public-assistance payments – where such payments are liable to be withheld or reduced if the would-be gambler conserved his assets – permits the individual to gamble with dollars that do not fully represent sacrifices of consumption to him. Finally, there is the gambling behavior that would generally be regarded as pathological; this would be associated with subnormal or aberrant mental conditions.

[20] See note above concerning the effect of relief payments (consumption floor) upon the propensity to gamble. Also, ill-informed believers in hunches, and subnormal or aberrant mental types, will tend to have low income status.

[21] Friedman and Savage allege (*op. cit.*, pp. 63–6) that higher returns are received on (reflecting aversion to) moderate risks – and that the average returns to high-risk activities like auto-racing, piloting aircraft, business undertakings in untried fields, and the professions of law and medicine (?) are so low as to evidence an inclination in favor of bearing extreme risks. The evidence presented for these assertions is weak, to say the least. The following will illustrate one of the many problems of interpreting such data as exist: for high-risk occupations there is likely to be a selection bias (since those who overestimate the chance of success are more likely to enter) so that adverse average results are not necessarily evidence of risk preference.

[22] H. A. Latané, "Portfolio Balance – The Demand for Money, Bonds, and Stocks," *Southern Economic Journal*, vol. 29 (Oct. 1962).

[23] Most of the difference is realized in the form of capital gains. See *Historical Statistics of the United States, Colonial Times to 1957* (Washington, 1960), p. 657.

[24] F. Modigliani and M. H. Miller, "The Cost of Capital, Corporation Finance and the Theory of Investment," *American Economic Review*, vol. 48 (June 1958), p. 268.

[25] In their paper the assumption is made throughout that the expected yield on equities exceeds the yield on riskless bonds; they associate the premium with "financial risk" due at least in part to variance of outcome (p. 271). Modigliani

and Miller claim that their propositions do not depend upon any assumption about individual risk preferences (p. 279); this statement is correct on the level of the individual (who can maximize asset value regardless of potential risk preferences), but on the market level the existence of a premium reflects the need on balance for compensation to induce bearing of variability risk.

[26] It is assumed that the firm does not consume and has null endowment. Hence all funds for investment must be obtained from outside, and also the firm has no use for funds except to invest them. While actual firms do make use of "internal" funds, we regard such funds as distributed to stockholders and returned to the firm for reinvestment.

[27] Modigliani and Miller describe an "arbitrage" process which has the effect of enforcing this single-price law (pp. 69–71). While their argument has been the subject of controversy, it seems unexceptionable under the provisos of the model here discussed – in particular, under the assumption that the several types of claim do not diverge in tax status.

[28] That is, *after* the commitment of current funds (which being "sunk," do not enter into present worth) but *before* the payout of returns to investors.

[29] Consider the following analogy. Bread and butter are complements for most people, and possibly substitutes for some careful calorie-watchers – but, regardless, a package of bread and butter in competitive equilibrium must sell for the sum of the bread price and the butter price. Any divergence could only be due to a possible saving of transactions cost, but such costs are a form of "external drain" assumed away in our model. (The assumption of competitive conditions also rules out "tie-in sales" as a device for capitalizing on monopoly power.)

[30] The capital gains feature applies to both debt and equity securities, though in practice equity benefits more. The unique advantage to equity is the opportunity to reinvest via "retained earnings," escaping personal tax in the process. (In our analysis, the "retention" is a mere fiction – which is not the whole story, of course.)

[31] For a more complete analysis see J. Lintner, "Dividends, Earnings, Leverage, Stock Prices and the Supply of Capital to Corporations," *Review of Economics and Statistics*, vol. 44 (Aug. 1962). The result here differs from Lintner's in showing that uncertainty *alone* is not sufficient to negate the Modigliani-Miller theorem.

[32] Among the points of view not considered here are those which reject the market evidence on time preference or time productivity in favor of a "social discount rate" excogitated from value judgments or planners' time preferences. This point of view can be defended as a way of compensating for market bias due to private "myopia" or intertemporal "selfishness," but it raises issues beyond the scope of the Pareto-efficiency criterion. For discussions of this position see O. Eckstein, "A Survey of the Theory of Public Expenditure Criteria," my "Comment," and Eckstein's "Reply" in the National Bureau of Economic Research volume, *Public Finances: Needs, Sources, and Utilization*, Princeton University Press, 1961, and S. Marglin, "The Social Rate of Discount and the Optimal Rate of Investment," *Quarterly Journal of Economics*, vol. 77 (Feb. 1963).

[33] The argument is based on that offered in J. Hirshleifer, J. C. DeHaven and J. W. Milliman, *Water Supply: Economics, Technology, and Policy*, University of Chicago Press, 1960, pp. 139–50.

[34] It might be argued that the corporate income tax is an equalizing adjustment designed to compensate the community for certain costs imposed on it by the corporate form of business – in contrast with partnerships, proprietorships, cooperatives, government enterprises, etc. This argument raises issues which are best avoided here; the principle in contention remains the same, though in one case the divergence is only between 4 percent and 5 percent and in the other case between 4 and 8.5 percent.

[35] Many prominent theorists have repeated this argument. Among examples are the discussions of P. A. Samuelson and W. Vickrey at the *Principles of Efficiency* session, Papers and Proceedings of the 76th Annual Meeting, *American Economic Review*, vol. 54 (May 1964). See also, Robert M. Solow, *Capital Theory and the Rate of Return*, Chicago: Rand-McNally, 1964, pp. 70–1.

[36] Since $P_1 = 1/(1 + r_1)$.

[37] Since $P_{1a} = 1/(1 + r_{1a})$, and $P_{1b} = 1/(1 + r_{1b})$.

[38] This figure is derived as follows. Let x be the scale of return per dollar invested. We seek the averaged discount rate r_1^* such that the present-worth calculations in terms of r_1^* and the averaged returns lead to the same result as the explicit calculation in terms of the state-distributed returns and the corresponding r_{1a} and r_{1b}. We determine r_1^* in the equation: $-1 + 3x/(1 + r_{1a}) + x/(1 + r_{1b}) = -1 + 2x/(1 + r_1^*)$. With $r_{1a} = 150$ percent and $r_{1b} = 66.66$ percent the numerical result in the text is obtained.

[39] Precisely this error is committed in the so-called "basin account" doctrine. This theory, put forward by proponents of certain large river basin plans, maintains that benefit-cost evaluations of component projects should be ignored so long as the overall plan shows a surplus of benefits over costs. Federal legislation has adopted this doctrine for the gigantic Missouri Basin Project. See Report of the President's Water Resources Policy Commission, vol. 2, *Ten Rivers in America's Future*, Washington, 1950, p. 250.

[40] This may have been the assumption made in Arrow's original formulation of the state-preference model. See Arrow, *op cit.*, equation (5).

[41] In an unpublished paper, Kenneth Arrow has employed the somewhat more general assumption of multiple social states, but where the social incomes (endowments) for the several states are *uncorrelated* with the returns from incremental investments in the private states. This also leads to the result that private risks are (on the average) socially irrelevant, and so that market rates of return reflecting private risk aversion should not influence the government's discount rate.

[42] The most important such asset is labor power. Riskiness might deter both a Mr X and a Mr Y from investing to improve their personal labor capacities. Yet, the state-distributions of the returns from the two investments might in combination represent a certainty. This would suggest that Mr X and Mr Y form a partnership, so that each has 50 percent of the certain combination (i.e. each sells the other half his claims). But, it is possible that one or both will work less productively when he only receives 50 percent of the benefit of his personal efforts. This possibility would, therefore, inhibit such trading.

[43] One possible line of simplification is exemplified by the "good year/bad year" dichotomy in H. A. Latané, "Investment Criteria: A Three Asset Portfolio Balance Model," *Review of Economics and Statistics*, vol. 46 (Feb. 1964).

PART II

From Uncertainty Theory to Information Theory

6 The Bayesian Approach to Statistical Decision: An Exposition*

Background and comments

This article differs from all the other essays in the volume since it deals primarily with statistical decision theory. It falls naturally into place here because the Bayesian approach to statistical decision is crucial for the economic analysis of choice under uncertainty, and even more especially for the economics of information. In contrast with the so-called "classical" tradition which employs the long-established, yet ultimately unsatisfactory, tests-of-significance technique, the Bayesian approach permits explicit valuation of the expected costs and benefits of alternative actions. What is perhaps even more important, Bayes's Theorem shows us how to *revise* our probability beliefs in the light of new information. The actions under consideration can be "terminal" ones, where the problem is simply how best to adapt to one's existing state of ignorance, or instead they can be decisions to defer terminal action while setting out to obtain and make use of new evidence. This shift from a passive to an active mode – from simply coping with ignorance to actually taking steps designed to overcome it – corresponds to advancing analytically from the realm of the economics of uncertainty into the more difficult domain of the economics of information.

*This article originally appeared in *Journal of Business of the University of Chicago*, vol. 34 (Oct. 1961), pp. 471–89. The permission of the University of Chicago to reprint in this volume is gratefully acknowledged.

I would like to acknowledge the helpful suggestions and criticisms of Harry V. Roberts, while absolving him of responsibility for the views expressed and the errors remaining in the exposition.

6.1   INTRODUCTION

These notes are intended to serve as a guide to the recent ferment of ideas known generally as "the Bayesian approach" to statistical inference or decision. The discussion will presume some knowledge of the current standard or "classical" approach to the problem of inference as presented in modern elementary statistics textbooks. These new ideas, if accepted generally (and I think they ultimately will win such acceptance), will require a basic change in almost all statistical practice – at least at the relatively unsophisticated levels of "tests of significance" and "confidence-interval estimation." It is interesting that these theoretical developments have evolved in part out of the problems of *business* decision under uncertainty; in fact, Schlaifer's books – the only Bayesian texts currently available – are definitely oriented to the problem of rationalizing such business decisions. Secondarily, this paper may serve as a partial review of these texts.[1] Schlaifer's work cannot, in my opinion, be too highly recommended to the student or practitioner; what he has done, almost single-handedly, is to structure into a set of operational procedures a group of revolutionary ideas which, while subverting the old order of statistical inference, had not given practitioners or consumers of statistics anything to replace the old order with. I hope this exposition will illustrate the power and relevance of Bayesian techniques as developed by Schlaifer.[2] The central ideas underlying these procedures, it should be mentioned, derive primarily from the "subjectivist" or "personalist" probability theories recently expounded and developed by L. J. Savage.[3]

The crux of this statistical revolution is the explicit use of *a priori* information, in the form of a "subjective" probability distribution for the unknown parameter under investigation. The subjective probability distribution describes the decision-maker's state of information or degree of belief as to the several different conceivable values that the unknown parameter may take. The beliefs represented by the *prior* probability distribution are those held by the individual before the phase of the investigation under discussion; these subjective beliefs may, however, be based in part upon previous objective evidence. To cite a simple example, suppose that a certain stake of money rests upon the outcome of a single toss of a coin. My beliefs concerning the unknown parameter of that coin (the true proportion of heads in an infinitely long sequence of tosses) might be approximated in this particular situation somewhat as follows: suppose I think with probability 80 percent the coin is fair, but I assign a 10 percent chance to the true proportion of heads being only 0.4, and another 10 percent chance to the proportion being 0.6. In other words, I think most likely the coin is fair (or so close to fair as to make no difference); I do admit the possibility of some small degree of bias one way or the other, but there is no reason to suspect bias in one direction to be more likely than the other. In this case the use of the prior probability distribution to summarize both my degree of knowledge and my uncertainty has immediate intuitive appeal. The distribution may in turn depend upon my knowledge of the character of the individual supplying the coin (partly "subjective," partly "objective" perhaps), possibly upon my purely subjective personal optimism or pessimism, and perhaps also upon some observations of how the coin behaved on a number of earlier occasions. However formed, the Bayesian approach requires that for rational action I must have a personal state of belief attaching a fractional probability to each possible value of the unknown parameter, prior to acting – this is the prior distribution. The state of belief or knowledge might, of course, not be immediate and explicit in numerical form, but it could in principle be elicited by a suitable controlled experiment testing the individual's choices among various combinations of outcomes and rewards.

The *posterior* probability distribution summarizes the state of knowledge or belief of the individual after making use of the new information gained by sample evidence at the stage of the investigation under discussion. The approach as a whole is called Bayesian because of the crucial role played by Bayes's Theorem in indicating how a specified prior probability distribution, when combined with sample evidence, leads to a unique posterior distribution for the unknown parameter.

The "new" statistical revolution reviewed here follows hard upon the previous "objectivist" revolution, associated primarily with the work of R. A. Fisher, and of Neyman and Pearson, and characterized by the now classical apparatus of "levels of significance" for tests of hypotheses, and "confidence coefficients" for estimates. This "old" revolution eschewed any statements about probability distributions for the unknown parameter, and attempted to arrive at procedures for coming to decisions purely on the basis of the objective evidence, given certain prespecified risks of error that the individual was willing to accept. Without going into polemics in detail here, Bayesians allege that "subjective" considerations – the intensities of prior beliefs and the economic values of making correct or incorrect decisions – enter anyway into the "objectivist" analysis by way of specification of hypotheses and of the tolerated risks of error (or significance levels). The Bayesian procedure makes the subjective elements of the decision problem explicit, bringing them into the light so that they can be carefully examined to insure consistent and logical treatment. In short, it is nonsense to assert that we can come to a decision without using *both* prior knowledge or belief (which may itself incorporate a considerable body of objective evidence previously accumulated, together with judgmental factors) *and* current objective evidence; we will do best to admit this and devise our procedures accordingly.

In fairness to the theorists expounding the "objectivist" approach, it should be mentioned that the recent development of the topic of decision theory forms a natural connection with subjectivist ideas. Indeed, some of the objectionable features of the standard approach as presented in elementary textbooks (e.g. the exclusive concentration in testing situations upon only two more or less arbitrarily selected possible values for the unknown parameter) have at least in part been remedied on the theoretical level – though not to any noticeable extent in practical applications. These notes, therefore, contrast the Bayesian approach with what is almost certainly an exaggerated or caricatured version of modern classical *thinking*, but nevertheless a fairly accurate version of current standard *practice* on the elementary level.

6.2   TESTS OF HYPOTHESES

The classical solution

A situation in which the individual is called upon to decide between two competing hypotheses may well be regarded as the central or standard case exemplifying the modern classical approach. For reasons that will become clear later, in the Bayesian approach a simple point-estimation situation seems more central or standard, but the testing framework is most useful for illustrating the crucial differences between the two approaches. In the classical model, it is supposed that there are two competing hypotheses on which evidence will be brought to bear, the two hypotheses corresponding to a choice between only two actions. (This may be called a two-action situation.) For example, a heavily loaded plane must be granted or refused permission to take off; a lot being inspected by the purchaser must be accepted or rejected; a manufacturing process under investigation must be stopped or permitted to continue. While perhaps there are many possible values for the unknown parameter (many possible "states of the world"), a choice between only two decisions is possible. The classical textbook solution involves finding a decision rule which indicates what decision to take for each possible sample outcome. The decision rule is determined ultimately by stated risks of error, that is, values for the maximum acceptable conditional risks of making the wrong decision in one direction or the other. These conditional risks of error are measured at two specific values for the unknown parameter, one for which the first ("null") action is appropriate and one for which the second ("alternative") action is appropriate. The parameter values at which the measurements are to be taken, and the stated risks of error, are supposed to be somehow determined outside of, and prior to, the statistical analysis proper.

To provide a concrete illustration, we will imagine a sampling inspection situation. The analyst is to decide on the acceptability of a large lot (e.g. of ammunition for the Army) on the basis of the results in testing a small sample for the fraction defective. Here there are only two possible actions – accept or reject the lot – but many possible states of the world, since the unknown parameter (the proportion defective, P, in the lot) can be any of a great number of discrete values between 0 and 1, inclusive. The classical approach is somewhat as follows. Let us suppose that lots of 4 percent defective or less are acceptable, and of more than 4 percent unacceptable. (The specification of the borderline value is presumably based upon economic considerations, though the question is typically left somewhat vague in textbook presentations.) If so, we establish as our null hypothesis, $H_0 : P \leq 0.04$. This is to be tested against the alternative hypothesis, H_A, that $P > 0.04$. (These hypotheses are composite, however. For purposes of making calculations in terms of risks of error, it will later be necessary to specify particular parameter values within each of them.)

We must now decide on a decision rule, which involves selection of sampling method, sample size, and the critical sample outcome which divides those sample results leading to rejection of H_0 from those leading to acceptance. Throughout this analysis, we will consider only the method of simple random sampling (with replacement), and for the present we will assume the sample size n fixed at 50. This leaves only the critical sample value or rejection number, p_r (the proportion of defectives in a sample of 50 which, if attained or exceeded, is to cause rejection of H_0) to be determined. Figure 6.1 shows probabilities of error of two different decision rules – $p_r = 0.04$ (solid curves) and $p_r = 0.10$ (dashed curves) – as a function of different possible values of the unknown parameter P.[4] When $P \leq 0.04$, H_0 is true, so the only way we can err is in getting a sample result leading us to reject H_0. This is a type I error. It will be noted that in this range, the rule $p_r = 0.04$ leads to higher probabilities of error than the rule $p_r = 0.10$ – since, obviously, there is a higher probability of getting

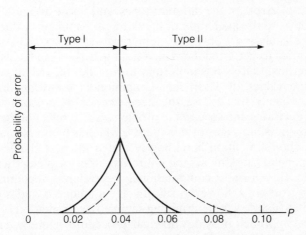

FIGURE 6.1 *Sketch of probability of error for specified decision rule, as a function of unknown parameter, P.*

misleading sample results of 0.04 or more than of 0.10 or more. When $P > 0.04$, H_0 is false, and the only way to err is in failing to reject H_0 (type II error). Here the rule $p_r = 0.10$ leads to greater risks of error, because it is easier to get the misleading sample results below 0.10 than sample results below 0.04.

To arrive at the best decision rule under classical procedures, it is necessary to fix the maximum acceptable risks of type I and type II errors for specific rather than composite null and alternative hypotheses. It is customary, in situations like this one, to fix the "level of significance" α (maximum acceptable risk of type I error) for the borderline value $P = 0.04$, considered as being within H_0; β (maximum acceptable risk of type II error) is to be fixed for some specific value within the composite H_A, but here no clear guide is given in existing presentations. Table 6.1 below shows, for all decision rules with $n = 50$ between the rule $p_r = 0$ (i.e. always reject H_0) and the rule $p_r = 0.12$, the implied α at $P = 0.04$ and the implied β at two arbitrarily selected values within $H_A : P = 0.05$ and $P = 0.06$. With information like that in this table (ordinarily, either β at $P = 0.05$ or β at $P = 0.06$ would be used, not both), the analyst is supposed to be able to select his decision rule on the basis of the acceptability to him of the α and β risks of error. Without going into a detailed analysis, we may add that, if he finds these errors too great, he can reduce all his conditional risks across the board by incurring greater sampling costs – increasing his sample size, or perhaps modifying the method of sampling (going to some form of sequential sampling, for example).

From the Bayesian point of view, this procedure is defective in a number of respects. First of all, the selection of α and β is left completely up in the air, whereas we do know and can put into the analysis at least some of the considerations that should govern the selection of α and β – the economic importance of errors of the different types, and (more arguably) our prior information as to the likelihood of the different parameter values. Second, limiting the analysis to only two numerical values for the states of the world in order to get a unique α and a unique β seems highly arbitrary, even dangerous – surely it is important to consider the risk of error for *all* the possible values of P. In fact, practitioners following the classical analysis are likely to confuse the necessity for a choice between two *actions* or decisions, intrinsic to the problem, with a selection between two of the many possible states of the world – which is by no means the same thing. (We should mention here, however, that the best classical thinking does recommend "looking at" the entire risk of error picture as shown in figure 6.1. But formal computational procedures recommended in elementary textbooks, however, still involve a unique α and a unique β.) Finally, when it comes to determining sample size or method of sampling, the classical approach provides no clear procedure whereby an optimum can be obtained by balancing the costs of sampling against the gains in terms of reduced risks of error.

We may remark that crude applications of classical techniques, especially for observational situations where sample size is fixed by the data available, generally involve deciding whether results do or do not represent "significant" divergences from the borderline value of H_0, measured exclusively in terms of an arbitrarily prespecified α, the levels commonly employed being either 5 percent or 1 percent. Table 6.1 illustrates how such procedures may lead to enormous risks of type II errors. This is not to say that any classical theorists recommend neglecting type II errors in such situations, but only that it remains common practice to do so.

The Bayesian solution

The aim of the Bayesian analysis, like that of the classical analysis, can be regarded as that of establishing the optimal decision rule: selecting sample method and size, and critical or rejection number. The Bayesian analysis makes precise and formal use of the risks of error (diagramed in figure 6.1) of each decision rule considered as a function of the possible values for the unknown parameter (possible states of the world). Usual procedure based on classical methods throws away most of this information, employing only the risks of error for two arbitrarily or, we may say, "subjectively" selected values of the parameter within the composite H_0 and H_A and thus requiring an additional arbitrary or "subjective" expression of choice among the (α, β) combinations available (as tabulated, for example, in table 6.1). The Bayesian method uses all the information in figure 6.1 for each decision rule considered (and recent classical thinking would concur here) – but, in addition, further information is required to calculate the best decision rule according to the Bayesian criterion: *select the decision rule that minimizes the expected loss.*

The first additional element of information needed is the conditional loss function, where loss is to be regarded as the opportunity cost (in the economic sense) of the error. That is to say, for each possible value of the parameter (state of the world) one of the two actions will be preferable. The opportunity loss associated with choosing the preferable action is zero; however, if the inferior action has been chosen, there will be a

TABLE 6.1 *Implied conditional risks of error, α and β, for decision rules with $n = 50$*

p_r	0	0.02	0.04	0.06	0.08	0.10	0.12
α (at $P = 0.04$)	1.0	0.8701	0.5995	0.3233	0.1391	0.0490	0.0144
β (at $P = 0.05$)	0	0.0769	0.2794	0.5405	0.7604	0.8964	0.9622
β (at $P = 0.06$)	0	0.0453	0.1900	0.4162	0.6473	0.8206	0.9224

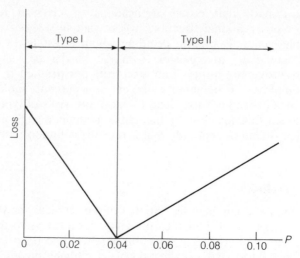

FIGURE 6.2   *Example of a loss function: loss owing to making wrong decision as a function of unknown parameter, P.*

positive opportunity cost or loss as compared with the result had the right decision been made. Figure 6.2 illustrates a conditional loss function for the sampling inspection problem here considered. We may note the following points: (1) The conditional loss function is derived solely from the economics of the problem and is independent of the decision rule considered (though, of course, the probabilities of incurring these losses do depend upon the decision rule). (2) Like the conditional risks of error, the conditional opportunity losses can be divided into type I and type II losses, the former applying over that range of the parameter where the null action or hypothesis is preferable or correct, and the latter where the alternative is correct.[5] (3) The student may think of losses as dollar values, although in certain problems it may be possible or necessary to use another "pay-off" dimension (e.g. bombs on target in a military operations research problem, lives saved in a medical experiment, or utility in the economists' sense). (4) There will typically be some break-even value for the unknown parameter at which we are indifferent between the two actions;[6] in figure 6.2, this value P_b is set at 0.04. (Note that the Bayesian approach makes it clear that this is not an arbitrary selection, but arises from the economics of the problem – our figure asserts that at the value for P of 0.3999, say, the action corresponding to H_0 is preferable; at $P = 0.0401$, the action corresponding to H_A is preferable.) (5) The figure illustrates a situation in which the loss due to making a wrong decision increases as P diverges from P_b. It is worse to incorrectly accept a lot when its fraction defective is, say, $P = 0.14$ than when $P = 0.08$, or to reject incorrectly a good lot with $P = 0.01$ than a somewhat less good lot with $P = 0.03$. (6) The figure shows the loss function as linear in each branch; this is only one of many possibilities.

Proponents of the classical approach would not, perhaps, deny that some such consideration of loss should enter into the determination of the specific values within H_0 and H_A to be employed in calculating α and β, and into the selection of the desired (α, β) combination as well; indeed, some have emphasized the concept of loss. Nevertheless, the classical approach provides no formal procedure for employing this information. However, it is on the next class of information required that the schools of thought crucially diverge; "prior probability" is the shibboleth. The classicists assert that to speak of probabilities for the unknown parameter is incorrect or meaningless (except possibly in certain very special situations). The parameter is not a random variable; any possible value considered for it either is or is not the correct one, and no probabilistic statements can be made. Bayesians reply that prior probabilities are a useful and logically consistent formalization of one's prior state of information about the unknown parameter. Users of the classical approach, if they are at all reasonable, will themselves take account of this information in their decisions. For example, reasonable men will insist on a higher level of significance (smaller α) before rejecting, on the basis of given sample evidence, a null hypothesis representing a strongly held belief as compared with a null hypothesis representing only a weak conjecture. By failing to formalize this information, classical analysts are in danger of making erroneous or inconsistent use of it.

Figure 6.3 illustrates a possible prior probability distribution[7] for the unknown parameter, P.[8] We now have all the information needed to come to a Bayesian solution here, the principle being to select that decision rule minimizing expected loss, where expected loss for a given decision rule $(d.r.)$ is given by the following formula:[9]

$$EL(d.r.) = \sum_P [(\text{probability of error} \mid P)$$

$$\times (\text{loss due to error} \mid P)$$

$$\times (\text{prior probability of } P)]$$

A point of considerable importance here is the assumption that expected values of loss are sufficient to guide decision. If loss is measured in dollars this implies, for example, that the individual in whose interest the analysis is conducted is indifferent between $500 certain, a 50 percent chance of $1,000, a 5 percent chance of $10,000, or a 0.5 percent chance of $100,000. But we would not ordinarily regard, say, a small businessman as unreasonable if he took a loss of $600 certain, or even perhaps $1,000 certain, in the form of an insurance premium on property worth $100,000 where the contingency insured against had a known probability of 0.5

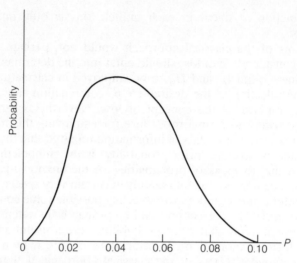

FIGURE 6.3   *Prior probability distribution for P.*

percent. On the other hand, it would seem unreasonable for General Motors to pay much more than the expected value as insurance on the (for it) very moderate loss contingency of $100,000. Such an argument, if accepted, implies that where only "moderate" contingencies of loss are involved, expected values of dollar loss may be at least a roughly satisfactory guide.[10]

Geometrically, the expected loss of a given decision rule could be pictured as the area under a curve showing, for each value of P on the horizontal axis, the product of the vertical heights for that value of P in figure 6.1 (conditional risk of error), figure 6.2 (conditional loss), and figure 6.3 (prior probability). However, the relationships are easier to interpret if we show, against the prior probabilities in figure 6.3, a figure 6.4 representing for each P the product of the vertical heights in figures 6.1 and 6.2. This product of the conditional risk of error and the conditional loss due to error will be called the conditional expected loss.

Figure 6.4 reveals a rather important point: if the true P is near P_b (here $P_b = 0.04$), it does not matter much if we make the wrong decision (the conditional expected loss is small, even though the conditional probability of error is large, because the conditional loss near P_b in figure 6.2 is almost zero). This is to be contrasted with the strong emphasis that the classical approach places upon the risk of error α at the borderline or limiting value of the composite H_0.[11]

It may be useful to students to work out a numerical solution for the example described above. Assuming a sample size of 50 with simple random sampling, the classical approach directs the analyst to choose his

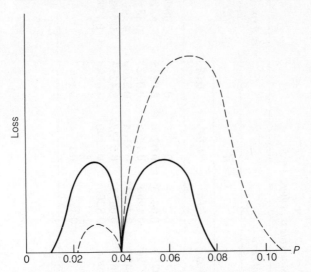

FIGURE 6.4 *Conditional expected loss (conditional probability of error × conditional loss owing to error) for two decision rules.*

decision rule on the basis of only the information contained in table 6.1 – and not all of that, if he is supposed to concentrate his attention upon the α at $P = 0.04$ and the β at some *one* of the values within H_A, where we have provided two values ($P = 0.05$ and 0.06) to choose from. We may also remark that, if a conventional 0.05 level of significance is used, the conditional risk of type II error will be in the neighborhood of 80 percent for $P = 0.06$ (90 percent for $P = 0.05$); if a 0.01 level of significance is used, the conditional risk of type II error for each of these two alternatives is over 90 percent!

While the classical analysis requires a direct intuitive fixing of the determinants of the decision rule, the Bayesian approach builds up a simple and elegant structure for its determination. The information required is summarized in table 6.2. The main body of the table shows, for each decision rule considered, the conditional probability of error for values of the unknown parameter by hundredths from 0 to 0.08 – of type I error for $P \leq 0.04$ and of type II error for $P > 0.04$.[12] This part of the table corresponds to figure 6.1, except that to make the computations easy we will allow only the nine discrete possible values for P shown. This limitation may be interpreted as an approximation – or, alternatively, it may simply be the case that only these discrete values are possible.

On the line below the main body of the table, the conditional losses of the two types of error are shown as a function of P. Since the conditional losses are independent of the decision rule, one line suffices to show them. This line corresponds to figure 6.2. The actual numbers are derived from

TABLE 6.2 *Bayesian computation to find best decision rule p_r, where $n = 50$*

| | Conditional probabilities of error | | | | | | | | | Expected loss (EL) |
| | Type I | | | | | Type II | | | | |
P	0	0.01	0.02	0.03	0.04	0.05	0.06	0.07	0.08	
$p_r = 0$	1.0	1.0	1.0	1.0	1.0	0	0	0	0	2.0000
0.02	0	0.3950	0.6358	0.7819	0.8701	0.0769	0.0453	0.0266	0.0155	0.6826
0.04	0	0.0894	0.2642	0.4447	0.5995	0.2794	0.1900	0.1265	0.0827	0.3852[1]
0.06	0	0.0138	0.0784	0.1892	0.3233	0.5405	0.4162	0.3108	0.2260	0.3984
0.08	0	0.0016	0.0178	0.0628	0.1391	0.7604	0.6473	0.5327	0.4253	0.5561
0.10	0	0.0001	0.0032	0.0168	0.0490	0.8964	0.8206	0.7290	0.6290	0.7288
Conditional loss	8	6	4	2	0	1	2	3	4	
Prior probabiiity	0.1	0.1	0.1	0.2	0.2	0.1	0.1	0.1	0.1	

[1] Minimum *EL*. (See discussion of table in text.)

the following expressions, where $L(R, p)$ is the conditional loss of rejecting as a function of P and $L(A, P)$ is the conditional loss of accepting as a function of P:

(Type I)

$$L(R, P) = \begin{cases} 0, \text{ for } P \geqq 0.04 \\ 200(0.04 - P), \text{ for } P < 0.04 \end{cases}$$

(Type II)

$$L(A, P) = \begin{cases} 0, \text{ for } P \leqq 0.04 \\ 100(P - 0.04), \text{ for } P > 0.04 \end{cases}$$

The bottom line shows the prior probabilities $Pr_0(P)$. This line corresponds to figure 6.3; however, for simplicity of computation, the probabilities in the table are assumed to be uniform over the discrete values of P from 0 to 0.08, except for a bulge at $P = 0.04$.

Finally, the right-hand column of table 6.2 shows the expected loss EL for each decision rule considered. The best decision rule is that for which EL attains its minimum: 0.3852 for the rule $p_r = 0.04$. As can be seen in table 6.2 (or table 6.1), this is equivalent to selecting an α of 0.5995, and a β of 0.2794 measuring at $P = 0.05$ or of 0.1900 measuring at $P = 0.06$ – values for α and β that unaided intuition would hardly be likely to hit upon using the classical approach.

Using this decision rule, we see that the sample result $p = 0.04$, for example, would lead to rejection of the null hypothesis, corresponding to rejection of the lot. This may seem surprising, since a population $P = 0.04$ would represent a (borderline) satisfactory lot. The explanation for the decision is that while, in this case, the prior probability distribution of table 6.2 is symmetrical about $P = 0.04$, the loss function in table 6.2 (see also figure 6.2) is not. Type I losses rise more rapidly than type II losses, thus making us more willing to commit type II errors than comparable type I errors – speaking loosely, more inclined to reject the null hypothesis than to accept it.

Throughout this analysis we have assumed the sampling method and sample size n fixed, so choice of a decision rule amounted to a choice of p_r. We will only comment briefly on the consequences of changing n. It is immediately clear that n affects only the conditional risks of error (fig. 6.1) which enter into both the classical and Bayesian procedures – figure 6.2 and 6.3 are unaffected. The selection of the sample size under the Bayesian approach follows directly from the basic principle of minimizing expected loss. In choosing the best decision rule for a given n, the minimum expected loss for that n, which we may denote EL^*, was determined. In principle, there is no difficulty finding EL^* for any n. It is necessary to establish whether an increase in n is justified, which will depend upon whether the reduction in expected loss achieved by the change in n is in excess of the additional sampling cost. The same principle applies to the choice of sampling method.

6.3 BAYES'S THEOREM AND THE GENERAL ESTIMATION PROBLEM

The classical approach to estimation

As has already been mentioned, under the Bayesian approach the point-estimation problem, or rather the analogue of what is called the point-estimation problem under the classical approach, can be regarded as the central or model circumstance for analysis. In Bayesian terminology, the problem is transmuted from the classical one of finding a single *best estimate* value for the unknown parameter to the more concrete or operational question of finding the *best action* to take in a many-action situation. (Different possible values of the parameter are interesting only insofar as different actions would then be optimal.) From this point of view, the two-action (testing) situation becomes a special case.

It is widely conceded that, under the classical approach, the problem of point estimation is in an unsatisfactory state. The traditional method has been to select estimators (functions of the sample data) for parameters on the basis of more or less arbitrary appealing characteristics: unbiasedness, consistency, and efficiency are the most familiar.[13] The difficulty is that the different criteria frequently indicate differing estimators for the same parameter, in which case we are left quite at sea. And even where all the criteria agree, we may still have doubts as to whether, for some purposes at least, another estimator might be superior.

In view of these difficulties, the classical approach has tended to emphasize confidence interval as opposed to point estimation. Textbooks will frequently have remarks to the effect that point estimates in themselves have little value and that what is useful is some assertion as to an interval which includes the parameter value, together with the "confidence" with which the assertion is made.

"Confidence" in the classical sense is not a probability of the assertion being correct (under classical principles, it either *is* or *is not* correct), but rather the probability that the interval-determining procedure will lead to correct results. We will not here go into the procedure itself, but will remark instead that it really represents an adaptation of the testing framework to an estimation situation. Thus it can be shown, for example, that a central interval of values for an unknown parameter based on given sample evidence and asserted with confidence $(1 - \gamma)$ – that is, excluding $\gamma/2$ probability on either tail – is equivalent to specifying a range of specific values for the null hypothesis that have the following property:

each such specific H_0 would not be rejected on the basis of the given sample evidence using a two-tailed significance level of γ (more specifically, if the rejection region for each such H_0 contained $\gamma/2$ probability on each tail).

The trouble with this, from the Bayesian point of view, is that if we have a many-action problem we usually *do* want a point estimate[14] to answer the question of which specific act of the many possible is the best to undertake. Assertions about intervals merely exclude certain extreme possibilities, without giving definite answers. Furthermore, if such assertions are made solely on the basis of the sample evidence with no consideration of economic loss or (again more arguably) prior belief, we may be led into serious error. It is not at all difficult to construct loss functions that make the usual method of conifdence-interval estimation very dubious: for example, suppose that losses owing to errors in one direction are much more serious than those owing to errors in the other direction. Also, most people would probably be unwilling to act on a confidence-interval assertion based on limited simple evidence if that evidence happened to be in conflict with strongly held views, acquired perhaps over a lifetime of experience. Their behavior in such cases cannot simply be dismissed as unreasonable. A partial classical reply could be made to the effect that such considerations indicate employing low values of $(1 - \gamma)$ in drawing inferences, and possibly establishing asymmetrical and/or non-central confidence intervals. But even waiving the objection about the need for a definite answer, the selection of the type of interval and of $(1 - \gamma)$ would then again require a kind of "subjective" judgment about loss due to error and about the weight of prior information that had best be made explicit.

Point estimation and Bayes's Theorem

For the reasons indicated, the Bayesian approach seems to indicate de-emphasizing confidence-interval estimation. Instead the problem is to select the best specific act (point estimate) of the many actions possible. The essential principle remains unchanged: choose that act which minimizes the expected loss.

In general, there may be as many actions as states of the world (values of the unknown parameter), or fewer. If there are just as many, there is a one-to-one correspondence between parameter value and action. If there are fewer, there must be a range of parameter values which call for the same action. At the minimum, the choices reduce down to those of the two-action problem.

As an intuitively appealing illustration of a many-action problem, it is helpful to think of a warehouse in which inventory must be stocked in advance to meet demand in a given time period. The quantity that will be demanded is the unknown parameter. Each possible quantity that might be stocked (the possible quantities might be continuous, like lengths of wire, or discontinuous, like number of replacement motors of a given type) is an action. We can have fewer actions than states of the world if, for example, warehouse size sets an upper limit upon the quantity we can stock. The loss function may be described in terms of the costs of understocking and overstocking, each of which might or might not be a function of the true parameter (it might possibly involve less loss to understock by two units when 100 are demanded than to understock by two when only ten are demanded). The only additional information needed to choose an action is the "subjective" probability distribution – the prior distribution before taking sample evidence, or the posterior distribution after doing so.

For parallelism with the testing discussion, however, we will continue to use, though adding some rather artifical simplifications, a sampling inspection framework. Here it will be assumed that there are only four possible states of the world (allowable values for P), with the prior probabilities $Pr(P)$ indicated in table 6.3. The prior probabilities here shown might really represent our beliefs about the true state of the world. If so, they indicate that any values for P other than those shown are believed to be impossible. An alternative interpretation is that this tabulation might be a quick four-point approximation of a much more detailed probability distribution for the unknown parameter. While such approximations may be of great practical usefulness in problem-solving, we will adopt the interpretation that the prior probabilities shown literally represent beliefs.

Table 6.4 shows how expected losses are calculated for each of the possible actions. The case illustrated in table 6.4 is a rather special one in the following ways. It is assumed that there are four possible actions, each appropriate for one of the four possible states of the world. We will symbolize the expression "act as if P were known to be 0.10" as "$A = 0.10$." Table 6.4 has been constructed employing a very simple loss function: the cost of error is assumed to be $1.00 per 0.01 divergence, direction being immaterial, between the true state of the world and the action or estimate. Symbolically, $L(A, P) = 100 |A - P|$, the vertical lines

TABLE 6.3 *Prior probability dis-*
tribution

Fraction defective (P)	*Prior probability (Pr[P])*
0.02	0.7
0.04	0.1
0.06	0.1
0.10	0.1

TABLE 6.4 *Conditional losses and calculation of expected loss using prior probability – before sampling (one-to-one correspondence between actions A and states of world P)*

Action	Conditional losses (dollars)				Expected loss (EL)
Prior probability State of world	0.7 $P=0.02$	0.1 $P=0.04$	0.1 $P=0.06$	0.1 $P=0.10$	
$A=0.02$	0	2	4	8	1.4[1]
0.04	2	0	2	6	2.2
0.06	4	2	0	4	3.4
0.10	8	6	4	0	6.6

[1] Minimum *EL*.

indicating absolute value. Making use of the losses there tabulated, and the (prior) probabilities shown across the top, we see that expected loss is minimal for $A = 0.02$, and we would act accordingly. Note that we do not say: "We *estimate* that P equals 0.02." Different loss functions would lead to different best actions ("estimates" in classical terminology); for example, if the loss function makes the cost of error equal to the square in dollars of the number of hundredths divergence, $A = 0.06$ is the best action. The loss function could also be made to weigh differently overestimates and under-estimates of P.

Let us now depart from the special assumption that there is a one-to-one correspondence between action and state of the world. In particular, let us suppose that the action denoted as $A = 0.10$ is inadmissible, so that the action denoted $A = 0.06$ becomes the best available if P were in fact 0.10. It is tempting to think that we can still use table 6.4, only now deleting the line corresponding to the inadmissible action $A = 0.10$; unfortunately, that would be quite erroneous.[15] The reason is that the loss function we are dealing with is supposed to represent *opportunity cost* in the economists' sense – that is, the loss due to inappropriate action as compared with the best action available. It follows that, if we delete the bottom line of table 6.4 corresponding to $A = 0.10$, we must now correct the conditional loss column for $P = 0.10$ to show losses in comparison with the best action remaining available (the one previously denoted $A = 0.06$). Once the one-to-one correspondence between action and state of the world is lost, it may possibly be misleading to name actions after corresponding states of the world. In table 6.5, therefore, the actions are named more abstractly by the symbols a_1, a_2, a_3. The one-to-one correspondence between action and state of world does, however, constitute a kind of ideal case; the loss function resulting from the inadmissibility of certain actions (fewer actions than states of the world) can easily be

TABLE 6.5 *Revised conditional losses and calculation of expected loss before sampling (no one-to-one correspondence between actions and states of world)*

Action	Conditional losses				Expected loss (EL)
Prior probability	0.7	0.1	0.1	0.1	
State of world	$P=0.02$	$P=0.04$	$P=0.06$	$P=0.10$	
α_1	0	2	4	4	1.0[1]
α_2	2	0	2	2	1.8
α_3	4	2	0	0	3.0

[1] Minimum EL.

derived by introducing the opportunity-cost idea. The crucial thing to remember is that, *for each state of the world*, the best admissible action is assigned zero loss and serves as the standard of comparison for the other actions. In short, the loss table is filled in vertically, not horizontally – measuring from the best action for each state of the world, not the best state of the world for each action. Comparing tables 6.4 and 6.5, we see that the three remaining actions each have less expected loss than before; roughly speaking, by limiting the range of admissible actions we have reduced the possible loss owing to inappropriate action, inappropriateness being measured by loss in comparison with the best action remaining available.

We now turn to the question of how sample evidence is used to transform prior probabilities to posterior probabilities. This is done with Bayes's Theorem which, given as inputs the prior probabilities for the parameter and the conditional probabilities of the sample result, logically determines what the posterior probabilities must be. Bayes's Theorem is not a particularly new discovery,[16] but until the refusal to admit the idea of a probability distribution for the unknown parameter is overcome the theorem cannot play any important role in statistical inference.

We will use the theorem in the following form, where $Pr(S_i \mid E)$ indicates the desired (posterior) probability of a particular state of world S_i being true (the probability that the unknown parameter has a certain particular value), given the sample evidence E.

$$Pr(S_i \mid E) = \frac{Pr(S_i \text{ and } E)}{Pr(E)} = \frac{Pr(S_i) \times Pr(E \mid S_i)}{\sum_j Pr(S_j) \times Pr(E \mid S_j)}$$

The first equality is the usual definition of a conditional probability as equal to the joint probability of the event and the condition (here $Pr[S_i$ and

E]) divided by the probability of the condition (here $Pr[E]$). Turning to the next equality, in the numerator the joint probability is decomposed, following a basic law of elementary probability, into the probability of S_i times the probability of the evidence E on the condition S_i. In the denominator, the unconditional (prior) probability of the evidence $Pr(E)$ has been broken up into the sum of the joint probabilities of E with every possible distinct state of the world S_j (this step is not explicitly shown),[17] and then each such joint probability has been decomposed in the same fashion as the numerator. The desired posterior probability $Pr(S_i | E)$ has now been expressed as a function of the prior probabilities $Pr(S_j)$ for the unknown parameter and the calculable conditional probabilities of the observed evidence for each such S_j.

Suppose that, in the one-to-one correspondence example discussed above, we have taken a sample of 50 and observed four defectives. Then table 6.6 illustrates the calculation of the posterior probabilities. The final decision is arrived at by going back to the conditional loss function of table 6.4, but now employing the *posterior* instead of the *prior* probabilities in weighing the conditional losses to find the expected loss. For our example the result of this calculation is summarized in table 6.7.

Note that our evidence, an observed sample with 8 percent defectives, has rather drastically shifted the subjective probabilities from their original heavy weight at the extreme low end of values for P to a less asymmetrical distribution with the bulk of the weight toward the high end. The best action has shifted correspondingly from $A = 0.02$ to $A = 0.06$. The student may be somewhat puzzled, however, by the fact that our expected loss for the best action has *increased*, from 1.4 using the prior probabilities to about

TABLE 6.6 *Bayes's Theorem calculation of posterior probabilities, sample result of four defectives in 50*

Fraction defective (P)	Prior probability $(Pr_0[P])$	Conditional probability $(Pr[E \mid P])$	Joint probability $(Pr[P$ and $E])$	Posterior probability $Pr(P$ and $E)$ $\dfrac{}{\sum\limits_{P} [Pr(P$ and $E)]}$
0.02	0.7	0.0146	0.0102	0.1868
0.04	0.1	0.0901	0.0090	0.1650
0.06	0.1	0.1733	0.0173	0.3169
0.10	0.1	0.1809	0.0181	0.3314
	1.0		0.0546	1.0

TABLE 6.7 *Expected losses in terms of posterior probabilities, after sample result of four defectives in 50*

Action (A)	Expected loss (EL)
0.02	4.2488
0.04	2.9958
0.06	2.4028[1]
0.10	3.7520

[1] Minimum *EL*.

2.4 using the posterior probabilities. That this must be correct, however, is evident from the following considerations. The prior probability distribution represented a rather confident belief that P lay at or near 0.02. Consequently, the zero conditional loss of the action $A = 0.02$ when $P = 0.02$ (note in table 6.4 that whenever A and P correspond, $L[A, P] = 0$) received the bulk (70 percent) of the probability weight. But our assumed sample result of four defectives in 50 was rather sharply at variance with these prior beliefs. Consequently, the posterior distribution, which represents a kind of compromise between prior beliefs and sample evidence, was somewhat closer to the uniform distribution which represents in a crude way what might be called "complete ignorance." In short, since we were highly confident *a priori*, our expected loss due to wrong action in the fact of uncertainty was small. *A posteriori*, we have less confidence or are "more ignorant" than before, in that our supposed previous knowledge now seems dubious; therefore, we now expect greater losses due to uncertainty.

The student may possibly be wondering at this point whether there is in general a gain of sampling over non-sampling, or of larger samples over smaller samples in view of this possibility that sampling may increase the expected loss. Intuition tells us that, as we increase sample size, expected loss should decrease – and the *expected value* of the expected loss after sampling does decrease. A particular sample result may lead to an increase of expected loss, but if we take *all possible* sample results and weigh these by their prior probabilities, expected loss on the average will decline. For brevity, we will say that *expected terminal loss*, $ETL(n)$ decreases as a function of sample size n (and, in particular, decreases when we go from a no-sampling situation, with $n = 0$, to some positive n).

I will not attempt to prove in general that expected terminal loss declines as a function of n. Instead, the simplest case will be worked out – a comparison of expected terminal loss before sampling, or $ETL(0)$, with expected terminal loss for $n = 1$, or $ETL(1)$. Table 6.8 illustrates the calculation of posterior probabilities for the two possible sample results, zero defective or one defective in the sample. We may remark that the more surprising sample result, one defective, creates a greater shift in the probability distribution that the less surprising result, which is what we would anticipate.

Table 6.9 shows us the expected loss for each action. Note that the less surprising result leaves the best action unchanged, while the sample of one showing a defective leads to a shift to an action corresponding to a higher estimated P.

Finally, the calculation of expected terminal loss is shown in table 6.10. Since, obviously, $ETL(0)$ is the same as the expected loss of the best action before sampling, the expected gain from sampling is the difference between 1.4 and 1.3883, or 0.0117.

It may be useful to remind the reader that the expression for the prior probability of the sample result or the evidence, $Pr_0(E)$, was developed in the course of explaining Bayes's Theorem: it is the sum of the joint probabilities of the observed evidence with each possible state of the world, or value of P. The numbers actually used came out of the calculation in table 6.8.

After this discussion, the student will have no difficulty seeing how the question of optimal sample size is determined in principle. If we are considering a sample of any given size, say 50, we must calculate for it the expected terminal loss $ETL(50)$. This amounts to considering separately each of the 51 different possible sample results, from zero defectives to 50 defectives, in tables like table 6.9 and table 6.10. While in general the computations may seem rather fierce, it may not be very difficult (especially, in two-action problems) to compare the incremental improvement in ETL with the incremental sampling cost. The optimal sample size, of course, is found by balancing reduction in expected terminal loss as n increases against increased cost of sampling – an increase in n is justified so long as, and only so long as, the reduction in ETL exceeds the increase in sampling cost.

We may summarize these considerations in the following simple formulas: $EVI(n) = ETL(0) - ETL(n)$. That is, the expected value of the information gained in taking a sample of size n is the expected loss without sampling minus the expected loss after drawing a sample of n. Second,

$$ETL(n) = \sum_i [EL^*(n, E_i) \times Pr(E_i)].$$

This says that the expected terminal loss associated with a sample size of n is the weighted sum of the resultant expected losses from the best action under each possible sample result E_i, the weights being the prior probabilities of the different sample results.

TABLE 6.8 Calculation of posterior probabilities for two sample outcomes (n = 1)

Parameter (P)	Prior probability $(Pr_0[P])$	One defective			Zero defective		
		Conditional probability	Joint probability	Posterior probability	Conditional probability	Joint probability	Posterior probability
0.02	0.7	0.02	0.014	0.4118	0.98	0.686	0.7101
0.04	0.1	0.04	0.004	0.1176	0.96	0.096	0.0994
0.06	0.1	0.06	0.006	0.1764	0.94	0.094	0.0973
0.10	0.1	0.10	0.010	0.2942	0.90	0.090	0.0932
	1.0		0.034	1.0		0.996	1.0

TABLE 6.9 *Expected loss of actions*

Action (A)	EL (n = 0)	EL (n = 1) One defective	EL (n = 1) Zero defective
0.02	1.4[a]	3.2944	1.3336[a]
0.04	2.2	2.9416[a]	2.1740
0.06	3.4	3.0592	3.4120
0.10	6.6	4.7056	6.6664

[a] Minimum *EL*.

TABLE 6.10 *Calculation of expected terminal loss (n = 1)*

Sample result (E)	Expected loss of best action (EL*)	Prior probability of sample (Pr₀[E])	Expected terminal loss
0	1.3336	0.966	1.2883
1	2.9416	0.034	0.1000
			1.3883

6.4 CONCLUDING REMARKS

I must regretfully admit that this summary article has not succeeded in giving the reader an adequate appreciation of the richness, relevance, and power of the Bayesian techniques in general. I have alluded scarcely, or not at all, to such topics as: the fruitful simplifications made possible by assuming particular prior distributions (e.g. normal) for the unknown parameter; the integration of the problems of selection of sample method (e.g. single, multiple, sequential), sample size, and best action into a common format of economic choice in terms of value of information and sampling cost; and the handling of sample bias due to such sources as measurement error and imperfect randomization.

What I have tried to convey, however, is the ease and simplicity with which the new approach solves those dual fundamental weaknesses of the classical position – what "criteria" to use in estimation (many-action) problems, and how to specify the tolerable risks of error in testing (two-action) problems. In each case, the solution falls naturally into place once we incorporate the two essential ideas of the new approach: (1) explicit and systematic use of the economic concept of opportunity cost to evaluate the worth of actions in comparison with the best possible action for the given states of the world, and (2) use of subjective probabilities to assign weights to the different possible states of the world, thus permitting determination of a definite best procedure for any situation.

Let me conclude, finally, by raising the question whether, having adopted this approach, we can regard statistics as reduced to a special branch of economics – namely, the economics of search for information – or is it economics that can now be regarded as a special branch of statistics, regarding the latter broadly as the logic of rational decision in general and the former as the logic of choice where information is given.

NOTES

[1] The original book is Robert Schlaifer, *Probability and Statistics for Business Decisions*, New York: McGraw-Hill Book Co., 1959. A somewhat condensed and simplified verison, more suitable for an elementary text, has since been published under the title *Introduction to Statistics for Business Decisions* (1961). A more advanced work, *Applied Statistical Decision Theory*, by Howard Raiffa and Robert Schlaifer, Boston: Division of Research, Harvard Business School, 1961, has recently appeared, but was unavailable to me during the period when this paper was prepared.

[2] The reader will also benefit from the article by Harry V. Roberts, "The New Business Statistics," *Journal of Business*, vol. 33 (Jan. 1960). Roberts' primary interest is in a critical evaluation of Schlaifer's contribution as an outgrowth and further development of the line of ideas known as "statistical decision theory"; the present article supplements Roberts' presentation with a fuller description and exposition of Bayesian techniques and their underlying logic. After drafting this manuscript, I learned of the (very) brief expository article by F. J. Anscombe, "Bayesian Statistics," *American Statistician*, vol. 25 (Feb. 1961), which the interested student will also profit from perusing.

[3] L. J. Savage, *The Foundations of Statistics*, New York: John Wiley & Sons, 1954. The book by I. J. Good, *Probability and the Weighing of Evidence*, London, 1950, should also be cited in this connection.

[4] Since the population is finite for this problem, the continuous curves drawn represent only an approximation. The true picture would show the probabilities of error as vertical bars for each discrete possible value of P. It will be noted that the risks of both kinds of error (for each decision rule) approach their maxima as P nears. 0.04.

[5] It is possible to dispense entirely with the terminology of null *versus* alternative hypotheses in the Bayesian approach; even using the classical approach, the distinction is not essential (some authors avoid it). In the classical approach, the distinction seems to apply only in selecting the specific values within the composite hypotheses at which to calculate α and β. Thus, we have seen that with H_0 defined as $P \leq 0.04$, α was calculated at the borderline value of $P = 0.04$ – while with H_A defined as $P > 0.04$, β was calculated for some P well within

this latter composite. This is the only departure from symmetry of treatment of the hypotheses in the classical method – and the Bayesian is completely symmetrical. It may be convenient to retain the term "null hypothesis," however, since statistical problems often appear as a choice between taking or not taking some positive action. For example, in a statistical quality control situation, the null hypothesis would be that the process is satisfactory so that no action is required – and the alternative hypothesis that something has gone wrong so that the process must be halted and inspected. An alternative interpretation is that the "null hypothesis" corresponds to the more conservative action – the decision which, if wrong, will have less drastic consequences than the other, if *it* should be wrong. On this interpretation, if the question arises of permitting a heavily loaded aircraft to take off, the null hypothesis would be that the plane *is* over-loaded – presumably, the risk of crashing is more drastic than the economic cost of underloading an aircraft. I depart from Schlaifer in preferring the "no-action" interpretation of null hypothesis to the "drastic-consequences" interpretation – the latter is difficult to define rigorously or to tie in with Bayesian ideas.

[6] This may not be strictly true when, as in this case, there are only a discrete number of possible states of the world. Thus, supposing that the lot size is 10,000, only values for P like 0.0399, 0.0400, 0.0401, etc., are possible; then it may be true that none of the possible values for P is the break-even value, one action being perhaps slightly but definitely preferable at $P = 0.0400$, and the other at 0.0401.

[7] The probability distribution shown is continuous although, as is also true for figures 6.1 and 6.2, the finiteness of the population size strictly calls for a discrete representation.

[8] Students who have had the notion of "subjective" probability drilled out of them often have difficulty recapturing this rather simple and direct idea. As mentioned above, such a distribution (whether prior or posterior) represents as of that moment a formal and consistent structuring of the individual's beliefs about the unknown value of the parameter. To cite but one example, suppose the unknown parameter is a binomial proportion P of successes in a certain popula-tion. Supposing that P may take any value in the continuum between 0 and 1 (population size is infinite), a particular individual might feel that he knows for certain that $0.001 \leq P \leq 0.010$, but that within this range no confidence of any kind in any value or any set of values over any others. This implies a uniform subjective probability distribution with the limits specified. Another individual might perhaps assign only 50 percent of probability to this range, 10 percent probability to the range below 0.001, and 40 percent probability to the range above 0.010; furthermore, within each subrange he may feel that some values are more likely than others. Operationally, we may imagine these subjective probabilities as being measured by the choices an individual makes when faced with certain betting options. Thus, offered a choice between a ticket guarantee-ing $100 if a coin of unknown properties turns up heads and a corresponding ticket for tails, most reasonable people would have no basis for choice – implying that 50 percent probability is attached to tails and 50 percent to heads, although the coin is not known to be "fair."

A point that sometimes bothers students is that the probability distribution for the unknown parameter expresses beliefs, but says nothing explicitly about the strength with which the beliefs are held. This is a mistake, however – the strength or confidence of beliefs that the parameter will take on particular values is precisely expressed by the probability distribution. In the example above, the individual who placed 100 percent probability on the parameter P being within the interval from 0.001 to 0.010 obviously has stronger or more confident beliefs about P than the individual who could attach only 50 percent probability to P falling within this same range.

[9] This formula is strictly appropriate only for a discrete number of possible states of the world (values of the unknown parameter P). The following verbal statement of the formula may be helpful. The expected loss for any specified decision rule, EL $(d.r.)$, is equal to the sum of a number of terms – one for each possible value, P, of the parameter – where each such term is the product of (1) the probability of error, given that P is the true parameter value, (2) the loss due to error, again given that P is the true value, and (3) the prior probability attached to P being the true value.

[10] A theoretically more satisfactory solution involves the substitution of a utility dimension for dollars in measuring pay-off or loss. It has recently been demonstrated that, if certain very reasonable postulates are accepted, it is rational for individuals to calculate solely in terms of expected values of utility. More precisely, it is rational for the individual to act as if (1) he attaches a number, called a utility, to each possible (dollar) outcome, and (2) in choosing between probabilistic alternatives, he selects that one for which the expected value of utility is the higher. For full discussion and citations, see Harry M. Markowitz, *Portfolio Selection* ("Cowles Foundation Monograph," no. 16 [New York: John Wiley & Sons, 1959]), pp. 205–42. Schlaifer outlines procedures, based on expected utility, to be used in those cases where expected value of loss is not a reliable guide.

[11] The Bayesian break-even value P_b would, most likely, be the limiting value of H_0 for a classical analyst, although perhaps there might be some question on this point. The reason for identifying the two is that, to use our example, the classical approach speaks of a type I "error" being committed if H_0 is rejected when $P \leqq 0.04$, implying that H_0 is the "correct" hypothesis or action in such cases, and that H_A is "correct" for $P > 0.04$. If the "correct" action is interpreted in a commonsense way as the choice involving smaller loss, the classical division between the composite H_0 and H_A corresponds to the Bayesian division between that range of P for which one action is preferable (has less expected loss) and that for which the other is preferable. This makes P_b equivalent to the limiting value of H_0.

[12] It is immaterial how we treat the specific value $P = 0.04$, i.e., whether we consider it to be part of H_0 or of H_A. Since 0.04 is the break-even value P_b, the conditional loss of either decision under it is zero, so that whichever risk of error we consider will be canceled out when we multiply by the loss.

[13] These concepts, which we will not attempt to describe here, all refer to differing aspects of the sampling distribution of the estimator function with respect to the parameter value.

[14] As indicated above, it is not really a point *estimate* that a Bayesian seeks but a best *action*, which under the Bayesian criterion of minimizing expected loss will depend upon the entire subjective probability distribution for the parameter. The Bayesian should not say "I estimate that the parameter has this specified value," but rather "The expected loss will be minimized if I act as I would if I

knew for certain that the parameter has this value." In general, there will be such a unique certainty-equivalent only when there is a one-to-one correspondence between actions and states of the world (see below).

[15] I must confess to having committed this error in an earlier version of these notes that received considerable private circulation.

[16] Thomas Bayes, "An Essay toward Solving a Problem in the Doctrine of Chances," *Philosophical Transactions*, vol. 53 (1763).

[17] If there are k possible distinct states of the world S_j, then $Pr(E) = Pr(E$ and $S_1) + Pr(E$ and $S_2) + Pr(E$ and $S_3) + \ldots + Pr(E$ and $S_k)$.

7 The Analytics of Uncertainty and Information: An Expository Survey*

with John G. Riley

Background and comments

This article was co-authored with my colleague, John G. Riley, who has kindly consented to its being reprinted in this volume. It was commissioned for publication in *Journal of Economic Literature* as a broad survey of the economics of uncertainty and information.

The basic development of the economics of uncertainty ("passive" adaptation to one's initial condition of ignorance) makes use of the state-preference approach covered in chapters 4 and 5. And in the extension to the realm of the economics of information ("active" adaptation that aims at overcoming ignorance), Bayes's Theorem as discussed in chapter 6 plays a crucial role in allowing a systematic treatment of the value of new evidence.

*This article appeared in *Journal of Economic Literature*, vol. 17, (Dec. 1979), pp. 1375–421. The permission of the American Economic Association and of my co-author, John G. Riley, to reprint in this volume is gratefully acknowledged.

Among the very large number of people who provided comments and suggestions, we would like to thank most especially Fritz Machlup, Robert A. Jones, Mark Perlman, and Richard J. Zeckhauser. Hirshleifer's work on this paper was supported in part by National Science Foundation grant No. SOC75-15697 and by a grant from the Foundation of Research in Economics and Education. Riley's work was supported in part by National Science Foundation grant No. SOC79-07573.

That human endeavors are constrained by our limited and uncertain knowledge of the world has always been recognized by leading economic thinkers, far too numerous to be cited here. (An extended historical bibliography is contained in a forthcoming treatise by Fritz Machlup [1979].) But despite this longstanding *recognition*, until relatively recently there was no rigorous foundation for the *analysis* of individual decision-making and market equilibrium under uncertainty. This foundation lacking, the standard analytical models of our textbooks (typified by the familiar apparatus of supply and demand) made no explicit provision for uncertainty. It is not surprising, therefore, that the world of affairs often found academic economics to be of little operational value.

Recent explosive progress in the economics of uncertainty has changed this picture. The subject now flourishes not only in economics departments, but in professional schools and programs oriented toward business, government and administration, and public policy. In the world of commerce, stockmarket analysts now regularly report measures of share-price uncertainty devised by economic theorists. Even in government and the law, formal analysis of uncertainty is beginning to appear in dealing with such problems as safety and health, allowable return on investment, and income distribution. And academic economists, armed with the new developments in the economics of uncertainty, are much more successfully analyzing previously intractable phenomena such as insurance, research and invention, advertising, speculation, and the functioning of financial markets.

It will be impossible to provide any adequate review here of all the important developments under the headings of uncertainty and information. What we hope to do is to expound the central underlying ideas in non-technical fashion; to introduce the novel tools of analysis that have proved fruitful in this area; and to go somewhat more deeply into selected applications in order to convey some impression of the potential richness and power of the theory. Wherever possible, we will provide citations to major branches of the literature that we have been unable to survey here.

The theoretical developments that have brought about this intellectual revolution have two main foundation stones: (1) the theory of preference for uncertain contingencies and in particular the "expected-utility theorem" of John von Neumann and Oskar Morgenstern (1944), and (2) the formulation of the ultimate goods or objects of choice in an uncertain universe as *contingent* consumption claims: entitlements to particular commodities or commodity baskets valid only under specified "states of the world" (more briefly, "states") (Arrow, 1953, 1964; Debreu, 1959). Just as intertemporal analysis requires subscripting commodity claims *by date*, uncertainty analysis requires subscripting commodity claims *by state*. Among objects of choice so defined, as we shall see, production and exchange and consumption all take on recognizable forms as generalizations of the corresponding processes in the familiar world of certainty.

An alternative conceptualization of the objects of choice under uncertainty runs in terms of the *statistical parameters* of the probability distributions of commodity or income claims. In that formulation it is assumed that individuals prefer greater *mean* income but smaller *variance* of income; attention may or may not be paid to higher moments of the distribution (Markowitz, 1959). It has been shown that the more general "state-preference" representation of the objects of choice under uncertainty can be reduced to such a "parameter-preference" representation by making a number of specializing assumptions (Tobin, 1958; Borch, 1968; Feldstein, 1969). In the particularly simple form of choice between mean return and variance of return on investment, the parameter-preference model has provided the basis for important modern developments in the theory of finance (Markowitz, 1959; Sharpe, 1964; Lintner, 1965; Mossin, 1966). We will not be able to pursue the parameter-preference approach here; for recent surveys see Jensen (1972) and Merton (1988).

The modern analytical literature on uncertainty and information divides into two rather distinct branches. The first branch deals with *market uncertainty*. Each individual is supposed to be fully certain about his own endowment and productive opportunities; what he is unsure about are the supply-demand offers of other economic agents. In consequence, on the individual level the search for trading partners and at the market level disequilibrium and price dynamics take the center stage – replacing the traditional assumption of costless exchange at market-clearing prices (Stigler, 1961, 1962; McCall, 1965). Explicit analysis of market uncertainty is leading toward a more realistic treatment of market "imperfections," with implications not only for microeconomics but for macroeconomics as well (Phelps, 1970). The second branch of literature deals with *technological uncertainty* or (a preferable designation) *event uncertainty*. Here individuals are uncertain not about the terms on which they might make market exchanges but rather about exogenous events – such as resource endowments (will the wheat crop be large or small?) or productive opportunities (will fusion power be available?) or public policy (will taxes be cut?). Put another way, market uncertainty concerns the *endogenous* variables of the economic system, event uncertainty the *exogenous* data.

The present survey is limited to the relatively more tractable topic of *event uncertainty*. This limitation permits us to employ the simpler traditional model of perfect markets in which all dealings take place costlessly at equilibrium prices. Recent studies of the complex search and disequilibrium phenomena that emerge under market uncertainty are reviewed in Rothschild (1973) and Lippman and McCall (1976).

The paper is divided into two main parts, the first covering the economics of *uncertainty* and the second the economics of *information*. The two categories correspond to what might be called passive *versus* active responses to our limitations of knowledge. In section 7.1 individuals may be said to *adapt* to the fact of uncertainty; in section 7.2 they are allowed also to *overcome* uncertainty by engaging in informational activities.

7.1   THE ECONOMICS OF UNCERTAINTY

Decision under uncertainty

In decision-making under uncertainty the individual chooses among *acts*, while Nature may metaphorically be said to "choose" among *states*. In principle both acts and states may be defined over a continuum, but for simplicity here a discrete representation will ordinarily be employed. Table 7.1 pictures an especially simple 2 × 2 situation. The individual's alternative acts $a = (1,2)$ are shown along the left margin, and Nature's alternative states $s = (1,2)$ across the top. The body of the table shows the *consequences c* resulting from the interaction of each possible act and state.

More generally, the individual's decision problem requires him to specify: (1) *a set of acts* $a = (1,...,A)$; (2) *a probability function* expressing his beliefs $\pi(s)$ as to Nature's choice of state $s = (1,...,S)$; (3) *a consequence function* $c(a,s)$ showing outcomes under all combinations of acts and states; and, finally (4) a preference-scaling or *utility function* $v(c)$ defined over consequences. Using these as elements, the "expected-utility rule" (see below) enables him to order the available acts in terms of preferences, i.e. to assign a utility function over *acts* $u(a)$ so as to determine the one most highly preferred.

The menu of acts

We shall consider here two main classes of acts: *terminal*, and non-terminal or *informational*.

Terminal actions represent making the best of one's existing combination of information and ignorance. For example, you might decide whether or not to take an umbrella on the basis of your past history of having been

TABLE 7.1   *Consequences of alternative acts and states*

		States		*Utility of acts*
		$s = 1$	$s = 2$	
Acts	$a = 1$	c_{11}	c_{12}	u_1
	$a = 2$	c_{21}	c_{22}	u_2
Beliefs as to states		π_1	π_2	

caught in the rain. In statistical theory, terminal action is exemplified by the balancing of type I and type II errors in coming to a decision (whether to accept or reject the null hypothesis) on the basis of the evidence or data now in hand. In contrast with the classical statistical problem, which may be likened to the decision situation of an isolated Robinson Crusoe, in the world of affairs studied by economists there are interpersonal arrangements – insurance contracts, futures markets, guarantees and collateral, the corporation and other forms of combined enterprise – which serve to widen the terminal-act options available to individuals. These market processes provide a variety of ways for *sharing* risks and returns among the decision-making agents in the economy.

Informational actions are non-terminal in that a final decision is deferred while awaiting or actively seeking new evidence which will, it is anticipated, reduce uncertainty. In statistics, informational actions involve decisions as to new data to be collected: choice of sampling technique, sample size, etc. Again, in the world of affairs, interpersonal transactions open up ways of acquiring information apart from the sampling techniques studied in statistics: information may be purchased, or inferred by monitoring the behavior of others, or even stolen. To a degree, information acquisition and dissemination have become specialized functions (the "knowledge industry" [Machlup, 1962]) whose practitioners are rewarded by exchanges with other economic agents in the economy.

Section 7.1 of this paper will, apart from introductory discussions, cover only *terminal actions* – decisions made under fixed probability beliefs ("the economics of uncertainty"). The enlarged range of issues generated by admitting also non-terminal actions will be examined in section 7.2 ("the economics of information").

The probability function

We will assume that each individual is able to represent his *beliefs* as to the likelihood of the different states of the world (e.g. as to whether Nature will choose Rain or Shine) by a "subjective" probability distribution (Fisher, 1912, ch. 16; Savage, 1954). That is, an assignment to each state of a number between zero and one (end-points not excluded) whose sum equals unity. Subjective *certainty* would be represented by attaching the full probabilistic weight of unity to only one of the outcomes. The degree of subjective *uncertainty* is reflected in the dispersion of probability weights over the possible states.

Frank Knight (1921) attempted to distinguish between "risk" and "uncertainty," depending upon whether probability estimates are or are not calculable on the basis of an objective classification of instances. At times he suggested (1921, pp. 20, 226) that the probability concept is inapplicable under true uncertainty, for example, to such questions as whether or not a cure for cancer will be discovered in the next decade. It will not be possible to review here the philosophical and operational underpinnings of the probability concept. For our purposes, it is sufficient that the "subjective" or "degree of belief" interpretation has proved fruitful even for Knightian uncertainty situations. But elsewhere Knight's discussion is much more in line with modern developments, as when he suggests (1921, p. 227) that a man's actions may depend upon his estimate of the chance that his beliefs are correct – or, we shall say, upon his *confidence* in his beliefs. We will show explicitly in section 7.2 that degree of confidence is an essential element in *non-terminal* (informational) actions; the estimated value of acquiring information varies inversely with prior confidence.

The consequence function
By *consequence* is meant a full definition of all relevant characteristics of the individual's environment resulting from the interaction of the specified act and state. A consequence can be regarded as a multi-commodity multi-date consumption basket. However, we will sometimes assume that it corresponds simply to the amount of a single summary variable like income.

In the case of a *terminal* action, the consequences contingent upon each state might either be certain or probabilistic – depending upon the definition of "states of the world" for the problem at hand. If the states are defined deterministically, as in "Coin shows Heads" *versus* "Coin shows Tails," and supposing the act is "Bet on Heads," the contingent consequences are the simple certainties "Win" in the one state and "Lose" in the other. But states of the world might sometimes represent alternative probabilistic processes. For example, the two alternative states might be "Coin is fair (has 50 percent chance of coming up Heads)" *versus* "Coin is biased to come up Heads with 75 percent chance." In this situation the act "Bet on Heads" will have probabilistic consequences: 50 percent chance of winning in one state of the world, 75 percent chance in the other.

For an *informational* action, on the other hand, the consequences will in general be probabilistic even if the states of the world are defined deterministically, since acquisition of information does not ordinarily eliminate all uncertainty. If the states are Rain *versus* Shine, and the informational action is "Look at barometer," the consequences will only be improved likelihoods of behaving appropriately – since the barometer reading is not a perfect predictor of Rain or Shine.

The utility function and the expected-utility rule
In the theory of decision under uncertainty, utility as an index of preference attaches both to consequences c and to acts a. We distinguish the two by the notations $v(c)$ and $u(a)$, the problem being to derive the $u(a)$ for evaluating actions from the primitive preference scaling $v(c)$ for consequences.

To choose an act is to choose a row of the consequence matrix, as in table 7.1. Given the assignment of probabilities to states, this is also choice of a probability distribution or "prospect." A convenient notation for the prospect associated with an act a, whose consequences $c_a = (c_{a1}, \ldots, c_{aS})$ are to be received with respective probabilities $\pi = (\pi_1, \ldots, \pi_S)$, is:

$$a \equiv (c_{a1}, \ldots, c_{aS}; \pi_1, \ldots, \pi_S).$$

The connection between the utility ordering of acts and the preference scaling of consequences is provided by the Neumann-Morgenstern "expected-utility rule":

$$u(a) \equiv \pi_1 v(c_{a1}) + \ldots + \pi_S v(c_{aS}) \equiv \sum_{s=1}^{S} \pi_s v(c_{as}). \tag{7.1}$$

That is, the utility of each act $u(a)$ is the mathematical expectation or probability-weighted average of the utilities of the associated consequences $v(c_{as})$.

The expected-utility rule is of course a very specific and special procedure for inferring preferences $u(a)$ over acts from the primitive preference scaling of consequences $v(c)$. What is its justification? It turns out that the expected-utility rule is usable *if and only if the $v(c)$ function is determined in a particular way that has been termed the assignment of "cardinal" utilities to consequences.* More specifically, the underlying theorem can be stated as follows:

> Given certain "postulates of rational choice," there is a way of assigning a cardinal preference-scaling function $v(c)$ over consequences such that the preference ranking of any pair of prospects a', a'' coincides with the ranking under the expected-utility rule.

The "postulates of rational choice" therefore justify the *joint* use of cardinal utilities and the expected-utility rule in dealing with choices among risky prospects – a point worth emphasizing, since it would be quite invalid to infer that the theorem warrants or provides a cardinal utility measure for choices *not* involving risk (see the discussions in Baumol, 1951; Alchian, 1953; Strotz, 1953).

The "postulates of rational choice" serving as basis for the theorem have been set forth in a number of different ways in the literature (Friedman and Savage, 1948; Luce and Raiffa, 1957; Markowitz, 1959; Marschak, 1968) and involve technicalities that cannot be pursued here. Instead, what follows is an informal presentation (based mainly on Schlaifer, 1959) illustrating, by direct construction, the development of a personal cardinal preference-scaling function for use with the expected-utility rule (equation 7.1).

For the purposes of this discussion, we will assume that the contingent consequences c are certainties and also that c represents simply the quantity of generalized income. Let $\check{c}$ represent the worst consequence (lowest level of income) contemplated by the individual, and $\hat{c}$ the best consequence (highest level of income). As "cardinal" preference scales allow free choice of zero and unit interval, we can let $v(\hat{c}) = 0$ and $v(\hat{\hat{c}}) = 1$. Now consider some intermediate level of income c^*. We can suppose that the individual is indifferent between (assigns equal utility to) having c^* for certain *versus* having some particular chance of success π^* in a "reference lottery" involving $\hat{c}$ and $\hat{\hat{c}}$. What numerical value can we attach to this common level of utility to allow use of the expected-utility rule? The answer is, simply, the probability π^* of success in the reference lottery. Making use of prospect notation:

$$u(c^*) \equiv u(\hat{\hat{c}}, \hat{c}; \pi^*, 1 - \pi^*) \equiv \pi^*. \tag{7.2}$$

Figure 7.1 illustrates a situation in which $\hat{c} = 0$, $\hat{\hat{c}} = 1{,}000$, $c^* = 250$, and $\pi^* = \frac{1}{2}$. That is, this individual is indifferent between a sure income of \$250 and a 50 percent chance of winning in a lottery whose alternative outcomes are \$1,000 or nothing. Then the utility assigned to the sure consequence \$250 is just $\frac{1}{2}$, so $v(250) = 0.5$. Repeating this process, the reference-lottery technique generates the individual's entire $v(c)$ curve of figure 7.1, which is his preference-scaling function for consequences.

The expected-utility rule, combined with the constructed $v(c)$ function, works because the latter is *scaled as a probability*. The formula (7.1) for

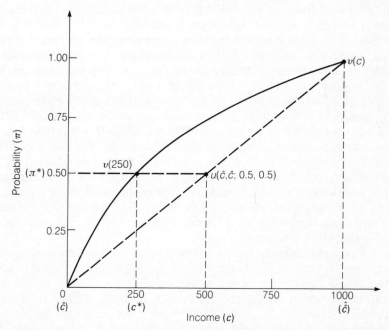

FIGURE 7.1 *The preference-scaling function v(c) derived by the "reference-lottery technique."*

finding an overall $u(a)$ by weighting the utilities of contingent consequences $v(c)$ is exactly the formula for finding the overall probability associated with a set of contingent probabilities.

We have foregone presenting a formal statement of the "postulates of rational choice" that underly the expected-utility rule. But a few comments are in order here:

(1) We have assumed that the $v(c)$ scale is unique, applicable to every state of the world. This will be reconsidered below under the heading of "state-dependent utility."

(2) We have implicitly ruled out complementarities in utility, whereby a higher income c_s in a state s might affect the v score attached to income c_t in another state t. The justification is that c_s and c_t are not to be received *in combination* but only *as alternatives*; no complementarity can exist because c_s and c_t can never be enjoyed simultaneously.

(3) While we have emphasized that $v(c)$ should be intuitively thought of as scaled in terms of probability, any fixed positive linear transformation of the $v(c)$ scale would be equally satisfactory – because cardinality permits free choice of zero and unit interval.

Risk- aversion and the risk-bearing optimum of the individual

The "concave" form of the cardinal preference-scaling $v(c)$ function in figure 7.1 shows diminishing marginal utility of income, $v''(c) < 0$, for this individual. Such a person is said to be *risk-averse*: he would always prefer a sure consequence (level of certain income) to any probabilistic mixture of consequences (lottery or prospect) having the same mathematical expectation. Figure 7.1 illustrated a situation where the reference lottery with equal chances of $1,000 or zero (and thus with a mathematical expectation of $500) is the utility equivalent of a sure income of only $250. Such a person must then prefer a sure income of $500 to this risky lottery whose mathematical expectation is $500. It is intuitively evident that this generalizes: any point P on a concave $v(c)$ curve will lie *above* the corresponding (vertically aligned) point along the straight line connecting any pair of positions on $v(c)$ that bracket P. The point *on the curve* represents the utility of a given sure income; the vertically aligned point *on the straight line* represents the utility of a lottery with a mathematical expectation equal to that given amount.

It follows immediately that a risk-averse individual endowed with a given sure income would never accept a *fair gamble*, a lottery whose mathematical expectation of net return equals zero (since it would shift him from a position *on* the $v(c)$ curve to a vertically aligned point on a straight line below it). A gamble would have to be somewhat better than fair, offer some positive mean return (just how much depends upon his degree of risk-aversion) to be acceptable. On the other hand an individual whose $v(c)$ function had the opposite "convex" curvature, representing *increasing* marginal utility of income, $v(c) > 0$, would be happy to accept any fair gamble and even, up to a point, gambles worse than fair (offering a negative mean return). Such an individual is said to display *risk preference*. An individual on the borderline, with a $v(c)$ function that is linear (constant marginal utility of income or $v''(c) = 0$) is said to be *risk-neutral*. A risk-neutral individual would accept, reject, or be indifferent to gambles that are respectively better than fair, worse than fair, or just fair.

It might be thought that the "concave" $v(c)$ function of figure 7.1 applies only to one psychological type of person, or perhaps only to people at particular times or stages in the life cycle, so that the world would consist of a mixture of risk-averse, risk-neutral, and risk-preferring types. But the observed fact of *diversification of assets* suggests that risk aversion is normal. An individual who is risk-neutral, for example, would plunge all of his wealth in that single asset which – regardless of its riskiness – offered the highest mathematical expectation of return. But we scarcely ever see this behavior pattern, and do observe more typically that individuals hold a variety of assets, thereby reducing their risk of ending up with an extremely low level of income.

What of the seemingly opposed evidence that fair gambles (and, indeed, gambles generally worse than fair) are accepted by bettors at Las Vegas and elsewhere? There have been some attempts to construct preference-scaling functions $v(c)$ that would be consistent with gambling over certain ranges of income *and* with avoiding gambles over other ranges (Friedman and Savage, 1948; Markowitz, 1952). These constructs run against the difficulty that if gambles are available on a fair or nearly fair basis, no one could ever be at an optimum in any risk-preferring range of his $v(c)$ curve. To leave such a range, individuals would accept even enormous riches-or-ruin gambles. Such behavior is surely rare, and there is no indication of ranges of income that are thus depopulated. Except in more or less pathological cases, therefore, gambling at fair or adverse odds appears to be a recreational rather than income-status-determining activity for individuals. As evidence, we observe that actual gambling as in Las Vegas is mostly of a repetitive small-stakes nature, more or less guaranteed *not* to change income status in the long run.

That risk aversion is the normal situation is indicated in a different way by figure 7.2. Here the familiar-looking indifference curves u^0, u', u'',…show the expected utilities of gambles, for the individual characterized by the preference-scaling function $v(c)$ in figure 7.1, in *state-claim* space. Following Arrow's formulation (1953, 1964), the commodities c_1 and c_2 on the two axes represent claims to income (claims to the unique consumption good) *contingent* upon the occurrence of the subscripted state of the world. (For simplicity here, we assume only two states, s_1 and s_2, with corresponding fixed probabilities π_1 and $\pi_2 \equiv 1 - \pi_1$.) Then the expected-utility equation (7.1) takes the special form (7.1'):

$$u \equiv \pi_1 v(c_1) + \pi_2 v(c_2). \tag{7.1'}$$

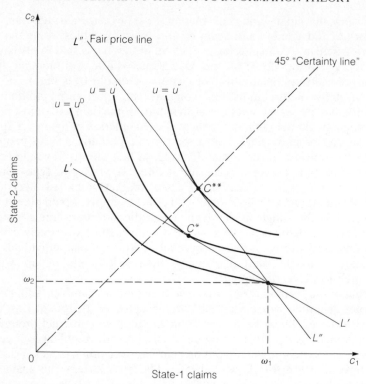

FIGURE 7.2 *The preference map in contingent consumption or state-claim space (probability fixed).*

This family of equations corresponds to the indifference curves of the diagram. The indifference-curve slopes in figure 7.2 are related to the marginal utilities $v'(c)$ via:

$$\left.\frac{dc_2}{dc_1}\right|_{du=0} \equiv -\frac{\pi_1 v'(c_1)}{\pi_2 v'(c_2)}. \tag{7.3}$$

It is elementary though tedious to show that the indifference curves have the normal "convex to the origin" curvature if and only if $v''(c) < 0$ – i.e. only if the preference-scaling function $v(c)$ is concave.

Now let us suppose that the individual is a price-taker in a market where contingent claims c_1 and c_2 can be exchanged in the ratio P_1/P_2. He has an initial endowment position (ω_1, ω_2) in state-claim space, his starting portfolio of contingent income claims – a risky position in the diagram, since $\omega_1 \neq \omega_2$. The price ratio, together with the endowment position, determined his budget line $L'L'$ in figure 7.2. It is then geometrically evident that, given the standard indifference-curve curvature that stems from risk aversion, the risk-bearing optimum position C^* will normally be in the interior – i.e. the individual will want to "diversify" his holdings of state-claims. Following standard techniques, C^* along the budget line is the tangency determined by the condition:

$$-\frac{dc_2}{dc_1}\bigg|_{du=0} \equiv \frac{\pi_1 v'(c_1)}{\pi_2 v'(c_2)} = \frac{P_1}{P_2}. \tag{7.4}$$

We can arrive at a much stronger result for the special case where the price ratio P_1/P_2 equals the probability ratio π_1/π_2. Since the condition for "fair" gambles can be expressed as $\pi_1\Delta c_1 + \pi_2\Delta c_2 = 0$ – the mathematical expectation of gain is zero – and since in market exchange $\Delta c_2/\Delta c_1 \equiv -P_1/P_2$, this equality of the price ratio and the probability ratio corresponds to the market offering fair gambles. Then the condition (7.4) simplifies to:

$$\frac{v'(c_1)}{v'(c_2)} = 1. \tag{7.4'}$$

Given the state-independent form of the $v(c)$ curve as in figure 7.1, equation (7.4') corresponds to a solution where $c_1 = c_2$ – i.e. to a tangency optimum like C^{**} at the intersection of the budget line $L''L''$ with the 45° "certainty line" in figure 7.2.

Thus, confirming our earlier result, starting from a certainty position the individual would never accept any gamble at fair odds. And, if endowed with a risky situation he would use the fair-odds condition to "insure" by moving to a certainty position. That is, he would accept just that risky contract, offering income in one state in exchange for income in another, which exactly offsets his endowed gamble. (Correspondingly, if the market odds are not fair, the individual *would* accept some risk so that C^* would lie off the 45° line.) Note that mere acceptance of a risky contract does not tell us whether the individual is moving away or toward a certainty position (enlarging or reducing his risk exposure) – the riskiness of his *endowment* position must also be taken into account.

A natural next step would be to explore the responses of the individual's risk-bearing optimum C^* (and thus of his implied state-claim transactions) to a variety of parametric shifts: to changes in prices, in probability beliefs, in the size of endowed income and its state-distribution, and in the riskiness of the prospects available to him. It has proved useful to define measures of *relative* and *absolute risk aversion* (Pratt, 1964; Arrow, 1965) that help characterize the individual's response to such parametric shifts. Limited space unfortunately precludes coverage of this large topic.

Market equilibrium under uncertainty

We now shift the level of analysis, from the decisions of the individual to market interactions and the conditions of equilibrium. Recall however that we are not dealing with what is called *market uncertainty* (with its characteristic phenomena of search and of trading at non-clearing prices). Rather, we are dealing with *event uncertainty*. And we shall generally be assuming perfect but not necessarily complete markets: trading in consumption claims contingent upon alternative states of the world takes place at market-clearing prices, but not all definable claims may be separately tradable.

Risk-sharing

If both parties in some transaction are risk-averse, they will generally contract to share the total risks and returns. This can be illustrated by the Edgeworth box in figure 7.3 (Brainard and Dolbear, 1971; Marshall, 1976), which for concreteness may be thought of as illustrating a "share-cropping" problem (Cheung, 1969a; Reid, 1976). The alternative states of

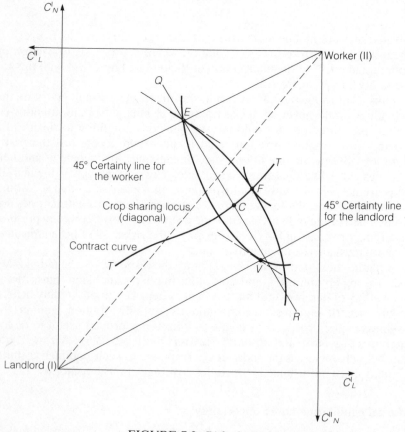

FIGURE 7.3 *Risk-sharing.*

the world are "good crop" or non-loss state N and "bad crop" or loss state L, with associated contingent claims c_N and c_L. Because of the difference in social totals of income in the two states, the box is vertically elongated.

Given agreed-upon probabilities π_L, $\pi_N(\pi_N = 1 - \pi_L)$, the indifference curves for each agent have the same absolute slope π_L/π_N along their respective 45° certainty lines. It is obvious that the two traders (landlord I and worker II) cannot both attain certainty positions. At a position like E the landlord is bearing all the risk (the worker is receiving a fixed wage independent of which state obtains). At a position like V the opposite holds; the landlord is receiving a fixed rent regardless of state, while the worker bears the risk. Starting from a position like E, state-claim trading will lead to an equilibrium at a point like C on the contract curve TT within the region of mutual advantage. It is geometrically evident that the contract curve necessarily lies between the two 45° certainty lines, so some of the risk will be borne by each party.

If the individuals were constrained to strict *proportionate* crop-sharing, the equilibrium would have to lie along the main diagonal of the Edgeworth box. (This would represent a kind of "incomplete market" for the trading of contingent claims.) Such a solution would not in general be Pareto-optimal, but it might be a rather close approximation of a point on the contract curve. Proportionate sharing in a world of unequal social totals of income would be strictly consistent with a Pareto-optimal solution only if conjoined with side payments from one party to another.

Insurance

The Edgeworth box interaction in figure 7.3 can be given another interpretation: the risk-sharing that takes place there can be regarded as "mutual insurance." Indeed, all insurance is best thought of as mutual (Marshall, 1974a; 1974b); insurance companies are only intermediaries in the risk-sharing process. We will be providing here a relatively extended discussion of insurance markets in order to illustrate in somewhat greater depth a number of the salient issues of uncertainty theory.

In the insurance context, once again the Edgeworth box will in general be elongated; we can imagine a social "loss" state of the world L (e.g. an earthquake occurs) *versus* a "non-loss" state N. From any given endowment point like E, price-taking traders arrive at a risk-sharing equilibrium like C on the contract curve. The absolute slope ($= P_L/P_N$) of the equilibrium market line (QR) exceeds the absolute slope of the dashed lines representing the fair prices or probability ratio ($= \pi_L/\pi_N$). That is, claims to income in the less affluent state L command a relatively high price, the marginal utility of income in that state being higher in equation (7.4) for the representative individual.

In economic analyses of insurance there has been a tendency to assume that fair or "actuarial" insurance terms would be normal were it not for transaction costs ("loading") (Ehrlich and Becker, 1972). In what follows we shall survey some of the major elements, transaction costs aside, that generally lead to *non-fair* equilibrium prices.

Social risk   Suppose two individuals I and II have equal initial incomes, but there is a hazard that will surely impose a fixed loss ξ on exactly one of them (with fixed, but not necessarily equal probabilities for each). The Edgeworth box would be square. Then the two 45° lines collapse into the single main 45° diagonal, which also becomes the contract curve. Here there is private risk without social risk. The two states of the world are "loss strikes I" *versus* "loss strikes II." Each party will want to exchange income in *his* non-loss state (the "premium") for compensation to be received in his loss state (the "indemnity"). The equilibrium price ratio (premium/indemnity ratio) corresponds to the respective probabilities; at these fair prices, all private risk is eliminated by mutual insurance.

Apart from this extreme special case of perfect negative correlation of risks, *four* distinct states of the world can be defined in a two-party situation – the loss may be suffered by neither person, by I alone, by II alone, or by both. And the social total of losses can be 0, 1, or 2. Evidently, there is no way of arranging affairs so that everyone can have the same income regardless of state; universal *full insurance* (whereby everyone attains his "certainty line") is generally impossible. It follows that equilibrium prices cannot be "fair"; each person's premium/indemnity ratio must exceed the odds that he will suffer a loss.

For larger insurance pools with M members, the Law of Large Numbers is sometimes thought to justify treating the *per-capita* loss $\gamma \equiv (1/M)\Sigma_i \xi_i$ as approximately constant over states. As M increases, the variance of γ declines and thus the error committed by assuming away social risk diminishes. Nevertheless this error does *not* tend toward zero unless the separate risks are on average uncorrelated (Markowitz, 1959, p. 111). If the variance of loss has the same value σ^2 for each individual, and if the correlations between all pairs of risks equal some common r (which can only hold if $r \geq 0$), the variance of the *per-capita* loss γ equals:

$$\sigma_\gamma^2 = \frac{1}{M^2}(M\sigma^2 + M(M-1)r\sigma^2). \tag{7.5}$$

In the limit as M increases, the variance of *per-capita* loss approaches the value $r\sigma^2$, which remains positive unless $r = 0$.

We see, therefore, that social risk is not exclusively due to small numbers; it persists even with large numbers if risks are on average correlated. In the language of portfolio theory, risks have a "diversifiable" element, which can be eliminated by purchasing shares in many separate securities (equivalent to mutual insurance among a large number of individuals) and an "undiversifiable" element due to the average correlation between risks. It follows then that a particular asset will be more valuable the less is the correlation of *its* returns over states with the aggregate returns of all assets together – the variability of which is the source of undiversifiable risk. As this concept is applied in modern investment theory, the correlation of returns on each particular security with the returns from the market portfolio consisting of all securities together is indicated by that security's "beta" parameter (Sharpe, 1978, ch. 6). Securities with low or, even better, negative betas trade at relatively high prices (i.e. investors are satisfied with low expected rates of return on these assets) because they provide their holders with relatively large returns in just those states of the world where aggregate incomes are low (where marginal utilities are high).

The social risk phenomenon therefore provides two reasons why insurance prices may not be fair or actuarial, so that purchase of coverage is ordinarily less than complete: (1) if the number of risks in the insurance pool is small, so that the Law of Large Numbers cannot fully work, or (2) even with large numbers, if risks are on average correlated.

State-dependent utilities   Our discussion to this point has been based upon the unique state-independent preference-scaling function of figure 7.1. More generally, however, the utility we attach to income c may vary with the state of the world. In the insurance context, we may have a $v_N(c)$ curve for the non-loss state N and a separate (lower) $v_L(c)$ curve for the loss state L (figure 7.4a). This will be appropriate wherever the object insured cannot be regarded simply as an income-equivalent – for example if it is an irreplaceable heirloom, or your own life, or your child's. There is no contradiction with the development above that led to the picture in figure 7.1, for there it was assumed (merely as a simplification) that utility was a function of a single generalized "income" commodity c. Here utility is a function of both c and an "heirloom" variable h, where $h = 0$ defines the loss state L and $h = 1$ the non-loss state N. Hence the two curves $v_N(c)$ and $v_L(c)$ do not represent distinct utility functions, but different sections through a single $v(c, h)$ function.

With state-dependent utility, the 45° *income* certainty line (ICL) is no longer the individual's utility certainty locus (UCL). Someone on the 45° line would not be indifferent as to whether state N or L occurs. In figure 7.4b, the UCL lies toward the c_L axis, since the individual requires more income in state L than in state N if he is to "fully insure utility" (Cook and Graham, 1977).

The individual optimization condition will, apart from the N or L subscripts attaching to the marginal utilities v', have the same form as equation (7.4):

$$\frac{\pi_L v'_L(c_L)}{\pi_N v'_N(c_N)} = \frac{P_L}{P_N}. \tag{7.6}$$

Assuming, as a benchmark, that prices are fair, (7.6) reduces to:

$$v'_L(c_L) = v'_N(c_N). \tag{7.6'}$$

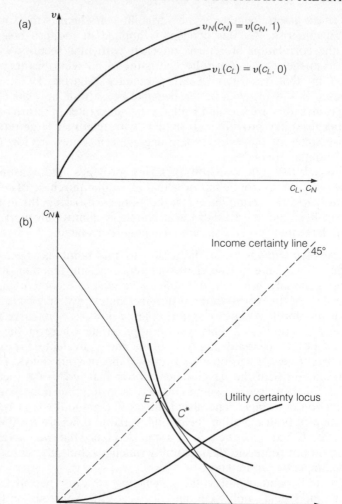

FIGURE 7.4 *(a) State-dependent utility, and (b) "Heirloom" insurance.*

With actuarial insurance available, the individual thus equates his marginal utilities in the two states as before, but these marginal utilities are now slopes along differing $v(c)$ curves.

With uncertainty only over the possible loss of the "heirloom," the individual has an initial endowment point E on the 45° income certainty line. Therefore insurance against the loss state is optimal, at actuarial prices, if and only if the indifference curve through E is steeper at this point than the budget line, that is if:

$$v'_L(c_E) = \frac{\partial v}{\partial c}(c_E, 0) > v'_N(c_E) = \frac{\partial v}{\partial c}(c_E, 1).$$

The desirability of insuring against the loss state thus depends upon whether or not income c and the "heirloom" variable h are Edgeworth substitutes – i.e. whether the cross-derivative of the two-dimensional cardinal preference-scaling function $v(c, h)$ is negative. For an heirloom such as an ancestral painting with negligible cash value it is hard to establish an *a priori* case either way. We can thus expect to find that some people insure such objects while others, similarly situated, do not.

But suppose $h = 0$ represents a major injury. Then the marginal utility of income will probably be higher in the loss state (one "needs" income c more than before). In such cases the optimum C^* lies to the southeast of the income certainty line, though not necessarily southeast of the utility certainty locus. The individual will buy insurance against injury, but not necessarily so much as to be "fully insured" in the sense of not caring whether or not the injury occurs.

The situation is very different if the variable h represents the life of one's child. It then seems plausible that h and c are complements; if your child dies $(h = 0)$ you have *less* need for income, since you planned to spend it largely on him. In such a case it is optimal to transfer income from the loss state to the non-loss state. That is, to "reverse insure" – to bet that the loss would not occur. (Contractually, instead of insuring your child's life you might buy a life annuity for him.)

We see that once allowance is made for state-dependent utility, it can no longer be presumed that individuals offered actuarial insurance terms will move to certainty positions – either certainty with respect to income, or with respect to utility.

Adverse selection and moral hazard   We now turn back to the simple assumption of state-independent utility, and also assume away social risk, in order to isolate another force operating upon individual decisions and market equilibrium: the inability of insurers to perfectly monitor the behavior or identify the risk status of insureds. (Since this is a kind of *informational* problem, our analysis here has close ties with topics to be taken up in section 7.2 below.)

To stick to essentials, we need only consider two risk classes with the same initial wealth ω and facing the same potential loss ξ. In the absence of insurance the high-risk class, with loss probability π', has an expected utility of $\pi' v(\omega - \xi) + (1 - \pi')v(\omega)$. This is represented by the distance $A'B'$ in figure 7.5. If members of this risk class are identifiable by the insurers (by the other members of the mutual insurance pool), fair insurance will result in their being offered full coverage for a premium of $\pi'\xi$, equal to the mathematical expectation of loss. These individuals then choose certainty position C' in figure 7.5 (equivalent to being on the 45°

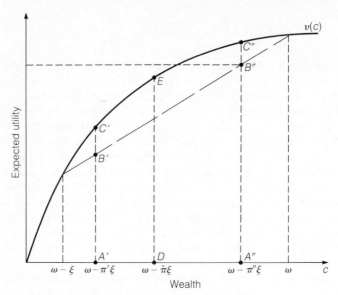

FIGURE 7.5 *Adverse selection.*

line in figure 7.2). Expected utility is $v(\omega - \pi'\xi)$, equal to the distance $A'C'$ in the diagram.

Similarly, if members of a low-risk class with loss probability π'' can be identified, insurance at actuarial terms will raise their expected utility from $A''B''$ to $A''C''$.

But what if the insurers have no way of distinguishing individuals belonging to different risk classes? Suppose they offer insurance on a full-coverage-or-none basis, initially using the average probability of loss $\bar{\pi}$. The resulting expected utility of those purchasing the insurance, $v(\omega - \bar{\pi}\xi)$, is given by the distance DE in figure 7.5. The high-risk class would be getting a bargain, but the low-risk class *may* (as shown here) be better off without any coverage $(A''B'' > DE)$. If so, the latter drop out of the insurance pool; only the high risks insure. The premium in equilibrium would of course be $\pi'\xi$, reflecting the loss probability of the high-risk class.

This is the problem of *adverse selection*. While we have described it in the insurance context, it is a much more general phenomenon. Whenever buyers can only observe average quality, there is a tendency for sellers not fully rewarded for high quality to withdraw from the market. In one extreme model, Akerlof (1970) showed that even if the used cars in existence represent a merit continuum, only the lowest-quality "lemons" would actually be traded.

More generally, however, the equilibrium may not be quite so extreme. With somewhat greater risk aversion, in figure 7.5 the $v(c)$ curve might have warranted participation even of the low-risk class in the insurance pool, at prices based on the average odds $\bar{\pi}$. With a risk continuum also, the pool of participants may include everyone from the lowest quality up to some cut-off point (Zeckhauser, 1974). Returning to figure 7.5, suppose now that the risks are distributed over a range of loss probabilities, the interval $[\pi'', \pi']$. Since insurance yields an expected-utility gain of $B'C'$ to the highest-risk class, those with not too dissimilar loss probabilities are also better off purchasing the same type of policy. Such participation lowers the average probability of loss and improves the actuarial premium, thereby drawing still better risks into the insurance pool. The process continues until the marginal risk class is just indifferent between no coverage and full coverage at a premium reflecting the average probability of loss for all those in the pool.

So far we have been assuming, in effect, a world of pure exchange: we have allowed people to *trade* risks (to engage in mutual insurance) but not to *modify* risks by productive activities. Such modifications might take the form of committing resources to *loss reduction* (reducing the gap between c_N and c_L) or to *loss prevention* (reducing the loss-probability π_L) (Ehrlich and Becker, 1972; Marshall, 1976) – apart from or in addition to purchase of market insurance. More commonly the problem is viewed the other way. Might individuals who purchase insurance be inclined not to undertake protective measures that would reduce the scale or chance of loss? This is what is called *moral hazard*.

Since efficient prices are proportioned only to the *probability* of loss, if π_L is known and fixed there is no need for insurers to guard against inadequate loss-reduction activity by price-taking risk-owners; the decisions of the insureds lead automatically to a Pareto-efficient *production and distribution* of risks (Marshall, 1976). And if π_L is variable but subject to costless monitoring by insurers, prices would respond appropriately and thus would continue to induce efficient loss-prevention activity as well as market risk-sharing transactions (Spence and Zeckhauser, 1971). Another way of looking at this is to note that, in principle, variation of *probability* of loss is equivalent to variations in the *amounts* of loss under a suitably extensive specification of states of the world (Hirshleifer, 1970, p. 217). Thus, with perfect monitoring, insurance terms can always be based upon the fixed probabilities of the true underlying states. If insurers could offer suitably different premium/indemnity ratios for losses under perfectly observable contingencies like a 10-foot flood, a 20-foot flood, etc., they need not be concerned with how high a dike the insured chooses to build.

Realistically speaking, however, monitoring of states will be imperfect. Insurers cannot be certain about the true flood hazards, fire hazards, or medical hazards experienced by insureds. Consequently, very often contracts have to be written in terms of "result-states" (Marshall, 1976) – actual observed losses – rather than the true underlying states. Then, if in the extreme case price did not respond at all to loss-prevention activity, no such activity would be undertaken.

Insurers have two main ways of coping with the problem (Arrow, 1963; Pauly, 1968; Zeckhauser, 1970). The first is to require the insured party to bear some portion of the risk, for example, by a "deductible" provision (indemnity will be less than the loss by a fixed amount) or by "coinsurance" (indemnity will be a proper fraction of the loss). Then insurance will be provided, but moral hazard persists in that insureds will engage in less preventive activity than would be efficient with costless monitoring. In addition, risk-spreading through insurance is less than ideal. The second way of coping is to price insurance in accordance with the *actual loss-prevention behavior* of insureds (the height of the dike built), the idea being that to monitor behavior may be monitoring the underlying states. Again, as this process is subject to slippage and uncertainty, there is less preventive activity and less risk-spreading through insurance than would be optimal.

Complete and incomplete market regimes, the stockmarket economy, and optimal production decisions

We have briefly alluded above to the possibility that, under uncertainty, a *complete* set of markets may not be available to economic agents. More formally, a regime of complete contingent markets (CCM) will exist if, with S distinct states of the world, the S elementary state-claims $c_s(s = 1,...,S)$ are all separately tradable. In such a regime each individual i with endowment $\omega^i \equiv (\omega^i_1,...,\omega^i_S)$ and facing prices $P \equiv (P_1,...,P_S)$ chooses some vector of trades t^i satisfying $P \cdot t^i = 0$. Equating marginal rates of substitution with the corresponding price ratios, the necessary condition for a utility-maximizing consumption choice of $c^i \equiv \omega^i + t^i$ is then:

$$\frac{\pi_S v'(c^i_S)}{\pi_1 v'(c^i_1)} = \frac{P_s}{P_1} \text{ for all } s. \tag{7.7}$$

This is of course a generalization of equation (7.4) above. More generally, trading in any S distinct *assets* representing combinations or packages of the c_s-claims will also constitute a CCM regime provided the assets are linearly independent (i.e. that none of them can be expressed as a linear combination of the others). For, any desired vector c^i can then be attained by holding an appropriate combinations of the S assets.

There is however a rather large gap between the CCM model and reality. Given the infinite variety of conceivable contingencies of economic interest (possible inventions, disasters, political developments, taste changes, etc.), in practice market regimes will necessarily be severely incomplete. Economic agents cannot in fact trade, directly or indirectly, in every distinct contingent claim. There are a number of different incomplete market regimes, some of which will be studied in more detail in section 7.2. For example, it might be the case that for some or all commodities only *certainty* claims rather than *contingent* claims are tradable: one might be able to contract to deliver wheat, but there might be no effective market in wheat contingent upon the Republicans winning the next election.

We will consider here one interesting regime of incomplete markets: a "stockmarket economy." Here each individual i has an untradable endowment $\omega^i = (\omega_1^i, \ldots, \omega_S^i)$ plus endowed amounts of tradable *shares* $(\bar{\alpha}_1^i, \ldots, \bar{\alpha}_F^i)$ of the F firms in the economy. Each firm corresponds to a state-claim vector $\omega^f = (\omega_1^f, \ldots \omega_S^f)$.

If each firm's holding has market value V_f, the individual's decision problem is to choose a portfolio $(\alpha_1^i, \ldots, \alpha_F^i)$ subject to his marketable wealth constraint:

$$\Sigma_f \alpha_f^i V_f = \Sigma_f \bar{\alpha}_f^i V_f. \tag{7.8}$$

His final consumption is $c^i \equiv \omega^i + t^i$ where:

$$t^i = \Sigma_f (\alpha_f^i - \bar{\alpha}_f^i) \omega^f. \tag{7.9}$$

The individual then chooses a portfolio to maximize:

$$u(\alpha_1^i, \ldots, \alpha_F^i) = \Sigma_s \pi_s v(c_s^i) \tag{7.10}$$

subject to (7.8) and (7.9). To achieve this he expands or contracts his holdings in the different firms until the expected marginal utility of a dollar invested in each asset is equated to his expected marginal utility of wealth, λ^i, that is:

$$\frac{\Sigma_s \pi_s v'(c_s^i) \omega_s^f}{V_f} = \lambda^i, \tag{7.11}$$

for all f and all i.

This directly implies:

$$\frac{\Sigma_s \pi_s v'(c_s^i) \omega_s^f}{\Sigma_s \pi_s v'(c_s^i) \omega_s^1} = \frac{V_f}{V_1} \tag{7.12}$$

for all f and i.

This relation, in comparison with (7.7), indicates an optimization constrained by the set of assets or claims packages (firms $f = 1, \ldots, F$) through which trading may take place. Unless the set of tradable assets constitutes a complete contingent market (which cannot be the case if $F < S$, or more generally if the F asset vectors fail to span the full S-dimensional space), it will not in general be possible for individuals to achieve the Pareto-efficient vector of net trades by purchase and sale of shares. However, it can be shown that the stockmarket economy is efficient in the restricted sense of achieving Pareto-preferred allocations of the tradable shares of different firms (Diamond, 1976).

Two related questions have received considerable attention: (1) will shareholders in general be *unanimous* in support of the firm's production decision, and (2) if so, will the optimal decision be such as to maximize the firm's *market value* V_f? In the simpler model of certainty choices, it is well-known that unanimous support for maximization of market value follows when a "separation theorem" holds. If there are perfect competitive markets and no technological externalities among firms, maximization of firm value implies that every shareowner's wealth and thus his consumption opportunities will be maximized. In the absence of the stated conditions, the separation theorem does not, in general, hold. For example, if the firm has significant monopoly power, the shareowner must balance increases in wealth against the loss he suffers as a consumer having to pay higher prices. And if differing shareowners have different tastes or endowments, the failure of separation will imply non-unanimity as well.

Very much the same holds for the firm's decisions in a world of uncertainty. In a stockmarket economy, in particular, shareowners will unanimously support value maximization if the firm's decision can have only a negligible perceived effect upon their marginal utilities in the different states. This condition will be violated if the firm can have a significant effect upon the aggregate supply of claims to any particular state s, akin to its having a degree of monopoly over c_s-claims. As an important special case, the condition will fail if the productive options before the firm enable it to create otherwise unavailable patterns (ratios) of state-claims. And again, unanimity fails if there is technological interdependence between this firm and any other firm, since there generally will be overlapping ownership between the two (Diamond, 1967; Ekern and Wilson, 1974; DeAngelo, 1979).

Other applications

In this section we have provided a relatively extensive treatment of insurance; under that heading we have been able to expound and illustrate, in rather simple format, most of the basic ideas of modern uncertainty theory. (Of course, we have scarcely been able to hint at the many exciting developments of a more advanced nature.) We have also referred briefly to other applications of uncertainty theory such as sharecropping and portfolio selection. A number of other significant applications can only be mentioned here: (1) optimal contracts between agent and principal, for example, to elicit ideal performance on the part of corporate managers (Marschak and Radner, 1972; Harris and Raviv, 1978; Shavell, 1978; Cheung, 1969b; Groves, 1973; Alchian and Demsetz, 1972; Jensen and Meckling, 1976; Zorn, 1978); (2) corporate finance and, in particular, the balance between debt and equity funding (Modigliani and Miller, 1958; Lintner, 1962; Hirshleifer, 1966; Fama and Miller, 1972, ch. 4); (3) optimal behavior and equilibrium with respect to accidents (Vickrey, 1968; Calabresi, 1970; Baumol, 1972; Diamond, 1974); (4) the "value of life" appropriate for risk-taking decisions (Mishan, 1971; Thaler and

Rosen, 1976; Conley, 1976; Schelling, 1968; Jones-Lee, 1976; Linner-ooth, 1979; Bergstrom, 1974); and (5) choice of discount rate for public investment (Hirshleifer, 1966; Arrow and Lind, 1970; Sandmo, 1972; Bailey and Jensen, 1972; Mayshar, 1977).

7.2   THE ECONOMICS OF INFORMATION

In section 7.1 individuals were limited to terminal actions, permitting them only to *adapt* to uncertainty. In this section we examine the consequences of informational actions, which allow them to *overcome* uncertainty. Paralleling the sequence of topics in section 7.1, we first analyze the optimizing choices of the decision-making unit. We then cover market equilibrium and, in particular, the interrelated prior and posterior equilibria associated with the receipt of *public* information. This is followed by a discussion of the incentives to seek out *private* information, as in inventive effort. We then examine processes by which information is revealed in market prices. Finally, there is a brief discussion of rational expectations and informational efficiency.

Informational decision-making

Acquisition of information
We continue to assume that the set of acts $a = (1,...,A)$, the set of states of the world $s = (1,...,S)$, and the associated consequences $c(a,s)$ are all known to the individual. He has, as before, a prior probability distribution of initial beliefs π_s as to the states of the world. The new element is that he can acquire information, receiving one of a known set of possible *messages* $m = (1,...,M)$ that in general will lead to a revision of probability beliefs. And thus in turn, to a possible revised choice of action.

In the extreme case, a message m might be *conclusive* as to the occurrence of some particular state s^* – in which case the revised or posterior belief distribution will attach probability of unity to state s^* and zero to all other states. More generally, the warranted revised probability belief $\pi_{s.m}$ attaching to state s after receiving message m is determined by Bayes' Theorem:

$$\pi_{s.m} = \Pr\{s \mid m\} = \frac{\Pr\{m \mid s\}\Pr\{s\}}{\Pr\{m\}} = \frac{q_{m.s}\pi_s}{q_m}. \qquad (7.13)$$

The probability q_m of receiving message m is related to the conditional probabilities or "likelihoods" $q_{m.s}$ (of receiving message m in each state s) by:

$$q_m = \sum_{s=1}^{S} q_{m.s}\pi_s. \qquad (7.14)$$

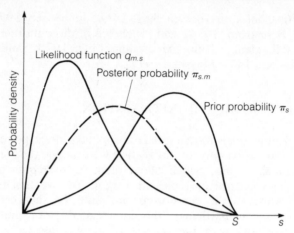

FIGURE 7.6 *Bayesian probability recalculation.*

Figure 7.6 is a suggestive illustration of Bayesian recalculation of probabilities on the basis of a given message m, where the possible states of the world are a continuum of values of s from zero to some upper limit S. In the prior distribution pictured, the bulk of the initial probability weight is assumed to lie toward the high end. But, as the likelihood function indicates, a message (evidence) has been received that is much more likely if s has a small rather than a large value. The posterior probability distribution is a compromise or average of the other two curves, derived by multiplying (for each s) the prior probability π_s and the likelihood $q_{m.s}$ – as indicated in the numerator of equation (7.13) – and then rescaling by the denominator factor so that the probability integral comes to unity.

The individual's *confidence* in his initial beliefs is indicated by the "tightness" of his prior probability distribution – the degree to which he approaches assigning 100 percent prior probability to some single possible value for s. Evidently, the higher the prior confidence the more the posterior probability distribution will resemble the prior for any given weight of evidence. As we shall see in detail below, *greater confidence implies attaching lesser value to acquiring evidence.*

We now turn to the revision of optimal terminal actions consequent upon acquisition of information. The terminal-action decision problem outlined above, for any given set of probability beliefs π, can be written:

$$\max_{(a)} u(a;\pi) = \sum_{s=1}^{S} \pi_s v(c_{as}).$$ (7.15)

The values of *informational* actions are essentially based upon the expected utility gains from shifting to better choices among the set of *terminal* actions. In particular, denote as a_0 the optimal terminal action that would be chosen before receiving any message – i.e. using the prior probabilities π_s in equation (7.15). If now a particular message m is received, the decision-maker would use (7.15) again, but with revised probabilities $\pi_{s.m}$ possibly leading to a new choice of terminal action a_m. Then Δ_m, the "value of the message m" can be written:

$$\Delta_m = u(a_m, \pi_{s.m}) - u(a_0, \pi_{s.m}). \qquad (7.16)$$

Note that Δ_m, which is necessarily non-negative, is an *ex post* valuation. It represents the expected gain from revision of best action, estimated in terms of the revised probabilities.

However, the decision to seek information must necessarily be made *ex ante*. One is never in the position of choosing whether or not to receive the particular message m; the essence of the problem is that the information-seeker does not know in advance which of the set of possible messages $m = (1,\ldots, M)$ he will obtain. What the agent can actually purchase is not a particular message but an *information service* μ generating a probability distribution of messages m (Marschak and Miyasawa, 1968).

An information service μ is "objectively" characterized by its matrix of likelihoods $Q = \lfloor q_{m.s} \rfloor$. As we have seen, matrix Q together with the individual's subjective prior probability vector $\pi = [\pi_s]$ imply a posterior probability matrix $\Pi = [\pi_{s.m}]$ and message probability vector $q = [q_m]$. Then (Π, q) represents a *personal* characterization of μ. Utilizing the message probabilities, the individual can calculate the *value $\Delta(\mu)$ of the information service* to him as the expectation of its associated message values Δ_m:

$$\Delta(\mu) = E(\Delta_m) = \Sigma_m q_m [u(a_m, \pi_{s.m}) - u(a_0, \pi_{s.m})]. \qquad (7.16)$$

Since, as already indicated, each Δ_m represented by the bracket in (7.16) is non-negative, an information service can never lower the agent's expected utility (before allowing for the cost of acquiring that service).

In figure 7.7 the determination of $\Delta(\mu)$ is illustrated for a special case in which there are two states of the world $(s = 1, 2)$, three available terminal actions $(a = 1, 2, 3)$, and an information service μ with two possible messages $(m = 1, 2)$. In the diagram utility is measured vertically, while the probabilities of the two states are scaled along the horizontal axes. Each possible assignment of probabilities to states is represented by a point along AB, a $135°$ line in the base plane whose equation is simply $\pi_1 + \pi_2 = 1$.

The utilities of consequences $v(c_{a1})$ attaching to the different actions if state 1 occurs are indicated by the points labelled $v(c_{11})$, $v(c_{21})$, and $v(c_{31})$ lying vertically above A in the diagram. Similarly, the utilities of outcomes in state 2 $(v(c_{a2})$ for $a = 1, 2, 3)$ lie above point B. The expected utility $u(a; \pi)$ of any action a given any probability vector π is indicated by the vertical distance from the point $\pi = (\pi_1, \pi_2)$ along AB to the line joining $v(c_{a1})$ and $v(c_{a2})$ for that action. In the diagram, if π is the *prior* pro-

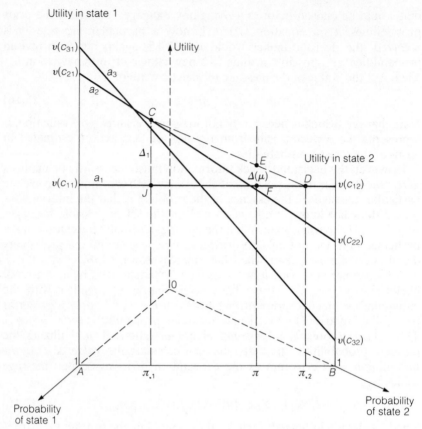

FIGURE 7.7   *The value of information.*

bability vector, then the best terminal action is $a = 1$ and the associated utility is indicated by the height of point F above the base plane.

Suppose for simplicity that the information service μ is costlessly acquired. Each of the possible messages $m = 1, 2$ will lead to a revised probability vector $\pi_{.m} = (\pi_{1.m}, \pi_{2.m})$. If $m = 1$, the revised optimal action in figure 7.7 is $a = 2$ (point C) with Δ_1 (*ex post* utility gain over $a = 1$) equal to the vertical distance CJ. If $m = 2$, the best action in the diagram remains $a = 1$ (point D), so $\Delta_2 = 0$. Weighting Δ_1 and Δ_2 by the message probabilities q_1 and q_2, the value $\Delta(\mu)$ of the information service is represented by the vertical distance EF above the point π along the line AB.

Figure 7.7 also helps us see why higher prior confidence implies lower value of information. Higher confidence – a tighter prior probability distribution in figure 7.6 – means that any given message or evidence will have a smaller impact upon the posterior probabilities. Then, in figure 7.7, the posterior probability vectors $\pi_{.1}$ and $\pi_{.2}$ would both lie closer to the original π. It is evident that the effect (if any) can only be to shrink the distance EF that represents the expected value of acquiring evidence.

One information service $(\hat{\Pi}, \hat{q})$ is said to be "more informative" than another (Π, q), from the point of view of an economic agent, if it yields sometimes higher and never lower expected utility regardless of the menu of actions (Marschak, 1971). Between some information services an informativeness ordering is clearly possible: a random sample of two, we know, must be more informative than a sample of one. But, in general, informativeness can only be partially ordered. The condition for $(\hat{\Pi}, \hat{q})$ to be more informative than (Π, q) is that the posterior probability vector associated with each message under the latter must be a convex combination of the posterior probabilities under the more informative service. For example, with two messages in each case, $(\hat{\Pi}, \hat{q})$ is more informative than (Π, q) if for some α, β between zero and unity:

$$\pi_{.1} = \alpha\hat{\pi}_{.1} + (1 - \alpha)\hat{\pi}_{.2},$$

and   (7.17)

$$\pi_{.2} = \beta\hat{\pi}_{.1} + (1 - \beta)\hat{\pi}_{.2}.$$

One interpretation of these conditions is that the recipient of the information service (Π, q) knows that the true messages 1 and 2 would imply revised probabilities $\hat{\pi}_{.1}$ and $\hat{\pi}_{.2}$. However the messages have become garbled in transmission, so that he is not sure which message he has actually received. For example, his received message 1 has chance $(1 - \alpha)$ of really being the true message 2.

These conditions are easily visualized in terms of figure 7.7, which pictures a particular information service (Π, q) leading to posterior probability vectors $\pi_{.1}$ and $\pi_{.2}$. Suppose an alternative information service $(\hat{\Pi}, \hat{q})$ also had two possible messages 1 and 2, but $\hat{\pi}_{.1}$ were to lie to the left of $\pi_{.1}$ and $\hat{\pi}_{.2}$ to the right of $\pi_{.2}$. The alternative service must lead to higher utility so long as there is any change in best conditional action under either message. If on the other hand the two posterior probability vectors of one service do not bracket the two posterior vectors of another, which one will be found "more informative" by an individual might depend upon the specifics of his personal situation.

Figure 7.7 also illustrates a general "non-concavity" (condition of *increasing* marginal returns) in the valuation of information services (Radner and Stiglz, 1976). Starting with the null information service with posterior probabilities equal to the prior π, suppose a slightly informative $\hat{\mu}$ comes along with posterior probabilities $\hat{\pi}_{.1}$ just barely to the left of π and $\hat{\pi}_{.2}$ barely to the right. If the probability revisions are small, neither message changes the associated best action and there can be no utility gain. So the *marginal* return of improved information may be zero over a certain range, before becoming positive at the point where the improvement begins to affect action.

A number of interesting complications, which unfortunately cannot be pursued here, arise when the informational decision process has multipersonal aspects. One important example is the use of "expert opinion" – the problems being to disentangle what is genuinely new in the information provided, and also to allow for possible conflict of interest between expert and client (Shavell, 1976; Pearl, 1978; Green, 1982). Other issues arise when a *group* of people must jointly make an information decision (Raiffa, 1968, ch. 8). The problems here stem once again from possible conflicts of interest (differences in utilities attached to consequences), but also from conflicts of opinion (differences in probability beliefs). Depending upon the circumstances, these factors may lead either to overinvestment or underinvestment in information.

Other informational activities

So far, under the heading of informational action we have only considered the *acquisition* of evidence – as by generation of sample data (the production of socially "new" information) or the receipt of expert advice (the interpersonal transfer of "old" information). But other types of informational activities can also be very important. The possibility of acquiring information from others, as discussed in connection with expert opinion above, immediately suggests the reverse activity – the *dissemination* of information to other economic agents. This might be done for a price, as when one is hired as an expert, but (as we shall see below) sometimes it may pay to disseminate gratuitously, or even to incur cost to "push" information to others (Hirshleifer, 1973). Advertising is an obvious example. There is also a choice between disseminating publicly ("publishing"), or else privately to a select audience. As a question of authenticity might arise in all such cases, the receiver of information may devote effort to the process of *evaluation*, possibly assisted by *authentication* activities (or hampered by *deception* activities) on the part of the disseminator. There is also the possibility of unintended dissemination, achieved by *espionage* or *monitoring* on the part of information-seekers – possibly leading to countermeasures in the form of *security* (secrecy-maintaining) activities by the possessors of information.

Finally, there are classes of activities, apart from those involved with acquisition or dissemination of information, that are indirect consequences of informational patterns. Wagering, for example, typically follows from differences of opinion in a situation where conclusive information is anticipated (so as to determine who wins and who loses). *Speculation* is a somewhat analogous activity, which turns on a prospective revision of prices in consequence of the arrival of information. Another form of activity, which will be considered in the next section below, involves the adoption of more or less "flexible" positions in anticipation of ability to make use of future information when it arrives.

Emergent information and the value of flexibility
In the sections preceding we thought of information as being newly generated by an informational action like a sampling experiment or, alternatively, as acquired from others via a transaction like the purchase of expert opinion. But in some cases information may autonomously *emerge* simply with the passage of time, without requiring any direct action by recipients. Tomorrow's weather is uncertain today, but the uncertainty will be reduced as more meteorological data flow in and will in due course be conclusively resolved when tomorrow arrives. Direct informational actions might still be useful, by providing knowledge *earlier* than it would autonomously arrive. But under conditions of emergent information, one might choose a kind of indirect informational action – adopting a flexible position and *waiting* before taking terminal action.

Suppose a choice must be made now between immediate terminal action and awaiting emergent information. This choice can only be interesting where there is a trade-off between two costs: (1) a cost of waiting, *versus* (2) an "irreversible" element in the possible loss suffered from mistaken early commitment. Exactly these elements have been involved in analysing the benefit of actions that irreversibly transform the environment (Arrow and Fisher, 1974; Henry, 1974) and in discussions of the value of "liquidity" (Marschak, 1949; Hirshleifer, 1972) or of "flexibility" (Marschak and Nelson, 1962; Jones and Ostroy, 1976).

To illustrate these ideas, consider again figure 7.7. Suppose an action is to be chosen in each of two time periods ($t = 0, 1$), but information is to emerge that might improve the decision at $t = 1$. Let the pay-off to the different actions be the same in each period. With no cost of switching, the diagram shows that the best action at $t = 0$ is a_1. At $t = 1$ this action will again be optimal unless message 1 is received, in which case a_2 becomes superior.

However, suppose that the cost of switching from action a_1 to a_2 exceeds the cost of switching from a_2 to a_1. So a_2 is the more "flexible" choice. If a_2 is chosen at $t = 0$ there would be an initial-period loss in expected utility. But if this cost is sufficiently small relative to the differential in switching cost and the expected value of the emerging information, a_2 may become the preferred initial-period action. Here the initial-period loss (reduction in pay-off due to choice of a_2) is the cost of waiting (or of maintaining flexibility); the counterbalancing "irreversible" loss, due to early commitment to a_1, is the extra cost of switching should that be required.

Public information and market equilibrium

Emergence of new public information will affect prices. In particular, relative market values will rise for those assets paying off more handsomely in states of the world now regarded as more likely. The anticipated arrival of public information requires economic agents to contemplate market exchanges in two distinct rounds – *trading prior to and posterior to receipt of the message*. The equilibria of the two trading rounds will generally be interrelated, but the form of the relationship depends upon the completeness of markets (see above) in each round.

Equilibrium in complete versus incomplete market regimes

In section 7.1 we mainly considered models with S states of the world and a single consumptive good c. In the realm of the *economics* of *uncertainty*, where arrival of public information is not anticipated, a regime of complete contingent markets (CCM) was said to exist if all the distinct c_s-claims (S in number) are separately tradable at prices P_s. (Trading in any set of S linearly independent asset combinations of the underlying c_s-claims would also constitute a CCM regime, but we will generally ignore this complication.) In equilibrium, the optimality condition (7.7) holding for each individual can conveniently be repeated here:

$$\frac{\pi_s v'(c_S)}{\pi_1 v'(c_1)} = \frac{P_s}{P_1} \quad (s = 2, \ldots, S). \qquad (7.18)$$

To achieve this condition, individuals will generally undertake *productive transformations* (e.g. loss-reduction and loss-prevention activities) as well as *market exchanges* (e.g. purchase of insurance).

Now consider that public information is expected to arrive before the close of trading. We will generally be assuming. however, that the message is not timely enough to permit *productive* adaptations to the changed probabilities. For example, a message as to increased flood danger comes in time to affect the market terms of flood-insurance transactions, but not in time to permit construction of dikes.

As an initial special case, assume it is known that the message will be *conclusive* as to which state of the world will obtain. Then to each and every state s corresponds exactly one message m. In these circumstances complete contingent markets (CCM) in the *prior round* will, just as before, provide for separate trading in the S distinct c_s-claims at prices P_s. Under the timing assumption of the previous paragraph, posterior trading is in general possible. But such trading would be meaningless in this special case; once it becomes known that some single state s^* is the true one, c_{s^*} is the only state-claim retaining any market value, and there is nothing available for exchanging against it. So equations (7.18) in the prior round are the *only* relevant conditions of equilibrium.

A more interesting model, continuing to assume that traders anticipate *conclusive* information, allows for multiple consumptive goods $g = 1, \ldots, G$. Here a regime of complete contingent markets (CCM) in the prior round would allow trading in the $G \cdot S$ different claims c_{gs} – claims to any good g under any state s – at prices P_{gs}. After the conclusive message arrives that some state s^* will obtain, complete *posterior* markets would permit exchanges among the G commodity claims c_{gs^*}. But suppose for the moment that individuals were not aware, in their prior-round dealings, of this possibility of posterior trading. Then the prior-round optimality conditions would have included ratios of the following form, where g' and g'' are any two goods:

$$\frac{\dfrac{\partial v}{\partial c_{g's}}}{\dfrac{\partial v}{\partial c_{g''s}}} = \frac{P_{g's}}{P_{g''s}}. \tag{7.19}$$

Note that π_s, whatever its value may be, is not involved in the optimality condition between different goods *contingent upon* state s. It follows that receipt of the incoming message, revising the probabilities π_s (in this particular case, making $\pi_{s^*} = 1$) does not affect this condition. Therefore the price ratio on the right-hand-side of (7.19) continues to sustain the solution arrived at in the prior round.

Thus we see that even though posterior exchanges are *possible* among the G remaining tradable claims c_{gs^*}, with CCM in the prior round no one will find such exchanges *advantageous*. Trading in the G posterior claims is "not needed" if there have been markets for $G \cdot S$ prior claims. We must however emphasize a very important qualification to this result: prior-round traders must *correctly forecast* that the price ratio on the right-hand-side of (7.19) will remain unchanged in the posterior round. If they mistakenly thought that it would change, they would be led to make "erroneous" prior-round transactions, affecting the market equilibrium and thus requiring corrective posterior-round transactions. The result would be a loss of efficiency. So CCM in the prior round (without posterior trading) suffices for Pareto optimality, but subject to a proviso of "correct conditional price forecasting" (Hirshleifer, 1977). (This proviso corresponds to one of the meanings of that Delphic phrase, "rational expectations," to be discussed below.)

We can now generalize still further to the case where messages are *not conclusive* as to the advent of any particlar state. With complete contingent markets in the prior round, there would be $G \cdot S \cdot M$ distinct tradable claims c_{gsm}. And there remain $G \cdot S$ valid claims c_{gsm^*} in the posterior round after receipt of message m^*. But here also it is not difficult to verify that CCM in the prior round permits every agent to attain his optimum at one fell swoop – provided once again that everyone correctly predicts that the relevant posterior-round price ratios are unchanged (Feiger, 1976). So quite generally, given "correct conditional price forecasting" and a CCM regime for prior-round trading, posterior-round markets are available but not necessary for Pareto efficiency.

Very interesting and important issues arise, however, when we analyze prior-round market regimes that are *incomplete* (as of course they actually must be in the world). To maintain simplicity, we will however return to the particular case of *conclusive* information. Then the set of M messages collapses into the set of S states so that individuals are concerned only with c_{gs} claims, $G \cdot S$ in number.

Among the many possible patterns of market incompleteness, three will be briefly discussed here.

Absence of prior-round markets   Total absence of prior-round markets is of course the most extreme form of incompleteness. In effect, what has happened is that the information arrives before *any* exchanges have taken place, while individuals are still at their endowment positions.

This situation has aroused considerable interest, as it implies the surprising result that incoming public information may be socially disadvantageous in the sense that everyone in the economy might be willing to pay *not* to have it! (Hirshleifer, 1971; Marshall, 1974a; Zeckhauser, 1974; Hakansson, Kunkel and Ohlson, 1979.) As among a group of traders who would otherwise have mutually insured against fire, a conclusive message (as to whose houses would actually burn down) would negate the possibility of mutually advantageous risk-sharing through insurance. The prospective arrival of such information prior to the opening of markets imposes an undiversifiable wealth-redistribution risk on the economy; no one can hedge against the price impact of the message to be received. (On the other hand, if earlier arrival of information permits more effective *productive* adaptations, as in loss-reduction measures against fire, this socially valuable feature must be weighed against elimination of the ability to spread risks.)

Numeraire contingent markets (NCM)   Suppose instead that there is prior-round trading, but only in contingent claims to a *single* commodity – which might as well be taken as the numeraire good $g = 1$. In the prior market, individuals cannot purchase claims to *any* good contingent upon state s, but can purchase claims to (say) *corn* contingent upon state s. Under this numeraire contingent markets (NCM) regime, these purchases are in effect side-bets as to which state of the world is going to obtain, whose outcome will determine the individual's posterior wealth. After receipt of the message, of course, the individual will use his enhanced or reduced wealth to purchase a preferred consumption basket in the *posterior* round of trading.

Arrow (1964) has shown that the same equilibrium allocation as indicated by conditions (7.19) under CCM (with prior trading in $G \cdot S$ claims) is achievable under NCM with prior contingent trading only in the S claims to a single commodity. But given the prior-round incompleteness of this NCM regime, the availability of G markets in the posterior round becomes now quite essential. And once again, we must also specify the important proviso of "correct conditional price forecasting." Furthermore, this proviso here becomes more stringent than under CCM, where the correct forecast was simply "no change" from the prior price ratio P_{gs*}/P_{1s*} to the posterior ratio $P_{g \cdot s*}/P_{1 \cdot s*}$ (for the particular state $s*$ pointed to by the incoming message). Here, under NCM, the correct price forecast *is not in general computable from data available to traders in the prior round* (Radner, 1968; Drèze, 1970–1). The conditional relative supplies and demands determining the posterior ratios $P_{g \cdot s*}/P_{1 \cdot s*}$ are not publicly "visible" in the prior round, where only claims to $g = 1$ are being traded. (Only the absence of utility complementarities between the numeraire and other goods could make the non-computability of posterior prices irrelevant for prior decisions.)

Futures markets (FM)   The CCM and NCM regimes both allow trading in state-contingent claims. Such trading does take place to some extent in the actual world, directly as in some insurance transactions or indirectly via trading in assets like corporate shares that can be regarded as packages of state-claims. But most of the trading observed in the world represents exchange of *unconditional* claims to goods. In a market regime allowing only the exchange of unconditional claims to G consumptive goods, under conclusive emergent information the prior and posterior rounds can be respectively identified with current "futures" markets *versus* later "spot" markets.

Under such a regime of unconditional or, as we shall say, futures markets (FM) there will be just G tradable claims in the prior round followed by possible re-trading in the same claims in the posterior round. Since it is reasonable to assume that $G < S$ (there are many more conceivable contingencies than goods), it is evident that the $G + G$ markets in two rounds under FM cannot in general achieve the same efficiency as the $S + G$ markets under NCM (or, *a fortiori*, as the $G \cdot S$ plus G markets under CCM) (Townsend, 1978).

This negative conclusion is somewhat mitigated, however, once we allow for the fact that emergent information in the world is only rarely *conclusive*. If improved though not yet conclusive public information emerges repeatedly, the multiplication of rounds of trading recreated after each informational input increases the effectiveness of FM relative to NCM and CCM. (Once again, the proviso as to correct conditional price forecasting retains its relevance and is indeed increasingly difficult of achievement.) Also, in general, multiple rounds can only partially offset market incompleteness, so that full Pareto efficiency is not achieved. More troubling, there may be different *self-fulfilling predictions* about prices in future trading round, leading to different equilibrium allocations – and these allocations may be Pareto-rankable (Hart, 1975).

Speculation
The term "speculation" has caused a good deal of confusion. Some authors loosely apply the word to arbitrage between markets, or to storage of

goods over time or carriage over space – activities that do not involve uncertainty in any essential way. For our purposes, speculation is purchase with the intention of re-sale, or sale with the intent of re-purchase, where the *uncertainty of the future spot price* is a source of both risk and gain. The probabilistic variability of price is in turn *due to anticipated emergence of information.* Each possible message (in the conclusive information case that we shall be assuming here, this is equivalent to the advent of a single possible state) leads to an associated equilibrium posterior price vector, benefiting agents who adopted trading positions generating relatively high conditional wealths for that state.

Among the possible determinants of speculative activity, John Maynard Keynes (1930) and John Hicks (1946) followed by many others have emphasized differential *risk aversion.* In their view, in the prior round of a futures markets (FM) regime the relatively risk-tolerant speculators accept risks of price variability from relatively risk-intolerant "hedgers." In the prior trading round, speculators buy commodity futures, achieving on average a small gain (excess of later mean spot price over futures price), which represents the return they receive from suppliers unwilling to bear the price risk. For example, a wheat-grower hedges by accepting a firm price now from a speculator, both of them anticipating that the unknown spot price will on average be a little higher. Later developments along this line (Houthakker, 1957, 1968; Cootner, 1968) have brought out that hedgers can be on either side of the futures market; speculators need bear only the imbalance between "long" and "short" hedgers' commitments, so that the risk-compensating average price movement could go either way. In contrast with these views, Holbrook Working (1953; 1962) has denied that there is any systematic difference as to risk-tolerance between those conventionally called speculators and hedgers. Working emphasizes, instead, differences of *belief* (optimism or pessimism) as motivating futures trading.

The Keynes–Hicks concentration upon aversion to "price risk" is seriously misleading. Individuals' prior-round trading decisions are affected by "quantity risk" (variability of endowments over states) as well as by price risk (McKinnon, 1967). Indeed, from the social point of view, price uncertainty is the (inverse) reflection of an underlying uncertainty as to the future aggregate commodity totals. And these risks tend to be offsetting, reducing the need to engage in prior-round hedging activity. For example, when the crop of a representative wheat-grower is big (good news) he will find that the wheat price tends to be low (bad news) and vice versa. In a futures markets (FM) regime it is in general not possible to divest oneself of *quantity risk* (since only certainty claims can be traded); consequently, traders might well find it preferable *not* to hedge against the offsetting *price risk.*

In a world where people have a spectrum of beliefs as to probabilities of future states, an individual's speculative activity proper (his adoption of a trading position in anticipation of arriving public information that will change market prices) depends in a rather complex way upon the degree of deviation of his beliefs from average opinion, upon his willingness to tolerate risks, and upon his endowment position conjoined with the trading limitations imposed by a regime of incomplete markets (Hirshleifer, 1975, 1977). With regard to the first of these determinants, a speculator with strongly deviant beliefs thinks that *others* will be surprised by the incoming message (and thus will be forced to make unanticipated posterior transactions). He will in consequence have adopted a trading position enabling him to benefit from these transactions. With regard to the second determinant, degree of risk aversion affects the *scale* of preferred speculative exposure. As to the regime of markets, we saw in the preceding section that (assuming "correct conditional price forecasting") re-trading possibilities are not needed under complete conditional markets (CCM). Thus, incompleteness of prior-round markets is also a necessary condition for speculation (Salant, 1976; Feiger, 1976).

The economics of research and invention

Research and invention activities are prime instances of the *informational* actions studied, on the level of the individual economic agent, above. We are not dealing here with situations like those examined in the previous section where public information simply emerges with the passage of time. Since Nature will not autonomously reveal her secret, it must be sought out by costly (generally private) search for the still-unknown "message." The topic of concern here however is not the informational decisions of an isolated Robinson Crusoe, but rather of individuals in a market environment facing rivalrous competition from some agents, but also having opportunities for mutually advantageous exchanges with others. In particular, as we shall see, successful private search generally leads to more or less universal dissemination of the discovery, with price impacts akin to that of the public information studied in the previous section.

The central problem considered by modern analysts (Machlup, 1968; Arrow, 1962) has been the conflict between the social goals of *achieving efficient use of information once produced* versus *providing ideal motivation for production of information*. With regard to optimal use, already produced information is a "public good" in the sense that its availability to any member of society does not reduce the amount that could be made available to others. Then any barrier to use, as may stem from legal enforcement of patents or copyrights or property in trade secrets, is inefficient. On the other hand, as in the standard public-good situation, there will be inadequate motivation to invest in production of information if the product cannot be reduced to legally protected property.

Under ideal conditions the efficient-use problem could be solved by charging perfectly discriminating fees to license (non-exclusively) all uses of a given idea. If the discoverer were granted full property rights in the idea, as by a perpetual copyright or patent, he in turn would have the optimal incentive to produce (search for) ideas. But in practice owners of copyrights or patents cannot impose perfectly discriminating royalty-fee structures on licensees. A patentee might instead maximize returns by granting *exclusive* licenses (in which case the social value of the excluded uses is of course lost) or by imposing fee structures that distort the marginal production decisions of licensees. On the other side of the picture, because of the elusiveness of property in ideas, there is uncertainty and unreliability in the legal protection of patents and copyrights, and even less protection for trade secrets not covered by patent or copyright. The result is that unlicensed uses often escape control. Short of ideal conditions there will be losses from *both* underproduction and underutilization, and in practice something of a trade-off: provision of greater legal protection to inventors tends to ameliorate the underproduction problem, but to worsen the underutilization problem.

More recent investigations have indicated, however, that not all the important elements of the picture have been captured by this analysis. These newer results turn upon the possibility of *over*investment in the production of ideas ("a rush to invent").

The first such factor is the *fugitive resource* (or *common-property resource*) nature of undiscovered ideas (Barzel, 1968). For concreteness, we can use as metaphor the "over-fishing" model of Gordon (1954). Suppose there are perfect property rights in fish caught, but complete free entry into fishing (i.e. there are no property rights that exclude others from engaging in fishing as an activity). Then in competitive equilibrium there will be over-fishing; private marginal cost will equal price, but the true social marginal cost in fishing exceeds the private marginal cost. The reason is that a certain fraction of each fisherman's catch consists of fish that would have been caught anyway, by other fishermen – so the true social product of fishing effort is less than appears in private calculations. The upshot is that too many fish are caught, too soon. Among the remedies discussed in the fugitive-resource literature are the imposition of taxes or production quotas to reduce the amount of fishing activity, or alternatively the assignment of exclusive property rights to engage in such activity.

This last point may be clarified by explicitly distinguishing rights *in* fish (the right to exclude others from a fish you have caught) from rights *of* fishing (the right to exclude others from competing with you in fishing activity). Assuming fully protected rights *in* fish, the fugitive-resource problem can be solved by also vesting rights *of* fishing – for example, by auctioning the right to exclusively exploit a fishery. Indeed, once rights *of* fishing are defined such an auction would tend to occur of its own, via Coase-Theorem negotiations. In the context of research, the equivalent distinction is between a right *in* an idea and a right *of* engaging in search for an idea. Again, one might imagine auctioning off the right *of* searching for an idea – for example, the right of inventing an alloy with specified properties. As the lowest-cost inventor would bid highest for this right, the "rush to invent" problem would be solved (Cheung, 1979a, b).

In research, the difficulty of defining the nature of an "uncaught" idea seems to make the assignment of rights *of* searching for them unfeasible. (Even in fishing, it is often impractical to define exclusive rights *of* hunting for such a wandering resource.) In contrast with fishing, however, property rights *in* ideas when caught are also very far from perfect. But, in the circumstances, this is not necessarily bad; being somewhat like a tax on inventive activity, defective rights *in* ideas reduce what otherwise might be an excessive "rush to invent."

Recapitulating at this point, we have seen two distinct possible justifications for limiting property rights in ideas – for example, by granting patents only for a term of years. The first is that some protection to inventors is traded off against protection of users of invention. The second is that the "rush to invent" tendency is moderated by reducing the capturable value of the invention itself.

There is still another motivation that may lead to excessive devotion of resources to invention. Ideas of course vary enormously in their significance, and some among them will have far-reaching consequences. This opens up a new channel of reward for inventors. Instead of, or possibly in addition to, selling the information via patent license or otherwise, an inventor might be able to *speculate* by taking long or short positions in assets whose values will be affected by the invention (Hirshleifer, 1971). An oil firm that has developed a new method of deep recovery might, for example, reap a speculative pay-off by buying up options on tracts whose petroleum now lies too deep to be recovered. One important implication of the speculative reward of invention is that it motivates the possessor of information to disseminate it widely and even gratuitously, after having made his speculative commitment.

Looking at this more generally, individual ideas will – unlike individual fish, or whole boatloads of fish – often have important *pecuniary* externalities. The "ideal conditions" referred to above, which would have reserved for the inventor the entirety of the technological benefit flowing from his idea, would then generally lead to *overcompensation* if the inventor could also capture some fraction of the pecuniary externalities as well.

There are classes of research activity for which the reward element stemming from the technological benefit is negligible, where the potential pecuniary return is almost the whole picture. Stockmarket research ("security analysis"), whether engaged in by full-time professionals or by ordinary investors, is essentially of this nature (Fama and Laffer, 1971). While there may be a technological benefit (improvement in society's productive opportunities) due to accurate security analysis, the reward reaped by security *analysts* stems almost entirely from the pecuniary revaluations – the correctly interpreted rises or falls in the stock prices themselves.

Recognition of the "rush to invent" problem, while undermining the traditional argument for patents (or other forms of protection for discoverers of ideas) that was based upon a presumption of *underinvestment* in research, does not warrant going to the other extreme. It would not be in order to conclude that patent protection is *not* justified, but only that the arguments pro and con are more complex than had previously been realized.

Informational advantage and market revelation of information

In the preceding sections we have considered situations in which an individual could profit by timely publication of knowledge in his private possession. For example, an agent obtaining new information might transact at existing prices (take a speculative position), planning to sell out at the revised prices that ensue once he publicly discloses his knowledge. But there are two problems here. First, the agent must be able to move to a trading position (make a speculative commitment) without thereby revealing his secret – this is the problem of *information leakage*. Second, at the disclosure stage he must be able to authenticate the information he is trying to publicize – that is the problem of *signalling*. We shall consider these two problems, in reverse order, in the sections following.

Signalling

The particular signalling problem that has aroused greatest interest arises when sellers of a higher-quality product or service are attempting to convey that message (that their product *is* high quality) to buyers. Of course, any seller is motivated to *claim* that his is a high-quality product. Signalling as a solution to this difficulty takes place when sellers of truly higher-quality products engage in some activity *that would not be rational for those selling lower-quality products.* Any activity is a potential signal if sellers of higher-quality products can engage in it at lower marginal cost (or higher marginal return) than producers of lower-quality products. For example, it has been argued (Nelson, 1974, 1975) that advertising tends to be especially advantageous for producers of higher-quality goods, in contexts where *repeat purchases* are a significant consideration. Since the high-quality firm will be acquiring a pool of satisfied customers, its marginal advertising cost per unit of sales will be lower. Even if there is zero information content in the advertising itself, a message is thus being conveyed: *that the product is worth promoting.*

For the labor market Spence (1974), Stiglitz (1975), and Riley (1976, 1979b) have argued that educational credentials constitute signals with regard to jobs in which productivity is difficult to determine. As long as there is a negative correlation between productivity and the (money and time) costs involved in achieving any education level, *the marginal cost of education is lower for the higher-quality workers*. The latter are then able to signal by attaining higher educational credentials. On the other side of the market, the process complementary to signalling is called *screening*; employers are able to use education signals to *screen* for quality differentials.

Rothschild and Stiglitz (1976) and Wilson (1977) make parallel arguments for the insurance market. In section 7.1, we saw how, in the absence of ability to distinguish between better and poorer risks, insurance premiums reflect the average risk quality. Hence *adverse selection* occurs, with lower-quality risk classes tending to insure more than others. However, the higher the probability of loss, the higher is the marginal loss in utility associated with accepting less than full coverage. Thus, the marginal cost of accepting a large "deductible" is greater for low-quality risks (those with high loss probabilities). In effect, then, high-quality risks can signal by willingness to accept a big deductible. Insurance companies can thus screen for differences in risk: policies with large deductibles can be offered at the low premiums appropriate for high-quality risks, while others with smaller deductibles but steeper premiums will be appropriate for and purchased by low-quality risks.

In contrast to the autonomously emergent information situations examined above, in signalling models the flow of information from seller to buyer is generated endogenously. This has important consequences for the stability of informational equilibria. It has been established that unless the gap between the quality of different products is sufficiently large, there is no Cournot-Nash equilibrium (Rothschild and Stiglitz, 1976; Riley, 1975, 1979a). That is, starting from a situation in which all traders adopt some complementary signalling/screening pattern, there is always an alternative that yields someone greater profit.

Figure 7.8 illustrates this for the simple case in which there are only two quality levels of the item for sale (insurance risk, consumer good, labor service, etc.). For concreteness we shall use the labor market interpretation. The dashed indifference curves $u_1(e, w)$ represent, for a low-quality (low marginal productivity) worker, equivalent combinations of the price of his labor services (lifetimes earnings) w and the level e of signalling activity (education). For a high-quality worker the solid indifference curves $u_2(e, w)$ will be applicable. The lesser slope of the latter indicates the condition for signalling to come about: that a more qualified worker can more easily or cheaply acquire the educational attainment that serves as signal. Put the other way, for any offer profile of lifetime earnings as related to educational credentials e, the higher-quality worker would be willing to acquire more e.

It is supposed here that, with full information, buyers (employers) would be willing to pay the marginal products θ_1 for the low-quality worker and

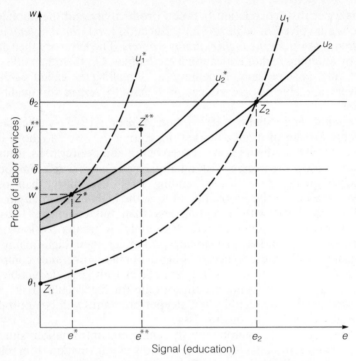

FIGURE 7.8 *Reactive signalling equilibrium.*

θ_2 for the high-quality worker. If only average quality were known, however, their maximum offer is $\bar{\theta}$. Suppose that initially all workers are offered the same signal-wage pair $Z^* = \langle e^*, w^* \rangle$ as depicted in figure 7.8, where w^* is no greater than $\bar{\theta}$.

The low-quality workers would then be on their indifference curve u_1^*, and the high-quality workers on u_2^*. Some firm would then be motivated to make the new offer Z^{**}. For, this would attract only the high-quality workers and, since $w^{**} < \theta_2$, such an offer would generate a positive profit. This proves that the position Z^*, pooling the different quality levels, is not a Cournot-Nash equilibrium.

Alternatively, suppose the two classes of workers are successfully separated with the pair of offers $Z_1 = \langle 0, \theta_1 \rangle$ and $Z_2 = \langle e_2, \theta_2 \rangle$ depicted in figure 7.8. Acting as price-takers, the lower-quality workers will accept the offer Z_1 and the higher-quality workers the offer Z_2. On the other side of the market the buyers, also acting as price-takers, find that the products purchased have the anticipated characteristics. The pair of offers $\{Z_1, Z_2\}$ is thus an equilibrium in the Walrasian sense (and in the sense of Spence [1974]). It is also efficient in the sense that all other pairs of offers (more generally all other wage schedules) that yield zero profit and that separate workers provide lower utility to the high-quality workers.

However, this equilibrium does not have the Cournot-Nash stability property either. A firm can now enter offering the signal-wage pair Z^*, which is strictly preferred by both classes of workers and yields an expected profit to the entering firm. As we have already seen that an offer like Z^* is not itself an equilibrium, there is no Cournot-Nash equilibrium.

How then would such a market behave? Plausibly, in the absence of collusion, each buyer would eventually expect some *reaction* by other agents to changes in his own list of offers. Suppose that a new offer would be profitable in the absence of any reaction, but leads to loss once another buyer reacts with a strictly profitable counteroffer. Suppose furthermore that the latter's response is riskless, in the sense that *further* response by any other buyers would not impose losses on the first reactor. Then it seems reasonable that the potential initial "defector" would eventually recognize that his new offer would bring on such a reaction, and hence would be deterred from making it. This suggests the following strategic equilibrium concept (Riley, 1979b), which builds on the development by Wilson (1977).

REACTIVE EQUILIBRIUM: *A set of offers is a reactive equilibrium if, for any additional offer that yields an expected gain to the agent making the offer, there is another that yields a gain to a second agent and losses to the first. Moreover, no further addition to or withdrawal from the set of offers generates losses to the second agent.*

The general derivation of the existence and uniqueness of the reactive equilibrium is somewhat delicate. However, it is relatively easy to check that, in figure 7.8, $\{Z_1, Z_2\}$ is a reactive equilibrium. The initial "defector" must make an offer like Z^* to generate an expected profit. But then another buyer can counter with Z^{**}, thereby attracting away some high-quality workers. As this process continues, θ will fall until Z^* generates losses, while Z^{**} remains strictly profitable, since $w^{**} < \theta_2$.

To conclude, the endogenous revelation of information via markets is, after all, explainable as a non-cooperative equilibrium phenomenon. While in general there is no Cournot-Nash equilibrium, recognition of reasonable reactions by other agents always results in a stable equilibrium.

Informational inferences from market prices

We now consider the problem of *information leakage*. Above, the process of speculation was interpreted as largely due to differences of information and belief. Nevertheless, the problem of *leakage* did not arise there because no trader regarded any other individual's knowledge or beliefs as intrinsically superior to his own. Here, we will suppose instead, everyone recognizes that some traders do and others do not possess an *informa-*

tional advantage. (Though traders with an informational advantage may not be publicly identified as such.) In the preceding section, better-informed individuals were seeking to *overcome* the informational disparity by signalling to potential trading partners. In this section, in contrast, the better-informed individuals are trying to *capitalize* on the disparity, by adopting a speculative position before their informational advantage disappears.

For concreteness, we can imagine that an information service μ is available which, at a certain price k, will (non-exclusively) provide any purchaser with conclusive information as to which state of the world will obtain. Initially, all the potential traders (speculators) may be assumed to have the same beliefs. But *anyone* can become better informed, and *everyone* knows that this is the case. The first, rather obvious point is that the speculative profit to those who become better-informed will decrease the larger the number purchasing the information. Figure 7.9 illustrates a two-state situation. An individual has an endowment $E = (\omega_1, \omega_2)$ and beliefs (π_1, π_2). With initial state-claim prices (P_1, P_2), his optimal consumption point is C_0. If he purchases information at a price k (to be

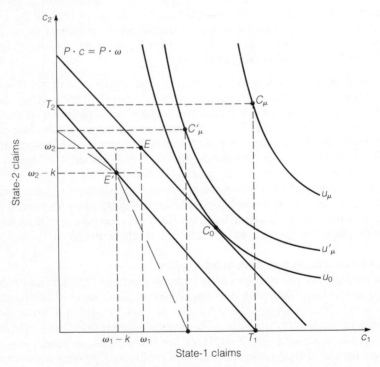

FIGURE 7.9 *Trading by informed agents.*

paid regardless of state), his endowment shifts to $E' = (\omega_1 - k, \omega_2 - k)$. He then anticipates that with probability π_1 he will learn that the true state is $s = 1$. In this case he will exchange all his state-2 claims for additional consumption in state 1 (point T_1). Similarly, with probability π_2 he anticipates learning that the true state is $s = 2$, in which case he sells all his state-1 claims (point T_2). The final consumption vector C_μ yields him an expected utility gain of $u_\mu - u_0$.

But, of course, the higher expected utility associated with the information service μ attracts other individuals. If the message is that the true state is $s = 1$, *all* the informed individuals will be in the market purchasing state-1 claims. This pushes up the relative price of these claims (steeper dashed budget line through E'). Similarly if the true state is $s = 2$ the price of state-2 claims is bid up (flatter dashed budget line). Final consumption is thus lower in each state, reducing the expected utility of informed agents from u_μ to u'_μ. As there is still a gain over u_0, purchase of information continues – until the utility gain due to informed trading is exactly offset by the cost k of obtaining and processing the information.

So far, it looks as if there may be an equilibrium in terms of a fraction of traders that choose to become informed. But there is a further complication. Should the true state be $s = 1$, as long as any traders at all are buying the information, the price of state-1 claims will tend to rise in comparison with the initial uninformed situation – and, of course, the reverse if $s = 2$ is going to obtain. So individuals not purchasing the information can *infer* it, simply by observing the movement of market prices! (Green, 1973, 1977; Grossman and Stiglitz, 1976.) They will therefore speculate in the same direction as those who have paid to become informed. With sufficiently hair-trigger reaction functions on the part of the uninformed, there will not even be a gross profit to those choosing to buy the information – so that, on net, these latter must lose.

In general, of course, prices may depend upon a great number of unknown or partially known determinants or parameters, apart from the uncertain element here that defines the state (e.g. the weather). But the same general result will continue to hold, so long as the price vector $p(I)$, which would prevail if *all* agents had all the available information I, differs for each different I. Then the function $p(I)$ is invertible, and $I = f^{-1}(p)$. That is, the information can be computed from the prices; or, the price vector p is a sufficient statistic for I (Kihlstrom and Mirman, 1975; Grossman, 1977). With a finite number of states, it is almost certainly the case that even in very incomplete markets the function $p(I)$ is invertible (Radner, 1979). Thus there is almost certainly a "fulfilled-expectations" equilibrium in which each agent correctly infers aggregate information from the price vector p. (As above, however, this conclusion relies on a rather extreme "correct conditional price forecasting" assumption, in which each trader is able to *compute* the equilibrium price vector associated with each state of the world.)

As in the case of the signalling models considered above, there is a market externality here that tends to break down any equilibrium in which information is obtained only at a cost. If none are informed, there is potential profit in becoming informed; yet if anyone invests in information and trades accordingly, he loses in comparison with those who have not invested. The "reactive equilibrium" here would evidently be the corner solution with no informational investments. However, in contrast with the signalling case, an interior solution can be obtained by introducing noise or lags. If only imperfect information about the state of nature can be inferred by observing prices (as will generally be the case with a continuum of states [Grossman, 1977; Jordan, 1976]), or if the informed individual can make his commitments before the uninformed can fully react, there will tend to be an equilibrium *fraction* of traders who choose to become informed.

Rational expectations and informational efficiency

There is much confusion about both the logical meaning and the descriptive realism of the interrelated concepts of "rational expectations" and "informational efficiency."

The original idea of rational expectations is that anticipations "are essentially the same as the predictions of the relevant economic theory" (Muth, 1961, p. 316). This can be visualized in a very simple temporal model without *exogenous* uncertainty – that is, a world where present and future endowed supplies, productive opportunities, utility functions, etc., are all perfectly known and determinate. In such a world there would, in general, be trading at different dates. And since the relative supply–demand situations for the various goods may change as the economy moves on its world-line, there is no reason to expect the *spot* price ratios to remain constant over time.

Suppose that, despite universal knowledge of the exogenous data, traders have divergent beliefs about the implied solution values for *endogenous* variables – in particular, about future spot prices. This possiblity is of interest in connection with the problem of incompleteness of market regimes discussed above. For concreteness, think of a two-period world. *Complete* markets at the current date (the analog of *complete conditional* markets as discussed earlier, but in the absence of exogenous uncertainty there is only one state) would provide for trading in the $2G$ claims c_{tg} at prices P_{tg}^0 – where the first subscript represents the effective date of the claim ($t = 0, 1$) and the second designates the good ($g = 1, ..., G$), while the superscript indicates the *trading date*. In an *incomplete* market regime with *no* futures markets, the future-dated claims c_{1g} would not be tradable at $t = 0$, so that the prices P_{1g}^0 would not exist. (In either case, however, there could be later spot trading at $t = 1$, at prices P_{1g}^1.)

In either market regime, individuals' trading decisions today will depend upon their anticipations as to the later spot prices P_{1g}^1, since there will in general be both productive interdependencies (e.g. storage possibilities) and utility complementaries between the two dates. And, in consequence, the equilibrium prices in today's and tomorrow's markets will generally both depend upon the anticipations that the individuals hold today. But following a familiar theme of the previous discussion, a *complete* regime at $t = 0$ makes "correct price forecasting" for $t = 1$ easy: "no change" will be the correct prediction. That is, if all traders forecast that the *later spot* price ratios will equal the *current futures* price ratios ($P_{1g'}^0/P_{1g''}^0 = P_{1g'}^1/P_{1g''}^1$) and make their current trading decisions accordingly, their anticipations will be borne out.

It is thus the absence of futures markets that creates the forecasting problem envisaged by the rational expectations literature (Arrow, 1978). We have seen that, strictly speaking, with incomplete markets today individuals cannot compute (from information privately available to them) tomorrow's spot prices necessary to guide today's productive and consumptive decisions. The model of rational expectations nevertheless assumes that, at least on average, they *can* do so. Each person in effect makes a guess on the basis of his private bit of information (as well as his general knowledge of relationships such as the law of supply and demand), and the errors of the various independent guesses balance out in the aggregate: "...allowing for cross-sectional differences in expectations is a simple matter, because their aggregate effect is negligible as long as the deviation from the rational forecast...is not strongly correlated with those of the others" (Muth, 1961, p. 321.)

The central idea of rational expectations can of course be applied more generally than in our bare-bones illustrative example: there can be more than two dates, not *all* futures markets need be lacking, individuals can have subjective probability distributions rather than simple point estimates for the unknown future spot prices, and finally some agreed patterns of exogenous uncertainty might be introduced – as in a random shift factor for future supply and/or demand. These generalizations lead to complications that cannot be pursued here. But even in the simplest version the assumption remains a strong one, whose virtue is in enabling us to close our intertemporal models and force out solutions. We shall not attempt to comment here on the descriptive validity of these models; just how validity might be tested is not at all evident and has been the subject of controversy. One interesting point brought out by Arrow (1978) is that the rational-expectations assumption in effect stands on its head the famous argument by Friedrich. A Hayek (1945) about the informational function of the market system. Hayek's view was that market prices convey to traders all they need to know about the vastly detailed particular circumstances of other economic agents. Without a price system, a central planner would require an impossibly elaborate data-gathering and data-analysing scheme to reproduce its results. But rational expectations implies that the price signals from the missing markets are not needed after all; traders can, at least on average, reproduce the missing signals on their own!

In these microeconomic applications, rational expectations essentially means correct prediction of the prices that will reign given different objective exogenous contingencies – what we have called "correct conditional price forecasting." No restrictions are placed upon subjective beliefs as to the probabilities of the different states. In contrast, a central feature of *macro*economic applications (Lucas, 1972; Sargent and Wallace, 1975) has been that individuals are not only superior econometricians but clairvoyant about events as well. Frank H. Knight seems to have anticipated this view: "We are so built that what seems to us reasonable is likely to be confirmed by experience, or we could not live in the world at all" (1921, p. 227). In the present context, it is supposed that in addition to being able to analyse the macroeconomic effects of any given monetary policy, individuals can also decipher the actual monetary rule being followed.

This Lincolnesque idea that "the people can't be fooled" may be based upon viewing the underlying world process as stochastically stationary, so that individuals can gradually learn both about the effects of events upon prices and about the probability distribution of events. However, this learning evolution does not imply that beliefs would be on average correct except in the limit.

Prices in an economy will be related to the knowledge and beliefs of all participating traders – possibly weighted by endowed wealths, degree of risk aversion, etc. Under the heading of *informational efficiency*, the issue has been raised as to whether prices "fully reflect" people's current information (Fama, 1970).

Unfortunately, the meaning of the term "fully reflect" has proved elusive. Mark E. Rubinstein has proposed that information be said to be already reflected in prices if, upon arrival of the message, traders have no incentive to revise portfolios (1975). On this definition, he shows that prices can almost never "fully reflect information." As follows from the earlier section on public information and market equilibrium, there are two main reasons: (1) even with agreed beliefs, incomplete regimes of *prior* markets generally make posterior trading (portfolio revision) unavoidable, and (2) with diverging beliefs and consequent speculative prior trading, it will be necessary to close out speculative positions in the posterior round.

The most widely held interpretation – what has been called the "weak form" of the proposition – is that markets are "informationally efficient" if, as a pragmatic matter, there is no way to make a profit (more precisely, to achieve an expected utility gain) from information already in the public domain. In particular, there is no way to outsmart the stockmarket by detecting patterns of price movement in the historic record.

This interpretation in effect asserts that, at least on average, individuals can *process* available information correctly. (While cost of processing may prevent perfect adjustment, errors tend to cancel out.) More specifically, this has been taken to imply that prices should follow a *martingale* process. That is, except perhaps for time and risk adjustment factors, the price today should be the mathematical expectation of the price tomorrow (Samuelson, 1965). However, it has been shown that even supposing known or agreed probabilities (without which it would be impossible to calculate mathematical expectations), only under very special conditions does a martingale in prices result (Woodward, 1979). First of all, prices are *ratios*: if a given ratio followed the martingale property, in general its reciprocal (the ratio taken the other way) would not. And even if expressed in terms of some standard numeraire commodity, prices would not follow a martingale unless there were no utility complementaries between the numeraire and other goods (Salant, 1976). It has also sometimes been argued that failure of prices to follow a martingale would by definition create an arbitrage-like profit opportunity in the sense of a positive expectation of gain from holding an asset, over and above the normal interest yield. But, as we have seen from our earlier discussion of private and social risks, a higher *mathematical expectation* of income does not in general represent higher *expected utility*, so this argument is erroneous.

The "strong form" of the efficient market hypothesis has been taken to mean that even *private* information cannot be profitably used (compare our discussion of "information leakage" above). This form of the hypothesis does not seem consistent with the evidence – for example, of gains from insider trading (surveyed in Copeland and Weston [1979, ch. 9]). As for the "weak form," numerous econometric studies have concluded that it is not possible to reject the hypothesis that price changes are independent of past prices. However, there does not yet seem to be a sufficiently well-specified model to allow testing the hypothesis that price changes are independent of *all* public information (but see Figlewski [1979]).

Informational activities, finally, have an unusual relation to economic equilibrium. Information generation is in large part a disequilibrium-creating process [Schumpeter, (1911) 1936], and information dissemination a disequilibrium-repairing process. The two are intertwined, as we have seen, in very complex ways. It does not yet seem that we are very close to having an efficiency concept that can usefully be employed to measure the dynamically optimal level of such activities.

REFERENCES

Akerlof, George, A. "The Market for 'Lemons': Qualitative Uncertainty and the Market Mechanism," *Quarterly Journal of Economics*, vol. 84 (Aug. 1970), pp. 488–500.

Alchian, Armen A. "The Meaning of Utility Measurement," *American Economic Review*, vol. 43 (March 1953), pp. 26–50.

—— and Demsetz, H. "Production, Information Costs, and Economic Organization," *American Economic Review*, vol. 62 (Dec. 1972), pp. 777–95.

Arrow, Kenneth J. "Le Role des Valeurs Boursières pour la Répartition la Meilleure des Risques," in *International Colloqium on Econometrics* (1952), Paris: Centre National de la Recherche Scientifique, (1953).

—— "Economic Welfare and the Allocation of Resources for Invention," in *The Rate and Direction of Inventive Activity: Economic and Social Factors*, Universities–NBER Conference Series, Princeton, NJ: Princeton University Press (1962), pp. 609–25.

—— "Uncertainty and the Welfare Economics of Medical Care," *American Economic Review*, vol. 53 (Dec. 1963), pp. 941–73.

—— "The Role of Securities in the Optimal Allocation of Risk-Bearing," *Review of Economic Studies*, vol. 31 (April 1964), pp. 91–6.

—— *Aspects of the Theory of Risk-Bearing*, Helsinki: Yrjö Jahnssonin Säätio (1965).

—— "The Future and the Present in Economic Life," *Economic Inquiry*, vol. 16 (April 1978), pp. 157–69.

—— and Fisher, Anthony C. "Environmental Preservation, Uncertainty and Irreversibility," *Quarterly Journal of Economics*, vol. 88 (May 1974), pp. 312–19.

—— and Lind, Robert C. "Uncertainty and the Evaluation of Public Investment," *American Economic Review*, vol. 60 (June 1970), pp. 364–78.

Bailey, Martin J. and Jensen, Michael C. "Risk and the Discount Rate for Public Investment," in M. C. Jensen, *Studies in the Theory of Capital Markets*, New York: Praeger (1972), pp. 269–93.

Barzel, Yoram "Optimal Timing of Innovations," *Review of Economics and Statistics*, vol. 50 (Aug. 1968), pp. 348–55.

Baumol, William "The Neumann–Morgenstern Utility Index: An Ordinalist View," *Journal of Political Economy*, vol. 59 (Feb. 1951), pp. 61–6.

—— "On Taxation and the Control of Externalities," *American Economic Review*, vol. 62 (June 1972), pp. 307–22.

Bergstrom, Theodore "Preference and Choice in Matters of Life and Death," in Jack Hirshleifer, Theodore Bergstrom, and Edward Rappaport, *Applying Cost-benefit Concepts to Projects which Alter Human Mortality*, UCLA School of Engineering and Applied Science, ENG—7478 (Nov. 1974).

Borch, Karl "Indifference Curves and Uncertainty," *Swedish Journal of Economics*, vol. 70 (March 1968), pp. 19–24.

Brainard, William C. and F. Trenery Dolbear Jr, "Social Risk and Financial Markets," *American Economic Review*, (May 1971), vol. 61 (2), pp. 360–70.

Calabresi, Guido *The Costs of Accidents: A Legal and Economic Analysis*, New Haven: Yale University Press (1970).

Cheung, Steven N. S. *The Theory of Share Tenancy: With Special Application to Asian Agriculture and the First Phase of Taiwan Land Reform*, Chicago: University of Chicago Press (1969a).

—— "Transaction Costs, Risk Aversion and the Choice of Contractual Arrangements," *Journal of Law and Economics*, vol. 12 (April 1969b), pp. 23–42.

—— "Property Rights and Inventions," University of Washington Institute of Economic Research, Report no. 79–11, (1979a).

—— "The Right to Invent and the Right to an Invention," University of Washington Institute of Economic Research, Report no. 79-13, (1979b).

Conley, Bryan C. "The Value of Human Life in the Demand for Safety," *American Economic Review*, vol. 66 (March 1976), pp. 45-55.

Cook, Phillip J. and Graham, Daniel A. "The Demand for Insurance and Protection: The Case of Irreplaceable Commodities," *Quarterly Journal of Economics*, vol. 91 (Feb. 1977), pp. 143-56.

Cootner, Paul H. "Speculation, Hedging and Arbitrage," in *International Encyclopedia of the Social Sciences*, vol. 15 (1968), New York: Macmillan, Free Press, pp. 117-21.

Copeland, Thomas E. and Weston, J. Fred *Financial Theory and Corporate Policy*, Reading, Mass.: Addison-Wesley (1979).

DeAngelo, Harry *Three Essays in Financial Economics*, UCLA, Ph.D. dissertation, (1979).

Debreu, Gerard *Theory of Value: An Axiomatic Analysis of Economic Equilibrium*, New York: Wiley and Sons (1959).

Diamond, Peter A. "The Role of a Stock Market in a General Equilibrium Model with Technological Uncertainty," *American Economic Review*, vol. 57 (Sept. 1967), pp. 759-76.

—— "Accident Law and Resource Allocation," *Bell Journal of Economics*, vol. 5 (Autumn 1974), pp. 366-405.

Drèze, Jacques H. "Market Allocation Under Uncertainty," *European Economic Review*, vol. 2 (Winter 1970-1), pp. 133-65.

Ehrlich, Isaac and Becker, Gary S. "Market Insurance, Self-Insurance, and Self-Protection," *Journal of Political Economy*, vol. 80 (July-Aug. 1972), pp. 623-48.

Ekern, Steinar and Wilson, Robert "On the Theory of the Firm in an Economy with Incomplete Markets," *Bell Journal of Economics*, vol. 5 (Spring 1974), pp. 171-80.

Fama, Eugene F. "Efficient Capital Markets: A Review of Theory and Empirical Work," *Journal of Finance*, vol. 25 (May 1970), pp. 383-417.

—— and Laffer, Arthur B. "Information and Capital Markets," *Journal of Business*, vol. 44 (July 1971), pp. 289-98.

—— and Miller, Merton H. *The Theory of Finance*, New York: Holt, Rinehart & Winston (1972).

Feiger, George "What Is Speculation?" *Quarterly Journal of Economics*, vol. 90 (Nov. 1976), pp. 677-88.

Feldstein, Martin S. "Mean-Variance Analysis in the Theory of Liquidity Preference and Portfolio Selection," *Review of Economic Studies*, vol. 36 (Jan. 1969), pp. 5-12.

Figlewski, Stephen "Subjective Information and Market Efficiency in a Betting Market," *Journal of Political Economy*, vol. 87 (Feb. 1979), pp. 75-88.

Fisher, Irving *The Nature of Capital and Income*, New York: Macmillan (1912).

—— *The Theory of Interest*, New York: Macmillan (1930).

Friedman, Milton and Savage, Leonard J. "The Utility Analysis of Choices Involving Risks," *Journal of Political Economy*, vol. 56 (Aug. 1948), pp. 279-304.

Gordon, H. Scott "The Economic Theory of a Common Property Resource: The Fishery," *Journal of Political Economy*, vol. 62 (April 1954), pp. 124-42.

Green, Jerry *Information, Efficiency and Equilibrium*, Harvard Institute of Economic Research, Discussion Paper no. 284 (March 1973).

—— "The Non-existence of Informational Equilibria," *Review of Economic Studies*, vol. 44 (Oct. 1977), pp. 451–63.

—— "Statistical Decision Theory Requiring Incentives for Information Transfer," in J. J. McCall, *The Economics of Information and Uncertainty*, Universities–NBER Conference Series, Chicago (1982).

Grossman, Sanford J. "The Existence of Futures Markets, Noisy Rational Expectations and Informational Externalities," *Review of Economic Studies*, vol. 44 (Oct. 1977), pp. 431–49.

—— and Stiglitz, Joseph E. "Information and Competitive Price Systems," *American Economic Review*, vol. 66 (May 1976), pp. 246–53.

Groves, Theodore "Incentives in Teams," *Econometrica*, vol. 41 (July 1973), pp. 617–31.

Hakansson, Nils H., Kunkel, J. Gregory and Ohlson, James A. "Sufficient and Necessary Conditions for Information to Have Social Value in Pure Exchange," School of Business Administration, University of California, Berkeley (June 1979).

Harris, Milton and Raviv, Artur "Some Results on Incentive Contracts with Applications to Education and Employment, Health Insurance, and Law Enforcement," *American Economic Review*, vol. 68 (March 1978), pp. 20–30.

Hart, Oliver D. "On the Optimality of Equilibrium when the Market Structure is Incomplete," *Journal of Economic Theory*, vol. 11 (Dec. 1975), pp. 418–43.

Hayek, Friedrich A. "The Use of Knowledge in Society," *American Economic Review*, vol. 35 (Sept. 1945), pp. 519–30.

Henry, Claude "Investment Decisions Under Uncertainty: The 'Irreversibility Effect'," *American Economic Review*, vol. 64 (Dec. 1974), pp. 1006–12.

Hicks, John *Value and Capital*, second edition, Oxford: Oxford University Press, Clarendon Press (1946).

Hirshleifer, Jack "Investment Decision Under Uncertainty: Applications of the State-Preference Approach," *Quarterly Journal of Economics*, vol. 80 (May 1966), pp. 252–77. (Reprinted in this volume, ch. 6.)

—— *Investment, Interest and Capital*, Englewood Cliffs, NJ: Prentice-Hall (1970).

—— "The Private and Social Value of Information and the Reward to Inventive Activity," *American Economic Review*, vol. 61 (Sept. 1971), pp. 561–74. (Reprinted in this volume, ch. 9.)

—— "Liquidity, Uncertainty, and the Accumulation of Information," in C. F. Carter and J. L. Ford, *Uncertainty and Expectations in Economics: Essays in Honour of G. L. S. Shackle*, Oxford: Blackwell (1972), pp. 136–47. (Reprinted in this volume, ch. 8.)

—— "Where Are We in the Theory of Information?", *American Economic Review*, vol. 63 (May 1973), pp. 31–9.

—— "Speculation and Equilibrium: Information, Risk, and Markets," *Quarterly Journal of Economics*, vol. 89 (Nov. 1975), pp. 519–42. (Reprinted in this volume, ch. 10.)

—— "The Theory of Speculation Under Alternative Regimes of Markets," *Journal of Finance*, vol. 32 (Sept. 1977), pp. 975–99. (Reprinted in this volume, ch. 11.)

Houthakker, Hendrik S. "Can Speculators Forecast Prices?" *Review of Economics and Statistics*, vol. 39 (May 1957), pp. 143–51.

—— "Normal Backwardation," in J. N. Wolfe, *Value, Capital, and Growth: Papers in Honour of Sir John Hicks*, Edinburgh: Edinburgh University Press (1968), pp. 193–214.

Jensen, Michael C., "Capital Markets: Theory and Evidence," *Bell Journal of Economics*, vol. 3 (Autumn 1972), pp. 357–98.

—— and Meckling, William H. "Theory of the Firm: Managerial Behavior, Agency Costs and Ownership Structure," *Journal of Finance and Economics*, vol. 3 (Oct. 1976), pp. 305–60.

Jones, Robert A. and Ostroy, Joseph "Uncertainty and Flexibility," UCLA Discussion Paper no. 73 (July 1976).

Jones-Lee, Michael W. *The Value of Life: An Economic Analysis*, Chicago: University of Chicago Press (1976).

Jordan, James S. *Expectations Equilibrium and Informational Efficiency for Stochastic Environments*, University of Minnesota, Center for Economic Research, Discussion Paper no. 71, (Aug. 1976).

Keynes, John Maynard *A Treatise on Money*, New York: Harcourt Brace (1930).

Kihlstrom, Richard E. and Mirman, Leonard J. "Information and Market Equilibrium," *Bell Journal of Economics*, vol. 6 (Spring 1975), pp. 357–76.

Knight, Frank H. *Risk, Uncertainty and Profit*, New York: Houghton Mifflin (1921).

Linnerooth, Joanne "The Value of Human Life: A Review of the Models," *Economic Inquiry*, vol. 17 (Jan. 1979), pp. 52–74.

Lintner, John "Dividends, Earnings, Leverage, Stock Prices and the Supply of Capital to Corporations," *Review of Economics and Statistics*, vol. 44 (Aug. 1962), pp. 243–69.

—— "The Valuation of Risk Assets and the Selection of Risky Investments in Stock Portfolios and Capital Budgets," *Review of Economics and Statistics*, vol. 47 (Feb. 1965), pp. 13–37.

Lippman, Steven A. and McCall, John J. "The Economics of Job Search: A Survey," *Economic Inquiry*, vol. 14 (June 1976), pp. 155–89.

Lucas, Robert E., Jr "Expectations and the Neutrality of Money," *Journal of Economic Theory*, vol. 4 (April 1972), pp. 103–24.

Luce, R. Duncan and Raiffa, Howard *Games and Decisions: Introduction and Critical Survey*, New York: Wiley and Sons (1957).

Machlup, Fritz *The Production and Distribution of Knowledge in the United States*, Princeton, NJ: Princeton University Press (1962).

—— "Patents," *International Encyclopedia of the Social Sciences*, vol. 11 (1968), New York: Macmillan, Free Press, pp. 461–72.

—— "The Economics of Knowledge and Information," Part Seven of *Knowledge: Its Creation, Distribution, and Economic Significance*, unpublished manuscript (1979).

Markowitz, Harry M. "The Utility of Wealth," *Journal of Political Economy*, vol. 60 (April 1952), pp. 151–58.

—— *Portfolio Selection: Efficient Diversification of Investments*, Cowles Foundation for Research in Economics, Yale University, Monograph 16, New York: Wiley and Sons (1959).

Marschak, Jacob "Role of Liquidity under Complete and Incomplete Information," *American Economic Review*, vol. 39 (May 1949), pp. 182–95.

—— "Decision-Making: Economic Aspects," *International Encyclopedia of the Social Sciences*, vol. 4 (1968), New York: Macmillan, Free Press, pp. 42–55.

—— "Economics of Information Systems," in M. D. Intriligator, *Frontiers of*

Quantitative Economics, Amsterdam: North-Holland (1971), pp. 32-107.

—— and Koichi Miyasawa "Economic Comparability of Information Systems," *International Economic Review*, vol. 9 (June 1968), pp. 137-74.

—— and Roy Radner *The Economic Theory of Teams*, Cowles Foundation for Research in Economics, monograph no. 22, New Haven: Yale University Press (1972).

Marschak, Thomas and Nelson, Richard "Flexibility, Uncertainty, and Economic Theory," *Metroeconomica*, vol. 14 (April-Dec. 1962), pp. 42-58.

Marshall, John M. "Private Incentives and Public Information," *American Economic Review*, vol. 64 (June 1974a), pp. 373-90.

—— "Insurance Theory: Reserves *versus* Mutuality," *Economic Inquiry*, vol. 12 (Dec. 1974b), pp. 476-92.

—— "Moral Hazard," *American Economic Review*, vol. 66 (Dec. 1976), pp. 880-90.

Mayshar, Joram "Should Government Subsidize Risky Private Projects?" *American Economic Review*, vol. 67 (March 1977), pp. 20-28.

McCall, John J. "The Economics of Information and Optimal Stopping Rules," *Journal of Business*, vol. 38 (July 1965), pp. 300-17.

McKinnon, Ronald I. "Futures Markets, Buffer Stocks, and Income Stability for Primary Producers," *Journal of Political Economy*, vol. 75 (Dec. 1967), pp. 844-61.

Merton, Robert C. "Investment Theory," in K. J. Arrow and M. D. Intriligator, *Handbook of Mathematical Economics*, Amsterdam: North-Holland (1988).

Mishan, Ezra J. "Evaluation of Life and Limb," *Journal of Political Economy*, vol. 79 (July-Aug. 1971), pp. 687-705.

Modigliani, Franco and Miller, Merton H. "The Cost of Capital, Corporation Finance and the Theory of Investment," *American Economic Review*, vol. 48 (June 1958), pp. 261-97.

Mossin, Jan "Equilibrium in a Capital Asset Market," *Econometrica*, vol. 34 (Oct. 1966), pp. 768-83.

Muth, John F. "Rational Expectations and the Theory of Price Movements," *Econometrica*, vol. 29 (July 1961), pp. 315-35.

Nelson, Phillip "Advertising as Information," *Journal of Political Economy*, vol. 82 (July-Aug. 1974), pp. 729-54.

—— "The Economic Consequences of Advertising," *Journal of Business*, vol. 48 (April 1975), pp. 213-41.

Von Neumann, John and Morgenstern, Oskar *Theory of Games and Economic Behavior*, Princeton, NJ: Princeton University Press (1944).

Pauly, Mark V. "The Economics of Moral Hazard: Comment," *American Economic Review*, vol. 58 (June 1968), pp. 531-36.

Pearl, Judea "An Economic Basis for Certain Methods of Evaluating Probabilistic Forecasts," *International Journal of Man-Machine Studies*, vol. 10 (1978), pp. 175-83.

Phelps, Edmund S. et al. *Microeconomic Foundations of Employment and Inflation Theory*, New York: Norton (1970).

Pratt, John W. "Risk Aversion in the Small and in the Large," *Econometrica*, vol. 32 (Jan.-April 1965), pp. 122-36.

Radner, Roy "Competitive Equilibrium under Uncertainty," *Econometrica*, vol. 36 (Jan. 1968), pp. 31-58.

—— "Rational Expectations Equilibrium: Generic Existence and the Information Revealed by Prices," *Econometrica*, vol. 47 (May 1979), pp. 655-78.

—— and Stiglitz, Joseph E. "A Nonconcavity in the Value of Information," unpublished manuscript, (July 1976).

Raiffa, Howard *Decision Analysis: Introductory Lectures on Choices under Uncertainty*, Reading, Mass.: Addison-Wesley (1968).

Reid, Joseph D., Jr "Sharecropping and Agricultural Uncertainty," *Economic Development and Cultural Change*, vol. 24 (April 1976), pp. 549-76.

Riley, John G. "Competitive Signalling," *Journal of Economic Theory*, vol. 10 (April 1975), pp. 174-86.

—— "Information, Screening and Human Capital," *American Economic Review*, vol. 66 (May 1976), pp. 254-60.

—— "Informational Equilibrium," *Econometrica*, vol. 47 (March 1979a), pp. 331-59.

—— "Testing the Educational Screening Hypothesis," *Journal of Political Economy*, vol. 87 (Oct. 1979b), Part 2, pp. 227-44.

Rothschild, Michael "Models of Market Organization with Imperfect Information: A Survey," *Journal of Political Economy*, vol. 81 (Nov.-Dec. 1973), pp. 1283-308.

—— and Stiglitz, Joseph E. "Increasing Risk: I. A Definition," *Journal of Economic Theory*, vol. 2 (Sept. 1970), pp. 225-43.

—— and —— "Increasing Risk: II. Economic Consequences," *Journal of Economic Theory*, vol. 3 (March 1971), pp. 66-84.

—— and —— "Equilibrium in Competitive Insurance Markets: An Essay on the Economics of Imperfect Information," *Quarterly Journal of Economics*, vol. 90 (Nov. 1976), pp. 629-49.

Rubinstein, Mark E. "Securities Market Efficiency in an Arrow-Debreu Economy," *American Economic Review*, vol. 65 (Dec. 1975), pp. 812-24.

Salant, Stephen W. "Hirshleifer on Speculation," *Quarterly Journal of Economics*, vol. 90 (Nov. 1976), pp. 667-76.

Samuelson, Paul A. "Proof that Properly Anticipated Prices Fluctuate Randomly," *Industrial Management Review*, vol. 6 (Spring 1965), pp. 41-9.

Sandmo, Agnar "Discount Rates for Public Investment under Uncertainty," *International Economic Review*, vol. 13 (June 1972), pp. 287-302.

Sargent, Thomas J. and Wallace, Neil "'Rational' Expectations, the Optimal Monetary Instrument, and the Optimal Money Supply Rule," *Journal of Political Economy*, vol. 83 (April 1975), pp. 241-54.

Savage, Leonard J. *The Foundations of Statistics*, New York: Wiley (1954).

Schelling, Thomas C. "The Life You Save May Be Your Own," in S. B. Chase, Jr, *Problems in Public Expenditures Analysis*, Washington DC: Brookings Institution (1968), pp. 127-62.

Schlaifer, Robert *Probability and Statistics for Business Decisions*, New York: McGraw-Hill (1959).

Schumpeter, Joseph A. *The Theory of Economic Development* (transl. from the German by Redvers Opie), Cambridge, Mass: Harvard University Press (1911, 1936).

Sharpe, William, F. "Capital Asset Prices: A Theory of Market Equilibrium under Conditions of Risk," *Journal of Finance*, vol. 19 (Sept. 1964), pp. 425-42.

—— *Investments*, Englewood Cliffs, NJ: Prentice-Hall (1978).

Shavell, Steven "On Valuable Opinion and the Efficiency of the Price System under Uncertainty," Harvard Institute of Economic Research, Discussion Paper no. 458 (March 1976).

—— "Do Managers Use Their Information Efficiently?" *American Economic Review*, vol. 68 (Dec. 1978), pp. 935–7.

Spence, A. Michael *Market Signalling: Informational Transfer in Hiring and Related Processes*, Cambridge, Mass: Harvard University Press (1974).

—— and Richard Zeckhauser, "Insurance, Information, and Individual Action," *American Economic Review*, vol. 61 (May 1971), pp. 380–7.

Stigler, George J. "The Economics of Information," *Journal of Political Economy*, vol. 69 (June 1961), pp. 213–25.

—— "Information in the Labor Market," *Journal of Political Economy*, vol. 70 (Oct. 1962), pp. 94–105.

Stiglitz, Joseph E. "The Theory of 'Screening', Education, and the Distribution of Income," *American Economic Review*, vol. 65 (June 1975), pp. 283–300.

Strotz, Robert H. "Cardinal Utility," *American Economic Review*, vol. 43 (May 1953), pp. 384–97.

Thaler, Richard H. and Rosen, Sherwin "The Value of Saving a Life: Evidence from the Labor Market," in N. E. Terleckyj, *Household Production and Consumption: Papers*, National Bureau of Economic Research, Studies in Income and Wealth, vol. 40, New York: NBER (1976), pp. 265–98.

Tobin, James "Liquidity Preference as Behavior Towards Risk," *Review of Economic Studies*, vol. 25 (Feb. 1958), pp. 65–86.

Townsend, Robert M. "On the Optimality of Forward Markets," *American Economic Review*, vol. 68 (March 1978), pp. 54–66.

Vickrey, William "Automobile Accidents, Tort Law, Externalities, and Insurance: An Economist's Critique," *Law and Contemporary Problems*, vol. 33 (Summer 1968), pp. 464–87.

Wilson, Charles A. "A Model of Insurance Markets with Incomplete Information," *Journal of Economic Theory*, vol. 16 (Dec. 1977), pp. 167–207.

Woodward, Susan E. *Two Essays in the Theory of Competitive Markets for Contingent Claims*, UCLA, Ph.D. dissertation (1979).

Working, Holbrook "Futures Trading and Hedging," *American Economic Review*, vol. 43 (June 1953), pp. 314–43.

—— "New Concepts Concerning Futures Markets and Prices," *American Economic Review*, vol. 52 (June 1962), pp. 431–59.

Zeckhauser, Richard "Medical Insurance: A Case Study of the Tradeoff between Risk Spreading and Appropriate Incentives," *Journal of Economic Theory*, vol. 2 (March 1970), pp. 10–26.

—— "Risk Spreading and Distribution," in H. M. Hochman and G. E. Peterson, *Redistribution through Public Choice*, New York: Columbia University Press (1974), pp. 206–28.

Zorn, Thomas S. *Information Differences, the Stockmarket, and Management Incentives*, UCLA Ph.D. dissertation (1978).

PART III

Applications of the Economic Theory of Information

8 Liquidity, Uncertainty, and the Accumulation of Information*

Background and comments

This article originally appeared in a collection of papers honoring a distinguished and innovative thinker in the area of the economics of information, G. L. S. Shackle.

The question addressed is the nature and significance of the concept of *liquidity*. Liquidity is interpreted here as equivalent to "flexibility," in the sense of ability to revise plans on the basis of later information without incurring extra costs. It is this sort of liquidity that is sacrificed when an agent makes long-term commitments that are not perfectly revocable. The article shows that individuals' *anticipations today*, of *information that will be arriving at later dates* to better guide investments, are the major source of the extra-high rate of return required to induce people to make long-term investments. Or, more generally, of the normally rising term structure of interest rates. The paper goes more deeply into the determinants of positive or negative liquidity in this sense, showing that a crucial role is played also by the intertemporal distribution of risky endowments and the prospects for transformation of them through productive processes like storage over time.

*This article originally appeared in C. F. Carter and J. L. Ford (eds), *Uncertainty and Expectations in Economics: Essays in Honour of G. L. S. Shackle* (Oxford: Basil Blackwell, 1972).

The research underlying this paper was undertaken while the author held a National Science Foundation Fellowship at the Catholic University of Louvain. Research and clerical assistance were provided by the Center for Operations Research and Econometrics at Louvain. Further clerical assistance was provided by the Western Management Science Institute, UCLA. Thanks are particularly due to Jacques Drèze for corrections and suggestions.

In the standard economic theory of value, market-clearing prices exist for all commodities. In such a model, all commodities are equally and perfectly "liquid." Clearly, the problem of imperfect liquidity arises only when one or more of the ground rules of the neoclassical model no longer obtain.

8.1   SOURCES OF ILLIQUIDITY[1]

The most obvious source of illiquidity is the fact that commodities are not in general perfectly and costlessly *marketable*, i.e. transaction costs exist in real-world asset markets. For one thing, limitations of information may prevent buyers and sellers from finding one another. Or, through misunderstanding or stubborness, they might not succeed in arriving at a bargain even when a mutually advantageous trade between them is possible. Then an individual transactor will find himself in the position of balancing the conjectural net advantage of further search and consequent negotiation against the alternative of accepting the best available offer now in hand. Since the costs and likely benefits of search and negotiations are in part a function of the nature of the commodity (its degree of standardization, its storability, portability, etc.), assets will vary in marketability. Marketability may also be affected by considerations other than the physical nature of the commodity. Tax provisions represent an obvious example: exchanges of some commodities, but not others, may be burdened by transaction duties – sales taxes, capital-gains taxes, etc. There may also be impaired marketability where a personal element attaches to an asset's productivity. In the case of a business firm whose success is associated with the personality of the proprietor, the sale-price of the physical assets of the firm will be low relative to the capitalization of the income yield to the present owner.

In the present paper, however, this entire range of phenomenon is set aside. It will be assumed that costless competitive markets *do* exist, so that all commodities are perfectly marketable. The purpose behind this unrealistic assumption is to facilitate the analysis of another distinct source of illiquidity, quite apart from impaired marketability. This second source of illiquidity is connected with inability to revise plans for consumption and investment in the light of later and better knowledge. Such a loss of flexibility will be accepted, and illiquid assets held, only if (as will be seen below) these investments have an offsetting advantage in productivity, i.e. less liquid assets will be associated with a higher rate of yield.

The source of illiquidity considered here is associated with the length of the period to "maturity" of the asset. Maturity is an unambiguous concept only for assets possessing a *point-input point-output* payment pattern. Examples include some financial assets, such as bills sold at discount (but not stocks or interest-bearing bonds), and some physical assets, such as trees grown for timber (but not trees grown for fruit). The central principle involved will stand out most clearly if we deal here only with such assets, with their unique encashment dates. Illiquid assets then are those characterized by a relatively large discount for "premature" realization; this corresponds to a relatively high time-rate of return if the asset is held rather than so realized. It remains to be shown just what are the underlying forces making this come about, and in particular why the time-rate of discount is greater on long-maturity assets – so that these tend to earn a higher rate of yield than short-maturity assets.[2]

In examining this question, a connection will be shown between *physical* illiquidity and *market* illiquidity. However, it is essential to distinguish the two in considering investments. A recently planted tree will be a highly illiquid asset in the physical sense, for it may be many years before any significant fraction of the ultimate timber yield can be realized even by early cutting. But it may be that the asset has perfect market liquidity – if title to such a tree can be immediately converted into money at a price representing only a normal time-discount of the future value at maturity.

8.2 INTERTEMPORAL CHOICE UNDER UNCERTAINTY

A time-state model of choice under uncertainty[3] will be employed to examine the forces determining the liquidity "premiums" enjoyed by short-maturity assets in market equilibrium. The bearing of the following necessary conditions will be elucidated: (1) *Uncertainty*, of a type that is at least partially dispelled by the unfolding of events over time. (There must also, of course, be market aversion to uncertainty.) (2) *Ability to defer* consumption-investment decisions, so that the reduction of uncertainty (accumulation of information) can be utilized. (3) At least partial *physical irreversibility* of longer-maturity productive investments, so that only the shorter-maturity investments can fully benefit from the possibility of reconsideration.

The time-state model used here has, as illustrated below, four marketable commodities: certain claims c_0 to consumption at time-0 ("the present"); contingent claims c_{1a} and c_{1b} to consumption at time-1, such claims being valid if and only if state-a or state-b, respectively, obtains at time-1; and certain claims c_2 to consumption at time-2.[4] A unit of *certain* dated income will be expressed as c_0, c_1, or c_2 – where any particular numerical value given for c_1 indicates that *both* c_{1a} and c_{1b} have that same numerical value. The very special nature of this model is not really as restrictive as appears. The principles remain the same if the number of uncertain states is increased or if uncertainty is admitted at a number of future dates up to some terminal horizon.[5]

Date: 0   1   2

Commodities: c_0 $\begin{matrix} c_{1a} \\ \\ c_{1b} \end{matrix}$ c_2

At this point a formal definition of liquidity-premiums can be provided. Let P_0, P_1, and P_2 symbolize the prices of unit claims to certain incomes at the respective dates, all these prices being determined at $t=0$. Let c_0 be the numeraire commodity, with $P_0 = 1$. A premium (which may or may not be a *liquidity*-premium) on the shorter-maturity asset will be said to exist at $t=0$ if the ratio P_1/P_0 exceeds the ratio P_2/P_1 – or, equivalently, if $(P_1/P_0)^2$ exceeds P_2/P_0.

The same relationships can be translated into interest-rate equivalents, where "riskless" interest rates (the only rates to be considered here) are defined in terms of prices of certain incomes of the various dates.

$$P_1 = \frac{1}{1 + r_1}$$

$$P_2 = \frac{1}{(1 + r_2)(1 + r_1)} = \frac{1}{(1 + R_2)^2} .$$

(8.1)

Here the lower-case symbols represent "short-term" interest rates, $1 + r_1$ being the discounting factor translating certain income at time-1 into its equivalent at time-0 and $1 + r_2$ the factor translating certain income at time-2 into the immediately preceding time-1. The upper-case symbol represents a "long-term" rate, $1 + R_2$ being the discounting factor which (when properly compounded) translates income at time-2 into present income at time-0. Then a premium on the *prices* of short-term assets would correspond to a premium on the pecuniary *yields* of the long-term assets, so that R_2 exceeds r_1 – or, equivalently, the "deferred" short-term rate r_2 would exceed the current short-term rate r_1.

Finally, we can define P_{1a} and P_{1b} as the prices of the respective contingent claims at time-1, where

$$P_1 = P_{1a} + P_{1b},$$

(8.2)

since a unit certain claim at a given date is obtained only by purchasing unit contingent claims covering each contingency at that date.

By an extension of the familiar Neumann–Morgenstern procedure to intertemporal risky choices, a cardinal function $v(c_0, c_1, c_2)$ spanning consumption at different dates and satisfying the expected-utility rule can be established.[6] Then:

$$U = \sum_{s=1}^{S} \pi_s v(c_{0s}, c_{1s}, c_{2s}),$$

(8.3)

where s is an index running over the S possible *sequences* of time-states, π_s is the probability of the sequence, while c_{ts} is the consumption at time-t associated with the sequence-s. In the particularly simple model used here, there are but two such sequences: c_0, c_{1a}, c_2 and c_0, c_{1b}, c_2. The sequence-probabilities correspond simply to the state-probabilities at time-1. These may be denoted π_a and π_b. So the utility function specializes to:

$$U = \pi_a v(c_0, c_{1a}, c_2) + \pi_b v(c_0, c_{1b}, c_2). \tag{8.3a}$$

To carry the analysis further, let us assume that a community of "representative individuals" with identical tastes and opportunities exists – each having the same endowment vector $(y_0, y_{1a}, y_{1b}, y_2)$ over the four commodities. Let us suppose initially the world is one of pure exchange, excluding all intertemporal productive possibilities. Among the excluded possibilities is simple storage, which (as a way of moving real income forward over time) represents one type of intertemporal productive transformation. In the absence of productive possibilities, a "sustaining" price vector must emerge making each representative individual just willing to hold his endowment combination – thus, no exchange actually takes place. The sustaining prices, with $P_0 = 1$, are given by:

$$P_{1a} = \frac{\partial c_0}{\partial c_{1a}}\bigg|_U = \frac{\pi_a v'_{1a}}{v'_0}$$

$$P_{1b} = \frac{\partial c_0}{\partial c_{1b}}\bigg|_U = \frac{\pi_b v'_{1b}}{v'_0} \tag{8.4}$$

$$P_2 = \frac{\partial c_0}{\partial c_2}\bigg|_U = \frac{v'_2}{v'_0}$$

where the derivatives are to be evaluated at the endowed quantities.

Consider the following numerical example. Let the v-function of (8.3a) be:

$$v(c_0, c_1, c_2) = \sum_{t=0}^{2} \ln c_t. \tag{8.5}$$

Then

$$U = \pi_a(\ln c_0 + \ln c_{1a} + \ln c_2) + \pi_b(\ln c_0 + \ln c_{1b} + \ln c_2) \tag{8.6}$$

$$= \ln c_0 + \pi_a \ln c_{1a} + \pi_b \ln c_{1b} + \ln c_2.$$

Let $\pi_a = \pi_b = \frac{1}{2}$, and the endowment vector $(y, y_{1a}, y_{1b}, y_2) = (100, 150, 75, 100)$. With $P_0 = 1$, the sustaining prices are $P_{1a} = \frac{1}{3}$, $P_{1b} = \frac{2}{3}$ (so that $P_1 = P_{1a} + P_{1b} = 1$), and $P_2 = 1$ (see table 8.1). The numerical example has evidently been constructed to make all the interest rates zero; since

TABLE 8.1 *Pure-exchange solution*

| | Quantities | | | Prices | | | Marginal utilities | |
t:	0	1	2	0	1	2	0	1	2
		150			1/3			0.0033	
	100		100	1		1	0.01		0.01
		75			2/3			0.0067	
					—			—	
					1			0.01	
					Discount rates				
					—	0%	0%		

$R_2 = r_1$, *no liquidity premium initially exists.* That is, riskless short-maturity assets (claims to c_1) are discounted at the same time-rate (0 percent) as long-maturity assets (claims to c_2).

Now, continuing in the context of the numerical example, suppose that the possibility of production is admitted in the form of costless and riskless intertemporal *storage*. Thus, arrangements can be made to transform at par units of c_0 into units of c_1 or of c_2, and units of c_1 into c_2. But, any such decisions are to be made *now* (at time-0), in ignorance of which state will actually obtain at time-1. Then it is evident that no storage will actually take place, the solution remaining unchanged from that shown in table 8.1. In particular, the ruling prices remain the same and, consequently, there is no liquidity premium. For, from the point of view of any individual, the possibility of physical storage transformations at par are no more favorable on the margin than the possibilities of exchange transformations already available at the price ratios $P_1/P_0 = P_2/P_1 = 1$. Or, in terms of the marginal utilities, we can see that $U_0' = 1/c_0 = 0.01$, $U_1' = U_{1a}' + U_{1b}' = \frac{1}{2}v_{1a}' + \frac{1}{2}v_{1b}' = \frac{1}{2}(1/150) + \frac{1}{2}(1/75) = 0.01$, and also $U_2' = 1/c_2 = 0.01$ – all the marginal utilities being already equal, there is no point in storage transformations.

The situation is quite different, however, if it is possible for the individual to defer the decision as to storage transformations between time-1 and time-2 until *after* learning which of the contingencies has been realized at the former date. It is then evident that if the better-endowed state-*a* obtains at time-1, storage would take place – in the example of table 8.1, if y_1 were known to equal 150, we would have $U_1' = v_{1a}' = 1/150 < U_2' = 1/100$ instead of $U_1' = \frac{1}{2}v_{1a}' + \frac{1}{2}v_{1b}' = 0.01 = U_2'$. On the other hand, if state-*b* obtains, there is no incentive for storage since $y_{1b} = 75$ as against $y_2 = 100$, and $U_1' = 1/75$ would be greater than U_2'. The possibility of taking advantage of later information thus lends a certain flexibility to time-1 claims (short-term assets) viewed at time-0. We would expect that, for the original decision at time-0, individuals would desire to transfer consumption from both c_0 and c_2 toward c_1. But, since storage is one-directional over time, the transformation from c_2 to c_1 cannot physically take place. The lessened desire to hold c_2 should then reveal itself in a fall in P_2 relative to P_1 – i.e. in a liquidity-premium for the shorter-maturity claims. On the other hand, since storage from time-0 to time-1 is possible, we would expect such storage to occur – minimizing the tendency of the price P_1 to rise relative to P_0.

These relationships can be illustrated by obtaining a solution for the numerical example when storage is permitted. Note first that c_2 being no longer immutable, we must respecify the sequences entering into the calculation of utility as c_0, c_{1a}, c_{2a} and c_0, c_{1b}, c_{2b} – where c_{2a} benefits from storage transfers from time-1 when state-a obtains. Then:

$$U = \pi_a v(c_0, c_{1a}, c_{2a}) + \pi_b v(c_0, c_{1b}, c_{2b}). \tag{8.7}$$

Now, it is evident from the symmetry of the v-function in the form (8.5) that the storage transfers that take place at time-1 when state-a obtains will be such as to equalize c_{1a} and c_{2a}. If we symbolize storage at time-0 by z_0, and storage at time-state-$1a$ by z_{1a}, we know that $z_{1a} = \frac{1}{2}(y_{1a} + z_0 - y_2)$. Hence the optimum may be found by maximizing utility with respect to the single variable z_0.

$$\frac{dU}{dz_0} = v_0' \frac{dc_0}{dz_0} + \pi_a v_{1a}' \frac{dc_{1a}}{dz_0} + \pi_a v_{2a}' \frac{dc_{2a}}{dz_0} + \pi_b v_{1b}' \frac{dc_{1b}}{dz_0} + \pi_b v_{2b}' \frac{dc_{2b}}{dz_0}.$$

Since $dc_0/dz_0 = -1$, $dc_{1a}/dz_0 = dc_{2a}/dz_0 = \frac{1}{2}, dc_{1b}/dz_0 = 1$, and $dc_{2b}/dz_0 = 0$, we obtain:

$$v_0' = \frac{1}{2}\pi_a(v_{1a}' + v_{2a}') + \pi_b v_{1b}'.$$

This says that storage z_0 takes place up to the point where the marginal utility of c_0 equals the indicated weighted average of the marginal utilities of c_{1a}, c_{2a}, and c_{1b}.

Making the numerical substitutions,[7] the optimal storage at time-0 is approximately $z_0 = 3.3$. The implied prices and quantities are shown in table 8.2. Thus, $1 = P_1/P_0 > P_2/P_1 = 0.865$, so that a liquidity-premium exists. In terms of interest rates, $r_1 = 0$ percent while $R_2 = 7.5$ percent.[8] It will be noted that even though the relative values of P_{1a} and P_{1b} change, their sum remains equal to unity. This is of course imposed by the possibility of storage transfers at par between c_0 and c_1.

We can now review the three conditions indicated earlier as being necessary for the emergence of a liquidity-premium.

Uncertainty: Evidently, without uncertainty there would be no need for flexibility.

Ability to defer decisions: In the absence of this condition there could be no flexibility, however great the need. We saw above how, in two models

TABLE 8.2 *Solution with storage, deferrable decisions*

	Quantities			Prices		
t:	0	1	2	0	1	2
	96.7	126.65	126.65	1	0.382	0.382
		78.3	100		0.618	0.483
					1	0.865
				Discount rates		
				—	0%	7.5%

TABLE 8.3 *Time-state sequences*

		With storage only			With reverse-storage only		
	t:	0	1	2	0	1	2
			125	125		150	100
		100			100		
			75	100		87½	87½
Marginal utility		0.01	0.0107	0.009	0.01	0.009	0.0107
Direction of desired transfer		⟶			⟵		

otherwise exactly alike, a liquidity-premium arose only in the one permitting the deferring of decisions.

Physical irreversibility. The necessity of this condition was not underlined above, and it is rarely noted in the literature. But its implications are quite interesting. We could indeed imagine a world in which investment transfers in the form of storage could not take place, but where the reverse of costless storage – anticipatory physical realization of future claims at par – could be engaged in.[9] The time-state-sequence implications of the storage *versus* the "reverse-storage" assumptions are illustrated in table 8.3. The table shows two comparable situations, where consumptions are balanced by storage or reverse-storage respectively between time-1 and time-2 (on the basis of the information as to which state obtains at time-1) but without going through the computations necessary to optimize consumption at

TABLE 8.4 *Time-state sequences*

	With storage only			With storage and reverse-storage		
t:	0	1	2	0	1	2
		125	125		125	125
	100			100		
		75	100		$87\frac{1}{2}$	$87\frac{1}{2}$
Marginal utility	0.01	0.0107	0.009	0.1	0.0097	0.0097

time-0. However, the marginal utilities at each date indicate the direction of the optimal transfer to be made at time-0.

The situations are close to mirror images of one another. With the indicated disparity of the marginal utilities in the storage situation, transfers via storage from time-0 to time-1 were called for. In the reverse-storage situation, transfers from time-1 to time-0 would be optimal. Furthermore, under reverse-storage the "liquidity-premium" would evidently attach to the time-2 claims: P_2/P_1 will exceed P_1/P_0!

We are rather more interested, however, in comparing storage alone with a situation where *both* storage and reverse storage would be possible. This is shown in table 8.4, again before any adjustment of consumption at time-0. Note that in the numerical example allowing both storage and reverse-storage, there is only a very slight discrepancy in the marginal utilities – calling for a small transfer of consumption to time-0. There is no liquidity premium, since all the prices would equalize at unity after this transfer.[10]

8.3 CONCLUSIONS

The implication of all this is that the physical irreversibility of claims to future incomes – the comparative unavailability in the real world of reverse-storage transformations or, *a fortiori*, of disinvestments yielding a net surplus at earlier dates – is a necessary condition for the liquidity premium represented by an excess of P_1/P_0 over P_2/P_1.

We may now remark on the potentialities of market liquidity as a substitute for physical liquidity. In the "representative-individual" model used up to this point, the market provided no additional source of liquidity: everyone's situation being identical, no pair of individuals could find their respective desires or resources complementing one another so as to permit trade. But in the real world, individuals and their situations are not identical. In particular, their incomes for given time-states will be imperfectly correlated: one individual's poorer-endowed state might be associated with another's better-endowed state. Then the existence of markets for assets will tend to reduce the realization discounts on physical investments like trees grown for timber. For, the arrival of a set of circumstances causing one individual to seek early realization may coincide with another individual's desiring to augment his productive investments to achieve more future return. Nevertheless, we would not expect this levelling or cancelling tendency for aggregate state-incomes to work out perfectly, since there is considerable positive correlation due to widespread social events like prosperity *versus* depression or war *versus* peace. So the existence of markets dilutes, without eliminating entirely, the effect of the irreversibility of physical investments that represents a necessary condition for the liquidity premium.

The counter-balancing force, upon which we must place the bulk of the explanation as to why people do after all hold long-term assets, is *productivity*. This force was masked in our examples above, where the net yield on physical investments was fixed by assumption at 0 percent. But if a continuum of investments of differing yields were available, the tendency of R_2 to rise above r_1 would represent a higher marginal rate of real yield on long-term investments. (This does not mean that long-term investments are *intrinsically* more productive, in any philosophical or essential sense – but only that the cut-off rate of return will be higher on the long-terms.) In the numerical example illustrated by table 8.2, at equilibrium $r_1 = 0$ percent while $R_2 = 7.5$ percent. However, with storage the only productive possibility, there was no way of earning 7.5 percent on long-term physical investments – hence, the only transformations entering into the solution were short-term transfers from c_0 to c_1 via storage. But with a continuum of short-term and long-term marginal investment yields, consumptive sacrifice at time-0 would be distributed between "liquid" but lower-yielding short-term investments and "illiquid" but higher-yielding long-term investments.

To sum up, the great advantage of short-term assets, given risk aversion and an uncertain world, is that they facilitate the utilization of new information about the environment as it becomes available over time. For the information to be usable, it must be possible to defer some decisions, or to reconsider tentative decisions. In order for the reconsideration opportunity to be peculiarly advantageous for holders of short-term as opposed to long-term assets, there must be limits on the *physical* reversibility of long-terms. In somewhat diluted form – due to divergences of individual tastes and opportunities, and imperfect correlation of better- and poorer-endowed states – these limits on physical reversibility pass over into impairments of market realizations of long-term assets at "premature" dates. And finally, to assure that the information is purchased at a positive price, i.e. to preclude the corner solution in which *no* long-term investments are undertaken, there must exist a real marginal time-rate of yield on long-terms greater than that on short-terms.

NOTES

[1] For a related discussion, see J. Marschak, "Role of Liquidity under Complete and Incomplete Information," *American Economic Review*, Papers and Proceedings, May 1949, esp. pp. 182–3.

[2] For evidence on this point, see R. A. Kessel, *The Cyclical Behavior of the Term Structure of Interest Rates*, National Bureau of Economic Research, Occasional Paper 91 (1965).

[3] K. J. Arrow, "The Role of Securities in the Optimal Allocation of Risk-Bearing," *Review of Economic Studies*, April 1964; G. Debreu, *Theory of Value*, New York: Wiley 1959, ch. 7; J. Hirshleifer, "Investment Decision under Uncertainty: Choice-Theoretic Approaches," *Quarterly Journal of Economics*, Nov. 1965.

[4] This model is that employed in H. A. John Green, "Uncertainty and the 'Expectations Hypothesis'," *Review of Economic Studies*, Oct. 1967. Green cites an earlier version of this paper as one of his sources, while this revised version in turn makes use of certain of his ideas.

[5] Green, *op. cit.*, p. 388.

[6] The procedure involved is illustrated in J. H. Drèze and F. Modigliani, "Epargne et Consommation en Avenir Aléatoire," *Cahiers du Séminaire d'Econométrie*, vol. 9 (1966), pp. 7–33.

[7] Here $v_0' = 1/(y_0 - z_0) = 1/(100 - z_0)$; $v_{1a}' = 1/(y_{1a} + z_0 - z_{1a}) = 1/\frac{1}{2}(y_{1a} + z_0 + y_2) = 2/(250 + z_0)$; $v_{2a}' = v_{1a}'$; $v_{1b}' = 1/(y_{1b} + z_0) = 1/(75 + z_0)$; and $\pi_a = \pi_b = \frac{1}{2}$.

[8] $1/(1 + R_2)^2 = 0.865$ implies $R_2 = 0.075$.

[9] In such a world the individual might be endowed with a set of perishable dated rations, so constituted that any unit can be consumed equally well before the specified date – but if it were attempted to defer consumption until after that date, the ration would be useless.

[10] The optimal transfer to c_0 is about 1.4, so that the solution would be $c_0 = 101.4$, $c_{1a} = c_{2a} = 123.6$, $c_{1b} = c_{2b} = 86.1$.

9 The Private and Social Value of Information and the Reward to Inventive Activity*

Background and comments

This paper has received a good deal of attention, owing perhaps to the "paradoxical" demonstration that public information may have zero or even negative social value – in the sense that every member of the community might be willing to agree beforehand to suppress the information, even at positive cost. The reason, as will be explained below, is that premature revelation of public information may deprive people of the opportunity to balance their portfolios so as to spread their individual risks.

More generally, the paper shows that there is typically a divergence between the private value and the social value of information, since information may be privately sought for its distributive rather than productive advantages. It follows that informational activity, and notably the process of invention, may well be carried on beyond efficient levels. While not conclusive of itself, this consideration weakens the traditional argument made on behalf of the patent system.

*This article originally appeared in *American Economic Review*, vol. 61 (Sept. 1971), pp. 561–74. The permission of the American Economic Association to reprint in this volume is gratefully acknowledged.

This article is an abbreviation of a report with the same title prepared for the Western Management Science Institute, UCLA (1970b). The research at WMSI was supported by the National Science Foundation and the Office of Naval Research. Valuable suggestions were contributed by Earl Thompson, Jacob Marschak, Ross M. Starr, and Joseph Ostroy.

A number of recent papers[1] have dealt with the economics of information in a context in which each individual is fully certain about his own endowment and productive opportunities. In those papers, the individual is imperfectly informed only about his market opportunities, i.e. about the supply-demand offers of *other* individuals. In consequence, costly patterns of search for trading partners replace the traditional assumption of costless exchange.

This paper deals with an entirely different aspect of the economics of information. We here revert to the textbook assumption that markets are perfect and costless. The individual is always fully acquainted with the supply-demand offers of all potential traders, and an equilibrium integrating all individuals' supply-demand offers is attained instantaneously. Individuals are unsure only about the size of their *own* commodity endowments and/or about the returns attainable from their *own* productive investments. They are subject to technological uncertainty rather than market uncertainty.[2]

Technological uncertainty brings immediately to mind the economics of research and invention. The traditional position has been that the excess of the social over the private value of new technological knowledge leads to underinvestment in inventive activity. The main reason is that information, viewed as a product, is only imperfectly appropriable by its discoverer.[3] But this paper will show that there is a hitherto unrecognized force operating in the opposite direction. What has been scarcely appreciated in the literature, if recognized at all, is the *distributive* aspect of access to superior information. It will be seen below how this advantage provides a motivation for the private acquisition and dissemination of technological information that is quite apart from – and may even exist in the absence of – any social usefulness of that information.[4]

9.1 FOREKNOWLEDGE *VERSUS* DISCOVERY

Within the category of technological (as opposed to market) information, different sorts of knowledge are associated with rather different private incentives and social efficiency conditions. This paper concentrates upon a distinction between what will be called foreknowledge on the one hand, and discovery on the other. The type of information represented by foreknowledge is exemplified by ability to successfully predict tomorrow's (or next year's) weather. Here we have a stochastic situation: with particular probabilities the future weather might be hot or cold, rainy or dry, etc. But whatever does actually occur will, in due time, be evident to all; the only aspect of information that may be of advantage is prior knowledge as to what will happen. Discovery, in contrast, is correct recognition of something that possibly already exists, though hidden from view. Examples include the determination of the properties of materials, of physical laws, even of mathematical attributes (e.g. the millionth digit in the decimal expansion of π). The essential point is that in such cases Nature will not autonomously reveal the information; only human action can extract it. Foreknowledge information is conceptually simpler to deal with, involving as it does only the value of *priority* in time of superior knowledge; this topic will be taken up first below.

9.2   ELEMENTS OF THE ECONOMICS OF FOREKNOWLEDGE

The analysis of the value of priority of information necessarily involves both temporality and uncertainty. For convenience, the simplest possible paradigm of choice will be employed. Suppose that there exists but a single physical good (corn). It will be assumed, however, that a number of different types of claims may be owned or traded – claims to corn at specified dates and under specified contingencies or "states of Nature."[5] It suffices to consider a particularly simple model in which the present (time-0) is certain, and the future consists of a single date (time-1) at which just one of two alternative states (a or b) will obtain. The marketable commodities of the analysis can be denoted c_0, c_{1a}, and c_{1b}: claims to corn valid at, and only at, the subscripted dates and states.

Each individual will have a utility function governing his preferences *now* for holdings of alternative combinations of these claims. Entering into this function will be his beliefs as to the probabilities π_a and π_b of the two states. It has been shown[6] that, under certain widely accepted assumptions, it is possible to find a cardinal intertemporal function $u(c_0, c_1)$ that (a) measures desirability of alternative *certain* dated consumption sequences and (b) is such that the von Neumann-Morgenstern expected-utility rule can be employed to order preferences among *risky* sequences of time-state claims, according to the formula:

$$U = \pi_a u(c_0, c_{1a}) + \pi_b u(c_0, c_{1b}). \tag{9.1}$$

This utility function exemplifies the property of "state-independence," i.e. the expected utility is a sum of distinct terms each of which is associated with only one particular state of the world.[7]   .

The utility function to be used below makes the further specification that $u(c_0, c_1)$ can be written in the special form $v(c_0) + \theta v(c_1)$, where θ is a fixed time-preference parameter characteristic of the individual, and v is a cardinal preference-scaling function for income valid for him at each state and date. The essential additional property underlying this specification may be called time-independence.[8] Given both state-independence and time-independence, the utility function becomes:

$$U = \pi_a(v_0 + \theta v_{1a}) + \pi_b(v_0 + \theta v_{1b}) = v_0 + \theta(\pi_a v_{1a} + \pi_b v_{1b}), \tag{9.2}$$

where v_0 is condensed notation for $v(c_0)$, and v_{1a} and v_{1b} are defined analogously.

The acquisition of information will take the form of warranted revisions in the probability estimates π_a and π_b that enter into preference functions and so guide decisions. In what follows it will be essential to distinguish *private* information (available only to a single individual) from *public* information (available to everyone) – intermediate cases will generally be ignored. It will also be important to keep in mind the distinction between information that is *prior* to, and information that is *posterior* to, the individual consumption-investment decisions that must be made at $t = 0$. Still another distinction is that between *sure* information (as to which future state will obtain) and merely *better* information – the latter would represent a sharper focusing of subjective probabilities that does not entirely eliminate uncertainty.

9.3   THE VALUE OF FOREKNOWLEDGE: PURE EXCHANGE

In a simplified world of pure exchange, all productive transformations among the quantities c_0, c_{1b}, and c_{1b} are ruled out – even simple storage. An individual dissatisfied with his endowment vector $Y = (y_0, y_{1a}, y_{1b})$ can modify it only by trading. Let us suppose a competitive world of "representative" individuals, characterized by identical probability beliefs and utility functions, and all holding identical endowments. Then no trading actually takes place; the price structure that emerges in market equilibrium must "sustain" the endowment pattern for every individual. Taking current corn as numeraire so that $P_0 = 1$, the sustaining prices must be:[9]

$$P_{1a} = \theta\pi_a v'_{1a}/v'_0 \text{ and } P_{1b} = \theta\pi_b v'_{1b}/v'_0. \tag{9.3}$$

Wealth in c_0 units may then be determined from the definition:

$$W_0 = P_0 c_0 + P_{1a}c_{1a} + P_{1b}c_{1b} \tag{9.4}$$

Finally, utility attained may be calculated by appropriate substitutions in (9.2). This is the base situation with which the results of changes in information will be compared.

For concreteness, a numerical illustration will be employed using a logarithmic preference-scaling function v (see table 9.1). Note that future state-a is assumed better endowed than state-b ($y_{1a} = 200$, $y_{1b} = 80$) as well as more probable ($\pi_a = 0.6$, $\pi_b = 0.4$). With c_0 as numeraire so that $P_0 = 1$, the parameters assumed lead to the solutions shown in column (4) for the sustaining prices ($P_{1a} = 0.3$ and $P_{1b} = 0.5$) and wealth ($W_0 = 200$). The expected utility ($U = 9.5370$) is worked out in table 9.2 (column 4).

Now, suppose that a single individual at time-0 secures *private*, *prior*, and *sure* information that state-a will obtain at time-1. Since one in-

TABLE 9.1 *Data and solution for numerical example*

Endowments	Prior beliefs	Preference parameters	Solution, base case
(1)	*(2)*	*(3)*	*(4)*
$y_0 = 100$	—	$\theta = 1$	$P_0 = 1$
$y_{1a} = 200$	$\pi_a = 0.6$	$v = \log_e c$	$P_{1a} = 0.3$
$y_{1b} = 80$	$\pi_b = 0.4$		$P_{1b} = 0.5$
			$W_0 = 200$

TABLE 9.2 *Private value of information*

	Consumptive choices[1]			Utility[2]		
Uncertainty[3]	State-a[4] to obtain	State-b[5] to obtain	Uncertainty	State-a to obtain	State-b to obtain
(1)	*(2)*	*(3)*	*(4)*	*(5)*	*(6)*
c_0	100	100	100	4.6052	4.6052	4.6052
c_{1a}	200	333.3	—	0.6(5.2983)	5.8091	—
c_{1b}	80	—	200	0.4(4.3821)	—	5.2983
Expected utility under uncertainty:				9.5370		
Conditional utility:					10.4143	9.9035
Expected utility given perfect information:[6]					10.2100	

[1] $P_{1a} = 0.3$, $P_{1b} = 0.5$, $W_0 = 200$.
[2] Computed according to: $U = \log_e c_0 + \pi_a \log_e c_{1a} + \pi_b \log_e c_{1b}$.
[3] $\pi_a = 0.6$, $\pi_b = 0.4$.
[4] $\pi_a = 1$, $\pi_b = 0$.
[5] $\pi_a = 0$, $\pi_b = 1$.
[6] Using prior weights $\pi_a = 0.6$, $\pi_b = 0.4$.

dividual's choices would only negligibly affect the ruling prices, he could realize essentially all the market value $P_{1b}y_{1b}$ of his c_{1b} endowment (which he alone knows to be worthless) for reallocation to the purchase of more c_0 and/or c_{1a}. In the numerical example, this amount is $P_{1b}y_{1b} = 0.5(80) = 40$. With the parameters assumed, it can be shown[10] that he will purchase just $40/P_{1a} = 133.3$ units of c_{1a} to add to his endowed 200 units (table 9.2, columns 2 and 5). If instead he were to learn that state-b will obtain, he would reallocate the entire value $P_{1a}y_{1a} = 60$ of his c_{1a} endowment to purchase $60/P_{1b} = 120$ units of c_{1b}. Table 9.2 also shows the expected utility given perfect information (and the consequent rearrangement of consumption) to be substantially higher than the expected utility under uncertainty. These expectations are calculated, of course, using the individual's prior probability estimates as to what the information will reveal.

We now come to the crucial contrast. What of the *social* value of the sure information just analysed above? Suppose that by a collective payment to some knowledgeable outsider, an entire community consisting of the representative individuals above could all simultaneously be informed as to which future state will obtain – how large a payment would they be justified in making? The answer is: none at all! Such information would be absolutely valueless to the community as a whole. Information is of value only if it can affect action. But with identical endowments, preferences, and beliefs in a world of pure exchange, all individuals must still end up holding their endowment time-state distributions. The only thing that could happen, given the new public information, is that prices shift immediately to permit "sustaining" the endowment vector in the face of the changed beliefs entering into the utility function. In the numerical example, sure public information that state-*a* will obtain, available *prior* to the decisions at $t = 0$, will cause P_{1a} to rise to 0.5 (while P_{1b}, of course, falls to zero). Sure public prior information that state-*b* will obtain raises P_{1b} to 1.25, while P_{1a} falls to zero. Table 9.3 confirms that in these circumstances the individual will choose the same consumptions with the same probabilities as in the original uncertainty situation.

One other very important consideration must now be taken into account. There is a possibility of still greater gain for the *privately* informed

TABLE 9.3 *Social value of information*

	Consumptive choices			Utility		
	Uncertainty[1]	State-a[2] to obtain	State-b[3] to obtain	Uncertainty	State-a to obtain	State-b to obtain
	(1)	(2)	(3)	(4)	(5)	(6)
c_0	100	100	100	4.6052	4.6052	4.6052
c_{1a}	200	200	—	0.6(5.2983)	5.2983	—
c_{1b}	80	—	80	0.4(4.3821)	—	4.3821
Expected utility under uncertainty:				9.5370		
Conditional utility:					9.9035	8.9873
Expected utility given perfect information:[4]					9.5370	

[1] $\pi_a = 0.6$, $\pi_b = 0.4$; $W_0 = 200$; $P_{1a} = 0.3$, $P_{1b} = 0.5$.
[2] $\pi_a = 1$, $\pi_b = 0$; $W_0 = 200$; $P_{1a} = 0.5$, $P_{1b} = 0$.
[3] $\pi_a = 0$, $\pi_b = 1$; $W_0 = 200$; $P_{1a} = 0$, $P_{1b} = 1.25$.
[4] Using prior weights $\pi_a = 0.6$, $\pi_b = 0.4$.

individual if he is permitted to speculate rather than merely move directly to his preferred consumptive position. Assuming private knowledge that state-a was to obtain, for example, an optimally speculating individual would first convert not just his c_{1b} holdings but rather *all* of his wealth $W_0 = 200$ to c_{1a} holdings at the old price relationships. The anticipation here is that the true information will become public, P_{1a} rising to 0.5 and wealth to 333.3, prior to the finalizing of the consumption-investment decisions at $t = 0$. Note that the individual with private information would have every incentive to publicize that information, *after* making his speculative commitment. The enormously enhanced private results achievable via speculation are detailed in table 9.4.

So far, two reaction modes of the privately informed individual have been considered: consumptive adaptation, and optimal speculation. A third and even more attractive possibility is *resale of the information* itself. The potential gain then becomes enormous, since the individual is no longer constrained by his personal commodity endowment. However, it may not be easy for an informed individual to authenticate possession of valuable foreknowledge for resale purposes. After all, anyone could *claim* to have such knowledge. Feasible and optimal resale strategies, and the market value of resold information, are issues that cannot be pursued here. The crucial point remains that *the community as a whole obtains no benefit, under pure exchange, from either the acquisition or the dissemination (by resale or otherwise) of private foreknowledge.*

The contrast between the private profitability and the social uselessness of foreknowledge may seem surprising. Information is widely considered

TABLE 9.4 *Private value of information, with speculation*

	Consumptive choices			Utility		
	Uncertainty[1]	State-a[2] to obtain	State-b[3] to obtain	Uncertainty	State-a to obtain	State-b to obtain
c_0	100	166.7	250	4.6052	5.1160	5.5215
c_{1a}	200	333.3	—	0.6(5.2983)	5.8091	—
c_{1b}	80	—	200	0.4(4.3821)	—	5.2983
Expected utility under uncertainty:				9.5370		
Conditional utility:					10.9251	10.8198
Expected utility given perfect information:[4]					10.8830	

[1] $\pi_a = 0.6$, $\pi_b = 0.4$; $W_0 = 200$; $P_{1a} = 0.3$, $P_{1b} = 0.5$.
[2] $\pi_a = 1$, $\pi_b = 0$; $W_0 = 333.3$; $P_{1a} = 0.5$, $P_{1b} = 0$.
[3] $\pi_a = 0$, $\pi_b = 1$; $W_0 = 500$; $P_{1a} = 0$, $P_{1b} = 1.25$.
[4] Using prior weights $\pi_a = 0.6$, $\pi_b = 0.4$.

to be a classic example of a "collective good," the type of commodity for which private incentives are supposed to lead to underprovision rather than over-provision on the market. Indeed, there may be something of a collective-good aspect to the *market* information alluded to earlier: information that helps improve an otherwise imperfect process of exchange. But the expenditure of real resources for the production of *technological* information is socially wasteful in pure exchange, as the expenditure of resources for an increase in the quantity of money by mining gold is wasteful, and for essentially the same reason. Just as a smaller quantity of money serves monetary functions as well as a larger, the price level adjusting correspondingly, so a larger amount of fore-knowledge serves no social purpose under pure exchange that the smaller amount did not.

9.4   THE VALUE OF FOREKNOWLEDGE: PRODUCTION AND EXCHANGE

Consider now the more realistic regime in which production and exchange both take place. Assume that endowments are just the same as before, for all individuals. But suppose that, in addition, each representative individual has a small discrete productive investment opportunity of the following form: exactly one unit of endowed c_0 may be sacrificed to produce additional income in either time-state-$1a$ or time-state-$1b$ (but not both). Suppose that the choice is between a yield of $2\frac{1}{2}$ units in state-a or $2\frac{1}{2}$ units in state-b. With the prices of the initial situation in the example above ($P_{1a} = 0.3$, $P_{1b} = 0.5$), every representative individual would choose the latter alternative; he would physically invest, transforming his endowment combination ($y_0 = 100$, $y_{1a} = 200$, $y_{1b} = 80$) into the attained combination ($c_0 = 99$, $c_0 = 200$, $c_{1b} = 82.5$). Since the scale of the collective investment is not infinitesimal, the prices change slightly but not by enough to modify the desirability of the selection made.

Suppose now that *one single* individual is given sure, prior, and private information that state-a will obtain. Here it would be socially desirable that this individual's investment sacrifice of c_0 (and everyone else's, as well) be redirected so as to produce c_{1a} instead of the useless c_{1b}. But if the information is private, the original prices must still be ruling so that the individual's incentives for production decisions remain unchanged. He will continue to invest for a c_{1b} return, despite knowing that the latter will turn out to be valueless. It is more profitable for him to commit the resources to c_{1b}, merely taking care to arrange in advance for the liquidation of the $2\frac{1}{2}$ units of c_{1b} (in addition, of course, to his endowed 80 units) at the currently ruling market prices. *Thus, as under the regime of pure exchange, private foreknowledge makes possible large private profit without leading to socially useful activity.* The individual would have just as much incentive as under pure exchange (even more, in fact) to expend real resources in generating socially useless private information.

What of the value of *public* information? If the information were made public that state-*a* would obtain, P_{1a} would jump to 0.5 (P_{1b} falling to zero). Then the individual investments would all be shifted so as to yield c_{1a} instead of c_{1b}. This, of course, is socially efficient behavior. *Public information as to which state will obtain is indeed of social value in a regime of production and exchange.* However, it remains true that the value of private foreknowledge is enormously greater to any individual than the value to him of public foreknowledge. In the example used here, public information enables the representative individual to attain the consumption sequence ($c_0 = 99$, $c_1 = 202.5$) with probability 0.6, or the sequence ($c_0 = 99$, $c_1 = 82.5$) with probability 0.4. Private information enables him to attain with probability 0.6 the sequence ($c = 99$, $c_1 = 337.5$) – based on converting his 82.5 units of c_{1b} at the original price ratio into 137.5 units of c_{1a} to be added to his endowed 200 units – or with probability 0.4 the sequence ($c_0 = 99$, $c_1 = 202.5$). Evidently, the possibilities with private information are far superior (still leaving aside the prospect of much greater gains through speculation and/or resale). Thus, the incentives for the use of resources to generate private information remain excessive.

What about speculation and resale? Having undertaken a speculative commitment, it is in the interest of the informed individual to publicize the information. Whether or not involved in speculation, the informed individual would find it advantageous wherever possible to resell the information. Under pure exchange, where foreknowledge is socially value-less, devotion of resources to dissemination is only a further social waste. In a regime of production, however, universal dissemination would improve the choice of investments. The partial dissemination that would ensue from private publicizing or through resale would also tend to shift prices and lead to some productive adaptation. Thus, *in a regime of production, the dissemination of information has social utility*, against which gain must be offset, of course, any resource cost of the dissemination process.

9.5   DISTRIBUTIVE CONSIDERATIONS, PUBLIC INFORMATION, AND HOMOGENEITY OF BELIEFS

The key factor underlying all the results obtained above is the distributive significance of private foreknowledge. When private information fails to lead to improved productive alignments (as must necessarily be the case in a world of pure exchange, and also in a regime of production unless there is dissemination effected in the interests of speculation or resale), it is evident that the individual's source of gain can only be at the expense of his fellows. But even where information is disseminated and does lead to improved productive commitments, the distributive transfer gain will surely be far greater than the relatively minor productive gain the individual might reap from the redirection of his own real investment commitments.

Will *public* information have distributive implications, and if so, will this consideration provide additional private motivation for the generation of public information? The nature and direction of possible distribution effects turn upon the timing of information acquisition in comparison with the schedule of trading. Two alternative timing patterns will be considered here: (1) The information is publicly released before the opening of trading, or (2) the individuals trade to their consumptive optimum positions prior to the release of the information, with another round of trading permitted afterward.[11] Both trading and generation of information are best regarded as essentially continuous interacting processes, so that the second timing pattern seems more acceptable.[12] But the first is useful in emphasizing certain aspects of reactions to public information.

We will therefore imagine, first, a situation of pure exchange in which the true state of the world is announced in advance of any market trading whatsoever – while individuals are still at their endowment positions. Announcement that state-a will obtain (or, more generally, release of any information tending to increase the probability π_a that individuals attach to state-a) will, of course, enhance the position of those disproportionately endowed with state-a claims. The rise in the price P_{1a} will enrich such individuals. It will also enhance the position of those whose tastes or beliefs previously inclined them in the direction of purchase of state-b claims. For, such individuals would otherwise have largely wasted their income endowments in the purchase of worthless state-b claims.

That public information has distributive implications does not, however, lead necessarily to the conclusion that private individuals will want to generate public information. Individuals disproportionately endowed with state-a claims, for example, cannot be sure in advance that the information will not point to state-b rather than state-a. And indeed, it can be shown that in the circumstances assumed here, risk-averse individuals will prefer that the information not be released.[13] For, the anticipation of public information becoming available in advance of trading adds a significant *distributive risk* to the underlying *technological risk* (as to which state will obtain). A community of such individuals would actually pay something to a knowledgeable outsider not to reveal, in advance of market trading, which state will obtain! (This conclusion would have to be modified somewhat under a regime of production and exchange; the gain from redirection of productive investments achieved in consequence of the public information would have to be offset against the increased distributive risk.)

Let us turn now to the more reasonable assumption that individuals have already optimally adapted their decisions to their opportunities prior to the release of new public information. Differences of endowments would no longer have any relevance, and so there would be no net incentive for or against the acquisition of socially neutral information under pure exchange. (And there would be an appropriately small incentive for any one individual to support the acquisition of beneficial public information in a world of production.) A similar argument can be made about differences in tastes or beliefs so long as the individuals may be presumed to have merely moved to their consumptive optimum positions, and not engaged in speculative behavior. But, we know that for individuals with superior information there is a strong incentive to take speculative positions. Now, differences of beliefs amount to the same thing as *each individual's thinking that he is in possession of superior information.* Such differences open up a new range of possibilities.

We saw above that it was privately rational, for a better informed individual, to expend resources for the dissemination of socially neutral information – after having adopted a speculative commitment. With inhomogeneity of beliefs every person may be better informed, in his own opinion! Thus, the generation of public information is (from his point of view) nothing other than the dissemination of information already privately available to him. He will expect to reap speculative profits from this process. But so will other individuals, with quite opposed opinions! We therefore have rather strong grounds to anticipate that in these circumstances excessive resources will be devoted to the generation of public information.

These considerations may be clarified by reference to a well-known activity for the generation of public information – horse racing. Viewed as a research activity, horse racing may be presumed to have a small positive social value: the identification of faster horses works "to improve the breed." This consideration is evidently a very minor motivating factor for the activity in comparison with the opportunity to speculate upon one's supposedly superior knowledge. Without differences of opinion, it is said, there would be no horse races. That is, the social value is insufficient to motivate the research – the activity is founded upon the contradictory expectations of speculative gain.

Suppose that it costs $100 in real resources to run a horse race, and that the social advantage of knowing which is the fastest horse is just $5. Evidently, if the race is run society is engaging in excessive research. Now imagine that the potential speculative gain, to an individual convinced that his horse is truly faster, is just $90 – he could still not earn enough, himself, to cover the costs of the race. But if several individuals are so convinced, each about his own horse, they may cooperate to stage the experiment. So conflict of beliefs may enormously compound the speculative factor that, even from the point of view of a single individual, tends to promote excessive investment in information-generating activity.

9.6   THE VALUE OF DISCOVERY INFORMATION

The acquisition of technological information usually refers to the detection of properties of Nature that permit the development of new tools or the utilization of new techniques. This is the type of information categorized as discovery above, in which Nature's secret will not be autonomously revealed but must be extracted by man. The necessity for human interposition makes the analysis of the value of discovery information somewhat more complex than the analysis of foreknowledge information.

For concreteness, consider the following situation. Suppose that if an alloy with an enormously high melting point of $X°$ can be created, extremely cheap thermonuclear power will become feasible. The underlying state of the world is not the result of a probabilistic process: such an alloy may in fact be possible to create (state-a) or may not (state-b). While this is not a stochastic situation, it has been shown to be useful even in such circumstances to summarize our uncertainty in the form of a probability distribution.[14] Thus, just as in the case of foreknowledge, we can assume that individuals assign probabilities π_a and π_b to the two underlying states of the world. However, even if the favorable state-a is the true one, Nature is not going to tell us herself. In the discovery situation, no news is bad news.

From the point of view of any individual, however, the picture may not look very different from that analyzed under the heading of foreknowledge. For any individual there is a certain probability π_A of "good news" (discovery of the alloy), due to the actions of other men if not of his own. We can think of a compound event A which consists of the joint happenings "State-a is true (the required alloy is possible) *and* this fact is successfully exploited (the alloy is created) within the time-period envisaged." Evidently, $\pi_A \leq \pi_a$, the probability of good news is generally less than the probability attached to the more favorable state of Nature. And similarly, if the event B is defined in a complementary way as representing "no news" (identical with "bad news" in the circumstances considered), we have $\pi_B \geq \pi_b$. The individual's decisions – for example, whether to invest in a productive process whose profitability will be highly sensitive to the prospect of cheap thermonuclear power – will run in terms of the probabilities of good and bad news rather than the probabilities attached to the states of nature.

With this modification, the analysis is essentially similar to what has gone before. We need only consider the more general regime of production and exchange. Given private, prior, and sure information of event A, the individual in a world of perfect markets would *not* adapt his productive decisions if he were sure the information would remain private until after the close of trading. For, prices of the time-state claims c_{1A} and c_{1B} (involving the observable states A and B, of course, not the "natural" states a and b which do not directly affect markets) will not have changed. However, as before it would be in his interest to speculate and/or resell the information, in which case prices will tend to shift. The obvious way of acquiring the private information in question is, of course, by performing techno-logical research.[15] By a now familiar argument we can show once again that the distributive advantage of private information provides an incentive for information-generating activity that may quite possibly be in excess of the social value of the information.

The conclusions reached in the analysis of foreknowledge with respect to public information again carry over to the discovery situation. Public information is socially valuable in redirecting productive decisions, and to that extent individuals will rationally combine (through government and other instruments) to generate public information (or, in some cases, it will pay even a single individual to do so). But disparities of beliefs (differences in probability estimates) may lead to agreement upon a procedure of generating public information where social costs exceed the social benefit.

9.7   IMPLICATIONS FOR PATENT POLICY

Eli Whitney obtained one of the first American patents, in 1794, for his cotton gin. With some business associates, he spent many years and invested considerable resources in the attempt to protect his patent and prosecute infringements. These efforts were largely fruitless. It is reason-able to infer that potential inventors, both before and after Whitney, have been deterred from searching for new knowledge by the fear of a similar outcome – hence the argument for effective patent protection. On the other hand, had Whitney succeeded in obtaining the terms he demanded from users of his idea, the enormous expansion that actually took place in the production and consumption of cotton would have been significantly hampered.[16] This conflict between the "static" disadvantage of a patent monopoly and the "dynamic" advantage of encouraging invention is quite properly emphasized in the traditional literature.[17]

But what seems to have been overlooked is that there were other routes to profit for Whitney. The cotton gin had obvious speculative implications for the price of cotton, the value of slaves and of cotton-bearing land, the business prospects of firms engaged in cotton warehousing and shipping, the site values of key points in the transport network that sprang up. There were also predictable implications for competitor industries (wool) and complementary ones (textiles, machinery). It seems very likely that some forethoughted individuals reaped speculative gains on these develop-ments, though apparently Whitney did not. And yet, he was the first in the know, the possessor of an unparalleled opportunity for speculative profit.

Alternatively, of course, Whitney could have attempted to keep his process secret except to those who bought the information from him.

The issues involved may be clarified by distinguishing the "technological" and "pecuniary" effects of invention. The technological effects are the improvements in production functions – interpreted in the widest sense to include the possible production of new commodities, the discovery of new resources, etc. – consequent upon the new idea. The pecuniary effects are the wealth shifts due to the price revaluations that take place upon release and/or utilization of the information. The pecuniary effects are purely redistributive.[18]

For concreteness, we can think in terms of a simple cost-reducing innovation. The technological benefit to society is, roughly, the integrated area between the old and new marginal-cost curves for the preinvention level of output plus, for any additional output, the area between the demand curve and the new marginal-cost curve. The holder of a (perpetual) patent could ideally extract, via a perfectly discriminatory fee policy, this entire technological benefit. Equivalence between the social and private benefits of innovation would thus induce the optimal amount of private inventive activity. Presumably, it is reasoning of this sort that underlies the economic case for patent protection. It is true that under a patent system there will, in general, be some shortfall in the return to the inventor, due to costs and risks in acquiring and enforcing his rights, their limited duration in time, and the infeasibility of a perfectly discriminatory fee policy. On the other side are the recognized disadvantages of patents: the social costs of the administrative-judicial process, the possible anti-competitive impact, and restriction of output due to the marginal burden of patent fees.[19] As a second-best kind of judgment, some degree of patent protection has seemed a reasonable compromise among the objectives sought.

But recognition of the unique position of the innovator for forecasting and consequently capturing portions of the *pecuniary* effects – the wealth transfers due to price revaluations – may put matters in a different light. The "ideal" case of the perfectly discriminating patent holder earning the entire technological benefit is no longer so ideal. For, the same inventor is in a position to reap speculative profits, too; counting these as well, he would clearly be overcompensated.

Consider now the opposite extreme. Do we have reason to believe that the potential speculative profits to the inventor, from the pecuniary effects that will follow release of the information at his unique disposal, will be so great that society need take no care to reserve for him any portion of the technological benefit of his innovation? The answer here is indeterminate. There is no logically necessary tie between the size of the technological benefit on the one hand, and the amplitude of the price shifts that create speculative opportunities on the other.[20]

Even if the prospective price revaluations are ample, however, there will be limitations to the inventor's capacity to profit from them. For, speculative profits are constrained by the magnitude of feasible speculative commitments. If the possessor of prior information acts alone, he is limited by what may be a puny wealth endowment. But if he tries to sell his information, in effect buying a share in a larger speculative pool, he will find it difficult to consummate such a transaction. The most important limitation of all has not heretofore been taken up in this paper, but must be considered in a policy discussion: imperfection of markets for time-state claims.[21] Given the inconceivably vast number of potential contingencies and the cost of establishing markets, the prospective speculator will find it costly or even impossible to purchase neutrality from "irrelevant" risks. Eli Whitney could not be *sure* that his gin would make cotton prices fall: while a considerable force would clearly be acting in that direction, a multitude of other contingencies might also have possibly affected the price of cotton. Such "uninsurable" risks gravely limit the speculation feasible with any degree of prudence.

We are left, therefore, in an agnostic position. The fundamental argument for patent protection is gravely weakened when it is recognized that the pecuniary effects of the invention are a potentially enormous source of return to the inventor, quite apart from the technological benefit that the patent system attempts to reserve for him. But we cannot show that no patent protection at all is warranted, that the profits from speculation or from resale[22] suffice for an appropriate inducement to invention. These profits may more than suffice, or they may fall substantially short; there is no necessary relation at all between the magnitudes of the technological and the pecuniary effects. Or, more precisely, between the magnitudes of that fraction of the technological effect that a patentee can capture and that fraction of the pecuniary effect that a speculator on prior information can capture.

9.8 SUMMARY

In the model of this paper, markets are assumed to be perfect. Uncertainty attaches only to individuals' perceptions of their endowments and productive opportunities (technological uncertainty). The private and social values of two main categories of technological information were considered: (1) foreknowledge of states of the world that will in time be revealed by Nature herself (e.g. the weather), and (2) discovery of hidden properties of Nature that can only be laid bare by human action.

Private information that remains private was shown to be of no social value – in the sense of being purely redistributive, not leading to any improvement in productive arrangements. There is an incentive for individuals to expend resources in a socially wasteful way in the generation of such information. Public information, in contrast, does affect productive decisions in a socially appropriate way. Speculative profits from the price revaluations to be anticipated provide the knowledgeable individual with an incentive to disseminate (publicize) his private information. Still greater profit is possible if the information can be resold. In a world of pure exchange, there will in general be private overinvestment in information: resources committed to acquisition and to dissemination are both wasted from the social point of view. In a world of production, however, the gains from productive rearrangements due to the information must be offset against the costs of acquisition and dissemination; there may or may not be private overinvestment.

Distributive considerations enter also into the motivation for the acquisition of *public* information. To the extent that the prospect of such information imposes a distributive risk upon individuals – due, for example, to possible revaluation of endowment holdings – there will be an aversion to socially neutral and even (to some degree) to socially beneficial public information. Probably more important is a force acting in the opposed direction. With inhomogeneous beliefs, individuals with differing opinions will tend each to believe that revelation of new information will favor his own speculative commitments. Hence, a group of such individuals might willingly cooperate in making expenditures far in excess of the social value of the information to be acquired.

The standard literature on the economics of research and invention argues that there tends to be private underinvestment in inventive activity, due mainly to the imperfect appropriability of knowledge. The contention made is that, even with a patent system, the inventor can only hope to capture some fraction of the technological benefits due to his discovery. This literature overlooks the consideration that there will be, aside from the technological benefits, pecuniary effects (wealth redistributions due to price revaluations) from the release of the new information. The innovator, first in the field with the information, is able through speculation or resale of the information to capture a portion of these pecuniary effects. This fact is socially useful in motivating release of the information. Even though practical considerations limit the effective scale and consequent impact of speculation and/or resale, the gains thus achievable eliminate any *a priori* anticipation of underinvestment in the generation of new technological knowledge.

REFERENCES

Alchian, A., "Information Costs, Pricing, and Resource Unemployment," in E. S. Phelps et al. (eds), *Microeconomic Foundations of Employment and Inflation Theory.* New York: W. W. Norton, 1970.

Arrow, K. J., "Economic Welfare and the Allocation of Resources for Invention," in *The Rate and Direction of Economic Activity: Economic and Social Factors,*

Universities – National Bureau Economic Research Conference series, Princeton 1962.

——, "Le Rôle des Valeurs Boursières pour le Repartition la Meilleure des Risques," *International Colloquium on Econometrics 1952*. Paris: Centre National de la Recherche Scientifique, 1953; translated as "The Role of Securities in the Optimal Allocation of Risk-Bearing," *Review of Economic Studies*, (April 1964) vol. 31, pp. 91–6.

——, "Discounting and Public Investment Criteria" in A. V. Kneese and S. C. Smith (eds), *Water Research*. John Hopkins Press: Baltimore, 1966.

——, "The Organization of Economic Activity: Issues Pertinent to the Choice of Market *versus* Nonmarket Allocation," in US Congress, Joint Economic Committee, *The Analysis and Evaluation of Public Expenditures: The PPB System*, a compendium of papers submitted to the Subcommittee on Economy in Government, 91st Congress, 1st session, Washington 1968, vol. 1, pp. 47–64.

Borch, K., "Equilibrium in a Reinsurance Market," *Econometrica*, vol. 30 (July 1962), pp. 424–44.

Debreu, G., *Theory of Value: An Axiomatic Analysis of Economic Equilibrium*. New York: John Wiley and Sons 1959.

Demsetz, H., "Information and Efficiency: Another Viewpoint," *Journal of Law and Economics*, vol. 12 (April 1969), pp. 1–22.

Diamond, P. A., "The Role of a Stock Market in a General Equilibrium Model with Technological Uncertainty," *American Economic Review*, vol. 57 (Sept. 1967), pp. 759–76.

Drèze, J. H. and Modigliani, F., "Epargne et Consommation en Avenir Aléatoire," *Cahiers du Seminaire d'Econometrie*, vol. 9 (1966), pp. 7–33.

Fama, E. F. and Laffer, A. B., "Information and Capital Markets," *Journal of Business of the University of Chicago*, vol. 44 (July 1971).

Hirshleifer, J., "Investment Decision under Uncertainty: Choice-Theoretic Approaches," *Quarterly Journal of Economics*, vol. 79 (Nov. 1965), pp. 509–36.

——, "Investment Decision under Uncertainty: Applications of the State-Preference Approach," *Quarterly Journal of Economics*, vol. 80 (May 1966), pp. 252–77.

——, (1970a) *Investment, Interest, and Capital*. Englewood Cliffs: Prentice-Hall, 1970.

——, (1970b) "The Private and Social Value of Information and the Reward to Inventive Activity," working paper no. 185, Western Management Science Institute, UCLA, April 1970.

Koopmans, T. *Three Essays on the State of Economic Science*. New York: McGraw-Hill, 1957.

Machlup, F., "Patents," *International Encyclopedia of the Social Sciences*, vol. 11 (1968), pp. 461–72.

Malone, D., *Dictionary of American Biography*. New York: Scribners: 1964.

Manne, H. G., *Insider Trading and the Stock Market*. New York 1966.

Marschak, J., (1968a) "Decision-making: Economic Aspects," *International Encyclopedia of the Social Sciences*, vol. 4 (1968), pp. 42–55.

—— (1968b) "Economics of Inquiring, Communicating, Deciding," *American Economic Review Proceedings*, vol. 58 (May 1968), pp. 1–18.

McKean, R. N., *Efficiency in Government through Systems Analysis*. New York: John Wiley and Sons, 1958.

Ozga, S. A., "Imperfect Markets through Lack of Knowledge," *Quarterly Journal of Economics*, vol. 74 (Feb. 1960), pp. 29–52.

Samuelson, P. A., "Intertemporal Price Equilibrium: A Prologue to the Theory of Speculation," *Welwirtschaftliches Archiv*, vol. 79 (Dec. 1957), pp. 181–219, reprinted in J. E. Stiglitz (ed.), *The Collected Scientific Papers of Paul A. Samuelson*, vol. 2. Cambridge, Mass: MIT Press, 1966, pp. 946–84.

Savage, L. J., *The Foundations of Statistics*. New York: John Wiley and Sons, 1954.

Starr, R. M., "The Effect of Individual Beliefs on the Achievement of Pareto Optimal Distribution under Uncertainty," working paper no. 127, Western Management Science Institute, UCLA, Oct. 1967.

Stigler, G., "The Economics of Information," *Journal of Political Economy*, vol. 69 (June 1961), pp. 213–25.

—, "Information in the Labor Market," *Journal of Political Economy*, vol. 70 (Oct. 1962) supp., pp. 94–105.

Thompson, E. A., "A Pareto Optimal Group Decision Process," in G. Tullock (ed.), *Papers on Non-Market Decision Making*, Charlottesville: Thomas Jefferson Center for Political Economy, University of Virginia, 1966.

NOTES

[1] See S. A. Ozga (1960), George Stigler (1961, 1962), and Armen Alchian (1970).

[2] These two types of uncertainty have been distinguished by a number of authors: see Tjalling Koopmans, (1957, pp. 161ff), Peter Diamond (1967), Jacob Marschak (1968b, p. 17).

[3] See Kenneth Arrow (1962, p. 619). The comment by Harold Demsetz is also of interest. On patents as a device to achieve appropriability, see Fritz Machlup (1968).

[4] In connection with policy debates over stock market "insider trading," Henry Manne (1966) has discussed the private and social gains attached to the dissemination of corporate information. A very recent article by Eugene F. Fama and Arthur B. Laffer (1971) emphasizes the differing motivations of insiders and outsiders for the generation of such information; their analysis, though in a partial-equilibrium context, in some ways parallels the treatment here.

[5] The conception of state-claims as commodities stems from the pioneering work of Arrow (1953, 1964). Gerard Debreu (1959, ch. 7) extended Arrow's model to multiple time-periods. The paradigm of choice involving time-state claims has been further developed by other authors, incuding Karl Borch (1962) and Hirshleifer (1965, 1966).

[6] See Jacques Drèze and Franco Modigliani (1966); Hirshleifer (1970a, ch. 8).

[7] *State-independence* is an implication of the von Neumann-Morgenstern postulate sometimes called "irrelevance of non-affected outcomes" – see Marschak (1968a). The key idea is that when we are dealing with *prospects* which promise to offer one consequence if state-*a* obtains and another if state-*b* obtains, we need not consider any relations of complementarity in preference. For there is never any question of receiving the *combined* consequences attached to the two states; the individual will necessarily receive one to the exclusion of the other.

[8] *Time-independence,* the absence of complementarity in preference between income at time-0 and income at time-1, does not have so compelling a justification as does state-independence. For the individual will indeed be receiving a combination of consequences over time. But, in the absence of any convincing reason for anticipating positive complementarity or its reverse, the assumption of zero complementarity may be a satisfactory simplification. The assumption is widely employed in the literature of intertemporal optimization (see e.g., Arrow, 1966, p. 20).

[9] The individual maximizes $U = v_0 + \theta(\pi_a v_{1a} + \pi_b v_{1b})$ subject to $P_0 c_0 + P_{1a} c_{1a} + P_{1b} c_{1b} = P_0 y_0 + P_{1a} y_{1a} + P_{1b} y_{1b}$. The usual Lagrangean conditions lead to $v_0' = \lambda P_0$; $v_{1a}' = \lambda P_{1a}/\theta\pi_a$; $v_{1b}' = \lambda P_{1b}/\theta\pi_b$. With $P_0 = 1$, and (since all individuals have identical preferences and opportunities) $c_0 = y_0$, $c_{1a} = y_{1a}$, and $c_{1b} = y_{1b}$, the results in the text are obtained.

[10] See Hirshleifer (1970b, pp. 9–11).

[11] If no trading were permitted once the information was revealed, individuals' consumptive baskets (here, holdings of c_0 and c_1) would in general be non-Pareto optimal. That is, differences across individuals in marginal rates of substitution between commodities would persist. Such a model has been studied by Ross Starr. The non-Pareto optimality stemming from informational differences has also been noted by Earl A. Thompson (1966, n. 5) and by Arrow (1969, pp. 54–6).

[12] The second timing pattern corresponds to the dictum that, at any moment of time, the market has already "discounted" (allowed for) all publicly available information.

[13] See Hirshleifer (1970b, pp. 20–2).

[14] See Leonard J. Savage (1954).

[15] This is not the only way. The information might be purchased (or stolen) from some other person.

[16] Whitney and his partners planned to retain all the ginning in their own hands, buying the raw product and selling the ginned cotton (Dumas Malone, 1964, vol. 10, p. 159).

[17] See Machlup (1968).

[18] For a discussion in the context of government resource-investment policy, see Roland McKean (1958, ch. 8).

[19] A perfectly discriminatory fee system would place no marginal burden and thus would not lead to any restriction of output.

[20] A relatively minor shift in locomotive technology, for example, might lead railroad planners to select an entirely different route for a new line, with drastic upward and downward shifts of land values. Paul Samuelson emphasizes (1966, p. 974) the disproportionality between the gain reaped by the first-in-time speculator and the social utility of his activity.

[21] This imperfection has been emphasized by Arrow (1962, and also 1969).

[22] Resale of information does not stand on quite the same footing as speculation. Speculation is an extra source of gain, whether or not patent has been obtained, whereas resale of information otherwise kept secret is an *alternative* to obtaining a patent.

10   Speculation and Equilibrium: Information, Risk, and Markets*

Background and comments

The three final essays in this volume all bear upon the topic of speculation. The first two articles are a related pair. Taken together they set forth what is, I believe, the first general-equilibrium model of hedging and speculation in the literature that takes proper account of the risk-balancing decisions of both producers and consumers of the speculative good as against all other goods, of the conditions of actual and prospective possession of information, and of the regime of market trading.

Although these articles have had a certain modest influence, I am somewhat chagrined that papers dealing with speculation theory in terms of ill-defined partial-equilibrium models continue to appear in the current literature. One still encounters articles, for example, which implicitly postulate that traders face price risks without there being any variability of quantitative endowments. The debate on the theme "Is speculation destabilizing?" provides a whole class of instances. It is shown here, as had already been argued by McKinnon, that there cannot be free-floating price risk; price as an endogenous variable can vary only in consequence of an underlying stochastic variability of one or more exogenous parameters of the economic system. Most typically, of course, it is the possible fluctuations of quantities (owing to the possibility of crop failure, for example) that drives the variability of prices. The quantity risks intrinsic to individuals' real endowments are always a countervailing factor to price risks – prices are high when crops are small, and vice versa. In consequence, it will be evident, models

*This article originally appeared in *Quarterly Journal of Economics*, vol. 89 (Nov. 1975), pp. 519–42. The permission of MIT Press and John Wiley and Sons Inc. to reprint in this volume is gratefully acknowledged.

Comments and suggestions by Ronald Britto, Harold Demsetz, Jacquest Drèze, Edward Gallick, and Susan Woodward are gratefully acknowledged. Particular thanks are due to Mark Rubinstein, who has cooperated with me in developing some applications of this model (1973), and to John M. Marshall, whose own work contains a number of parallels with the results here reported. Research support by the Western Management Science Institute, UCLA, is gratefully acknowledged.

that allow for price risk alone are bound to be seriously misleading. (In my earlier articles I had unaccountably neglected to cite McKinnon's prior work; the reference is now provided in the final essay of this volume.)

In the first of these papers on speculation, the basic theory is developed under a relatively ample regime of markets, one in which trading in contingent claims may take place. The essay that follows extends the analysis to more restricted and realistic trading regimes. The thrust of the paper is to refute the Keynes–Hicks contention dominating previous thought in this area: that speculation is mainly a consequence of differential risk aversion, so that futures markets serve the role of transferring price risks from more risk-averse "hedgers" to more risk-tolerant "speculators." It is shown here that while differential risk aversion does play some role, the choice of hedged *versus* speculative (i.e. of risk-reducing *versus* risk-increasing) market portfolios is most fundamentally sensitive to agents' differential *beliefs* as to the likelihood of more and less well-endowed states of the world – as had been argued, notably, by Holbrook Working.

A widely accepted view of the nature and function of speculative activity, associated most prominently with the names of J. M. Keynes and J. R. Hicks, underlies and informs most of the professional and theoretical literature on the subject. This standard conception interprets speculation as a *process for the transfer of price risks.*[1] In the Keynes-Hicks view speculators are characterized not by any special *knowledge or beliefs* but simply by their *willingness to tolerate risks* in comparison with their trading partners – the more risk-averse "hedgers." Holbrook Working has argued, in contrast, that both "hedging" and "speculative" commitments do depend upon differential knowledge or beliefs as to price prospects.[2] For Keynes and Hicks the social function of speculation is the shifting of price risks to those less averse to risk bearing; for Working it is the improvement in the accuracy with which market prices reflect informed opinions.[3]

Neither of these conflicting theories is grounded upon a proper foundation: a general-equilibrium model in which individuals' tastes, endowments, and beliefs in a world of uncertainty interact so as to generate a market equilibrium incorporating both speculative and non-speculative transactions. Even the most sophisticated theoretical formulations extant[4] are all partial-equilibrium analyses, in that individuals somehow possess postulated probability distributions for price changes. *But price is an endogenous variable of economic systems: general-equilibrium models must explain prices and price anticipations on the foundation of more fundamental determinants.* In the model of speculation presented here, prices and price anticipations are endogenous variables. The *exogenous* parameters are the standard ones of economic theory: preferences (including attitudes toward risk), opportunities (individuals' risk-distributed commodity endowments, and the extent of markets for trading risky contingencies), and knowledge or beliefs (as to the commodity endowments and the extent of trading). In the interests of simplicity a regime of pure exchange is assumed – ruling out productive transformations. For such a regime the model explains (1) who becomes a speculator and who a hedger, (2) what determines the scale of speculative-hedging commitments, and (3) how traders' behavior generates equilibrium prior prices and price *movements* in response to changes in information.

10.1   PRICE RISK *VERSUS* QUANTITY RISK

The key analytical failing of the speculation literature is its preoccupation with *price risk* while neglecting *quantity* risk. It is the interaction of these two uncertainties that risk-avoiding individuals must respond to in their hedging-speculative commitments.

Figure 10.1 is a representation of the conventional view, in which only price risk is taken into account. In a world of pure exchange with two

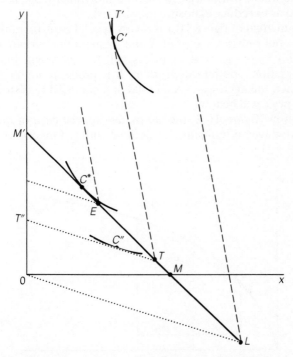

FIGURE 10.1 *Simple consumptive plan* versus *trading position, pure exchange – price risk only.*

commodities X and Y, let an individual's endowment position be at E. The currently ruling price ratio determines the budget line MM' through E, allowing a consumptive optimum at C^*. But suppose that prices may change before the close of trading. The individual might attach some non-zero probability to an upward shift in the price of X (suggesting by the steeper dashed market lines), and a complementary probability to a downward shift (suggested by the flatter dotted market lines). Rather than finalizing his consumption plan, he can therefore, if he chooses, move along MM' (i.e. while the initial prices are still ruling) not directly to C^* but to a *trading position* like T. From T, if the favorable shift of prices occurs, he attains the higher conditional consumptive optimum C'; with the unfavorable price shift, the lower conditional optimum C''. The trading in the "initial round" (along MM') corresponds, of course, to current dealing in futures contracts; the trading in the "final round" (along one or the other of the conditional posterior market lines TT' or TT'') corresponds to dealing at a later date in the spot market.

In this conventional view an individual is said to be *speculating* if he moves, in the initial round of trading, from the endowment position E to any trading position like T that enlarges his price risk.[5] *Hedging* would be trading in the initial round that moves the individual from E toward C^* along MM' so as to reduce exposure to price risk.

But the individual of figure 10.1 is a very special case: his endowment is not a *gamble*, but rather a vector of X and Y quantities certain. In general, quantity endowments as well as prices will be uncertain. Indeed, their stochastic variations are interdependent: It is precisely under those contingencies when the aggregate social total of a commodity is stochastically large that its price will be low.

Consider now (figure 10.2) the alternative special case of *quantity risk only*. Here we have an individual's "cardinal" utility function $v(z)$ defined

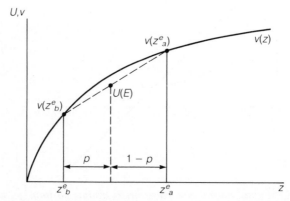

FIGURE 10.2   *A representation of state choice – quantity risk only.*

over a single risky commodity Z.[6] The concave curvature corresponds to *aversion to risk*, a property assumed in this paper always to hold. Let the individual be endowed with the gamble $E = (z_a^e, z_b^e)$, where $z_a^e > z_b^e$. This may be interpreted as follows. There are two alternative possible states of the world, a and b.[7] State-a is a situation of plenty (e.g. a good crop), state-b a situation of dearth. In a two-state world the endowment position appears as a *pair* of points on the horizontal axis of figure 10.2. If the individual attaches subjective probability p to state-a and $1 - p$ to state-b, the overall desirability of the endowment position is determined by the expected-utility rule:

$$U(E) = pv(z_a^e) + (1 - p)v(z_b^e).$$

Geometrically, in figure 10.2 $U(E)$ is the point on the dashed line connecting $v(z_a^e)$ and $v(z_b^e)$ that divides the horizontal distance in proportion to the probabilities p and $1 - p$. The endowment gamble may be expressed in "prospect" notation as $E = [z_a^e, z_b^e; p, 1 - p]$.

To show the *interaction* of price risk and quantity risk, let us deal with a two-commodity world with Z risky and a second commodity N envisaged as riskless (i.e. N endowments are invariant over states of the world). All the quantity risk is therefore associated with commodity Z. In figure 10.3 the endowment vector in prospect notation is $E = [(n^e, z_a^e), (n^e, z_b^e); p, 1 - p]$. Here the first ("good crop") outcome is illustrated by the point in the base plane denoted $e_a = (100, 200)$ and the second ("poor crop") outcome by $e_b = (100, 80)$. As in figure 10.2 the endowment position appears as a *pair* of points (e_a, e_b) in the diagram of figure 10.3. The

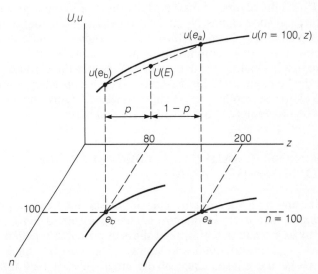

FIGURE 10.3 *Utility level of endowment position, with two commodities.*

absence of quantity risk with respect to the N commodity is reflected in the horizontal alignment of the e_a, e_b points along $n = 100$.

Since N is assumed riskless throughout, in what follows it will usually be convenient to use a somewhat condensed notation that expresses the endowment position as $E = (n^e; z_a^e, z_b^e) = (100; 200, 80)$. Similar notation will be used for trading positions T and consumptive positions C. (At times, however, it will become necessary to revert to the more complete prospect notation for the underlying gambles.)

The vertical axis measures a cardinal preference-scaling function $u(n, z)$ defined over the two commodities N and Z; this function can be arrived at by a natural generalization of the Friedman-Savage one-commodity development.[8] The expected-utility rule can then be set down in the generalized form:

$$U(n; z_a, z_b) = pu(n, z_a) + (1 - p)u(n, z_b).$$

In figure 10.3 we do not see the entire utility surface $u(n, z)$ but only the section that overlies the line $n = 100$ in the base plane. The utility of the endowment position is shown by the point $U(E)$ along the line connecting $u(e_a)$ and $u(e_b)$, weighted in accordance with probabilities p and $1 - p$ in complete analogy with the corresponding construction in figure 10.2.

In this analysis it is essential to specify the nature of the transactions permitted. The riskless commodity N is assumed always tradable; N will be taken as numeraire, so that $P_N \equiv 1$ always. As for the risky commodity Z, there are two interesting possibilities: (1) *Semicomplete Markets*: Here the *conditional* state claims to Z_a and Z_b are separately tradable against units of the riskless commodity N, leading to distinct contingency prices P_{Za} and P_{Zb}. (This regime of markets falls short of being *fully* complete in that conditional state claims N_a and N_b to the riskless commodity are not assumed tradable.) (2) *Certainty Markets*: Here only *unconditional* (certain) claims even to the risky commodity Z are tradable, so that markets can determine only a single price denoted P_Z. Whether the Certainty Markets model or the Semicomplete Markets model represents a better approximation to real world conditions remains arguable.[9] Only the more ample regime of Semicomplete Markets will be studied here.

10.2   NON-INFORMATIVE EQUILIBRIUM: SIMPLE CONSUMPTIVE GAMBLE

Speculative and hedging commitments are determined by the prospect of *price changes*. In the world of pure exchange assumed here, prices can change only as a result of widespread shifts in probability beliefs (as to the likelihoods of differently endowed states of the world).[10] Such shifts are assumed to be the consequence of the emergence of new information; hence, speculative or hedging behavior arises only in an "informative situation," where such emergence is anticipated. *In an informative situation there will be two interrelated market equilibria of prices – one prior to and the second posterior to the shift in probability beliefs.*

Consider first a *non*-informative situation, where no new information about state probabilities is anticipated before the close of trading. Since there is then no anticipation of price change, there will be no speculation or hedging. Rather, each person's decision problem is to choose a *simple consumptive$_e$ gamble*, i.e. to trade from his endowment gamble $E = (n^e; z_a^e, z_b^e)$ to a preferred consumptive gamble $C^* = (n^*; z_a^*, z_b^*)$ in the light of his utility function. Exchange will take place at market-clearing prices P_{Za} and P_{Zb}. The anticipated sequence of events can be indicated:

$$\begin{array}{l}\text{Endowment} \\ \text{gamble } E\end{array} \to \text{Trading} \to \begin{array}{l}\text{Consumptive} \\ \text{gamble } C^*\end{array} \to \begin{array}{l}\text{Nature's choice} \\ \text{of state-}a\text{ or -}b\end{array} \to \text{Consumption.}$$

The individual maximizes his expected utility:

$$U(n; z_a, z_b) = Eu(n, z) = pu(n, z_a) + (1 - p)u(n, z_b). \tag{10.1}$$

Note that there is no need to distinguish between n_a and n_b, which are necessarily equal under the regime of Semicomplete Markets. It will be assumed that the preference-scaling function can be written in additive form:

$$u(n, z) = u_n(n) + u_z(z). \tag{10.2}$$

At some modest cost in generality, this restriction provides great simplification by clearing away the intricacies of complementarity effects.

Under pure exchange the budget constraint is the wealth value of the endowment combination W^e:

$$n + P_{Za}z_a + P_{Zb}z_b = n^e + P_{Za}z_a^e + P_{Zb}z_b^e \equiv W^e. \tag{10.3}$$

The usual optimization technique leads to:

$$p\frac{\partial u/\partial z_a}{\partial u/\partial n} = P_{Za} \text{ and } (1-p)\frac{\partial u/\partial z_b}{\partial u/\partial n} = P_{Zb}. \qquad \begin{array}{l}\text{Consumptive} \\ \text{optimality} \\ \text{conditions}\end{array} \tag{10.4}$$

These conditions, together with the budget constraint (10.3), suffice to determine the individual's optimum simple consumptive gamble C^*. Also determined, of course, are the transactions he must execute to convert his endowment gamble E into C^*.

What are the factors governing the market prices P_{Za} and P_{Zb}? Supply and demand functions could be derived from (10.3) and (10.4) whose equality, summed over all individuals, would express the conditions of equilibrium. It will be convenient here, however, to introduce as a heuristic device the "representative individual." Apart from the possibly deviant trader to whom equations (10.3) and (10.4) apply and who as a single person is of negligible weight, everyone else is identical so that any one of them serves as a microcosm of the entire market. (The representative individual, like the Cheshire cat, will in due course disappear – except possibly for his grin!) In a world of pure exchange the equilibrium prices are then governed by the necessity of "sustaining" the representative endowment vector; since a representative individual can find no-one to trade with in a closed economy, his endowment vector must be his consumptive optimum.

Let the representative individual's utility function be denoted $\mu(n, z)$ and suppose that he assigns probabilities π and $1 - \pi$ to states-a and -b, respectively. Then the conditions determining prices are

$$\pi \frac{\partial \mu / \partial z_a^r}{\partial \mu / \partial n^r} = P_{Za} \text{ and } (1 - \pi) \frac{\partial \mu / \partial z_b^r}{\partial \mu / \partial n^r} = P_{Zb}. \quad \begin{matrix} \text{Sustaining} \\ \text{prices,} \\ \text{representative} \\ \text{individual} \end{matrix} \quad (10.5)$$

Here $((n'; z_a^r, z_b^r) \equiv R$ is both endowment vector and consumptive optimum for the representative individual. Note how the representative probability beliefs π, $1 - \pi$ and the representative marginal utilities (involving both the cross-commodity comparison $\partial u / \partial z$ versus $\partial \mu / \partial n$, and the intracommodity comparison $\partial \mu / \partial z_a$ versus $\partial \mu / \partial z_b$, that reflects degree of risk aversion) enter into the equilibrium price ratios. Without a representative individual, equilibrium prices would of course reflect some *average* measure of the various individuals' differing probability beliefs and some *average* measure of their respective marginal utilities.[11]

Numerical example 1

Consider an economy consisting of a great number of representative individuals – plus a single deviant person whose weight is negligible in determining prices. Suppose that all have endowment vectors $E = R = (100; 200, 80)$ and that all utility functions are $u = \mu = \log_e nz = \log_e n + \log_e z$. Let the representative individual's probability parameter (belief attached to the more prosperous state a) be $\pi = 0.6$, and the deviant's be $p = 0.7$. (Thus, the non-conforming individual here is *belief*-deviant and not endowment-deviant or utility-deviant.) Then, from equation (10.5) the prices are determined as $0.6(1/200)/(1/100) = 0.3 = P_{Za}$ and $0.4(1/80)/(1/100) = 0.5 = P_{Zb}$. It follows that all individuals have endowed wealths $W^e = 100 + 0.3(200) + 0.5(80) = 200$. The budget equation (10.3) becomes $n + 0.3z_a + 0.5z_b = 200$. For the deviant individual the consumptive optimality conditions take the form $0.7(1/z_a)/(1/n) = 0.3$ and $0.3(1/z_b)/(1/n) = 0.5$. These determine his simple consumptive optimum as the vector $C^* = (100; 233\frac{1}{3}, 60)$. As for the representative individual, it can be verified (by substituting his belief parameter π for p in equations (10.4)) that his consumptive optimum is identical with his endowment vector $R = (100; 200, 80)$.

In the numerical example the deviant individual attaching higher belief to the advent of state-a is willing to take more of a chance on state-a obtaining. But even the representative individual does not move to a riskless situation – indeed he cannot, because an inescapable quantity risk exists on the social level (the aggregate crop may be a good one or a poor one).

Now suppose that individuals have acted on the basis of a non-informative situation, interacting so as to generate a price equilibrium – after which new information is *unexpectedly* revealed that changes representative probability beliefs from π, $1 - \pi$ to π^*, $1 - \pi^*$. If markets are reopened, what will be the effect on prices? Using the device of a fully representative individual, we see immediately from (10.5) that

$$\frac{P_{Za}^*}{P_{Za}} = \frac{\pi^*}{\pi} \quad \text{and} \quad \frac{P_{Zb}^*}{P_{Zb}} = \frac{1 - \pi^*}{1 - \pi}. \tag{10.6}$$

In order to sustain the representative individual's position, *prices will move in simple proportion to changes in probability beliefs*. Furthermore, we can let our Cheshire cat, the representative individual assumption, fade away, and the proposition still holds true! We must still retain, however, the cat's grin in the form of agreement or *concordance of beliefs*,[12] so that essentially all the personal p's equal π before and π^* after the new information. The validity of (10.6), given agreed beliefs, is evident from the way in which personal probabilities p, $1 - p$ enter as multiplicative factors in the consumptive optimality conditions (10.4). The positions attained by individuals of agreed beliefs are sustained when beliefs change, the prices moving in such a way as to keep the gambles optimal given the new probability beliefs.[13]

10.3   INFORMATIVE EQUILIBRIUM: PRIOR-TRADING OPTIMUM AND COMPOUND CONSUMPTIVE GAMBLE

We are now ready to bring speculation (or hedging) into the picture. The traditional literature emphasizes, what is indeed an essential element, the "price risk" faced by transactors. But quantity risk also, and indeed in an uncertain world *always*, exists. Price risk, in contrast, exists only in an informative situation: where new evidence is expected to emerge, before the close of trading, so as to modify representative beliefs. (The situation could of course be regarded as informative by some traders and as non-informative by others, but we here assume no disagreement on this score.)

In an informative situation there will be *two distinct rounds of trading*, so that the sequence of events is

$$\text{Endowment} \rightarrow \text{Prior} \rightarrow \text{Speculative} \rightarrow \text{Emergence of}$$
$$\text{gamble } E \quad \text{trading} \quad \text{gamble } T^* \quad \text{information}$$
$$\text{round}$$

$$\rightarrow \text{Posterior} \rightarrow \text{Consumptive}$$
$$\text{trading} \quad \text{gamble } C^{**}.$$
$$\text{round}$$

After traders choose their final consumptive gambles, Nature as before selects the state, and then actual consumption takes place.

The individual's decision problem is now more complicated. In the *posterior* round of trading he will engage in portfolio revisions on the basis of known final prices. In the *prior* round of trading he will be facing known prior state-claim prices, which we may denote P^0_{Za} and P^0_{Zb}, *but he must take some account of the unknown posterior prices* $\mathbf{P}_{Za}$ *and* $\mathbf{P}_{Zb}$ *that will be ruling in the final round* after the new information emerges.

To carry the analysis further, the nature of the emergent information (as anticipated by traders) has to be specified. It will suffice to assume here the simplest possible information anticipations: posterior unanimity and certainty. Posterior *unanimity* means that the evidence forthcoming will be so overwhelming that no difference of opinion can afterward persist as to the probabilities of the two states; i.e. concordant and deviant beliefs will no longer diverge. Posterior *certainty* means that the personal belief parameter p (probability of state a) will then take on only one or the other of the limiting values $p' = \pi' = 1$ or else $p'' = \pi'' = 0$. In short, the information forthcoming is to be absolutely *conclusive* as to which state will obtain. But of course no-one can in general be certain in advance which way the information will point. Any trader will have to assign his same personal probability parameter p, that he attached to the likelihood of state a obtaining, to the likelihood that the conclusive evidence to emerge will convince everyone that state a is now certain.

The optimizing problem in an informative situation can be formulated as follows:

$$\underset{(T^*)}{\text{Max }} U = pu(n', z'_a) + (1-p)u(n'', z''_b) \text{ subject to} \tag{10.7a}$$

$$n' + \mathbf{P}'_{Za} z'_a = n^t + \mathbf{P}'_{Za} z^t_a \equiv W'$$

$$n'' + \mathbf{P}''_{Zb} z''_b = n^t + \mathbf{P}''_{Zb} z^t_b \equiv W'' \tag{10.7b}$$

$$n^t = P^0_{Za} z^t_a + P^0_{Zb} z^t_b = n^e + P^0_{Za} z^e_a + P^0_{Zb} z^e_b \equiv W^e.$$

Here n^t, z^t_a, z^t_b are the elements of the optimum trading vector T^* to which the individual can move in the initial round. The attainable trading vectors are constrained by endowed wealth W^e, as indicated in the third equation of (10.7b). The primed symbols are the posterior variables associated with the first information outcome $(\pi' = 1)$, and the double-primed symbols are those associated with the other outcome $(\pi'' = 0)$. The conditional posterior price $\mathbf{P}'_{Za}$ is the price for Z_a that would rule given the information result leading to $\pi' = 1$ (certainty of state-a); in this case, of course, the price of state-b claims must necessarily fall to zero, and hence no Z_b term enters in the first equation of (10.7b). Similarly, $\mathbf{P}''_{Zb}$ is the price of Z_b claims in the opposite case (certainty of state-b), so that no Z_a term need enter into the second equation of (10.7b).[14] W' and W'', defined as indicated above, will be called the *conditional posterior wealths*. The intermediate T^* position serves in the role of starting point or endowment position for the posterior trading that leads in the one case to the conditionally optimal n', z'_a point and in the other case to the corresponding n'', z''_b point. The overall choice may be regarded as selection of an optimum compound consumptive gamble that may be denoted in "prospect" form as $C^{**} = [(n', z'_a), (n'', z''_b); p, 1 - p]$. Note that the N consumptions, n' and n'', may differ with two rounds of trading even though N is riskless.

The crucial question is: Can anything be known about the conditional *posterior* prices that will help to guide *prior* trading? The answer is: Yes, sometimes![15] *In the special case where concordant beliefs represent essentially all the social weight*, it will be shown that *posterior and prior prices are related simply in proportion to the posterior and prior concordant probabilities*:

$$\frac{\mathbf{P}'_{Za}}{P^0_{Za}} = \frac{1}{\pi} \text{ and } \frac{\mathbf{P}''_{Zb}}{P^0_{Zb}} = \frac{1}{1 - \pi}. \quad \begin{array}{l}\text{Relation between} \\ \text{prior and posterior} \\ \text{prices}\end{array} \quad (10.8)$$

This very satisfying theorem has the possibly surprising corollary:

$$P^0_{Za} = P_{Za} \text{ and } P^0_{Zb} = P_{Zb}. \quad (10.8a)$$

That is, the prior trading prices in an informative situation will (given agreed beliefs) be simply equal to the state-claim prices that would have ruled had the situation been a noninformative one!

The essential idea underlying (10.8) and (10.8a) can be appreciated intuitively if we bring back the Cheshire cat, the heuristic device of a fully representative individual. Prices in both prior and posterior markets must be such as to sustain the endowment position of such an individual. To put it another way, prices must be such that for him the simple consumptive gamble C^* and the compound consumptive gamble C^{**} are the same and indeed identical with the endowment gamble R. For a representative individual not to find it advantageous to move in the initial round to a position inconsistent with R, equations (10.5) would have to hold for prior-round trading, i.e. if we substitute P^0_{Za} for P_{Za} and P^0_{Zb} for P_{Zb} as in (10.8a). And since there is no uncertainty in the posterior markets, to sustain the endowment position there the prices would have to be

$$\frac{\partial\mu/\partial z_a^r}{\partial\mu/\partial n^r} = \mathbf{P}_{Za}' \quad \text{and} \quad \frac{\partial\mu/\partial z_b^r}{\partial\mu/\partial n^r} = \mathbf{P}_{Zb}''.$$

Equations (10.8) follow directly, and (10.8a) has already been shown to hold in this representative-individual case.

Dropping the representative-individual assumption, we know that if $P_{Za}^0 = P_{Za}$ and $P_{Zb}^0 = P_{Zb}$ then in the initial round every trader *can* attain a T^* equal to his simple consumptive optimum C^*. If we assume concordant (homogeneous) beliefs, equation (10.6) holds for any agreed change in the probability parameter π (likelihood of state-a). With conclusive evidence the parameter can only become zero or unity; thus (10.8) is seen to be a special case of (10.6). So the C^* positions attained in the initial round are sustained: $C^{**} = C^*$. Equations (10.8) and (10.8a) are thus consistent with equilibrium, given only concordant beliefs.[16]

It is very interesting to note that the price-revision relation (10.8) is a *martingale* formula. That is, for either conditional state-claim the ratio (expectation of posterior price)/(prior price) is unity. Consider the state-a price. The ratio $\mathbf{P}_{Za}'/P_{Za}^0 = 1/\pi$, and this will occur (i.e. the information will point to state-a) with probability π (according to the beliefs of concordant individuals). But with corresponding probability $1 - \pi$ the information will conclusively point to state-b, and Z_a-claims will be worth zero. Hence $E(\mathbf{P}_{Za}'/P_{Za}^0) = 1$. A similar argument holds of course for prior and posterior prices of state-b claims. The relation can be very considerably generalized beyond the special case considered here. But note that what is a martingale according to the beliefs of a concordant individual *cannot* be one if deviant beliefs are used as probability weights.[17]

The optimizing problem of equations (10.7a) and (10.7b) can be reformulated in an illuminating way as a choice between conditional posterior *wealths*. Using (10.8), multiply the first equation of (8.7b) by π and the second by $1 - \pi$ to obtain the third. Thus, the three constraints are not independent. The relation between them may be expressed as

$$\pi W' + (1 - \pi) W'' = W^e. \tag{10.9}$$

That is, the endowed wealth can be regarded as the mathematical expectation (using the concordant prior probabilities) of the conditional posterior wealths. Then the problem can be expressed as

$$\underset{(W', W'')}{\text{Max}} \ U = pu'(W' \mid \mathbf{P}') + (1 - p)u''(W'' \mid \mathbf{P}''), \tag{10.10}$$

subject to (10.9) as constraint. Here u' and u'' are conditional utility elements expressed in "indirect" form as functions of the corresponding wealths, given the posterior price vectors symbolized by $\mathbf{P}'$ and $\mathbf{P}''$.[18]

The result is the following condition for optimal prior trading:

$$\frac{p}{1-p}\frac{du'/dW'}{du''/dW''}=\frac{\pi}{1-\pi}\ . \quad \begin{array}{l}\text{Trading}\\ \text{optimality}\\ \text{condition}\end{array} \qquad (10.11)$$

The trading optimality condition (10.11), together with the constraint (10.9), determines for each individual the pair of conditional posterior wealths W', W'' he must reach in the initial round to obtain the best compound gamble C^{**} within his opportunity set. With W' and W'' he would enter equations (10.7b) to find the elements n', z_a^t, z_b^t of the optimal trading vector T^*. But the *two* wealths are insufficient to determine all *three* elements of T^*. We therefore arrive at a *principle of trading indeterminacy*: In a regime of Semicomplete Markets for state-claims, the optimal trading position T^* depends only on attaining the correct conditional posterior wealths. A degree of freedom remains in which any *one* element of T^* can be arbitrarily selected.[19]

Numerical example 2

Continuing with the data of numerical example 1, consider a belief-deviant individual (of negligible social weight) in an informative situation. New (and conclusive) evidence as to which state will obtain is anticipated to emerge, before the final round of trading. With the utility function $u = \log_e nz$, conditional marginal utilities of posterior wealth can be shown to be $du'/dW' = 2/W'$ and $du''/dW'' = 2/W''$.[20] Then the trading optimality condition (10.11) takes the convenient form $p/(1-p) \times (W''/W') = \pi/(1-\pi)$. Together with (10.9), this leads to explicit equations for the optimal condition wealths: $W' = (p/\pi) W^e$ and $W'' = (1-p)/(1-\pi) W^e$. With $p = 0.7$, $\pi = 0.6$, and $W^e = 200$, we obtain numerically $W'' = 233\frac{1}{3}$ and $W'' = 150$. Fixing $n^t = 100$ (as is possible due to trading indeterminacy), we see that the optimal trading vector is $T^* = (n^t; z_a^t, z_b^t) = (100; 266\frac{2}{3}, 40)$. Using (10.8) and (10.8a), we see that the *posterior* prices are $\mathbf{P}' \equiv \mathbf{P}'_{Za} = P_{Za}/\pi = 0.3/0.6 = 0.5$, and $\mathbf{P}'' \equiv \mathbf{P}''_{Zb} = P_{Zb}/(1-\pi) = 0.5/0.4 = 1.25$. Then, the individual's conditional posterior optimum positions are found by standard Lagrangian procedures to be $C' = (n', z_a') = (116\frac{1}{3}, 233\frac{2}{3})$ and $C'' = (n'', z_b'') = (75, 60)$. His compound consumptive gamble can be written in prospect notation as $C^{**} = [(116\frac{1}{3}, 233\frac{2}{3}), (75, 60); 0.7, 0.3]$.

Figure 10.4 provides a geometrical interpretation of the interaction between price risk and quantity risk in the example above; it can be regarded as a generalization of figure 10.1. The *posterior* optimization problem takes place under conditions of certainty. Either state-a will be known to obtain, in which case $\mathbf{P}' = 0.5$ and the flatter (dashed) price lines in the N, Z plane will be relevant – or state-b will be known to obtain, with $\mathbf{P}'' = 1.25$ and the steeper (dotted) price lines relevant. There is price risk,

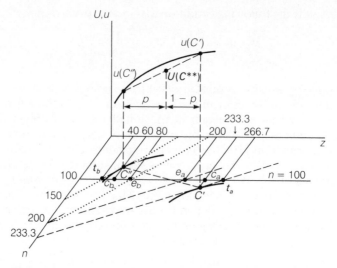

FIGURE 10.4   *Trading optimum for belief-deviant individual.*

just as in figure 10.1, since the individual does not know in advance which of the posterior prices will be ruling in the final round. But the same circumstances that lead to one or another outcome with respect to the posterior prices are also associated with a more or less favorable *quantitative* situation. Suppose that he were to remain with his endowment gamble, pictured as the pair of points e_a, e_b. Then the advent of state-a would be associated, at one and the same time, with the flatter price lines and the favorable quantity outcome $e_a = (100, 200)$, and the advent of state-b with the steeper price lines and the unfavorable $e_b = (100, 80)$.

In an informative situation this belief-deviant individual will not stand pat with his endowment gamble in the initial round. The prior trading opportunities are awkward to represent geometrically, since they involve combinations of three types of claims: N, Z_a, and Z_b. However, thanks to the principle of trading indeterminacy, we can hold $n = 100$ and consider only trading between Z_a and Z_b claims. Then prior trading permits the individual to *widen or narrow the gap* along $n = 100$ in comparison with his endowed point-pair e_a, e_b. Here the prior prices are in the ratio $P_{Zb}^0 / P_{Za}^0 = 3/5$ – so three units of Z_b can be exchanged in the initial round against five units of Z_a. The *simple* consumptive optimum C^* (one round of trading only) for the belief-deviant individual with $p = 0.7$ involves a widening of risk as shown by the location of the point-pair c_a, c_b, where $c_a = (100, 233\frac{1}{3})$ and $c_b = (100, 60)$. The trading optimum T^* (speculative position) involves this individual in still further risk widening to the point-pair t_a, t_b, where $t_a = (100, 266\frac{2}{3})$ and $t_b = (100, 40)$.

The final step is the posterior movement to the conditional optimum positions. If state-a obtains, the speculation has succeeded; the trader moves from t_a in the final round along the flatter price line to the indifference-curve tangency $C' = (n', z'_a) = (116\frac{2}{3}, 233\frac{1}{3})$. If state-$b$ obtains, the best attainable position is $C'' = (n'', z''_b) = (75, 60)$. The conditional utility levels attainable, $u(C')$ and $u(C'')$, do not lie over the $n = 100$ line so that the vertical section of the utility surface shown in figure 10.4 is not sliced the same way as the section pictured in figure 10.3. However, the expected utility $U(C^{**})$ of the compound consumptive gamble is arrived at similarly as the probability-weighted average along the dotted line connecting $u(C')$ and $u(C'')$.

While the trading optimality condition (10.11) is applicable for any individual, the development leading to (10.11) postulated an "almost-concordant world" in which individuals of agreed beliefs constituted essentially all the social weight in the market. For such concordant individuals, (10.11) reduces to the still simpler form:

$$\frac{du'}{dW'} = \frac{du''}{dW''}. \tag{10.12}$$

Using relation (10.12), it may be verified that *individuals with concordant beliefs will choose compound gambles* C^{**} *identical with their simple consumptive gambles* C^*. (In this sense, they will not be *speculating* – as will be explained below.) *This will be so even when utility functions or endowment positions diverge.* In their case $n' = n''$, and both are equal to the n^* entering into $C^* = (n^*; z^*_a, z^*_b)$. Similarly, $z'_a = z^*_a$ and $z''_b = z^*_b$.

To demonstrate this, it will be useful to set down the *posterior* optimization problems explicitly in Lagrangian form:

$$\text{Max } u(n', z'_a) - \lambda'(n' + \mathbf{P}'_{Za} z'_a - W')$$
$$\text{Max } u(n'', z''_b) - \lambda''(n'' + \mathbf{P}''_{Zb} z''_b - W'').$$

The conditions resulting are:

$$\lambda' = \frac{\partial u}{\partial n'} \text{ and } \lambda' \mathbf{P}'_{Za} = \frac{\partial u}{\partial z'_a} \tag{10.13a}$$

$$\lambda'' = \frac{\partial u}{\partial u''} \text{ and } \lambda'' \mathbf{P}''_{Zb} = \frac{\partial u}{\partial z''_b} \tag{10.13b}$$

Using (10.8) and (10.8a), we see that:

$$\pi \frac{\partial u/\partial z'_a}{\partial u/\partial n'} = P_{Za} \text{ and } (1 - \pi) \frac{\partial u/\partial z''_b}{\partial u/\partial n''} = P_{Zb}. \tag{10.14}$$

Equations (10.14), apart from substitution of the concordant belief parameter π for p, look almost the same as the consumptive optimality conditions (10.4) governing the choice of the individual's simple consumptive gamble. The only difference is the distinction between n' and n'' in the denominators of (10.14). But now note that in (10.13a) λ' can be identified with du/dW', the marginal utility payoff of relaxing the W' constraint, and similarly, λ'' can be identified with du/dW''. The equality in (10.12) of the derivatives du'/dW' and du''/dW'' in "indirect" form evidently involves the equality of the parametric "direct" derivatives du/dW' and du/dW''.[21] Hence $\lambda' = \lambda''$, $\partial u/\partial n' = \partial u/\partial n''$, and $n' = n''$. Thus the conditions (10.14) are the same as (10.4), so that $C^{**} = C^{*}$.[22]

Individuals can differ one from another with regard to *beliefs*, with regard to *endowment scale* and *composition*, and with regard to *utility functions* (of which risk aversion is an aspect). The proposition above shows that, in a world where concordant beliefs represent essentially all the social weight, only those deviating in *belief* will make use of the opportunity provided by an informative situation to choose an optimal gamble C^{**} that diverges from the simple consumptive gamble C^{*} they would have chosen in a noninformative situation. Conversely, contra Keynes and Hicks, differences in utility functions (or in endowments) *without* deviation from concordant beliefs will not lead to divergences between C^{*} and C^{**}.

10.4   CONCLUSION: DETERMINANTS OF SPECULATIVE-HEDGING BEHAVIOR

The conventional definition describes hedging as initial-round trading (at the known prior prices) tending to reduce the need for final-round trading (at the unknown posterior prices) – in short, as behavior tending to reduce exposure to price risk. Speculation is conventionally defined in the reverse way, as acceptance of price risk. These definitions seemed plausible enough in the situation described in figure 10.1, where no *quantity risk* was recognized and where only certain (unconditional) claims to commodities could be traded. In the more general situation considered here, however, exclusive concentration upon price risk is seriously misleading. *Speculators and hedgers are those using the prior market, in an informative situation, to achieve a compound consumptive gamble* C** *that differs from the simple consumptive gamble* C* *they would have chosen in a non-informative situation.* This definition involves the recognition that (1) consumptive positions chosen by all individuals will, in a world of uncertainty, generally be gambles ("quantity risk"), and (2) only individuals who anticipate the emergence of new information tending to modify prices before the close of trading ("price risk") envisage the possibility of using the anticipated price change so as to obtain consumptive gambles otherwise unattainble. The hedgers are then those who employ prior trading to reduce their overall risk (choose a compound C^{**} that is less risky than the simple gamble C^* they would otherwise have chosen), while the speculators are of course doing the reverse. Those who are neither hedgers nor speculators, who are content to have C^{**} in an informative situation identical with the C^* they would have chosen in a non-informative situation, may be called "investors."[23]

The crucial result attained in the analysis above can be stated: *Only those individuals deviating from representative beliefs in the market will hedge or speculate.* In particular, contra the Keynes–Hicks or "risk-transfer" theory, differences in degree of risk aversion alone will not lead to hedging or speculative behavior. For, while relatively risk-averse individuals will tend to select narrower consumptive gambles and relatively risk-tolerant individuals select wider gambles, in the absence of deviating beliefs choices of compound gambles C^{**} in an informative situation will not differ from the simple gambles C^* that would have been selected had the situation been non-informative.

Conversely, our results support the Working theory that emphasizes *differences of belief* as the key to hedging-speculation behavior. Those, and only those, whose beliefs as to what the emergent information will reveal diverge from representative opinion in the market, will regard themselves as able (on the average) to profit from anticipated price change. In an informative situation they will choose compound gambles C^{**} differing from their C^* gambles even if their risk tolerances (and all other aspects of their utility functions and endowment positions) conform with the representative situation in the market.

It is natural to associate speculation with *optimistic* opinion and hedging with *pessimistic* opinion as to the likelihood of more and less favorable states of the world. And indeed it is true that (as in numerical example 2 above) someone attaching a higher-than-representative probability belief to the more favorable state of the world will choose a relatively risky compound gamble C^{**} (i.e. one with a large gap between the state-dependent results). For, he expects to profit from the price change consequent upon the emergence of new information that he anticipates will validate his own prior beliefs. And it is also true that someone who (over a certain range) is pessimistic tends to hedge – to trade in the prior round so as to achieve a relatively safe C^{**} gamble, safer still than the conservative C^* gamble such an individual would have been inclined to accept in a non-informative situation. However, there is another factor at work that disrupts a simple correlation of the optimism-pessimism parameter with speculation-hedging behavior. As the degree of pessimism parametrically increases, the associated belief-deviant behavior will become more conservative only up to a point; pessimism that is sufficiently extreme will actually dictate a widening of risk once again! For, with very extreme pessimistic beliefs, it can be shown that the individual will find it attractive to gamble in such a way as to make himself better off should the *unfavorable* state of the world obtain.[24]

Attitudes toward risk are not, however, entirely without effect. For, given the necessary condition of belief deviance, the *scale* of the compound gamble accepted (in an informative situation) will be positively associated with the degree of risk tolerance that characterizes the individual's utility function. The formal development is straightforward and need not be expounded here.

10.5   LIMITATIONS AND GENERALIZATIONS

The assumptions of just two commodities and two states of the world are innocuous simplifications; everything will generalize in these respects. And posterior certainty can be relaxed without fundamental change. However, the following are not mere simplifications: (1) independence of the commodities in preference (zero complementarity); (2) concordant (homogeneous) prior beliefs constituting essentially all the weight in the market; (3) agreement as to informative or non-informative situation; (4) Semicomplete Markets.

The main function of the zero-complementarity assumption was to permit the replacement of the regime of fully Complete Markets by the regime of Semicomplete Markets. If complementarity effects are second-order in magnitude (as against comparisons of the direct marginal utilities), the general results here would continue in substance to hold without requiring absolute independence in demand.

The assumption of concordant beliefs (except possibly for deviant individuals of negligible social weight) is, however, a very strong one. As a practical matter, one would want to interpret *agreed* belief as some kind of *average* belief (weighted by endowed wealth). Such an interpretation is not strictly permissible, as the formal analysis requires literally agreed beliefs. But shifts in average beliefs would surely have effects on prices substantially similar to changes in agreed beliefs. On the other hand, one important difference does have to be recognized. Where beliefs generally vary, essentially everyone may be "deviant" from the average opinion and so would tend to engage in some hedging-speculation behavior in an informative situation. Hence, while relaxing the concordance assumption does not substantially affect *price changes* between prior and posterior trading rounds, we would expect to observe a significantly greater *volume of prior transactions* than would be accounted for by the theory above.[25]

What if, in a world of concordant beliefs as to the underlying state probabilities, there were disagreements as to whether the situation was informative or not? All individuals who regard the situation as non-informative would of course be attempting to move to their simple consumptive optimum positions C^* in the initial round, rather than to trading positions T^*. However, since (from equations 10.8a) the prior prices P_{Za}^0 and P_{Zb}^0 in an informative situation are, respectively, the same as the P_{Za} and P_{Zb} of a non-informative situation, the compound gambles C^{**} being sought by the one concordant group are identical with the simple gambles C^* being sought by the other. So this divergence does not in any way disturb the equilibrium of prices – prior or posterior.

Finally, as to the assumption of a regime of Semicomplete Markets, the degree to which this is an inessential simplification of a system of *fully* Complete Markets has already been commented on. What is much more important and interesting, however, is not consideration of a still more ample set of markets but rather comparison with a regime of substantially *curtailed* trading opportunities in the presence of uncertainty. As indicated initially, the most interesting alternative assumption is to go to the opposite extreme, to a regime of Certainty Markets. Here we would be dealing with a world in which individuals were, in general, endowed with gambles over states (quantity risk), but in which, nevertheless, market trading was permitted only in certainty claims to commodities, regardless of whether the commodity itself is risky or riskless. In models of such a world there are some interesting parallels, yet significant divergences, as to the determinants of speculative-hedging behavior.[26]

NOTES

[1] J. M. Keynes, *A Treatise on Money*, New York: Harcourt, Brace and Company, 1930, vol. 2, ch. 29; J. R. Hicks, *Value and Capital*, 2nd ed., London: Oxford University Press, 1946, pp. 137–9; H. Houthakker, "Can Speculators Forecast Prices?" *Review of Economics and Statistics*, vol. 39 (May 1957), pp. 143–51; H. Houthakker, "Normal Backwardation," in J. N. Wolfe, ed., *Value, Capital and Growth*, Edinburgh: Edinburgh University Press, 1968; P. H. Cootner, "Speculation, Hedging, and Arbitrage," *International Encyclopedia of the Social Sciences*, vol. 15, 1968; L. G. Telser, "A Theory of Speculation Relating Profitability and Stability," *Review of Economics and Statistics*, vol. 41 (Aug. 1959), pp. 295–301.

[2] H. Working, "Futures Trading and Hedging," *American Economic Review*, vol. 43 (June 1953), pp. 314–43, esp. p. 320.

[3] H. Working, "New Concepts Concerning Futures Markets and Prices," *American Economic Review*, vol. 52 (June 1962), pp. 431–59, esp. pp. 452–3. See also C. S. Rockwell, "Normal Backwardation, Forecasting and the Returns to Commodity Futures Traders," *Food Research Institute Studies*, vol. 7, Supplement (1967), pp. 107–10.

[4] See L. L. Johnson, "The Theory of Hedging and Speculation in Commodity Futures," *Review of Economic Studies*, vol. 27 (June 1960), pp. 139–51; M. S. Feldstein, "Uncertainty and Forward Exchange Speculation," *Review of Economics and Statistics*, vol. 50 (May 1968), pp. 182–92; and Houthakker, "Normal Backwardation."

[5] The point L is a limit upon speculative commitments. Individuals can move to trading positions involving negative holdings of one or more specific commodities, but not to trading positions in which conditional posterior net wealth becomes negative in any state of the world recognized as possible in the market. See J. Hirshleifer, "Foundations of the Theory of Speculation: Information, Risk, and Markets," Western Management Science Institute, UCLA, Working Paper no. 189, revised, June 1972, section 10.1.

[6] The best known reference is M. Friedman and L. J. Savage, "The Utility Analysis of Choices Involving Risk," *Journal of Political Economy*, vol. 56 (1948); reprinted in K. E. Boulding and G. J. Stigler, eds, *Readings in Price Theory*, Chicago: R. D. Irwin, 1952, pp. 74-6 (page citations are to the latter version). The underlying theoretical justification is in J. von Neumann and O. Morgenstern, *The Theory of Games and Economic Behavior*, 2nd ed., Princeton, NJ: Princeton University Press, 1947, pp. 15-31.

[7] In contrast with Johnson, *op. cit.*, and Houthakker, "Normal Backwardation," the *state-preference model* of uncertainty is adopted here; the ultimate objects of choice are conditional claims defined both as to commodity and state of the world. This model was first proposed by K. J. Arrow, "Le Rôle des Valeurs Boursières pour la Repartition la Meilleure des Risques," *Econometrie*, Paris, Centre Nationale de la Recherche Scientifique, vol. 11 (1953), pp. 41-7; translated as "The Role of Securities in the Optimal Allocation of Risk-Bearing," *Review of Economic Studies*, vol. 31 (April 1964), pp. 91-6; and has been developed and amplified by other authors including G. Debreu, *Theory of Value: An Axiomatic Analysis of Economic Equilibrium*, New York: Wiley and Sons, 1959; K. Borch, "Equilibrium in a Reinsurance Market," *Econometrica*, vol. 30 (July 1962), pp. 424-4; J. Hirshleifer, "Investment Decision Under Uncertainty: Choice-Theoretic Approaches," *Quarterly Journal of Economics*, vol. 79 (Nov. 1965), pp. 509-36; J. Hirshleifer, "Investment Decision Under Uncertainty: Applications of the State-Preference Approach," *Quarterly Journal of Economics*, vol. 80 (May 1966), pp. 252-77; R. Radner, "Competitive Equilibrium Under Uncertainty, *Econometrica*, vol. 36 (Jan. 1968), pp. 31-58; J. Drèze, "Market Allocation Under Uncertainty," *European Economic Rview*, vol. 2 (Winter 1970-1), pp. 133-65.

[8] For an illustration in an intertemporal context (where the two commodities are "present consumption" and "future consumption"), see J. Drèze and F. Modigliani, "Epargne et consommation en avenir aléatoire," *Cahiers du Seminaire d'Econometrie*, vol. 60 (1966); or J. Hirshleifer, *Investment, Interest, and Capital* (Englewood Cliffs, NJ: Prentice-Hall, 1970), pp. 236-40.

[9] The entities exchanged in markets are usually thought of as quantities of commodities certain. But in the securities markets, for example, there exist types of financial instruments – risk-graded bonds, preferreds, common shares, warrants, etc. – that permit investors to take portfolio positions reflecting, as desired, greater or lesser sensitivity of income to more and less prosperous states of the world. In the marketing of physical commodities, also, a farmer might arrange a crop-sharing contract instead of promising to deliver fixed quantities. Percent-of-sales or even more complex contingent arrangements are not uncommon in store rentals and other lease contracts. And, of course, all insurance represents the exchange of contingent claims. So, while a complete set of conditional state-claim markets does not exist in the "real world," neither does the opposite extreme hold true that only certainty claims can be traded.

[10] Holding constant individuals' utility functions and their state-distributed physical endowments of the two commodities.

[11] See, for example, J. Lintner, "The Aggregation of Investors' Diverse Judgments and Preferences in Purely Competitive Security Markets," *Journal of Financial and Quantitative Analysis*, vol. 4 (Dec. 1969), pp. 347–400, who develops such average measures in a mean *versus* variance model of uncertainty.

[12] The concordant or "homogeneous" beliefs assumption has been found to be a crucial simplification in mean-variance asset-pricing theory and empirical studies based thereon. See, for example, W. F. Sharpe, "Capital Asset Prices: A Theory of Market Equilibrium Under Conditions of Risk," *Journal of Finance*, vol. 29 (Sept. 1964), pp. 425–42; and "Risk Aversion in the Stock Market: Some Empirical Evidence," *Journal of Finance*, vol. 20 (Sept. 1965), pp. 416–22.

[13] We can now see that, insofar as choice of the simple consumptive optimum C^* is concerned, Semicomplete Markets are as satisfactory as a regime of fully Complete Markets in a world of individuals with agreed beliefs. Under Complete Markets the optimization problem would take the form,

$$\text{Max } U = p(n_a, z_a) + (1-p)u(n_b, z_b) \text{ subject to}$$

$$P_{Na}n_a + P_{Nb}n_b + P_{Za}z_a + P_{Zb}z_b = W^e.$$

The usual procedure leads to the following condition (among others):

$$\frac{1-p}{p}\frac{\partial u/\partial n_b}{\partial u/\partial n_a} = \frac{P_{Nb}}{P_{Na}}$$

For concordant individuals, $p = \pi$. Now if the price ratio P_{Nb}/P_{Na} were to exceed the probability ratio $(1-\pi)/\pi$, *all* individuals would attempt to make $\partial u/\partial n_b > \partial u/\partial n_a$, or $n_b < n_a$ (in the absence of complementarity in utility). But in the aggregate $\Sigma n_a = \Sigma n_b$, so this is impossible. Hence, individuals of agreed beliefs, with endowments and consumptive optima both characterized by $n_a = n_b$, have no need to trade separately in conditional N-claims. Belief-deviant individuals would, on the other hand, have a use for markets in conditional N-claims even though commodity N is riskless in the aggregate.

[14] The symbol $\mathbf{P}'_{Zb}$ would signify the conditional price of state-b claims given the first information outcome (that state-a will obtain). Evidently, $\mathbf{P}'_{Zb} = 0 = \mathbf{P}''_{Za}$, so we shall not need to use the symbols.

[15] Radner, *op. cit.*, has emphasized the essentially uncomputable nature of these posterior prices on the basis of the information available at prior dates. The results here are not in conflict, but show that the posterior prices are computable *in one significant special case.*

[16] We have not proved uniqueness of this equilibrium. (Indeed, even in *riskless* pure exchange uniqueness of the equilibrium price vector cannot generally be proved.) But note that with, for example, $P_{Za}^0 < P_{Za}$ there would be unbalanced substitution effects tending to raise the price of Z_a-claims again.

[17] Space permits only very brief allusion here to the extensive recent discussions of the martingale property, in association with the concepts of random walks and efficient markets. See, for example, E. F. Fama, "Efficient Capital Markets: A Review of Theory and Empirical Work," *Journal of Finance*, vol. 25 (May 1970), pp. 383–417; and P. A. Samuelson, "Proof That Properly Anticipated Prices Fluctuate Randomly," *Industrial Management Review*, vol. 6 (Spring 1965), pp.

41–9. In contrast with the result here, Fama's model does not actually lead to any expectational formula; he emphasizes (p. 384) that the "expected value is just one of many possible summary measures," without "any special importance" for market efficiency. Samuelson proves a purely probabilistic theorem (p. 44), indeed an exceedingly elementary one, in which he already assumes as an "Axiom" that futures prices are set at the prior expectation of terminal spot prices. In contrast, the analysis here *proves* the expectational theorem (Samuelson's "Axiom"), but only for the special case of concordant beliefs. In terms of the beliefs of nonconcordant individuals, it then necessarily follows that the martingale property *cannot* generally apply.

[18] A similar device is employed in Drèze, *op. cit.*, p. 138.

[19] It is shown in Hirshleifer, "Foundations of the Theory of Speculation: Information, Risk, and Markets," section 10.4, that this degree of freedom vanishes under market regimes more constrained than Semicomplete Markets.

[20] Given the first information outcome (state-a certain), the posterior optimization problem involves the standard tangency condition,

$$\left. \frac{-dn'}{dz'_a} \right|_{u'} \equiv n'/z'_a = \mathbf{P}'_{Za}$$

or, in condensed notation, $\mathbf{P}'$. The second condition is the budget constraint:

$$n' + \mathbf{P}z'_a = W'.$$

Since $n' = \mathbf{P}z'_a = W'/2$, then $u' = \log_e n' + \log_e z'_a = \log_e W'/2 + \log_e W'/2 - \log_e \mathbf{P}'$. So:

$$\frac{du'}{dW'} = \frac{2}{W'}.$$

By an analogous development:

$$\frac{du''}{dW''} = \frac{2}{W''}.$$

[21] Since u' and u'' are nothing but the original u now expressed as functions of the posterior wealth and price parameters. Then du'/dW', for example, is the derivative of u' holding posterior price at $\mathbf{P}_Z = \mathbf{P}_{Za}$. The conditional posterior optimization problem that leads to the condition $\lambda' = du'/dW'$ also holds $\mathbf{P}_Z$ constant at $\mathbf{P}_{Za}$, hence the derivatives denoted du/dW' and du'/dW' are identical. A similar argument holds of course for du/dW'' and du''/dW''.

[22] The following is an alternative formal development of this result, that achieves greater compactness (with some loss of intuitive appeal) by omitting the intermediate decision variables W', W''. Concordant individuals are postulated. (This development is mainly due to Mark Rubinstein.)

A. *Simple consumptive gamble*

$$\underset{(n, z_a, z_b)}{\text{Max}} \ \pi u(n, z_a) + (1 - \pi) u(n, z_b) - \lambda(n + P_{Za} z_a + P_{Zb} z_b - W^e)$$

First-order conditions: $\dfrac{\partial u}{\partial n} = \lambda, \ \pi \dfrac{\partial u}{\partial z_a} = \lambda P_{Za}, (1 - \pi) \dfrac{\partial u}{\partial z_b} = \lambda P_{Zb}$

$$\text{Optimality conditions:} \quad \frac{\partial u/\partial z_a}{\partial u/\partial n} = \frac{P_{Za}}{\pi}, \quad \frac{\partial u/\partial z_b}{\partial u/\partial n} = \frac{P_{Zb}}{1-\pi}.$$

B. *Compound consumptive gamble*

$$\max_{(n', z'_a, z'_b, z''_a, z''_b, n', n'')} \quad \pi u(n', z'_a) + (1-\pi) u(n'', z''_b)$$

$$- \pi \lambda'(n' + \mathbf{P}'_{Za} z'_a - n^t - \mathbf{P}'_{Za} z^t_a)$$

$$- (1-\pi) \lambda''(n'' + \mathbf{P}''_{Zb} z''_b - n^t - \mathbf{P}''_{Zb} z^t_b)$$

$$- \lambda^0(n^t + P^0_{Za} z^t_a + P^0_{Zb} z^t_b - W^e)$$

First-order conditions: $\quad \pi \lambda' \mathbf{P}'_{Za} = \lambda^0 P^0_{Za} \quad (1-\pi) \lambda'' \mathbf{P}''_{Zb} = \lambda^0 P^0_{Zb}$

$$\partial u/\partial z'_a = \lambda' \mathbf{P}'_{Za} \quad \partial u/\partial z''_b = \lambda'' \mathbf{P}''_{Zb}$$

$$\partial u/\partial n' = \lambda' \quad \partial u/\partial n'' = \lambda''$$

$$\pi \lambda' + (1-\pi) \lambda'' = \lambda^0$$

$$\text{Optimality conditions:} \quad \frac{\partial u/\partial z'_a}{\partial u/\partial n'} = \mathbf{P}'_{Za} \quad \frac{\partial u/\partial z''_b}{\partial u/\partial n''} = \mathbf{P}''_{Zb}.$$

It will be evident that if:

$$\mathbf{P}'_{Za} = \frac{P_{Za}}{\pi} \text{ and } \mathbf{P}''_{Zb} = \frac{P_{Zb}}{1-\pi},$$

the conditions under B are identical with those under A, with $n' = n''$. Hence the same solution is an equilibrium for both. Furthermore, $n' = n''$ leads immediately to $\lambda' = \lambda'' = \lambda^0$, from which $P^0_{Za} = P_{Za}$ and $P^0_{Zb} = P_{Zb}$ follow directly.

[23] In J. Hirshleifer and M. Rubinstein, "Speculation and Information in Securities Markets," UCLA Economics Department Discussion Paper no. 32, January 1973, the following more fundamental definition is proposed. An *investor* uses available markets to achieve identical contingent holdings over information-events, though his planned consumption may (and generally will) vary over states of the world. In contrast, of course, a speculator's holdings will be sensitive to information-events.

[24] Hirshleifer, "Foundations of the Theory of Speculation: Information, Risk, and Markets," pp. 26–8.

[25] Transaction costs, of course, would work in the opposite direction.

[26] An analysis appears in ibid., sections 10.4 and 10.5.

11   The Theory of Speculation Under Alternative Regimes of Markets*

Background and comments

As was indicated in the previous prefatory note, this essay supplements and completes the article reprinted in chapter 10. The problem dealt with here concerns the determinants of speculation and hedging in a general-equilibrium model with *incomplete regimes of markets* – most importantly, under a regime of "Unconditional Markets" where it is not possible to exchange contingent claims. However, this more realistic modelling is still subject to the main theme that speculation/hedging behavior is the resultant of the combined quantity risks and price risks faced by traders. Substantively, the adoption of speculative positions is shown to be highly sensitive to traders' beliefs (optimism or pessimism) and to the distribution of their endowment positions over the different states of the world.

*This article originally appeared in *Journal of Finance*, vol. 32 (Sept. 1977), pp. 975–99. The permission of the American Finance Association to reprint in this volume is gratefully acknowledged.

I would like to thank Jacques Drèze, Mark Rubinstein, Robert A. Jones, John Riley, Armen Alchian, and Holbrook Working for helpful comments and suggestions. Research support from the National Science Foundation is acknowledged.

Speculation is ordinarily understood to mean the purchase of a good for later re-sale rather than for use, or the temporary sale of a good with the intention of later re-purchase – in the hope of profiting from an intervening price change.

The best-known theory of speculation, associated most prominently with J. M. Keynes (1930, vol. 2, ch. 29) and J. R. Hicks (1946, pp. 137–9),[1] may be called the *risk-transfer hypothesis*. On this view, speculators are relatively risk-tolerant individuals who are rewarded for accepting price risks from more risk-averse "hedgers." A risk-averse trader who is or anticipates being long on the commodity (e.g. a farmer with a crop of wheat approaching harvest) may hedge by selling now, in a forward or "futures" market, for future delivery at a currently determined price. An individual who is or anticipates being short the commodity (e.g. a miller of wheat) may hedge by buying now for future delivery at such a known price. *Speculators* in the forward or futures market may be on the long or the short side of any single such transaction, but in aggregate their commitments must offset any net imbalance of the long and short *hedgers'* positions. In the Keynes-Hicks view the hedgers are divesting themselves of price risks; it is these price risks that are, correspondingly, being accepted by speculators.

An alternative explanation of speculation, due to Holbrook Working, denies any such fundamental difference between the motivations of what are conventionally called speculators and hedgers. According to this alternative *knowledgeable-forecasting hypothesis*, what may look like risk-transfer behavior is only the interaction of traders with more and less optimistic *beliefs* about approaching developments that will affect prices. An individual who expects prices to rise will make speculative purchases; one who expects them to fall will sell. On this view, futures markets do not serve mainly to facilitate the transfer of risk. Rather, they provide an instrumentality whereby a consensus of beliefs about future supply-demand influences is brought to bear (by the establishment of a current price for later deliveries) upon current production-consumption decisions (Working, 1953, 1962; see also Rockwell, 1967).

The first question to be addressed here is the logic of these hypotheses as to the fundamental nature of speculation. A second question is the closely related issue of the equilibrium pattern of price movements over time. Is the normal relation between current prices of futures contracts and the later spot prices such as to reward speculators for bearing price risks? Or is the current futures price merely the mathematical expectation of the spot price ultimately realized (Fama, 1970, pp. 584; Samuelson, 1965), so that there is no reward (on average) for bearing price risk?[2] And, apart from the possible role of risk-transfer, how does the pattern of price movements reflect the relation between current consensus opinion and later revealed actuality emphasized by the knowledgeable-forecasting theory?

A predecessor paper to this one[3] developed a general-equilibrium model of the speculative process that led to the following key propositions:

A Contra the Keynes-Hicks theory, *differences in risk-tolerances alone do not motivate speculative trading.* If all individuals shared the same beliefs there would be no speculation – even if traders had different degrees of risk aversion. However, given differences of belief so that speculation occurs, the extent of an individual's speculative commitments will vary with his risk-tolerance.

B If "concordant beliefs" exist (in a sense to be explained below), *apart from time-discount the current price will be the mathematical expectation of the stochastically varying spot price to be realized.* That is, in terms of these probabilities prices will be a "martingale."

These propositions are too strong in that, like almost all the useful propositions of economic theory, they derive from a model that is a conscious oversimplification of reality. The fundamental nature of the conceptualization of speculation employed here, and of the "idealizing assumptions" leading to the above propositions, will be set forth in the section following. The main thrust of the present paper will be to examine the robustness of propositions A and B above with respect to *modifications of the regime of markets postulated for trading under uncertainty.*

11.1 FUNDAMENTALS OF SPECULATION, AND IDEALIZING ASSUMPTIONS

Several not-yet-generally comprehended fundamentals of speculation, that underly the analysis of this paper, will be asserted here with very brief commentary.[4]

1 *Speculation occurs only in "informative situations."* Earlier theorists have not, generally speaking, appreciated the crucial role of the *conditions of information emergence* for speculative behavior. Speculation is premised upon anticipations of price changes. In a world of uncertainty, for each set of individual's beliefs (over contingencies affecting the to-be-realized later "spot" prices) there is a corresponding equilibrium for current "futures" prices; "futures" prices can change only if beliefs change.[5] Speculation occurs therefore only in "informative situations," where some or all traders anticipate that additional public information[6] – as to factors influencing future supply and demand, and thereby the later spot prices – will emerge so as to modify beliefs before the close of trading. In such a situation some traders may transact away from their endowment positions (portfolios), not to their final productive-consumptive choices but instead to *trading* positions. Their intention is thus to revise portfolios, to attain their final positions by re-trading in the "futures" (or later spot) markets on more advantageous terms after the anticipated price shift has occurred. These

traders are the speculators. As we shall see, this term properly includes those ordinarily called hedgers. (Section 11.5 will show that portfolio revision is *not* ultimately the essential sign of speculative activity. For the present, however, we can use planning for portfolio revision as a working definition.)

2 *In informative situations individuals must adjust both to "price risk" and "quantity risk."* Given an informative situation, the prospect of stochastic price change generates the "price risk" that the traditional speculation literature emphasizes. But price is an endogenous variable: price uncertainty is necessarily the resultant of an underlying uncertainty about the exogenous elements determining demand and supply influences upon price. In the simplest case price uncertainty reflects merely a corresponding stochastic variability of the aggregate of individuals' commodity endowments. For example, the wheat price will be high if the crop (and, therefore, the average wheat endowment per individual) turns out to be small; price will be low if the crop (average wheat endowment) turns out big.[7] *It is therefore not price risk alone that governs individuals' speculative/ hedging behavior, but the interaction of price risk with quantity risk.* In its preoccupation with price risk, the traditional speculation literature has overlooked the even more fundamental influence of quantity risk upon traders' decisions.

3 *In an informative situation there are two interrelated market equilibria.* The prospect of information emergence implies that there will be two distinct, though of course interrelated, market equilibria. The first is associated with the "prior-round" trading that occurs before the anticipated public information emerges, the second with the "posterior-round" trading that takes place afterward. In the prior round, traders' commitments (transactional movements from endowment positions to trading positions) take place in the face of uncertainty as to quantity endowments and posterior prices – though, of course, the prior-round price vector is itself deterministic. In posterior trading the underlying quantity uncertainty has been at least partially resolved. If, as will mainly be assumed below, the emergent information is *conclusive* as to the state of the world, the uncertainty will be fully resolved before posterior trading begins. In this special case the prior-round/posterior-round dichotomy corresponds to the distinction between futures and later spot markets. Section 11.4 contains comments on the consequences of successive *partial* (less than conclusive) information injections – leading to a multiple sequence of prior and posterior trading rounds in futures markets before uncertainty is ultimately resolved and spot trading begins.

4 *Speculative behavior is conditioned upon the scope of markets.* The traditional speculation literature allows trading only in simple certainty claims to commodities. This will be called here a regime of "Unconditional Markets" (UM).[8] In contrast, the predecessor paper cited above studied a regime called "Semi-Complete Markets" (SCM).[9] Consider a world of two

goods N and Z, and two states of the world a and b, where N is riskless (all individuals' N-endowments are uniform over states) but Z is risky (individuals' Z_a and Z_b endowments generally differ). Then under Semi-Complete Markets (SCM) the marketable claims are the trio N, Z_a, and Z_b. (The riskless commodity N would naturally serve as numeraire.) Under Unconditional Markets (UM) only certainty claims N and ζ (the latter being a $1:1$ package of Z_a and Z_b entitlements) can be traded. Another regime of interest is "Fully Complete Markets" (FCM), with trading permitted in all *four* defineable claims N_a, N_b, Z_a, and Z_b. While Fully Complete Markets would seem a more natural polar case than SCM to oppose to the regime of Unconditional Markets, there can in fact be no speculation (in the ordinary sense of planned portfolio revision after emergence of information) under FCM! In the prior round each trader would be able to buy a portfolio covering his desired consumption baskets in the light of the alternative possible information-events as well as over the different state-contingencies. Then, even if a posterior market were available, no-one would need to use it.[10]

Other interesting structures of markets can be defined. Under "Equity Markets" (EM), against unconditional claims to numeraire N could be traded unit shares ω defined as entitlements to a *proportionate* interest in the aggregate social endowment of Z, whatever that might turn out to be. It would be as if all the production of the risky good Z were carried out by a single firm, in the presence of a securities market where stock in that firm could be purchased and sold against the numeraire commodity N.[11] The EM regime, like the UM regime, has only two classes of tradable claims – but EM, unlike UM, does permit some trading in risky contingencies.

Most significant from the theoretical point of view is the regime that might be called "Numeraire Contingency Markets" (NCM), where only N_a and N_b claims can be exchanged in the prior round. Here there is no prior trading in the risky commodity Z at all, but only what are in effect side-bets in numeraire (money) units as to whether the feast or the famine state of the world is going to obtain. As we shall see, in the special case of *conclusive* information the NCM regime provides all the prior-round markets needed by traders to achieve their optimal gambles.[12]

To complete the preliminaries several of the "idealizing assumptions' will be listed here: (1) The standard theoretical postulates (costless trading, price-taking behavior, instantaneous market-clearing) necessary to assure that all transactions take place at equilibrium prices. (2) Just two goods, N riskless and Z risky – and two states of the world a and b reflected in the size of Z-endowments. (This assumption is relaxed in section 11.4.) (3) All individuals have state-independent, additive utility functions in N and Z, i.e. there is zero complementarity in preference.[13] (4) There is no "real time" intervening between prior and posterior trading. This assumption isolates the effect of informational emergence from time-involved processes like growth, depreciation, storage, utility time-discount, etc. Mere passage of time can create patterns of price movement that have nothing to do with speculation, so long as *uncertainty* is not involved. (5) The most radical of the idealizing assumptions to be employed here is that prices will reflect "concordant" beliefs in the market. This means that essentially all the market weight in price determination will be contributed by traders who share identical prior probability beliefs about which state of the world will obtain. This does not mean that belief-deviant traders are rare or unimportant, but only that they cancel one another out so far as effects on prices are concerned. In practice one would want to interpret "concordant" beliefs as *average* beliefs, though this translation is not strictly warranted.[14]

Because of the oversimplifications involved in these and certain other assumptions (in particular, one called "correct conditional forecasting" to be discussed below), the statements summarized in propositions A and B are obviously too sweeping. Even if the model were valid in the sense of providing a useable representation of speculation phenomena, the propositions should be interpreted in a rather more modest sense such as: (A') Speculators are *primarily* individuals whose probability beliefs (rather than whose risk-tolerances) deviate from those more typical of individuals in the market. (B') The price-revision relation between prior and posterior rounds of trading (between futures and later spot prices) will *approximate* a martingale when calculated in terms of "concordant" probability beliefs (in practice, in terms of a suitable average of traders' beliefs).

11.2   THE NON-INFORMATIVE SITUATION IN ALTERNATIVE MARKET REGIMES

As a base point let us consider first the solutions obtained under alternative market regimes for a *non*-informative situation. Here since traders do not anticipate the emergence of information leading to any price change before the close of trading, there is only one trading round. So no portfolio revision (and hence no speculation) takes place. Each individual moves at once to his optimum consumptive position (which is, in general, a gamble over possible states of the world).

A trader's endowment, also in general a gamble, can be expressed in "prospect notation" as:

$$E \equiv [(n_a^e, z_a^e), (n_b^e, z_b^e); p, 1 - p]. \tag{11.1}$$

That is, with subjective probability belief p the individual anticipates the particular endowment vector n_a^e, z_a^e associated with the advent of state-a; he assigns, of course, the complementary probability $1 - p$ to the endowment vector n_b^e, z_b^e associated with state-b. But since commodity N is riskless, the N-endowment is invariant over states – i.e. $n_a^e = n_b^e = n^e$.

Using this feature, and suppressing the probability parameter p, it will sometimes be convenient to employ the more compact notation:

$$E \equiv (n^e; z_a^e, z_b^e). \tag{11.1'}$$

The individual's problem is to select among "simple consumptive gambles" C, expressed (in the two alternative notations) as:

$$C \equiv [(n, z_a), (n, z_b); p, (1-p)] \equiv (n; z_a, z_b). \tag{11.2}$$

The individual maximizes his expected state-independent utility:

$$U(C) \equiv U(n; z_a, z_b) \equiv pu(n, z_a) + (1-p)u(n, z_b). \tag{11.3}$$

The difference between market regimes is manifested to the individual in the form of the trading opportunities available. Under Semi-Complete Markets (SCM) his budget constraint is the wealth-value of the endowment combination:

$$n + P_{Za} z_a + P_{Zb} z_b = n^e + P_{Za} z_a^e + P_{Zb} z_a^e \equiv W^e. \quad \text{Budget equation (SCM)} \tag{11.4}$$

That is, he may buy or sell any desired numbers of units of the contingent claims Z_a or Z_b, each having its own price in terms of the numeraire commodity N. Maximizing expected utility subject to this constraint leads to:

$$p \frac{\partial u / \partial z_a}{\partial u / \partial n} = P_{Za} \quad \text{and} \quad (1-p) \frac{\partial u / \partial z_b}{\partial u / \partial n} = P_{Zb}. \quad \text{Optimality conditions (SCM)} \tag{11.5}$$

Given the additivity and state-independence assumptions, the denominators in the two equations are equal.

Finally, the market-clearing conditions serve to determine the equilibrium prices P_{Za} and P_{Zb}:

$$\Sigma n = \Sigma n^e, \Sigma z_a = \Sigma z_a^e, \Sigma z_b = \Sigma z_b^e. \quad \text{Equilibrium conditions (SCM)} \tag{11.6}$$

Of course, one of these conditions is implied by the other two.

Under the more restricted regime of Unconditional Markets (UM), however, the trading constraint is quite different. Already, under SCM, trading in conditional claims to the *riskless* commodity N was ruled out. Under UM there is no trading in conditional claims even to the risky commodity Z; only unconditional rights to either N or Z may be exchanged. A unit *unconditional* right to Z, symbolized as ζ, can be regarded as a sandwich consisting of unit conditional claims to Z in each possible state. P_ζ, the unit price of the sandwich, can evidently be interpreted as the price of Z in this market regime $(P_\zeta \equiv P_Z)$. In general, however, we would not expect P_ζ under UM to equal the sum $P_{Za} + P_{Zb}$ of the conditional prices under SCM. It follows that, in general, individuals would not attain the same optimal consumptive gambles C^* as in SCM. In

particular, under UM individuals with inconvenient endowment compositions will generally find it impossible to move to their SCM-preferred
gambles when Z_a, Z_b claims can be bought and sold only in a $1:1$ ratio.

This difficulty expresses itself in the form of the budget constraint.
Endowed wealth, interpreted as the *market* value of endowment, is no
longer the effective bound on attainable combinations under UM. The
restrictions on trading can make endowment compositions partially (or
even wholly) unmarketable. The individual must therefore account
separately for all the commodities:

$$\begin{cases} n + P_\zeta \zeta = n^e \\ z_a - \zeta = z_a^e \\ z_b - \zeta = z_b^e. \end{cases} \quad \text{Budget constraints (UM)} \tag{11.7}$$

And in consequence, the optimality conditions reduce to the single
equation:

$$p \frac{\partial u/\partial z_a}{\partial u/\partial n} + (1-p) \frac{\partial u/\partial z_b}{\partial u/\partial n} = P_\zeta. \quad \text{Optimality condition (UM)} \tag{11.8}$$

The market-clearing conditions (either implying the other) can here be
expressed as:

$$\Sigma n = \Sigma n^e \text{ and } \Sigma \zeta = 0. \quad \text{Equilibrium condition (UM)} \tag{11.9}$$

Numerical example 1

Assume that the economy consists of two equally numerous classes of
individuals, differing only in endowment composition. Specifically,
suppose as shown in part 1 of table 11.1 that we can think of a typical pair
as a microcosm – consisting of a "representative supplier" of the risky
commodity Z with endowment $E = (n^e; z_a^e, z_b^e) = (0; 400, 160)$ and a
"representative demander" of Z with endowment $E = (200; 0, 0)$. Suppose
in addition that everyone has the identical utility function $u(n, z) = \log_e nz$.
Finally, let all have concordant beliefs (so that all the individual p's equal a
common value π), assigning the common probability parameter
$p = \pi = 0.6$ to state-a and $1 - p = 1 - \pi = 0.4$ to state-b. Then, under Semi-
Complete Markets (SCM), the equilibrium contingent-claim prices (in
terms of N as numeraire) can be shown to be $P_{Za} = 0.3$ and $P_{Zb} = 0.5$. At
these solution prices everyone has equal endowed wealth: $W^e = 200$.
Consequently, all end up with the same optimal consumptive gamble
$C^* = (n^*; z_a^*, z_b^*) = (100; 200, 80)$. These results, and the trading implied,
are shown in the upper panel of part 1 of table 11.1.

In the regime of Unconditional Markets (UM), shown in the lower panel
of part 1, the result is quite different. The market-clearing price for the
package ζ (i.e. for an unconditional claim to Z) works out as $P_\zeta = 0.9439$.

TABLE 11.1 Endowments, transactions, and simple consumptive gambles in non-informative situation under two market regimes

	Endowment (E) $n^e; z_a^e z_b^e$		Trading $\Delta n; \Delta z_a; \Delta z_b$		Consumptive optimum (C*) $n^*; z_a^* z_b^*$	
Part 1: Representative supplier-demander pair with concordant beliefs ($\pi = 0.6$)						
Semi-complete markets (SCM)[1]						
Supplier	0; 400, 160		+100; −200,	−80	100; 200,	80
Demander	200; 0, 0		−100; +200,	+80	100; 200,	80
Totals	200; 400, 160				200; 400,	160
Unconditional markets (UM)[2]						
Supplier	0; 400, 160		+100; −105.9,	−105.9	100; 294.1,	54.1
Demander	200; 0, 0		−100; +105.9,	+105.9	100; 105.9,	105.9
Totals	200; 400, 160				200; 400,	160
Part 2: Traders with representative endowments and deviant beliefs						
Semi-complete markets (SCM)[1]						
Optimist ($p=0.7$)	100; 200, 80		0; +33.3,	−20	100; 233.3,	60
Pessimist ($p=0.5$)	100; 200, 80		0; −33.3,	+20	100; 166.7,	100
Unconditional markets (UM)[2]						
Optimist ($p=0.7$)	100; 200, 80		+13.3; −14.1,	−14.1	113.3;185.9,	65.9
Pessimist ($p=0.5$)	100; 200, 80		+3.6; −3.8,	−3.8	103.6;196.2,	76.2

[1] SCM equilibrium prices: $P_{Za} = 0.3$, $P_{Zb} = 0.5$.
[2] UM equilibrium price: $P_\zeta = 0.9439$.

This price is higher than the sum of the contingent-claim prices under SCM obtained above ($P_\zeta = 0.9439 > P_{Za} + P_{Zb} = 0.3 + 0.5 = 0.8$), as may be explained as follows. The supplier of Z wishes to sell off some Z-claims for the N-claims he lacks. But his endowed state-contingent holdings of $Z(z_a^e = 400, z_b^e = 160)$ are highly unbalanced, which is an undesirable feature from the point of view of risk aversion. He would have preferred to sell more of Z_a than of Z_b claims, as was possible under SCM. Selling units of ζ (certainty claims to Z) under UM does provide him with the N he desires, but only by further increasing the *relative* disproportion of his retained Z-holdings. Since the supplier is therefore somewhat reluctant to sell Z-claims in the 1:1 ratio dictated by UM, whereas the demander has no such reluctance in buying (since his endowment situation is already balanced at $z_a^e = z_b^e = 0$), the consequence is a relatively high price P_ζ.

At the equilibrium $P_\zeta = 0.9439$ the supplier sells about 105.9 ζ-units (whereas, under SCM he would have sold 200 units of Z_a at $P_{Za} = 0.3$ and 80 units of Z_b at $P_{Zb} = 0.5$). The demander in either case pays just 100 units of N. The two classes of traders do not reach the same consumptive gambles under UM. The supplier of Z attains $C^* = (100; 294.1, 54.1)$, while for the demander of Z the consumptive optimum is $(100; 105.9, 105.9)$. In utility terms the Z-supplier ends up somewhat better off, the Z-demander somewhat worse off. It can be shown that the loss of the latter is greater than the gain to the former. If the alternative of Semi-Complete Markets were available, those doing better under SCM would be able to compensate those who gain under Unconditional Markets.

The numerical example above indicated a loss in efficiency under the regime of Unconditional Markets. This loss, due to the restriction imposed upon the consumption baskets attainable by individuals, is quite a general consequence of impaired trading opportunities. As compared with UM, a *costless* shift to a regime of Semi-Complete Markets (SCM) will (with appropriate compensation) generally be Pareto-preferred. Of course, providing the additional markets will in general be costly. Before coming to absolute conclusions as to efficiency the added expense would have to be weighed against the inefficiency of impaired trading.

It is of interest to compare UM with the Equity markets (EM) regime. Under EM, as in UM, the Z_a, Z_b claims are tradable only jointly. But the ratio of the elements of the $Z_a : Z_b$ of the sandwich is not 1:1 but is, instead, equal to the ratio of the social totals $\bar{Z}_a : \bar{Z}_b$. Define the unit EM claim ω as the right to receive Z_a and Z_b in the respective amounts $Z_a/100$ and $\bar{Z}_b/100$. Thus, an ω-entitlement is a claim to 1 percent of society's Z-output in either state. Then, by analogy with the preceding:

$$n + P_\omega \omega = n^e$$

$$z_a - \bar{Z}_a \omega / 100 = z_a^e \quad \text{Budget Constraints (EM)} \qquad (11.10)$$

$$z_b - \bar{Z}_b \omega / 100 = z_b^e.$$

$$\frac{p\bar{Z}_a}{100}\frac{\partial u/\partial z_a}{\partial u/\partial n} + \frac{(1-p)\bar{Z}_b}{100}\frac{\partial u/\partial z_b}{\partial u/\partial n} = P_\omega. \quad \text{Optimality condition (EM) (11.11)}$$

$$\Sigma n = \Sigma n^e \quad \text{and} \quad \Sigma\omega = 0. \quad \text{Equilibrium condition (EM)} \qquad (11.12)$$

Considering table 11.1 once again, let us now ask what would happen under Equity Markets (EM)? The unit claim ω would be a sandwich in the amounts Z_a, $Z_b = 4, 1.6$. In the example here, the SCM optimum *could* be attained under EM – there is no efficiency loss! A trade between the parties of 50 ω-units, at the price $P_\omega = 4P_{Za} + 1.6P_{Zb} = 2$, would do the trick. But this is clearly an artifact, a result of the special construction of the example – in particular, of the conditions that the utility functions are homothetic and identical, together with the fact that all the individual Z-endowments are in the same proportions as are the social totals (and therefore as the elements of ω). More generally, the optimum achievable under SCM could no more be attained under EM than under UM, and for the same reason: the fixity of the proportions of the trading unit or sandwich. It seems a plausible conjecture that EM would commonly do better than UM, however, i.e. would get closer to the SCM solution. If the society can at least roughly be dichotomized into "suppliers" (who want to trade off *both* Z_a and Z_b), and "demanders" (who want to acquire some of both), then EM will tend to do better – since the trading unit ω will at least roughly reflect the relative $Z_a : Z_b$ proportions that the one party wants to sell and other wants to buy. It is possible, however, to construct cases – in particular, where some individuals are specialized in state-a endowments and others in state-b – where UM does better than EM. In any case, it can be seen that the Equity Markets regime is *qualitatively* similar to Unconditional Markets in its working. For this reason, and in the interest of space saving, henceforth the main analysis will be limited to the traditional UM regime in comparison with the SCM regime.

Let us briefly consider the impact of divergences in endowment position, in probability beliefs, and in risk-aversion upon the non-informative individual solutions obtained in these two market regimes.

1 As to endowment position, the budget equation (11.4) shows that under SCM only the individual's endowed wealth W^e – and not the detailed composition thereof – will affect his achieved consumptive gamble. Under UM, in contrast, the significance of the specific commodity-state composition of endowments is revealed by the necessity of accounting separately as in (11.7) for all the goods entering into the utility function.

2 As to probability beliefs, the form of (11.5) shows that under SCM a belief-deviant individual assigning relatively high belief p_s to any state-s will accept a proportionately lower $\partial u/\partial z_s$ for that state – implying a correspondingly larger purchase of contingent Z_s-claims to that state. Inability to trade separately in Z_s-claims means that under UM traders can no longer achieve an exact inverse proportionality between p_s and $\partial u/\partial z_s$.

In part 1 of table 11.1, the individuals constituting the supplier-demander pair had divergent endowments but concordant beliefs. In part 2 are shown individuals with *representative* endowments (that are a cross-section of the social commodity totals) but *deviant* beliefs. In particular, we have an "optimist" who assigns probability $p = 0.7$ to the advent of state-a, and a "pessimist" who assigns $p = 0.5$ – in contrast with the $\pi = 0.6$ belief of the concordant individuals. The upper panel of part 2 shows how the consumptive solutions for the optimist and pessimist diverge, in the expected directions, from the C^* optimum positions of the concordant individuals. The lower panel of part 2 shows the behavior of these deviant individuals under the more constrained regime UM. Here the high market price of Z-claims, as derived from the behavior of the concordant individuals shown in part 1 of the table ($P_\zeta = 0.9439$), induces both the optimist and pessimist to sell a number of units of ζ for more N-claims. Apart from this effect, it will be seen that the $1:1$ linkage of the Z_a and Z_b claims impairs – indeed, practically eliminates – the ability of the individuals to move from their endowment positions $E = (100; 200, 80)$ to anything like their preferred consumptive gambles C^* achievable under SCM.

3   Finally, as to risk-aversion, a greater degree of risk tolerance means a smaller change in $\partial u / \partial z$ for a given quantitative difference in the amount of Z held in the different states. Then (11.5) implies that, under SCM, a more risk-tolerant individual would be willing to hold relatively more of the more plentiful Z_a-claims and relatively less of the less plentiful Z_b-claims – in short, the perfectly reasonable result that a more risk-tolerant trader would accept a wider risk than the typical individual. Under Unconditional Markets the result is somewhat different. The UM regime does not permit a relatively risk-tolerant trader to widen (or a relatively risk-averse trader to narrow) his *absolute* Z-risk. Whatever the individual's endowed discrepancy between z_a^e and z_b^e may be, this discrepancy is preserved when Z-claims can only be traded on $1:1$ basis. Equation (11.8) shows that the individual will equate a *weighted average* of his marginal utilities to the market price. Suppose a risk-averse individual tried to decrease his risk exposure by moving more heavily into N, thus holding less of the risky commodity Z. But in reducing the absolute scale of his Z-holdings, he is increasing their *relative* disproportion. And, in fact, it can be shown that under UM more risk-averse individuals will purchase relatively *more* of the risky commodity as a kind of insurance against the bad state-b contingency.[15]

11.3   THE INFORMATIVE SITUATION IN ALTERNATIVE MARKET REGIMES: EMERGENCE OF SPECULATION

In an *informative* situation, the anticipated emergence of new information affecting prices divides trading into a prior round and a posterior round.

Then some or all individuals may be induced to speculate, i.e. to adopt *trading positions* – portfolio holdings in the prior round that do not correspond to consumptive desires but rather to hopes for potential profit consequent upon anticipated price revisions. Of course, speculators will ultimately (in the posterior round) make trades permitting them to end up with desired consumptive gambles at the enhanced or diminished levels of wealth stemming from their degree of speculative success.

Continue to assume, for simplicity, that the emergent information will be *conclusive* as to which state is going to obtain. Then, under Semi-Complete Markets (SCM), a trader's optimizing problem can be formulated as:

$$\text{Max } U = pu(n', z_a') + (1 - p)u(n'', z_b'') \quad \text{subject to} \qquad (11.13a)$$

$$\begin{cases} n' + P_{Za}' z_a' = n' + P_{Za}' z_a' \equiv W' \\ n'' + P_{Zb}'' z_b'' = n' + P_{Zb}'' z_b' \equiv W'' \\ n' + p_{Za}^0 z_a' + P_{Zb}^0 z_b' = n^e + P_{Za}^0 z_a^e + P_{Zb}^0 z_b^e \equiv W^e. \end{cases} \qquad (11.13b)$$

The optimal trading position $T^* = (n'; z_a', z_b')$ is arrived at by the individual subject to the prior-round market prices denoted P_{Za}^0 and P_{Zb}^0. The effective constraint in this round, represented by the third equation of (11.13b), is the level of endowed wealth W^e. As for the posterior round, one or the other of the constraints in the first two equations of (11.13b) will be effective. If state-a obtains the single-primed symbols of the first equation show the effective wealth W' (the posterior market value of the trading position), the choice variables n' and z_a', and the posterior price P_{Za}' (the price of numeraire N remains unity, and Z_b-claims have become valueless). Similarly, the double-primed sybmols of the second equation represent the variables conditional upon the advent of state-b, with only the price P_{Zb}'' appearing.

Taking the two rounds of trading together, in an informative situation the individual can be regarded as selecting a "compound consumptive gamble" that may be denoted in prospect form as $D = [(n', z_a'), (n'', z_b''); p, 1 - p]$. In the compound gamble permitted by the two rounds of trading, n' and n'' may differ – something that could not be achieved in a single round of trading under Semi-Complete Markets.[16]

The posterior-round optimality conditions under SCM have the simple form:

$$\frac{\partial u/\partial z_a'}{\partial u/\partial n'} = P_{Za}' \quad \text{and} \quad \frac{\partial u/\partial z_b''}{\partial u/\partial n''} = P_{Zb}''. \quad \begin{array}{l} \text{Posterior-round optimality} \\ \text{conditions (SCM)} \end{array} \qquad (11.14)$$

Since there is posterior certainty, the probability belief parameter no longer plays any role.

For the prior-round optimality conditions, on the other hand, we must face the awkward problem that the choice of optimal trading position T^*

depends not only upon the prior-round prices P_{Za}^0 and P_{Zb}^0 but also upon the posterior prices P'_{Za} and P''_{Zb}. But these latter have not yet been determined; indeed, one of them will never actually be realized, since only one state or the other is going to be observed! What information will traders have as to posterior prices to guide them in their prior-round decisions? In general, conditional posterior prices are not actually *computable* from public prior data (see Radner, 1968). But there is one set of anticipations – called here "correct conditional forecasting" – which, if universally held, will be self-fulfilling and thus consistent with equilibrium.[17] Specifically, suppose that traders anticipate that *prices will move in proportion to changes in concordant beliefs:*[18]

$$\frac{P'_{Za}}{P_{Za}^0} = \frac{1}{\pi} \text{ and } \frac{P''_{Zb}}{P_{Zb}^0} = \frac{1}{1-\pi}. \tag{11.15}$$

(The numerator of unity on the right-hand-side of each equation corresponds to posterior certainty, i.e. the information is to be conclusive.) Note that these anticipations concerning price revisions immediately imply the martingale property, calculated in terms of concordant beliefs. (The same price revisions would not be a martingale calculated in terms of any other set of beliefs.)

If (11.15) holds true the third constraint of (11.13b) can be reformulated as a relation among the endowed and conditional wealths:

$$\pi W' + (1 - \pi) W'' = W^e. \tag{11.16}$$

This leads to a simple condition for optimal *prior* trading:

$$\frac{p}{1-p} \frac{du'/dW'}{du''/dW''} = \frac{\pi}{1-\pi}. \quad \text{Prior-round optimality condition (SCM)} \tag{11.17}$$

Thus, optimal prior trading involves determining the conditional posterior wealths W', W''. With W' and W'' the trader can enter the first two equations of (11.13b) to find the elements n', z'_a, z'_b of his optimal trading position T^*. But, as a point that will take on considerable significance below, note that the *two* wealths are insufficient to uniquely determine the *three* elements of T^*. In prior-round trading under SCM there is a degree of freedom; any one element of T^* can be arbitrarily selected.

It remains to be shown just what the equilibrium prior-round prices P_{Za}^0 and P_{Zb}^0 will be. Under the assumption of concordant beliefs the result is very neat:

$$P_{Za}^0 = P_{Za} \text{ and } P_{Zb}^0 = P_{Zb}. \tag{11.18}$$

That is, the prior-round prices in an informative situation are simply equal to the state-claim prices that *would* have ruled had the situation been non-informative!

This may be explained as follows. For individuals holding concordant beliefs, who account for essentially all the social weight in determining prices, equations (11.5) for the non-informative SCM optimum take the form

$$\pi \frac{\partial u/\partial z_a}{\partial u/\partial n} = P_{Za} \quad \text{and} \quad (1-\pi)\frac{\partial u/\partial z_b}{\partial u/\partial n} = P_{Zb}. \tag{11.5'}$$

But substituting the martingale condition (11.15) into (11.14) yields an exactly analogous result for the prior-round informative SCM optimum:

$$\pi \frac{\partial u/\partial z_a'}{\partial u/\partial n'} = P_{Za}^0 \quad \text{and} \quad (1-\pi)\frac{\partial u/\partial z_b''}{\partial u/\partial n''} = P_{Zb}^0. \tag{11.19}$$

Then if $z_a = z_a'$, $z_b = z_b''$, and $n' = n'' = n$, equation (11.18) follows.

The prior and posterior markets will be in equilibrium if prices are such that individuals of concordant beliefs (who account collectively for essentially all the social weight determining prices) find it optimal to achieve the same optimal consumptive baskets D^* under an informative situation as the C^* baskets they would have chosen had the situation been non-informative. And they will find it optimal to do so given "correct conditional forecasting." Put another way, prices will be a martingale if concordant-belief traders forecast that they will be!

Given the ruling prior-round prices P_{Za}^0 and P_{Zb}^0, an individual of concordant beliefs has a range of options as to T^*, any of which could achieve the desired conditional wealth-pair W', W''. In particular, he could stand pat with his endowment gamble in the prior round, using the posterior prices $P_{Za}' = P_{Za}^0/\pi$ or $P_{Zb}'' = P_{Zb}^0/(1-\pi)$ – depending upon which state obtains – to achieve $D^* = C^*$. Or, a single prior-round move from E to $C^* = D^*$ would suffice to achieve optimality, with no need for portfolio revision.[19] On the other hand, individuals of deviant beliefs would all find it advantageous to trade in both rounds under SCM, i.e. they will speculate.

So much for the regime of Semi-Complete Markets. How different are results for the regime of Unconditional Markets, where only certainty claims may be traded?

Maintaining the same assumptions as before except for the change in market regime, the decision problem of an individual with belief parameter p can be expressed by equations analogous to (11.13a) and (11.13b):

$$\text{Max } U = pu(n', z_a') + (1-p)u(n'', z_b'') \quad \text{subject to} \tag{11.19a}$$

$$\begin{cases} n' + P_\zeta' z_a' = n' + P_\zeta' z_a' \equiv W' \\ n'' + P_\zeta'' z_b'' = n' + P_\zeta'' z_b' \equiv W''. \end{cases} \tag{11.19b}$$

Of course, P_ζ' is the price of the same contingent claim as P_{Za}' under SCM, and P_ζ'' the same as P_{Zb}''.

We do not yet have the expression for the prior-round constraint, the analog of the third equation of (11.13b). It is more convenient to find an analog to the relation (11.16) among the wealths. In fact, using (11.15), (11.19b), and the budget accounting identities (11.10), we obtain:[20]

$$\pi W' + (1 - \pi) W'' = W^e + (P^0_{Za} + P^0_{Zb} - P^0_{\zeta}) \zeta. \tag{11.19c}$$

The symbol W^e here does not represent the *actual* market value of the endowment under Unconditional Markets (UM). Rather, it is the *hypothetical* value that the same endowment would have under Semi-Complete Markets (SCM). Similarly, P^0_{Za} and P^0_{Zb} are the corresponding hypothetical prior-round state-claim prices under SCM. The point of this development is that *if* the prior-round price of the unconditional Z-claim, P^0_{ζ}, satisfies $P^0_{\zeta} = P^0_{Za} + P^0_{Zb}$, then conditions (11.19) become literally identical with the conditions (11.13) governing choice of trading position T^* under SCM.

The upshot is that markets *must* clear if the unconditional prior-round price of the risky commodity Z is simply:

$$P^0_{\zeta} = P^0_{Za} + P^0_{Zb}. \tag{11.20}$$

This price must be consistent with equilibrium, as it leads back to the very same equilibrium achieved under Semi-Complete Markets! If (11.20) holds, *each individual will want and be able in the initial round to attain the same posterior conditional wealth-pair W', W'' that he could achieve in the prior round under SCM*. With the desired balance between W' and W'' achieved in selecting a trading position T^*, he will of course later engage in posterior-round transactions so as to reach the same compound consumptive gamble D^* that was optimal under SCM.

Martingale-type anticipations are involved once again in this equilibrium. For, it follows immediately from (11.15), (11.18), and (11.20) that:

$$P^0_{\zeta} = \pi P'_{\zeta} + (1 - \pi) P''_{\zeta} = \pi P'_{Za} + (1 - \pi) P''_{Zb}. \tag{11.21}$$

That is, if all traders make "correct conditional forecasts," and believe that the prior-round price of the unconditional claim to Z is the mathematical expectation (calculated in terms of concordant probabilities) of the posterior-round price, this belief will be self-fulfilling in market equilibrium!

Numerical example 2

Table 11.2 follows the pattern of table 11.1, but provides for the two rounds of trading under an informative situation. Only the E, T^*, and D^* positions are shown; the implied transactions can be inferred.

Part 1 covers the interaction of the same representative supplier-demander pair as in example 1. These individuals, with opposed endowments but concordant beliefs ($p = \pi = 0.6$), are supposed to represent a microcosm of the entire market. The upper panel of part 1 shows that,

TABLE 11.2 *Endowments, trading positions, and compound consumptive gambles in informative situation under two market regimes*

	Endowment (E) $n^c;\ z_a^c,\ z_b^c$	Desired posterior wealths $W',\ W''$	Trading position (T^*) $n^t;\ z_a^t,\ z_b^t$	Compound consumptive gamble $(D^*),$ $\begin{cases} n',\ z_y', \\ n'',\ z_b'' \end{cases}$
Part 1: Representative supplier-demander pair with concordant beliefs ($\pi = 0.6$)				
Semi-complete markets (SCM)[1]				
Supplier	0; 400, 160	200, 200	100; 200, 80	$\begin{cases} 100,\ 200 \\ 100,\ 80 \end{cases}$
Demander	200; 0, 0	200, 200	100; 200, 80	$\begin{cases} 100,\ 200 \\ 100,\ 80 \end{cases}$
Totals	200; 400, 160		200; 400, 160	
Unconditional markets (UM)[2]				
Supplier	0; 400, 160	200, 200	0; 400, 160	$\begin{cases} 100,\ 200 \\ 100,\ 80 \end{cases}$
Demander	200; 0, 0	200, 200	200; 0, 0	$\begin{cases} 100,\ 200 \\ 100,\ 80 \end{cases}$
Totals	200; 400, 160		200; 400, 160	

Part 2: Traders with representative endowments and deviant beliefs

Semi-complete markets (SCM)[1]

Optimist ($p = 0.7$)	100; 200, 80	233.3, 150	100; 266.7, 40	$\left\{\begin{array}{l} 116.7,\ 233.3 \\ 75,\quad 60 \end{array}\right.$
Pessimist ($p = 0.5$)	100; 200, 80	166.7, 250	100; 133.3, 120	$\left\{\begin{array}{l} 83.3,\ 166.7 \\ 125,\quad 100 \end{array}\right.$

Unconditional markets (UM)[2]

Optimist ($p = 0.7$)	100; 200, 80	233.3, 150	188.9; 88.9, 31.1	$\left\{\begin{array}{l} 116.7,\ 233.3 \\ 75,\quad 60 \end{array}\right.$
Pessimist ($p = 0.5$)	100; 200, 80	166.7, 250	11.1; 311.1, 191.1	$\left\{\begin{array}{l} 83.3,\ 166.7 \\ 125,\quad 100 \end{array}\right.$

[1] SCM prior-round equilibrium prices: $P^0_{Za} = 0.3$, $P^0_{Zb} = 0.5$. Posterior-round equilibrium prices: $P'_{Za} = 0.5$, $P''_{Zb} = 1.25$.
[2] UM prior-round equilibrium price: $P^0_\zeta = 0.8$. Posterior-round equilibrium prices: $P'_\zeta = 0.5$, $P''_\zeta = 1.25$.

under SCM, each of the pair attains a compound consumptive gamble D^* that is identical with the C^* achieved with a single trading round under SCM in example 1. Specifically, with equilibrium prior prices $P_{Za}^0 = P_{Za} = 0.3$ and $P_{Zb}^0 = P_{Zb} = 0.5$ as given by equation (11.18), and posterior prices $P'_{Za} = 0.5$ and $P''_{Zb} = 1.25$ as given by equation (11.15), the optimal conditional wealths determined by equation (11.17) are $W' = W'' = 200$. Both traders can achieve these by moving immediately, in the prior round, to the trading position $T^* = (100; 200, 80)$ – identical with the optimal simple consumptive gamble C^* achieved under a non-informative situation. Then neither would trade in the posterior round, with the result that $T^* = D^* = C^*$. Thus the efficient portfolios achieved by concordant traders in a non-informative situation under SCM are also attained in two trading rounds in an informative situation.

In the lower panel of part 1, the informative-situation results under UM are shown. The equilibrium conditional *posterior*-round prices here are $P'_\zeta(= P'_{Za}) = 0.5$ and $P''_\zeta(= P''_{Zb}) = 1.25$. The prior-round price implied by equation (11.21), the martingale proposition, is then $P_\zeta^0 = 0.8$ (in contrast with the $P_\zeta = 0.9439$ obtained in example 1 for the non-informative situation). In this case it so happens that the optimal wealth-pair of equation (11.17) – W', $W'' = 200, 200$ – can be achieved only by choosing $T^* = E$, i.e. *there will be no prior-round trading*. (This is, however, an accidental consequence of the particulars of this example. More generally, both prior and posterior trading will be called for on the part of concordant individuals under UM.) This trading position makes possible the achievement of the optimal compound consumptive gamble $D^* = [(100, 200), (100, 80)] = C^* = (100; 200, 80)$ even under the constrained UM market regime – in contrast with the inefficient result under UM where only a single trading round was permitted (part 1 of table 11.1).

Part 2 of table 11.2 shows the results in these markets regimes for individuals of representative endowments but deviant beliefs. In the upper panel of part 2, compare the trading positions T^* attained under SCM with the consumptive optimum positions C^* shown for a single trading round in table 11.1. (Here again, there is a degree of freedom that has been used to fix the first element $n' = 100$ of T^*). The key point to notice is that the two rounds of trading permit a heavier commitment to deviant beliefs. For the optimist assigning a relatively higher probability to state-a, the trading position $T^* = (100; 266.7, 40)$ backs his belief more heavily than the simple consumptive gamble under SCM, $C^* = (100; 233.3, 60)$. For the pessimist assigning a relatively higher probability to state-b, $T^* = (100; 133.3, 120)$ compares similarly with $C^* = (100; 166.7, 100)$. Note also that if the speculation is successful, the belief-deviant trader can attain relatively high consumptions of *both* N and Z – since with two rounds of trading the n' and n'' elements of the optimal D^* gamble can differ along with z'_a and z''_b.

The lower panel of part 2 shows, once again, that two rounds of trading under UM permit the achievement of the same wealth-pairs and so the same efficient consumptive gambles D^* as under SCM. Specifically, under UM the optimist trader – attaching a high probability to the favorable state of the world and therefore to the low posterior price $P'_Z = 0.5$ – *sells* 111.1 units of ζ for 88.9 units of N in the prior round, to achieve $T^* = (188.9; 88.9, -31.1)$. The pessimist trader, attaching relatively high probability to the unfavorable state of the world and high posterior price $P''_Z = 1.25$, instead takes advantage of the prior-round price to *buy* 111.1 units of ζ to as to achieve $T^* = (11.1; 311.1, 191.1)$. After emergence of the information, re-trading in the spot market allows each trader to move to one or other of the elements of the same D^* gamble as achievable under SCM. (Note, however, that under UM there is no degree of freedom left in the choice of trading position T^*.)

To sum up, the development in this section indicates that the opportunity to engage in both prior-round and posterior-round trading, afforded by the anticipated emergence of information, remedies the deficiency of the regime of Unconditional Markets that was observed for a *non*-informative situation. Specifically, in our model above *every trader – whether belief-deviant or not – was able to achieve in two trading rounds under UM the exact same consumptive gamble that was optimal under the more ample regime of Semi-Complete Markets (SCM).*

11.4   ADEQUACY OF MARKETS AS RELATED TO NUMBERS OF STATES AND GOODS

The key result derived for the model of the previous section was that the two rounds of trading in an informative situation allow every transactor, even under the incomplete Unconditional Markets regime, to achieve the same optimal consumptive gamble as was attainable under Semi-Complete Markets. But the preceding analysis specified a world of just two alternative states (a and b) and just two commodities (N and Z). This is too artificial to be acceptable without further consideration.

More generally, let S denote the number of states and G the number of goods. Then, in a non-informative situation – or in prior trading in an informative situation – under Semi-Complete Markets there will be dealing in $S(G-1)+1$ distinct claims or "contracts." (Contingent claims to $G-1$ different risky commodities will be traded, but only the single unconditional claim to the riskless numeraire commodity N.) In the posterior round, after the emergence of conclusive information, there is no more uncertainty. At that point trading takes place once again, but only in G contracts – one for each good. Under Unconditional Markets, in contrast, there will be trading in only the G unconditional contracts in the prior round, followed by a second posterior round involving the same G contracts.

The key feature of the development in section 11.5 is that, *for each individual in an informative situation to achieve his optimal gamble, all that he need determine in the prior trading round are his S conditional posterior wealths – one for each possible state of the world.* This is equivalent to saying that Numeraire Contingency Markets (NCM) as defined in section 11.1 above – essentially, the availability of S contracts in the prior round having the form of side-bets in numeraire units as to the advent of any of the S possible states of the world – would suffice.[22] In this round each individual would place his bets as to the state of the world s governing the endowment vector for each and every good. Upon emergence of the conclusive information as to which state has in fact obtained, his posterior wealth W_s would then become the budget constraint for consumptive purchases in the G contracts for goods. So $S + G$ contracts are all that are needed over the two rounds.

However, the extra degrees of freedom in the prior round provided by Semi-Complete Markets are of considerable interest. We saw in section 11.3 above that, with $G = S = 2$, under SCM the $S(G-1) + 1 = 3$ contracts in the prior round provided just one extra degree of freedom in choice of T^*. Since the restriction under Unconditional Markets (UM) to certainty trading in the risky commodity Z (the fact that Z_a and Z_b claims must be traded only in a $1:1$ ratio) used up just this one degree of freedom, the UM regime could achieve the same result as the SCM regime.

More generally, under SCM the excess number of prior-round contracts (the degrees of freedom d.f. in choice of T^*) will be:

$$\text{d.f.} = S(G-1) + 1 - S = S(G-2) + 1. \tag{11.22}$$

Under SCM there will *always* be such an excess for $G \geqslant 2$.[23] Under UM, the excess number of contracts is simply:

$$\text{d.f.} = G - S. \tag{11.23}$$

Since the number of potentially distinguishable states of the world S is infinite, it might be thought that under the more realistic UM regime there would generally be a deficiency of markets. To this there are several possible replies: (1) Given our limited mental capacities, the number of *actually distinguished* states entering into people's subjective calculations is likely to be a rather small figure. (2) While Unconditional Markets may be a closer approximation of real world actuality than Semi-Complete Markets, there is in fact *some* trading in conditional claims (e.g. in insurance markets). Such markets are likely to be provided just where it is most important to do so in terms of meeting perceived gaps in market adequacy. (3) Most important of all is the consideration that information will not ordinarily be arriving in one single injection. If *successive* informational inputs are anticipated, all but the last being less than conclusive, repeated rounds of trading become available for rebalancing of portfolios. Multiple trading rounds thus compensate for inadequacy of markets in any given round.[24] Since the arrival of information is often an essentially continuous process over time, the number of degrees of freedom available tends to rise without limit, even if there are only Unconditional Markets at any point in time. (An explicit analysis of the complex problem of sequential information inputs will not be provided here, however.)

The conclusion, therefore, is that the applicability of the key theoretical results obtained does not depend in any essential way upon the illustrative assumptions of $S = 2$ and $G = 2$ goods.

11.5   BEHAVIORAL IMPLICATIONS – SPECULATORS
         VERSUS HEDGERS

There is one significant difference in implications for trader behavior as between Semi-Complete Markets and Unconditional Markets. Under SCM anyone with *concordant* beliefs can, in the prior round of trading, choose a trading position T^* identical with his optimal consumptive gamble $D^* = C^*$. That is, he could move direclty to his consumptive optimum as soon as markets open, foregoing any opportunity for posterior trading at the changed prices to rule after emergence of the anticipated new information. And anyone with *deviant* beliefs would plan to deal in both the prior and the posterior markets; his prior-round choice of T^* would necessarily diverge from his ultimate consumptive choices. This distinction provided a simple identification of speculative behavior under the SCM regime: a speculator is one whose prior-round trading position is linked to *prospective portfolio revision* in the posterior round, whereas a non-speculator is one who need not plan for portfolio revision.

The identification of speculation with prospective portfolio revision does not hold for the UM regime! Here the limitations on marketing are such that posterior trading is in general necessary for everyone, whether of concordant beliefs or of deviant beliefs. Since under UM, typically, everyone will be revising portfolios, the working definition of speculation employed above for the SCM regime (planning for posterior portfolio revision) is not ultimately satisfactory. A more general definition, applicable to both SCM and UM market regimes, is as follows: A speculator is a trader who, in an informative situation, plans to deal in the prior and posterior rounds in such a way as to achieve a compound consumptive gamble D^* that differs from the simple consumptive C^* he would have chosen in a non-informative situation. Or, putting it less technically, a speculator is one who *plans to profit from emergent information*; for a non-speculator, on the other hand, planned contingent consumption is identical over information-events (but not, in general, over states of the world).[25]

What of the conventional view in the speculation literature that distinguishes between (a) risk-averse individuals who use the prior round of trading to *reduce their exposure to price risk* ("hedgers") *versus* (b) risk-tolerant individuals who trade so as to *increase their exposure to price risk* ("speculators")? Our analysis shows that this distinction is invalid. While relatively risk-tolerant individuals do (other things equal) seek wider gambles, if they hold representative beliefs their ultimate D^* gambles will not differ from the C^* gambles they would have chosen in a non-informative situation. They will therefore *not* be planning to profit from incoming information. Perhaps even more convincing a refutation, to increase one's exposure to *price risk* – in a world where *quantity risk* also exists (and is, indeed, as we have seen, an ultimate determinant of price risk) – is not necessarily to widen consumptive risk. Putting this the other way, a highly risk-averse trader will not, in general, accept an opportunity to "transfer" *price risks* even at fair odds! (Whereas a risk-averse individual would, by definition, always be willing to convert a *quantity risk* into a certainty at fair odds.) This is shown most clearly by a numerical illustration.

Numerical example 3

In table 11.2, the lower panel of part 1 illustrated an informative situation under a regime of Unconditional Markets (UM). At the equilibrium prior price $P^0_\zeta = 0.8$ there was no actual trading in the prior round ($T^* = E$ for both traders). Each individual does as well as possible by engaging in posterior trading only.

But this behavior would be regarded, in the conventional view, as failure to use the prior market ("futures" market) to divest price risk! The martingale property (11.21), with "correct conditional forecasting," shows that such divestment could be attained at fair odds – both traders agree that the prior-round price is the mathematical expectation of the unknown posterior price. This means that the representative demander and representative supplier here could, in the conventional view, mutually "hedge" without having to pay any premium at all to speculators. Why do they then not do so? Because the risk-aversion argument is plausibly yet incorrectly applied to the divesting of *price risk*. It is *quantity risk*, not price risk, that enters into the utility function; the divesting of price risk may actually increase the riskiness (and therefore reduce the desirability) of the overall consumptive gamble attainable. And, in particular, in this case any trading by an individual in the prior round – whether conventionally regarded as "hedging" or "speculating" – will preclude his ever attaining a consumptive gamble as desirable as the $D^* = (100; 200, 80)$ achievable by *not* trading in the prior round.

For traders with representative beliefs, the prior-round optimality condition (11.17) reduces to the simple form $du'/dW' = du''/dW''$ – implying, with (11.16), that $W' = W'' = 200$. But it is easy to see that, in this market regime, each individual can assure himself a conditional posterior wealth of 200 only by remaining at his endowment position. Suppose a demander was somehow induced to make a "hedging" purchase of ζ in the initial round, at the price $P^0_\zeta = 0.8$, or a supplier was similarly induced to "hedge" by sale of ζ in the prior round. It can be verified that this *must* lead to an inferior outcome for each, as compared with the "no-hedging" behavior that leads to the optimal conditional wealths $W' = W'' = 200$.

If a hedger cannot be defined in terms of divesting of price risk, does the hedger/speculator distinction then retain any meaning or applicability whatsoever? There is one natural reinterpretation that follows from the general definition of speculation arrived at here. In the spirit of this under-lying concept, we can define *hedgers* as that sub-class of speculators who trade with a view toward attaining D^* gambles that are *less risky* than their C^* gambles under SCM. The "speculators," where the word is used in contrast with "hedgers," are then those seeking *more risky D^** gambles.

As previously emphasized, the crucial role in speculative behavior is played by belief-deviance – by the degree of optimism $p - \pi$. We would anticipate that an optimistic individual, one for whom p exceeds the representative belief parameter π, would tend to adopt wider gambles – stake more of his resource upon state-a obtaining. That this is true, up to a point, is illustrated by the final numerical example below.

Numerical example 4

Table 11.3 shows the bearing of the belief parameter p upon the con-sumptive risks accepted by individuals. An informative situation under a regime of Unconditional Markets is assumed (where, following the analysis above, all traders achieve the same solutions as could be attained under Semi-Complete Markets). The numerical data are the same as in the preceding examples: (1) the representative belief parameter is $\pi = 0.6$; (2) the prior-round equilibrium price is $P_\zeta^0 = 0.8$, and the posterior-round conditional prices are $P'_\zeta = 0.5$ and $P''_\zeta = 1.25$; (3) all traders have utility function $u = \log_e nz$; (4) but five different endowment compositions are shown, all with wealth-values $W^e = 200$ (calculated in terms of the prices that *would* have ruled under Semi-Complete Markets, *not* in terms of the actual prices under UM).

The main results can be interpreted as follows. Looking at the simple consumptive gambles C^* achievable under SCM (recall that these will *not* in general be achievable in a single trading round under UM), we see that the "optimist" with $p = 0.7$ widens his gamble in the direction of the more prosperous state-a – in comparison with the individual of representative beliefs for whom $p = \pi = 0.6$. The "moderate pessimist" ($p = 0.5$) narrows his gamble, as one would expect. But note that the "extreme pessimist" ($p = 0.2$) is so confident about "bad news" (that state-b will obtain) as to widen his gamble in the direction of the latter state.

Consider now the compound consumptive gambles D^* achievable in two rounds of trading. Note, first, that for any *given* value of the belief parameter p the differently endowed traders all end up with the same D^*.

TABLE 11.3 Risks accepted, by degree of optimism/pessimism

	0.7 (Optimist)	0.6 (Representative)	0.5 (Moderate pessimist)	0.2 (Extreme pessimist)
Belief parameter $p =$				
Simple consumptive gambles (SCM)	$C^* = (n^*; z_a^*, z_b^*) = (100; 233\frac{1}{3}, 60)$	$(100; 200, 80)$	$(100; 166\frac{2}{3}, 100)$	$(100; 66\frac{2}{3}, 160)$
Desired posterior wealths	$W', W'' = 233\frac{1}{3}, 150$	$200, 200$	$166\frac{2}{3}, 250$	$66\frac{2}{3}, 400$
Prior-round trading (UM) of Z				
Endowments $E = (n^e; z_a^e, z_b^e)$				
1. $(100; 200, 80)$	$\zeta = -111\frac{1}{9}$	0	$111\frac{1}{9}$	$444\frac{4}{9}$
2. $(200; 0, 0)$	$\zeta = -111\frac{1}{9}$	0	$111\frac{1}{9}$	$444\frac{4}{9}$
3. $(0; 400, 160)$	$\zeta = -111\frac{1}{9}$	0	$111\frac{1}{9}$	$444\frac{4}{9}$
4. $(80; 400, 0)$	$\zeta = 155\frac{5}{9}$	$226\frac{6}{9}$	$377\frac{7}{9}$	$711\frac{1}{9}$
5. $(120; 0, 160)$	$\zeta = -377\frac{7}{9}$	$-266\frac{6}{9}$	$-155\frac{5}{9}$	$117\frac{7}{9}$
Elements of compound gambles $D^* = [C'; C''; p, 1-p]$	$C' = (n'; z') = (116\frac{2}{3}; 233\frac{1}{3})$ $C'' = (n''; z_b'') = (75, 60)$	$(100, 200)$ $(100, 80)$	$(83\frac{1}{3}, 166\frac{2}{3})$ $(125, 100)$	$(33\frac{1}{3}, 66\frac{2}{3})$ $(200, 160)$

But to achieve this identity of result the prior-round trading ζ (and also the trading positions T^* not shown in the table) must in general differ.

The initial-round purchases ζ do not vary, for any given p, as among the first three endowments tabulated (types 1, 2, and 3). The reason is that these individuals are already holding representative endowed *proportions* of the risky state-claims Z_a and Z_b. The other two cases, individuals with asymmetrical compositions of Z-claims over states (types 4 and 5), must arrange initial-round exchanges that balance Z_a and Z_b in the course of achieving the desired contingent wealth-pair W', W''. Subject to this proviso, the optimists ($p=0.7$) tend to be *sellers* of Z in the prior round. That is, they are optimistic about the social *quantity* of Z to be available for consumption, and so they expect on average a low price of Z in the posterior round.[26] Individuals of concordant beliefs ($p=\pi=0.6$) all end up with the optimal gamble $D^*=C^*=(100; 200, 80)$; here only endowment types 4 and 5 actually trade in the prior round (for the purpose of balancing their asymmetrical state-endowments). The moderate pessimists ($p=0.5$), and even more so the extreme pessimists ($p=0.2$), tend to be buyers of Z in the initial round; they attach greater belief to a Z-scarcity and hence to a higher posterior price.

11.6   SUMMARY

The widely accepted Keynes-Hicks theory explains hedging and speculation as the avoidance in the one case, and the acceptance in the other case, of price risk. We have found this explanation unacceptable, in view of the fact that it is the *interaction between price risk and quantity risk* that governs the overall hazard accepted or avoided by individuals. Failure to appreciate the significance of the quantitative uncertainty that underlies and is the main cause of stochastic variation of prices is the key failing to the traditional speculation literature. According to the definition proposed here, speculation and hedging consist of *trading in the prior and posterior markets* (in an informative situation, since only with anticipated emergence of new information can differences between posterior and prior prices be anticipated) *in such a way as to achieve compound consumptive gambles D^* that differ from the simple consumptive gambles C^* that would have been adopted in a non-informative situation.* The hedgers are those for whom the net effect of the prior trading activity is to make D^* less risky than C^*. – with the reverse holding for speculators, if the latter term is understood as opposed to hedging. Alternatively, it is sometimes terminologically more convenient to think of speculation as a wider category of activity (including all prior-market trading leading to divergences between C^* and D^*), in which case hedging becomes a special risk-reducing subclass of speculative behavior.

Among the factors studied here as possibly involved in the speculative decision are: (1) The individual's *beliefs* about the emergence and content of new information – which must logically bear a definite relation to his own prior estimates of the likelihood of alternative states of the world. (2) His *utility function*, involving both preferences as among different commodities and his degree of risk-tolerance (willingness to hold prospects yielding differential outcomes over the various states of the world). (3) The scale and composition of his *endowment*, as distributed over commodities and states of the world. (4) The extent of the *markets* available, and in particular whether or not conditional state-claims to commodities can be bought or sold separately.

Omitting the detailed qualifications (the "idealizing assumptions" of section 11.1, and the key "correct conditional forecasting" condition), the main results derivable from the models considered here can be summarized:

(A) Speculative trading is undertaken *only* by individuals whose opinions, as to the likelihood of future states of the world, diverge from representative beliefs in the market.

(B) Mutual equilibriation of prior-round and posterior-round prices requires that the price-revision relation be a martingale, calculated in terms of concordant beliefs.

These results are applicable not only for "unrealistic" market regimes permitting trading in contingent claims to risky commodities (Semi-Complete Markets) but also, subject to certain limitations, to regimes in which only certainty claims can be traded (Unconditional Markets) as assumed in the traditional speculation 'iterature.

As is always the case for theoretical models, because of the over-simplified assumptions these propositions could not be expected to be exactly applicable to actual behavior. But the main thrust of the results is to support the observation of Holbrook Working that speculative/hedging behavior is governed primarily by *differences of belief*, rather than by *differences of risk-tolerance* as postulated by the Keynes-Hicks risk-transfer theory.

REFERENCES

Arrow, K. J., "The Role of Securities in the Optimal Allocation of Risk-Bearing," *Review of Economic Studies*, vol. 31 (1964).

——, "On a Theorem of Arrow: Comment," *Review of Economic Studies*, vol. 42 (July 1975).

Cootner, P. H., "Speculation, Hedging, and Arbitrage," *International Encyclopedia of the Social Sciences*, vol. 15 (1968).

Diamond, P. A., "The Role of a Stock Market in a General Equilibrium Model with Technological Uncertainty," *American Economic Review*, vol. 57 (Sept. 1967).

Drèze, J. H., "Market Allocation Under Uncertainty," *European Economic Review*, vol. 2 (Winter 1970–1).

Fama, E. F., "Efficient Capital Markets: A Review of Theory and Empirical Work," *Journal of Finance*, vol. 25 (May 1970).

Feiger, George, "Speculation and Equilibrium: Comment," *Quarterly Journal of Economics*, vol. 90 (Nov. 1976).

Friedman, M., "In Defense of Destabilizing Speculation," in R. W. Pfouts (ed.), *Essays in Economics and Econometrics*, Chapel Hill, NC: University of North Carolina Press, 1960). Reprinted in M. Friedman, *The Optimum Quantity of Money and Other Essays*. Chicago: Aldine, 1969.

Hicks, J. R., *Value and Capital*, 2nd ed. London: Oxford University Press, 1946.

Hirshleifer, J., "The Private and Social Value of Information and the Reward to Inventive Activity," *American Economic Review*, vol. 61 (Sept. 1971).

——, "Foundations of the Theory of Speculation: Information, Risk, and Markets," Western Management Science Institute, UCLA, Working Paper no. 189 (revised, June 1972).

——, "Speculation and Equilibrium: Information, Risk, and Markets," *Quarterly Journal of Economics*, vol. 89 (Nov. 1975).

——, "Speculation and Equilibrium: Response," *Quarterly Journal of Economics*, vol. 90 (Nov. 1976).

Hirshleifer, J. and Rubinstein, M. E., "Speculation and Information in Securities Markets," *Proceedings – XX International Meeting, The Institute of Management Sciences*, vol. 2 Jerusalem: Academic Press, 1976.

Houthakker, H., "Can Speculators Forecast Prices?" *Review of Economics and Statistics*, vol. 39 (May 1957).

——, "Normal Backwardation," in J. N. Wolfe (ed.), *Value, Capital, and Growth*. Edinburgh University Press, 1968.

Keynes, J. M., *A Treatise on Money*. New York: Harcourt Brace, 1930.

Muth, J. F., "Rational Expectations and the Theory of Price Movements," *Econometrica*, vol. 29 (July 1961).

Radner, R., "Competitive Equilibrium Under Uncertainty," *Econometrica*, vol. 36 (Jan. 1968).

Rockwell, C. S., "Normal Backwardation, Forecasting, and the Returns to Commodity Futures Traders," *Food Research Institute Studies*, vol. 7 (1967), supplement.

Rubinstein, Mark E., "Securities Market Efficiency in an Arrow-Debreu Economy," *American Economic Review*, vol. 65 (Dec. 1975).

Salant, Stephen W., "Speculation and Equilibrium: Comment," *Quarterly Journal of Economics*, vol. 90 (Nov. 1976).

Samuelson, P. A., "Proof that Properly Anticipated Prices Fluctuate Randomly," *Industrial Management Review*, vol. 6 (Spring 1965).

Telser, L. G., "The Supply of Speculative Services in Wheat, Corn, and Soybeans," *Food Research Institute Studies*, vol. 7 (1967), supplement.

Working, H., "Futures Trading and Hedging," *American Economic Review*, vol. 43 (June 1953).

——, "New Concepts Concerning Futures Markets and Prices," *American Economic Review*, vol. 52 (June 1962).

NOTES

[1] Also see Houthakker (1947, 1968); Cootner (1968).

[2] If hedgers are mostly long the physical good (if they are predominantly suppliers or warehousers of the commodity) they must be mostly short in the futures market. Then the speculators must be net long in futures. This premise has led to the inference of "normal backwardation" – that prices of contracts tend to rise as delivery date approaches, thus rewarding the speculators for making early purchase commitments and thereby bearing the price risk. The evidence does not conclusively support normal backwardation, though the issue remains in debate (compare Houthakker, 1968; Rockwell, 1967; Telser 1967). Two main explanations for the supposed failure of normal backwardation have been proposed that are consistent with an underlying risk-transfer theory: (1) If hedgers were predominantly demanders rather than suppliers of the commodity, normal compensation for speculators would dictate a falling rather than a rising price trend over the life of the contract (Cootner, 1968, p. 119); or, (2) If speculators are not risk-averse on balance, no net compensation is required (Friedman, 1960). An alternative explanation, of course, would be that the risk-transfer theory is simply incorrect.

[3] Hirshleifer (1975). An earlier version was Hirshleifer (1972).

[4] Fuller exposition appears in Hirshleifer (1975).

[5] We are here making use of two of the idealizing assumptions to be mentioned below: that all trading takes place at equilibrium prices, and that decisions associated merely with the the the passage of time (e.g. storage activities) can be separated from speculation proper.

[6] If traders are atomistic, merely *private* information will only negligibly affect price. (See Hishleifer 1971, p. 564.)

[7] There are other exogenous infuences whose probabilistic variation might induce a corresponding stochastic distribution of prices. Among them are possible changes in tastes, technology, social institutions, etc. These factors will not be considered here.

[8] Called "Certainty Markets" in Hirshleifer (1975, p. 525).

[9] Ibid.

[10] See Feiger (1976). It is, however, possible to reinterpret the speculation concept for such a case. See Hirshleifer and Rubinstein (1976).

[11] A somewhat parallel conceptualization appears in Diamond (1967). Diamond's market regime provides for an arbitrary number of firms and corresponding tradable equity claims, and is in that respect more general than EM here. But his one-period one-commodity model does not permit speculative behavior, though he suggests that the interaction of "technological uncertainty" (quantity risk) and "price uncertainty" (price risk) does have to be taken into account in more general models.

[12] See Arrow (1964, sec. 3).

[13] For discussion of the additivity assumption, see the comment by Salant (1976) and reply by Hirshleifer (1976). The martingale theorem (proposition B) was derived, under the assumptions of a riskless commodity with state-independent additive utility, in Drèze (1970-1). Drèze did not consider the problem of speculation, however.

[14] Rubinstein (1975) defines a concept called "consensus beliefs" – a single probability distribution which, if unanimously held, would determine the same market prices as the actual heterogeneous beliefs of traders. In general, it is not possible to find a "consensus" or "representative" probability distribution as an average of individual beliefs.

[15] Personal communication from John G. Riley.

[16] Such a difference can be achieved, in a single trading round, only under Fully Complete Markets (FCM).

[17] A certain resemblance to the concept called "rational expectations" in Muth (1961) may be noted. See also Arrow (1975).

[18] It is only necessary that belief-concordant traders make "correct conditional forecasts" to achieve the price effects of (11.15), as these traders account for essentially all the social weight.

[19] Because of the degree of freedom in choice of elements of T^*, the individual *might* move in the prior round to a trading position having the same associated posterior wealths W' and W'' as D^*, yet requiring posterior trading to actually achieve D^*. But there is no advantage in not moving from E to D^* in one round of trading as described in the text. And any transaction costs, however minute, would make this direct movement strictly preferred.

[20] Multiplying the first equation of (11.19b) by π and the second by $1 - \pi$ and summing leads to:

$$\pi W' + (1 - \pi) W'' = \pi(n^t + P'_{Za}z^t_a) + (1 - \pi)(n^t + P''_{Zb}z^t_b)$$
$$= n^t + P^0_{Za}z_a + P^0_{Zb}z^t_b$$
$$= (n^e - P^0_Z\zeta) + P^0_{Za}(z^e_a + \zeta) + P^0_{Zb}(z^e_b + \zeta).$$

Equation (11.19c) then follows.

[21] As before, we will not attempt to show uniqueness.

[22] This is the result obtained in Arrow (1964, sec. 3), though not applied by him to the problem of speculation.

[23] This result assumes linear independence among the G goods with regard to posterior price distributions. If, for example, two goods had exactly proportional posterior prices over all possible states of the world, more contracts would be needed in the prior round. This qualification will henceforth be ignored.

[24] On this general point see Drèze (1970–1, pp. 144–5); Rubinstein (1975, p. 813, n. 3).

[25] Compare Hirshleifer and Rubinstein (1975, p. 799).

[26] A low price of Z is, of course, "bad news" for suppliers, other things equal. But other things are not equal, since the price is low precisely when the quantity available is great. Socially speaking, naturally, a large quantity available is "good news."

12   Two Models of Speculation and Information*

Background and comments

This essay, not previously published, enables me to end this volume on a somewhat lighter note.

The occasion was an article that appeared in *Econometrica* by the French economist, Jean Tirole. In the model of speculation developed in my essays reprinted in the preceding two chapters, *differences in belief* played a very central role. In contrast, Tirole's paper falls within a more recent tradition that looks with suspicion upon the idea that any belief differences at all can persist in a market economy. The underlying idea has been called the Groucho Marx Theorem – from Groucho's supposed statement, "I wouldn't be a member of any club that would admit me." Suppose that at the current price some particular trader wants to buy. It follows, according to this line of argument, that such a trader must have received private information that the price is going to go up. In which case, the rest of us should all refuse to sell! If so, no speculative trading based upon belief differences can ever occur. Or, put another way, all traders' beliefs will be brought into harmony by the market negotiation process (as Walras's auctioneer calls out possible prices) even though no trading actually takes place.

There is no doubt that such a process is at work, and thus that Tirole's critique has some merit. But the contention that all belief differences, and the market trading founded upon them, can thereby be eliminated is extreme indeed. After all, we still see betting at racetracks. More important, is it not residual differences of belief -- even after taking account of the information conveyed by market prices – that largely motivate those who choose to buy *versus* those who choose to sell General Motors stock, or buyers and sellers of wheat futures, or of forward contracts in foreign exchange? On the theoretical level, I argue more explicitly that the belief-equalization theorem can only hold under highly restrictive conditions, among them that all traders have identical prior beliefs (and common knowledge of that fact) and that there is no noise whatsoever in the market-signalling process. Absent these and other extreme specifications, individual belief differences will indeed persist to motivate speculative trading.

*UCLA Department of Economics Working Paper no. 329B (revised Sept. 1984).

I should add that the pleasantly informal tone of Tirole's paper enabled me to respond in kind, with appropriately chosen French-language quotations in a military vein to epitomize the friendly intellectual struggle going on. Determining the merits of the debate is left for the reader, in the hope that the task has been made a bit more agreeable than usual.

In a recent *Econometrica* paper, Jean Tirole (1982) asserted that what he called the Working–Hirshleifer–Feiger view of speculation was "internally inconsistent." His article goes on to present an alternative theoretical structure. The two competing formalizations differ interestingly in their modelling of the information-generation-plus-acquisition process, and it is this aspect that I mainly discuss here. I also will compare certain other features of the models. As to the accusation of internal inconsistency, I prefer to regard this as a momentary instance where ardent Gallic *élan* ("*De l'audace, encore de l'audace, et toujours de l'audace*" – Danton) has temporarily overbalanced Gallic cautionary *bon sens* ("*N'ayez pas de zèle*" – Not too much zeal, guys – Talleyrand). With reference to my papers (Hirshleifer, 1975, 1977), I take my stand with the Duke of Wellington: "There is no mistake; there has been no mistake; and there shall be no mistake."[1]

Turning now to the main issue, here are the key points in the information-tion modelling represented by what I shall be calling here the Hirshleifer–Salant–Feiger (HSF) model.[2] Think of events as occurring at three points of time, sufficiently close together so that no time-discounting is required:

(1) *Prior round of trading.* Here individuals with exogenously given portfolio endowments, tastes, attitudes toward risk, and generally differing prior probability beliefs (as to the content of public information to come) revise their endowed portfolios via market trading. (But consumption does not yet occur.) All such prior-round trading takes place at market-clearing equilibrium prices.

(2) *Emergence of information.* The public information anticipated in item 1 above, for example an authoritative government report about the prospective size of the wheat crop, now emerges, leading traders to revise their probability beliefs about the demand or supply of one or more commodities. In the extreme case (the only case I will consider further here) the information is *conclusive*, so that all traders must now agree in attaching probability of unity to one state of the world (one size of crop), probability zero to all other states.

(3) *Posterior round of trading.* Guided by their revised beliefs, traders go on to make their final revisions of portfolios (now under conditions of certainty, if the information-event was indeed conclusive). Again, all trades take place at market-clearing prices. Consumption then follows.

Before turning to how Tirole pictures information arrival, I should say something about the general structures of the competing formulations. The HSF model is one of *general equilibrium*: individuals start with endowments, preferences, etc., and end up choosing patterns of consumption that maximize utility. Tirole's main concern is with an extreme partial-equilibrium "pure trading" or (he sometimes says) "purely speculative" model. In this world no-one produces or consumes. In fact no-one has any intrinsic interest whatsoever in supplying or demanding commodities. Each person is simply looking for a chance to buy for less in order to sell for more – with the aim of maximizing "expected monetary gain" (if he is risk-neutral) or some risk-discounted adjustment thereof (if he is risk-averse). While Tirole does later try to extend the analysis to a more reasonable world, the incompleteness *à outrance* of his central model makes it difficult for it even to make contact with reality. On the other hand, his interesting theorems concerning what might be called "inferential information transmission" are in principle separable from this unsatisfactory feature, i.e. they could be incorporated into a more general theory.

While Tirole later generalizes his theory to a multi-date ("dynamic") version, his basic objection to the HSF arises in his simplest one-date ("static") model. Limiting attention to this case, therefore, his assumed sequence of events is:

(1) *Prior round of trading.* There is no prior round of trading (i.e. no trading occurs before arrival of information).
(2) *Emergence of information.* For Tirole, information arrives via a set of *private* signals (about the price vector p) received by the separate traders. While (he assumes) all traders have agreed prior beliefs, their generally heterogeneous signals should still, it might seem, lead to differing posterior beliefs. (*Mais non!* – as will be shortly seen.)
(3) *Posterior round of trading.* Everything of interest takes place here. More specifically, as in the Sherlock Holmes story what is of interest is that nothing takes place: there is no trading in the posterior round either!

Even in a strange world lacking productive or consumptive motives for exchange, it may seem surprising that no trading ever occurs – in view of the aforesaid differences in beliefs once individuals have received their private signals. The explanation, and Tirole makes a valid contribution here (see also Milgrom and Stokey, 1982), is that there is another source of information not yet accounted for: the very *willingness of others to trade* tells me something about the state of the market. And specifically, following a theme anticipated in Akerlof (1970) and Grossman and Stiglitz

(1976) and the adverse-selection literature generally, the visible eagerness of others to trade *may* (not must as Tirole claims) be sufficient basis for me not to do so. (Milgrom and Stokey [1982] call this the "Groucho Marx Theorem.") However, to see how this works one would have to specify, more fully than did Tirole, something about intra-period market "dynamics" in the proper sense of the word.[3]

Imagine a Walrasian auctioneer who cries out price *au hasard*. Suppose that I am a trader, named Hercule Poirot, that I am solely interested in turnaround profit, and that the initial price strikes me as too low in the light of my private signal. I decide to buy, and look for someone willing to sell. Imagine that I find a trading partner. So far so good. But then (the reasoning of course follows Aumann [1976]), I say to myself: "*Attendez, mon vieux*. Since we both, *lui et moi*, had the same priors, and since neither of us has any trading motive other than turnaround profit, he must have received an informative private down signal just as I was receiving my informative private up signal. Before finalizing my decision I should take account of this information of his which I have thus so cleverly deduced." *En effet*, his very willingness to sell makes me, Hercule, now less willing to buy. The other party, reasoning the same way, will similarly be less willing to sell. This mutual *recul*, carried to the limit, dictates that in the end no-one buys or sells.[4]

But Tirole's conclusion, that this process leads inevitably to agreed beliefs and thus to non-trading, is a special result with very little robustness. For one thing, and Tirole concedes this, it fails if traders' *priors* differ. And indeed, for the validity of the non-trading theorem something even stronger than agreed priors is needed: the parties' priors must not only be agreed but must be "common knowledge" in the sense of Aumann (1976) – i.e. each must know the other shares his beliefs, must know that the other knows he knows, etc.[5] This point is due to Guth (1984), who has also analyzed the implications for speculation theory of shared priors that are *not* "common knowledge." As a separate point, this inferential information transmission mechanism, in either Tirole's version or that of Milgrom and Stokey (1982), collapses immediately if any market participant engages in *strategic* behavior. Finally, if information generation and dissemination are "noisy," not all relevant information may be perfectly revealed by price, hence not all differences of belief ultimately eliminated (Diamond and Verrechia, 1981). Thus, for any or all of these very convincing reasons the parties may after all "agree to disagree," which implies that they will trade as assumed in the HSF models.

Returning to a comparison of the theories, it should be evident that a model whose implication is that no trading at all ever occurs is disastrously inadequate! Tirole therefore wisely turns (p. 1168) to what happens when his assumptions are relaxed. Some of his relaxations are relatively uninteresting, e.g. introducing irrational or risk-preferring agents, but others do point the way toward more satisfactory theories.

The most important relaxation occurs when Tirole abandons the assumption rather obscurely described as "absence of correlation between the initial position of traders and the market outcome." What this means is that Tirole would now admit into his world the fact that people have supplies of and demands for commodities, and so are interested in some-thing other than achieving trading gains. (*Cela va sans dire*, one would have thought!) Tirole draws from this relaxed model the inference that the market can provide "price insurance" to traders with risky positions. So, he goes on to conclude, his analysis "vindicates the Keynes–Hicks position" that speculative trading is a way to hedge price risks.

At this point Tirole's analysis does begin to make contact with the observed fact of speculative trading. And, certainly, the Keynes–Hicks price-insurance theory represents a part of the story. Nevertheless, owing to his exclusive concentration upon private signals that concern *market prices*, Tirole entirely misses the drastic flaw in the Keynes–Hicks analysis that initially motivated the HSF papers. To wit, that individuals with real supplies and demands for commodities do not face *price risks* only but also *quantity risks*, and indeed that in terms of social aggregates the quantity risks are the ultimate source of the price risks. (On this see also McKinnon [1967], Rolfo [1980], Britto [1984], Ho [1984].)

Consider a wheat farmer during the growing season. It is true that he faces a price risk at harvest time. *Other things equal*, therefore, he would indeed want to insure against this price risk, which he can do by selling at a known price today for delivery after harvest (i.e. he can sell "short" in the futures market). But other things are not equal. The typical farmer must face a physical *crop-size* risk as well as a *crop-price* risk (since prices vary, mainly, in consequence of crop-size fluctuations). Furthermore, and this is the crucial point, the two risks tend to be offsetting: the wheat price is generally high precisely when the typical farmer's wheat crop is stochas-tically small, while a low price will ordinarily be received just when his crop is big. Once this inverse interaction is taken into account, it is not at all clear that selling short – which hedges the price risk *alone* – is the optimal risk-balancing strategy for the farmer. Price risk is "needed," to a degree at least, because from a portfolio point of view it tends to balance out suppliers' intrinsic exposure to quantity risk.

In contrast with Tirole's partial-equilibrium model, and with the single-minded concern for price risk representing by the Keynes–Hicks view, the general-equilibrium modelling of the HSF formulation points to a number of interacting elements that contribute to speculative trading. The HSF papers emphasized that the wheat farmer's willingness to trade in the prior round will depend importantly upon his *beliefs* as to the probabilities of the good-crop *versus* bad-crop states of the world (and particularly upon the deviation of his beliefs from typical beliefs in the market), upon his *risk-tolerance*, and upon the *regime of available markets*. Later analysts pursuing the same or similar general-equilibrium approaches have demonstrated the significance of other parameters which also contribute to speculation/hedging decisions: the *covariance* of the farmer's own risky output with the market totals, the *elasticity of wheat demand*, and *transaction costs*.[6,7] Of course, analogous considerations will apply for the prior trading decisions of people on the other side of the market – consumers of wheat, millers, etc.

A second "relaxation" of interest concerns the postulate of identical priors. Here Tirole concedes the point that, where prior beliefs are not identical, trading would occur even in his arid "pure-trader" regime. So the Holbrook Working interpretation of speculative trading based on divergent beliefs, so airily dismissed earlier on, does reappear after all.

As Marshal Foch was wont to say, *"De quoi s'agit-il?"* – What's the bottom line? Tirole's paper is really an impossibility theorem about single-market transient price paths or "bubbles." It asks essentially whether, since a process of inferential information transmission will be taking place, "pure traders" in a zero-sum game can ever make money at one another's expense on the basis of differing *private* signals, the answer being negative in a particular idealized model. The HSF papers are in drastic contrast. They ignore possible bubbles, and describe the relationships that must hold between prior and posterior prices in a general-equilibrium comparative-static model – the prior/posterior dating being relative to the arrival of a *public* signal freely available to all traders.[8]

The lines of thought here are so dissimilar that they can scarcely be said even to be in disagreement. Tirole postulates private signals for agents with common priors, the HSF papers a public signal for agents with diverging priors. Tirole deals with intra-period informational transmission, HSF with inter-period comparative statics. Tirole employs an extreme partial-equilibrium ("pure-trading") approach, the HSF papers a general-equilibrium model in which consumption and production, and beliefs as to the content of forthcoming information, are what ultimately motivate trade. In one respect Tirole's analysis is the more general, to wit, in allowing for inferences about others' beliefs on the basis of their willingness to trade. This process of "inferential information transmission" should be incorporated into a truly general theory that would cover *both* comparative statics and the dynamic transient path of market trading.

REFERENCES

Akerlof, G., "The Market for 'Lemons': Qualitative Uncertainty and the Market Mechanism," *Quarterly Journal of Economics*, vol. 89 (Aug. 1970).

Anderson, R. W. and Danthine, J.-P., "Hedger Diversity in Futures Markets," *Economic Journal*, vol. 93 (May 1983).

Aumann, Robert J., "Agreeing to Disagree," *Annals of Statistics*, vol. 4 (1976), pp. 1236–9.

Baesel, J. and Grant, D., "Equilibrium in a Futures Market," *Southern Economic Journal*, vol. 49 (1982), pp. 320–9.

Britto, Ronald, "The Simultaneous Determination of Spot and Futures Prices in a Simple Model with Production Risk," *Quarterly Journal of Economics*, vol. 98 (May 1984).

Conroy, Robert M. and Rendleman, Richard J. Jr, "Pricing Commodities When Both Price and Output are Uncertain," *Journal of Futures Markets*, vol. 3 (1983), pp. 439–50.

Diamond, D. W. and Verrechia, R. E., "Information Aggregation in a Noisy Rational Expectations Economy," *Journal of Financial Economics*, vol. 9 (1981), pp. 221–35.

Feiger, George, "What is Speculation?" *Quarterly Journal of Economics*, vol. 90 (Nov. 1976).

Grossman, Sanford J. and Stiglitz, Joseph E., "Information and Competitive Price Systems," *American Economic Review*, vol. 66 (May 1976).

Guth, Michael A. S., "Intrinsic Uncertainty in the Contingent Claims Economy," 1984, unpublished manuscript.

Hirshleifer, David, "Risk, Equilibrium and Futures Markets," University of Chicago, Ph.D. dissertation, 1985.

Hirshleifer, J., "Speculation and Equilibrium: Information, Risk, and Markets," *Quarterly Journal of Economics*, vol. 89 (Nov. 1975).

——, "Reply to Comments on 'Speculation and Equilibrium: Information, Risk, and Markets'," *Quarterly Journal of Economics*, vol. 90 (Nov. 1976).

——, "The Theory of Speculation Under Alternative Regimes of Markets," *Journal of Finance*, vol. 32 (Sept. 1977).

Ho, Thomas, "Intertemporal Commodity Futures Hedging and the Production Decision," *Journal of Finance*, vol. 39 (June 1984), pp. 351–76.

Johnson, D. Gale, *Forward Prices for Agriculture*. Chicago: University of Chicago Press, 1947.

McKinnon, Ronald I., "Futures Markets, Buffer Stocks, and Income Stability for Primary Producers," *Journal of Political Economy*, vol. 75 (Dec. 1967).

Milgrom, Paul and Stokey, Nancy, "Information, Trade and Common Knowledge," *Journal of Economic Theory*, vol. 26 (1982), pp. 17–27.

Rolfo, Jacques, "Optimal Hedging Under Price and Quantity Uncertainty: The Case of a Cocoa Producer," *Journal of Political Economy*, vol. 88 (Feb. 1980).

Salant, Stephen W., "Hirshleifer on Speculation," *Quarterly Journal of Economics*, vol. 90 (Nov. 1976).

Salmon, Jon Wheaton, "The Emergence of Organized Futures Markets: The Distribution of Consumption Risk," UCLA, Ph.D. dissertation (1985).

Tirole, Jean, "On the Possibility of Speculation Under Rational Expectations," *Econometrica*, vol. 50 (Sept. 1982).

NOTES

[1] In a move suggested by Tirole's "seminar speaker" tale (his p. 1164), as a friendly challenge I hereby offer to bet a one-year subscription to *Econometrica* that he cannot demonstrate any internal inconsistency. Furthermore, as will become evident in note 4 below, this *défi américain* is no mere *gasconnade*. Following

Tirole's own logic, it is actually a kind of ontological proof of the validity of my argument!

[2] I use this label to call attention to the exchange in the *Quarterly Journal of Economics* (Feiger, 1976; Salant, 1976; Hirshleifer, 1976) which clarified, corrected, and generalized my original paper. Although Tirole refers also to the "Working theory," I do not feel justified in conscripting Holbrook Working's name as heavy artillery on my side of this clash. While the main thrust of the HSF theoretical results do tend to support his observations and insights relating to speculative markets (see note 8 below), in his correspondence with me Working has never specifically endorsed the models in question.

[3] Tirole unfortunately employs the terms "statics" and "dynamics" in a non-standard way. His "dynamics" refers to multi-date analysis, his "statics" to single-date analysis. This provides no terminology for the needed distinction between the analysis of equilibrium states and the analysis of transient paths or oscillations. In the standard terminology, we use "comparative statics" to analyze how a change in parametric underlying conditions modifies the equilibrium attained; we use "dynamics" if we are concerned with the specifics of the transition path. This distinction is quite crucial for the current discussion. For, in comparative-static analysis, a price change can *only* occur in consequence of underlying changes in supply or demand conditions – a key point in the HSF model. But Tirole is basically concerned with the possibility of "pure" price fluctuations (such as might emerge in "bubbles"), where mutually interacting anticipations about the prospective movement of prices of themselves (i.e. *without* any exogenous change in supply-demand determinants) feed back into the very price path thus generated.

[4] Thus, by his own logic, and following his "seminar speaker" tale, Tirole must now concede that I am correct! My unconditional willingness to bet (see the challenge in note 1), according to his theory, must make him recoil – leaving me in sole command of the field, like Napoleon at Austerlitz.

[5] Even the classic statement by Aumann (1976) appears defective on this score. Aumann emphasizes that the *posteriors* must be common knowledge; he requires only that the agents have the same priors. But the information-transmission process he describes will work only if the parties have common knowledge about their shared *priors* as well.

[6] See Britto (1984) for the bearing of demand elasticity in a general-equilibrium model of speculation, and D. Hirshleifer (1985) for an analytical integration of all three additional elements – elasticity, covariance, and transaction costs. An empirical study by Salmon (1985) has shown that differences among farmers with respect to *covariance* is a major determinant of the volume of desired prior trading and hence helps explain which futures markets have successfully come into existence in the United States.

[7] A number of other authors, employing partial-equilibrium models or a variety of other approaches to the speculation problem, have also recognized the importance of one or more of these determining elements. In particular, the role of demand elasticity has been addressed recently by Anderson and Danthine (1983) and Conroy and Rendleman (1983). The effect of covariance upon the risk faced by farmers (though usually formulated in terms of covariance with *price*, which is inversely associated with the more fundamental covariance with crop size) has long been discussed: see, e.g., Johnson (1947), McKinnon (1967), and Baesel and Grant (1982).

[8] An issue that might usefully be cleared away here concerns the distinction between a "theory" *versus* a particular application thereof. Tirole confuses the two categories when he asserts that Holbrook Working and the HSF authors have a "theory" that *differences in beliefs* are the key to speculative behavior. In the HSF general-equilibrium model not only differences of belief but also (e.g.) the distribution of commodity endowments over states of the world, individuals' utility functions (including their attitudes toward risk), and the scope of markets all play a role. What is true is that when certain idealized specifications are imposed – for example, that all individuals' utility functions are separable in the commodities, that all producers have perfectly correlated outputs – we can be led to stronger inferences such as that, absent belief differences, there would be no speculation. But the general-equilibrium modelling is on a different analytical level from this particular inference, whose validity depends also upon the "reasonableness" of the idealizing assumptions employed. I myself conjecture (but this is a personal opinion) that the requisite conditions are nearly enough satisfied for the inference to be *approximately* valid, thus providing a rationale for Working's observations about speculation in futures markets.

Name Index

Subject Index